Robert M. Levy is a federal magistrate judge in the District of New York. He was formerly the general counsel at New York Lawyers for the Public Interest, a public interest legal organization specializing in environmental justice and the rights of people with mental disabilities, and the senior staff attorney at the New York Civil Liberties Union. He is adjunct professor of law at Columbia, New York University and Brooklyn Law Schools, where he teaches courses in mental disability law. For seventeen years, he was plaintiffs' counsel in the *Willowbrook* case and has brought a wide range of individual and class action litigation to expand the rights of people with mental disabilities in institutional and community settings. He has received advocacy awards from the National Mental Health Consumers Association and the Benevolent Society for Retarded Citizens.

Leonard S. Rubenstein is executive director of Physicians for Human Rights. He was formerly executive director of the Bazelon Center for Mental Health Law (formerly the Mental Health Law Project), a national organization based in Washington, D.C., that for almost twenty-five years has advocated for protection of the rights of people with mental disabilities. He is also adjunct professor of law at Georgetown University Law Center in the Public Interest Law Scholars Program. He has litigated numerous class action cases establishing the rights of people with mental disabilities in institutions and in the community, published many articles, and lectured extensively on mental disability law. He has served on the American Bar Association's Commission on Mental and Physical Disability Law and has chaired the District of Columbia Bar's Health Law Section. He has served on the national board of the ACLU.

ALSO IN THIS SERIES

THE RIGHTS OF PEOPLE WITH

MENTAL DISABILITIES

The Authoritative ACLU Guide to
the Rights of People with Mental Illness
and Mental Retardation

A Completely Revised and Updated Edition
of *The Rights of Mental Patients*
and *The Rights of Mentally Retarded Persons*

Robert M. Levy
Leonard S. Rubenstein

General Editor of the Handbook Series
Norman Dorsen, President, ACLU 1976–1991

SOUTHERN ILLINOIS UNIVERSITY PRESS
CARBONDALE AND EDWARDSVILLE

Library of Congress Cataloging-in-Publication Data
Levy, Robert M. (Robert Morris)
The rights of people with mental disabilities : the authoritative ACLU
guide to the rights of people with mental illness and mental
retardation / Robert M. Levy, Leonard S. Rubenstein.
p. cm.—(An American Civil Liberties Union handbook)
"A completely
revised and updated edition of The rights of mental
patients and The rights of mentally retarded persons."
Includes bibliographical references.
1. Mental health laws—United States. I. Rubenstein, Leonard S.
II. Ennis, Bruce J., 1941–   Rights of mental patients.
III. Friedman, Paul R.   Rights of mentally retarded persons.
IV. Title. V. Series.
KF480.L48   1996
346.7301'38—dc20
[347.306138]   95-36408
ISBN 0-8093-1989-6 (cloth : alk. paper)   CIP
ISBN 0-8093-1990-X (pbk. : alk. paper)

The paper used in this publication meets the minimum requirements of
American National Standard for Information Sciences—Permanence of
Paper for Printed Library Materials, ANSI Z39.48-1984.

CONTENTS

PREFACE

This guide sets forth your rights under present law and offers suggestions on how they can be protected. It is one of a continuing series of handbooks published in cooperation with the American Civil Liberties Union (ACLU).

Surrounding these publications is the hope that Americans, informed of their rights, will be encouraged to exercise them. Through their exercise, rights are given life. If they are rarely used, they may be forgotten and violations may become routine.

This guide offers no assurances that your rights will be respected. The laws may change, and in some of the subjects covered in these pages, they change quite rapidly. An effort has been made to note those parts of the law where movement is taking place, but it is not always possible to predict accurately when the law *will* change.

Even if laws remain the same, their interpretation by courts and administrative officials often varies. In a federal system such as ours there is a built-in problem since state and federal laws differ, not to speak of the variations among states. In addition, there is much diversity in the ways in which particular courts and administrative officials interpret the same law at any given moment.

If you encounter what you consider to be a specific abuse of your rights, you should seek legal assistance. There are a number of agencies that may help you, among them ACLU affiliate offices, but bear in mind that the ACLU is a limited-purpose organization. In many communities there are federally funded legal service offices that provide assistance to persons who cannot afford the costs of legal representation.

In general, the rights that the ACLU defends are freedom of inquiry and expression; due process of law; equal protection under the law; and privacy. The authors in this series have discussed other rights (even though they sometimes fall outside the ACLU's usual concern) in order to provide as much guidance as possible.

These books have been planned as guides for the people directly affected: thus the question-and-answer format. (In some areas there are more detailed works available for experts.) These guides seek to raise the major issues and inform the nonspecialist of the basic law on the subject. The authors of these books are themselves specialists who understand the need for information at "street level."

If you encounter a specific legal problem in an area discussed in one of these handbooks, show the book to your attorney. Of course, he or she will not be able to rely exclusively on the handbook to provide you with adequate representation. But if your attorney hasn't had a great deal of experience in the specific area, the handbook can provide helpful suggestions on how to proceed.

NORMAN DORSEN, *General Editor*
Stokes Professor of Law
New York University School of Law

The principal purpose of this handbook, as well as others in this series, is to inform individuals of their legal rights. The authors from time to time suggest what the law should be, but their personal views are not necessarily those of the ACLU. For the ACLU's position on the issues discussed in this handbook, the reader should write to Public Education Department, ACLU, 132 West 43d Street, New York, NY 10036.

ANTECEDENTS AND ACKNOWLEDGMENTS

We owe a great debt to the predecessors of this book, *The Rights of Mental Patients* by Bruce Ennis and Loren Siegel, later revised by Bruce Ennis and Richard Emery, and *The Rights of Mentally Retarded Persons* by Paul Friedman, both written in the 1970s. Those volumes not only explained the rights that people with mental disabilities had at the time but also contributed to their evolution.

The authors have more contemporary debts as well. A special thanks to Susan Stefan for her critical and enlightening comments. We also thank colleagues who took the time to read and provide helpful suggestions on portions of the book within their field of expertise, including Joseph Bevilacqua, Kathleen Boundy, Bill Brooks, Ira Burnim, Julie Clark, Pam Cohen, George Diggle, Larry Gostin, Shelley Jackson, Chris Koyanagi, Ruth Lowenkron, and Bonnie Milstein. Natalie Ireland and Gwen Bean Armstrong tracked down sometimes elusive information, Caroline Ewing provided helpful research assistance, and Laura J. Lewis contributed insightful research and prose.

Although the list of heroes in the field, both celebrated and unsung, is too large to acknowledge here, several among them deserve particular mention: United States District Judge John R. Bartels, who began this work at an age when most people have already retired and whose dedication and compassion during eighteen years of overseeing the Willowbrook Consent Decree helped more than 5,400 individuals gain a life of dignity and respect and inspired countless others; United States District Judge Frank Johnson, whose courage in protecting the civil rights of Americans extended to people with disabilities; Bernard Carabello, who, after spending nearly twenty years of his life in Willowbrook, became an advocate for others still enmeshed in the system; Ken Donaldson and Howie the Harp, who fought so hard for the rights of all people with disabilities; and Florine Israel and Kathy Schwaninger, whose passing has left a void that will not easily be filled.

Rob Levy would like to give special thanks to Susan for her insight and encouragement and those countless gourmet meals when the burden of running a household fell solely on her, and to Katie for her wit and mastery of the computer and for loyally resisting the temptation to look for a new dad.

Len Rubenstein would like especially to thank Margaret for her support and her endless patience, and Alex and Jodie for tolerating computer deprivation.

THE RIGHTS OF PEOPLE
WITH MENTAL DISABILITIES

1

Introduction

Some paradox of our nature leads us, when once we have made our fellow men the objects of our enlightened interest, to go on to make them objects of our pity, then of our wisdom, ultimately of our coercion.

—Lionel Trilling

How Ideas about People with Mental Disabilities and Their Rights Have Evolved

When Congress passed the Americans with Disabilities Act, it found that people with disabilities "have been faced with restrictions and limitations, subjected to a history of purposeful unequal treatment, and relegated to a history of political powerlessness in our society based on characteristics that are beyond the control of such individuals and resulting from stereotypic assumptions not truly indicative of the individual ability of such individuals to participate in, and contribute to, society."[1] For no group has this statement been more true than for people with psychiatric and developmental disabilities, who have endured a long history of degradation, stigma, fear, and even hatred. The movement to establish and protect their rights has been a means of gaining fair and equal treatment and fostering the respect and dignity every human being deserves.

Two decisions of the United States Supreme Court involving people with mental retardation bracket the massive change in the law's attitudes toward people with mental disabilities. The first was written by Justice Oliver Wendell Holmes in 1927, at a time when people with mental retardation were referred to as "imbeciles," "idiots," and "mental defectives," and state legislatures enacted discriminatory laws prefaced with

1

findings declaring them to be a "blight on mankind" and "not much above the animal." Government publications described mentally retarded people as "a parasitic, predatory class," "a danger to the race," and "a blight and a misfortune both to themselves and to the public."[2] The goal was to contain and eliminate them, not to recognize their rights. Against that background, an institution in Virginia sought a court order authorizing the compulsory sterilization of Carrie Buck based on the allegation that she, her mother, and her daughter were mentally retarded. Writing for the Supreme Court, Justice Holmes described people with mental retardation as a "menace" who "sap the strength of the state" and concluded that the state had the duty and the authority to prevent its polity from being "swamped with incompetence." "It is better for all the world," he wrote, "if, instead of waiting to execute degenerate offspring for crime, or let them starve for their imbecility, society can prevent those who are manifestly unfit from continuing their kind." And in one of the most infamous sentences in the history of the Supreme Court, he concluded, "Three generations of imbeciles are enough."[3]

Almost half a century later, Justice Thurgood Marshall wrote a concurring opinion in *City of Cleburne v. Cleburne Living Center*,[4] in which the Supreme Court held that a city's effort to exclude people with mental retardation from its midst violated the equal protection clause of the Constitution. He eloquently reviewed the nation's history of discrimination, segregation, and mistreatment of people with mental disabilities, exemplified by their confinement in huge custodial institutions, the exclusion of children with disabilities from school, and the implementation of laws permitting involuntary sterilization. This history, Justice Marshall said, reflected nothing less than a "regime of state-mandated segregation . . . that in its virulence and bigotry rivaled, and indeed paralleled, the worst excesses of Jim Crow."[5]

By the time the *Cleburne* case was decided in 1985, the use of the Constitution to challenge coercive and discriminatory practices against people with mental disabilities had become commonplace.

What happened between 1927 and 1985? The legal rights movement for people with mental disabilities began in earnest in the early 1970s with the filing of class action lawsuits asserting that inhumane conditions in state psychiatric and mental retardation institutions violated residents' constitutional rights to treatment and protection from harm, and challenging the legal justifications used to institutionalize them in the first place.

At the time, more than half a million adults and children with mental disabilities were locked in state institutions, with little regard for their rights. Inspired by the civil rights movement, their lawyers argued that the United States Constitution guaranteed them the right to due process in the decision to institutionalize them; freedom from abuse and unreasonable restraint inside the institution; a clean, sanitary environment; nutritious food; adequate clothing; decent medical care; protection from harm; and appropriate treatment or habilitation to improve their mental condition or increase their skills.

Although the legal theories were new and untested, a number of judges eventually agreed and struck down state commitment statutes with vague standards and abbreviated procedural protections and ordered states to improve conditions and services inside institutions and, in some cases, provide treatment in the community. Thus, the legal rights movement for people with mental disabilities was launched. Responding to these judicial decisions, many state legislatures enacted new laws incorporating constitutional safeguards into the civil commitment process and curbing the delegation of governmental authority to the discretion of professionals.

The next stage of reform focused on the right to informed consent and freedom from exploitation: the right to be paid for institutional labor, to be free from experimental or dangerous treatments, to refuse intrusive forms of treatment such as psychotropic medication and aversive stimuli, to avoid involuntary sterilization, and more. The assertion of rights also inevitably led to claims for a right to alternatives to institutionalization. In mental retardation, the developmental model was taking hold, based on the belief that people with mental retardation could learn, acquire basic skills, and thrive outside institutions. In mental health, the community mental health movement was beginning to gain acceptance, premised on the notion that long-term custodial confinement was inappropriate and that the vast majority of people with mental disorders could benefit from treatment in a less restrictive environment than an institution.

By the time the *Cleburne* case was decided, litigation to correct inhumane institutional conditions had turned to advocacy for the development of community-based services as a means to advance social justice for people with mental disabilities. The focus had moved beyond due process of law to housing, income, community supports and an approach to treatment that recognizes personal autonomy and responsibility. Meanwhile, an increasing recognition of individual rights gradually became a part of the culture of many of the professionals who work in mental health and mental retardation programs, as well as administrators, legislators, families, and, to a lesser extent, the general public.

This assertion of rights, however, was not universally welcomed, for it challenged not only popular prejudices and governmental abuse but the control that administrators and clinicians had long exercised over the lives of people with mental disabilities. Rights activists, including a growing number of ex-patients, sought to limit or eliminate the authority of professionals to involuntarily hospitalize or medicate an individual. They challenged the accuracy of psychiatric diagnoses and predictions of future violent acts,[6] highlighted the dangers of antipsychotic medication, electroconvulsive therapy and other physical treatments for mental conditions, and questioned both the therapeutic and experimental uses of aversive behavior modification techniques. Some even questioned whether mental disorders exist at all.

In addition to protesting the erosion of their authority, some psychiatrists, and a number of relatives of people with mental illness, expressed misgivings about elevating the values of liberty and autonomy over benevolence and paternalism. They contended that the courts had gone too far in recognizing individual rights, claiming that it was often impossible to provide acutely ill individuals with the help they need, at times with tragic results. Some blamed homelessness among people with mental disorders on the lawyers who had championed their clients' constitutional rights. The shriller opponents ridiculed civil rights advocacy with slogans like "dying with your rights on."

Although the controversy over the rights of people with mental disabilities continues, the nature of the debate has changed with the emergence of new ideas about their place in society. Two developments have been central.

First, judicial recognition of the rights of people with mental disabilities coincided with the birth of a self-advocacy movement premised on the belief that people with mental disabilities should not remain the passive recipients of services selected by others, no matter how well intentioned. Rather, they should participate in designing services that respond to needs they can identify themselves. Although the idea seems straightforward, it challenged entrenched approaches that discounted the views of the recipient as products of cognitive deficits or a diseased mind. One of the founders of the self-advocacy movement, Rae Unzicker, wrote a long and angry poem about the experience of being devalued and labeled in this way. The first and last lines convey the loss of self-esteem and the pervasive sense of powerlessness that many individuals have experienced.

To be a mental patient is to be stigmatized, ostracized, socialized, patronized, psychiatrized.

To be a mental patient is to have everyone controlling your life but you. You're watched by your shrink, your social worker, your friends, your family. And then you're diagnosed as paranoid.

. . . .

To be a mental patient is not to die—even if you want to—and not to be hurt, and not to be scared, and not to be angry, and not to be vulnerable, and not to laugh too loud—because, if you do, you only prove that you are a mental patient even if you are not.

And so you become a no-thing, in a no-world, and you are not.[7]

The anger was channelled into advocacy through the creation of organizations whose names succinctly convey this perspective, such as On Our Own, named after a seminal book by Judi Chamberlin,[8] and People First.[9] These organizations have sought to enable people with mental disabilities to gain a sense of power over their own lives, by developing means of self-help and support and establishing mental health and mental retardation services responsive to their needs.

While still emerging, these voices have already been influential. By the mid-1980s, for example, government agencies responsible for funding, designing, and regulating mental disability services began to see the enormous value of listening to the people their programs were intended to benefit. A number of service providers began to survey the preferences of people with mental disabilities on the subject of housing and the design of services[10] and to work with them to develop new models for services. Most saw respect for individual choice not as a threat, but as a source of dignity and self-respect and an essential ingredient in fostering independence.

The second, related development concerns the new service models themselves. Thirty years ago, leading mental disability professionals rejected custodial care in favor of normalization and individual development, achieved through active treatment and training. Val Bradley, now chair of the President's Committee on Mental Retardation, has observed that as exciting as this thinking was, it was also limiting. She argues that in this "era of deinstitutionalization," the developmental model in mental retardation remained wedded to a notion of people with mental retardation as very different from the rest of society, possessed of rights, to be sure, but nevertheless to be molded in skills and behavior by professionals.[11] Under then-prevailing concepts, she explains, the key was to identify a person's behavioral and skill deficits and then address them through specialized interventions.

The problem with this model, Bradley maintains, is that it gives little attention to the individual's own goals. If true integration is to be achieved in what she termed the "era of community membership," services and supports must be designed to the maximum extent possible around an individual's choices rather than the fulfillment of a set of professionally determined expectations. Instead of placing "clients" in program slots, the goal must be to "ensure people with disabilities a quality of life that is congruous with the way society in general views good quality of life."[12] In programmatic terms, this approach means replacing group homes with normalized housing and appropriate supports, sheltered workshops with real jobs and, above all, setting goals through individual choices whenever possible, not by criteria imposed by others.

Similar changes are taking place in the field of mental health. The first generation of community-based services tended to emphasize plans for treatment, housing, and support services according to a professional assessment of the person's symptoms and level of functioning. For example, in many programs, an individual leaving a psychiatric hospital was "placed" in a time-limited transitional setting and then moved into other housing and support arrangements as the person's level of functioning increased or the time expired in the transitional placement. Though seemingly logical, this approach took no account of whether these individuals objected, as most people without mental disorders would, to being moved from their home according to some predetermined timetable; or whether they preferred permanent and stable housing. Nor did it attempt to ascertain whether the program and placement were consistent with the person's plans for returning to a productive and fulfilling life.

Instead of looking at mental disorders as a disease to be cured through predetermined medical and programmatic interventions, new models focus on the individual's often painful effort to obtain rehabilitation and to seek recovery. Dan Fisher describes the change this way:

The present mental health care system is based on an illness model in which an expert defines the problem as primarily a defective chemical mechanism in the patient's brain that needs to be repaired by the expert. This model reduces symptoms but interferes with the person's taking an active role in recovery. We are proposing a health-promoting system in which individuals define their own needs and are active collaborators with a variety of people in their unique biological, psychological, social and cultural context.[13]

This approach is consistent with other developments in mental health services that include personal support and rehabilitation as critical elements in recovery. Indeed, a whole new field, known as *psychosocial rehabilitation*, has sprung up to explore and develop these services. Such innovations as outpatient psychiatric crisis services and peer support as part of a program of recovery now coexist with more traditional medically based services.

The development of a self-advocacy movement and corresponding new concepts in the design and provision of services goes hand in hand with a profound change in the rights of people with mental disabilities. These rights first developed around involuntary confinement and forced treatment, the abuse and neglect of people living in institutions, and the entitlement to services. They were based on principles of procedural justice, protection from harm, and liberty.

In the era of community membership, with values stressing citizenship, inclusion, integration, and services built around an individual's particular needs, the right to be free from discrimination and to obtain reasonable accommodation for one's disability have become as important as due process. Inclusion and integration can be achieved only if the law recognizes that people with mental disabilities are fundamentally like other people and hence entitled to equality as well as fairness. In this analysis, the right to equality becomes the most critical right of all, subsuming all other rights. It means that people with mental disabilities must have the same right to liberty, autonomy, informed consent, and due process as all other members of society and that qualified people with mental disabilities may not be discriminated against in housing, employment, or the activities of civic life.

The right to equality inevitably clashes with stereotypes about the uniqueness of people with mental disabilities.[14] After all, the entire field of mental disability law or, for that matter, mental retardation and mental health services, would not exist were the people involved not perceived as different in very important ways. Viewed from another perspective, though, human beings differ from one another, and society accommodates these differences in numerous ways without defining people, or their rights, by these differences. The law of nondiscrimination against people with disabilities thus can recognize difference and yet seek equality. This is most easily illustrated in the field of physical disability. The inability of a person to walk is an impairment, but if public transportation and buildings are accessible, the physical difference has no social consequence—society simply accommodates it as part of the goal of equal participation. As we discuss in chapter 5, corresponding accommodations can also be made in the name of equality for persons with mental disabilities. As the law recognizes the necessity of these accommodations and applies principles of equality to people with mental disabilities, their rights will evolve once again.

The evolution of new rights and services does not mean that past practices have died out. In many areas the old ways still predominate, just as today most of the billions of Medicaid dollars spent on residential care for people with mental retardation still remain tied up in institutions larger than sixteen beds.[15] The struggle to enforce the rights to protection from harm, to liberty, and to due process still continues, as witnessed by persistent accounts of abuse and coercion of people with mental disabilities. The same spring that the *Cleburne* case was decided, Congress held hearings into allegations of abuse at a number of institutions for people with mental disabilities. In his opening statement, Senator Lowell Weicker reported on a six-month staff investigation of psychiatric and mental retardation facilities. "From the walls of the nurses' stations to the halls of Federal agencies, my staff has seen carefully written rules and procedures. But they have also seen fear in the eyes of patients and staff as they contemplate a long afternoon in the dayroom. . . . They have observed heavily drugged patients tied to their beds, left in hospital hallways, and soaked in their own urine . . . beatings of patients and residents by others including staff exist as an open secret of institutional life."[16] So anyone concerned with the rights of people with mental disabilities must take account of both the new rights to nondiscrimination and the rights recognized in the era of institutional confinement.

A Glossary of Key Terms

Mental Disability

The developments in the fields of mental retardation and mental health have had enormous consequences for the language we use. The growing use of the word *consumer* to describe people who interact with the mental health and mental retardation service systems recognizes the principle that people's needs and desires should drive the system of services in place of the idea of a flawed human being the system tries to fix. By the same token, it is no longer appropriate to identify people with mental disorders as "mental patients" because their lives embrace far more than their existence as a patient. Nor is it proper to speak of "the retarded" as though mental retardation defines a person's entire being.

Nevertheless, replacement words have been hard to find, since many words used to describe people with mental disabilities remain fraught with prejudice. Even "mental retardation" carries so much stigma that the leading advocacy organization in the field took the initials of its former name, Association for Retarded Citizens, and renamed itself "The Arc."

In mental health, the politics of language is based on competing scientific and ideological positions. Thus, in the face of suggestive but hardly conclusive scientific evidence, some people nevertheless describe mental illness as a "brain disease," in an effort to bring the field more respect as a science. Others view this development as misguided because it overstates the scientific case and tends to devalue the people who carry the "brain disease" label. On the other side of the debate, some people who were once institutionalized call themselves "survivors" to convey the sense that they have been victims of the mental health system.

Society is still searching for the right words to describe the nature of the consequences of these disorders. We use *mental disability*, a phrase most closely in harmony with the developments described and one accepted by the rehabilitation field. The word *disability* has gained wide acceptance because it goes beyond the narrowly medical approach that proved inadequate either to serve people with mental (or physical) disorders or to respect their rights. In particular, the use of the word *disability* conveys the social consequences of a condition. A person's condition, of itself, has no particular relevance to the law or the concept of rights unless it is used by society to exclude, punish, compel, or otherwise interfere with a person. Only when the condition has, or is thought to have, an impact on the person's place in society should the law be concerned with it. For example, the use of a wheelchair would not be considered of legal consequence except that we use stairs, escalators, and modes of transportation that are not accessible to a person in a wheelchair; the question then becomes how the law should respond to that social fact. The word *disability* conveys this relationship between a person's condition and the implications of that condition for the society. That is why Congress chose to name the landmark civil rights law in this area the Americans with Disabilities Act. For the same reasons, the term is also used in this book.

A person with a mental disability therefore is someone with a developmental disability—typically mental retardation—or a psychiatric disability.

Mental Retardation

This was once considered a simple concept: a developmental disability[17] characterized by significantly subaverage intelligence, usually in the lowest 2½ percent of the population. By the 1970s, IQ alone was considered insufficient to establish mental retardation, and two other factors were added to the definition: significant deficits in what was called "adaptive behavior" necessary to cope with the environment and evidence of onset as a child. "Mild," "moderate," "severe," and "profound" levels of mental retardation tended to be defined by IQ combined with deficiencies in adaptive behavior. These definitions spawned yet more controversy, both as to the significance and reliability of IQ tests and the means used to measure adaptive behavior.

Recognizing these and other problems, the American Association on Mental Retardation in 1992 substantially revised the definition again. The association's new definition of mental retardation is: "Mental retardation refers to substantial limitations in present functioning. It is characterized by significantly subaverage intellectual functioning existing concurrently with related limitations in two or more of the following applicable adaptive skill areas: communication, self-care, home living, social skills, community use, self-direction, health and safety, functional academics, leisure and work. Mental retardation manifests itself before age 18."[18]

The change replaces the concept of "adaptive behavior" with "adaptive skill areas," which are listed in order to be more precise about the deficits relative to an individual's ability to function in society. Moreover, the definition does not stand alone. It is accompanied by four "assumptions" that seek to convey the fluid and environmentally connected nature of the classification of a person as mentally retarded. The assumptions are as follows:

- Valid assessment considers cultural and linguistic diversity as well as differences in communication and behavioral factors.
- The existence of limitations in adaptive skills occurs within the context of community environments typical of the individual's age peers and is indexed to the person's individualized needs and strengths.
- Specific adaptive limitations often coexist with strengths in other adaptive skills or other persons' capabilities.
- With appropriate supports over a sustained period, the life functioning of the person with mental retardation will generally improve.

These assumptions, read in conjunction with the definition itself, are important to signal the significant shift in thinking about mental retardation that has taken place in the past two decades. First, the definition rejects the notion that mental retardation is a static condition and thus eliminates the four categories of retardation—mild, moderate, severe, and profound—that locked a person into a particular characterization. Second, it stresses that the environment in which a person lives and the support a person receives has a profound impact on a person's cognitive capacity and functional skills. Third, the definition casts doubt on programmatic approaches that rely on fixed categorization and demands person-centered program planning.

The implications of this new approach are significant. It suggests that labels such as "educable" or "trainable" are no longer valid. It also stresses reliance on individually tailored supports rather than fitting a person into a category that will dictate the type of facility appropriate for the individual. Above all, as two of the drafters of the new definition explain, it "establishes the goal of full adult status for individuals with mental retardation and full inclusion and participation in community life."[19]

Psychiatric Disability

If the definition of mental retardation is problematic, the language describing people with serious mental health conditions is even more complex and controversial. In 1976, when the last edition of *The Rights of Mental Patients* was published, the authors began by explaining the controversy over whether mental illness was a physiological process or disease or something else entirely. They added: "Even those who hold that 'mental illness' is a physical or psychological disease disagree about its causes. Some believe that mental illness is caused by chemical, hormonal or other physiological disorders; others that it is caused by genetic defects; and still others that it is caused by environmental factors, particularly by early childhood problems and traumas."[20]

Almost two decades, hundreds of millions of dollars of research, and a sea change in social policy later, much has been learned but fundamental questions remain unanswered. There is still no certainty as to what mental disorders are, what causes them, or why certain treatments for various conditions seem to work. The search for biological and genetic origins has brought suggestions and correlations but not the definitive answers researchers have sought. Often multiple factors seem to be at work that are not fully understood. Still, the field is far better able to describe some mental disorders than in the past. As a result, epidemiologists have become more sophisticated in estimating the prevalence of recognized mental disorders, and social scientists have been able to study the effectiveness of various interventions. The major epidemiological study of the one year prevalence of Americans diagnosed with particular disorders showed the following:

Disorder Prevalence	*Number* (rounded)
Schizophrenia 1.1%	1.75 million
Bipolar disorder 1.2%	1.9 million
Major depression 5.0%	7.95 million
Dysthymia	
(depression) 5.4%	8.6 million
Phobias 10.9%	17.3 million
Panic disorders 1.3%	2.1 million
Obsessive-compulsive 2.1%	3.3 million[21]

Individuals with these and related conditions may be described as persons with mental disorders. We use the term *psychiatric disability* when speaking of people who have mental disorders and whose rights are at stake on that account. When the context requires, though, we also use the more familiar terms of people with a *mental illness* or *mental disorder*. These words do not end the problem of description, since as will become clear in subsequent chapters, problems of accuracy in diagnosis, even racially biased labeling, continue to plague the mental health field. The Americans with Disabilities Act provides some guidance by making it clear that people who carry an erroneous label of disability have the same rights as people with properly identified disabilities. This book takes the same approach.

Rights

When we use the word *right*, we mean a valid, legally recognized claim or entitlement, encompassing both freedom from government interference or discriminatory treatment and an entitlement to a benefit or service. We focus primarily on what the courts and legislatures have recognized as rights but try to make clear what rights we believe ought to exist as well.

This book does not discuss rights in the criminal process. Although these rights are important, the subject is simply too vast to be included in this small volume.

NOTES

1. 42 U.S.C. § 12101(7).
2. This history is described and these quotations taken from documents cited in T. Cook, *The Americans with Disabilities Act: The Move to Integration*, 64 Temple Law Review 393, 399–403 (1991).
3. Buck v. Bell, 274 U.S. 200 (1927).
4. 473 U.S. 432 (1985).
5. City of Cleburne v. Cleburne Living Center, Inc., 473 U.S. at 462 (Marshall, J., concurring and dissenting in part).
6. Ennis & Litwack, *Psychiatry and the Presumption of Expertise: Flipping Coins in the Courtroom*, 62 California Law Review 693 (1974).
7. The entirety of the poem has appeared in a longer essay by Rae Unzicker, *On My Own: A Personal Journey Through Madness and Re-Emergence*, 13 Psychosocial Rehabilitation Journal 71 (1989) and reprinted in *The Experience of Recovery*.
8. Chamberlin, *On Our Own* (1979).
9. Bowen, *The Power of Self-Advocacy*, in *Creating Individual Supports for People with Developmental Disabilities* (Bradley, Ashbaugh & Blaney eds. 1994).
10. *See, e.g.*, Uttaro & Mechanic, *The NAMI Consumer Survey Analysis of Unmet Needs*, 45 Hospital and Community Psychiatry 372 (1994).

11. Bradley, *Evolution of a New Service Paradigm* in *Creating Individual Supports for People with Developmental Disabilities* (Bradley et al. eds. 1994).

12. *Id.* at 22.

13. Fisher, *Health Care Reform Based on an Empowerment Model of Recovery by People with Psychiatric Disabilities,* 45 Hospital and Community Psychiatry 913 (1994). *See also* Deegan, *Recovery: The Lived Experience of Rehabilitation,* in *The Experience of Recovery* (Spaniol & Koehler eds. 1994); Chamberlin & Rogers, *Planning a Community-Based Mental Health System: Perspective of Service Recipients,* 45 American Psychologist 1241 (1990).

14. Minow, *Making All the Difference: Inclusion, Exclusion and American Law* (1990).

15. Braddock et al., *The State of the States in Developmental Disabilities,* Institute on Disability and Human Development, University of Illinois at Chicago (1994).

16. *Care of Institutionalized Mentally Disabled Persons: Joint Hearings Before the Subcommittee on the Handicapped of the Senate Committee on Labor and Human Resources and the Subcommittee on Labor, Health and Human Services, Education and Related Agencies of the Senate Committee on Appropriations,* 99th Cong., 1st Sess.

17. Mental retardation is a developmental disability, but not all developmental disabilities involve mental retardation. The term *developmental disability* is used in different ways. It is often considered a disability attributable to a mental or physical impairment that manifests itself during the developmental period of life, usually before age twenty-two, and that results in limitations in major life activities. Developmental disabilities include mental retardation, epilepsy, cerebral palsy, and autism, among other conditions.

The definition in the federal Developmental Disabilities Act, 42 U.S.C. § 6001(5), is narrower, focusing on more severe disabilities. For a person at least five years old, that law defines developmental disability as a "severe chronic disability" that is attributable to a mental or physical impairment, is manifest before age twenty-two, is likely to continue indefinitely, results in "substantial functional limitations" in three or more areas of major life activity, and results in a need for special interdisciplinary services of extended duration.

18. Luckasson et al., *Mental Retardation: Definition, Classification, and Systems Support,* American Association on Mental Retardation (9th ed. 1992).

19. Luckasson & Spitalnik, *Political and Programmatic Shifts in the 1992 AAMR Definition of Mental Retardation,* in *Creating Individual Supports for People with Developmental Disabilities* (Bradley et al. eds. 1994).

20. Ennis & Emery, *The Rights of Mental Patients* (1976) at 15 (footnotes omitted).

21. Regier, Narrow, Rae, et al., *The DeFacto U.S. Mental and Addictive Disorders Service System: Epidemiological Catchment Area Prospective 1-Year Prevalence Rates of Disorders and Services,* 50 Archives of General Psychiatry 85 (1993).

11

Standards for Involuntary Commitment

No area of mental disability law arouses more controversy than civil commitment. By its very nature, involuntary institutionalization creates a conflict between the individual's right to liberty and government's twin powers to shield vulnerable citizens from harm and to protect society from danger. Although its purpose is therapeutic, the Supreme Court, for good reason, has termed involuntary commitment a "massive curtailment of liberty."[1] Individuals are held under lock and key, separated from family and friends, deprived of personal privacy, and subjected to the possibility of forced treatment with highly intrusive neuroleptic drugs that can have serious and potentially irreversible side effects. Commitment infringes the right to liberty, to freedom of association, to travel, to freedom from unreasonable searches and seizures, and to bodily autonomy. Yet, unlike criminal defendants, people facing commitment can be preventively detained for behavior that violates no law because the confinement is to an institution, not a prison, and the purpose is treatment, not punishment.

This chapter will discuss the theory underlying involuntary commitment, its history, and the legal standards for determining whether an individual can properly be committed. The discussion will focus first on people with psychiatric disabilities and then examine special issues involving people with developmental disabilities.

INVOLUNTARY COMMITMENT: HISTORY, CONTEXT, AND THEORY

Where does the state derive its authority for commitment?

The state has two sources of authority for involuntary commitment: its *parens patriae* power and its police power.

Parens patriae literally means "parent of the country" and refers to the traditional role of the state as "sovereign and guardian of persons under legal disability," such as minors and people with mental disabilities.[2] The concept of *parens patriae* developed in feudal England not so much to protect people with disabilities as to protect the king's property interests, and later those of his noblemen. It is only comparatively recently that this power has been invoked to justify involuntary institutionalization and treatment of people with mental disabilities. In the United States, the *parens patriae* power first came into wide use as a justification for involuntary treatment in the mid-nineteenth century, when a "cult of asylum swept the country"[3] and psychiatrists claimed that "moral treatment" in a remote institutional setting "held the secret to the cure of insanity."[4]

The *parens patriae* power authorizes the state to intervene in the lives of people who lack the capacity to take care of themselves, such as minors, the elderly and people with mental disabilities. The theory is that the state has an obligation to protect the interests of those who cannot do so themselves, even if this means overriding their decisions and, in some cases, confining them involuntarily for their own good. Without a finding of incapacity, however, there is no justification under the *parens patriae* power for so extensive an interference with the right to personal autonomy—a right that is otherwise guaranteed to all persons "of adult years and sound mind."[5] The *parens patriae* power is typically used to commit people whose mental disability makes them dangerous to themselves.

Many states nevertheless deviate from the principles underlying this authority and allow *parens patriae* commitments of people whose mental disability makes them dangerous to themselves without any finding of incapacity. Although such an omission expands the universe of people subject to involuntary confinement, it also means that commitment no longer strips people of their capacity to exercise basic civil rights such as voting, managing their money, and making decisions about certain kinds of treatment.

By contrast, the purpose of the police power is to protect society from potential harm. Criminal laws and public health codes that authorize compulsory vaccinations[6] or quarantines of people with contagious diseases[7] are among the most common exercises of this power. In the mental health context, the police power is typically invoked to commit people whose mental disability poses a danger to others. Unlike criminal defendants, people facing police power commitments can be confined without proof that they violated the criminal law or, under some state laws, on predictions of dangerousness without evidence that they committed a dangerous act.

What are the origins of institutionalization in the United States?[8]

Until the nineteenth century, there were very few public institutions for people with mental disabilities in the United States. Although the first institution in the colonies devoted exclusively to mental disabilities was established in 1773,[9] few others were built during the next sixty years. The first institution for people with mental retardation was not authorized until 1848, when Massachusetts approved a school for "pauper idiots."[10]

Lumping "fools" and "lunatics" together with vagabonds, beggars, and other social outcasts, eighteenth-century America dealt with mental disorders "as a problem of containment, not treatment."[11] People with mental disabilities were expected to look to their families for support. Many lived at home, some were boarded out to private households or confined in almshouses and jails, while others were banished from towns along with paupers and wandered the countryside.[12] In eighteenth-century New York, for example, a succession of laws provided that an "idle wandering vagabond" could be summarily confined to a house of corrections, whipped, or deported out of the jurisdiction.[13]

A wave of change swept the country in the decades before the Civil War, born of the conviction that institutions could cure "lunatics" and sufficiently train "idiots" to enable them to lead productive lives in their communities. For people with psychiatric disabilities, champions of institutions hailed the creation of places of peace and order, seeing in them true asylums—isolated from the frenzy and disorder of the cities—that would cure insanity by bringing a quiet "discipline to the victims of a disorganized society."[14] In their view, civilization itself was the cause of mental illness, and there was a "constant parallelism between the progress of society and the increase of mental disorders."[15] States assumed responsibility for these asylums and then enacted civil commitment laws to authorize the institutionalization of those deemed in need of care or treatment.

This optimism eventually faded as no cure was found for many of the residents who had been admitted with such high hopes. Soon more than half of the inmates of these institutions were classified as incurable, and by the 1860s it became clear that the asylum was not the panacea it had been presumed to be. As institutions filled with people deemed incurable, they inevitably became more custodial. Their new mission was to protect society from what many viewed as the unpredictable violence of the mentally disturbed and to stop the spread of madness by quarantining people with mental illness.[16] Ultimately, the asylum became "a dumping ground for social undesirables,"[17] with a significant immigrant and poor population. "The convenience of confining these people," Rothman concludes, "even without the possibility of cure, made the institution worth supporting after its original purpose was no longer attainable."[18] Then, as now, institutions serve at least in part as the repositories of unresolved social problems.

Despite revelations of inadequate conditions in these institutions, reformers were successful only in adding procedural safeguards to the admissions process. Standards for hospitalization remained the same: so long as a person remained in need of treatment, hospitalization would be permitted.

Institutions for people with mental retardation fared no better. Their populations swelled as more and more residents were deemed untrainable and their parents refused or were unable to keep them at home. By the end of the nineteenth century there were more custodial institutions than educational facilities for people with mental retardation.[19] With the advent of the eugenics movement at the turn of the century, mental retardation was increasingly seen as the cause of crime, poverty, and insanity, all of which were said to pass inevitably from one generation to another. The eugenicists' solution called for the use of involuntary commitment laws to enforce the strict segregation of mentally retarded people from society at large, in order to prevent them from propagating and thereby "nearly extinguish their race."[20]

Even after the hysteria of the eugenics movement receded in the 1930s and 1940s, the segregation continued, in part because there were no real community alternatives to institutions. Until the early 1970s, involuntary commitment received little attention from judges, legislators, or scholars; the institutions and the laws that enabled them to survive remained in place. To the extent that courts considered the constitutionality of state commitment laws, it was usually to evaluate the legality of confinement under criminal statutes.

What is deinstitutionalization and how did it take place in the United States?

To its proponents, deinstitutionalization is the dismantling of a system of oppressive and dehumanizing confinement that perpetuated the century-long segregation of people with mental disabilities. Its detractors view it as a principal cause of homelessness, the decline in the quality of American urban life, and the profound neglect of helpless and disturbed persons.[21]

The term itself is laden with ideological baggage, implying that an enduring part of the social fabric is being discarded and that institutions are in some way endemic to the social order. Advocates of deinstitutionalization, on the other hand, point to the relatively recent origins of institutional care in post-Jacksonian America and the unnatural separation of people with disabilities from the communities where they belong.

Deinstitutionalization began in earnest in the United States in the mid-1950s. Between 1955 and 1978 the average daily census in state mental institutions plummeted from 559,000 to 149,000[22] and has since dropped further to about 100,000 people today. Similarly, the population of developmental centers dropped from a daily average of 195,000 in 1967 to 139,432 in 1978 and 77,712 in 1992.

A number of forces have driven deinstitutionalization. First, the introduction of psychotropic drugs in the 1950s enabled institutions to reduce patients' psychotic symptoms and release them into the community. Second, revelations of scandalous conditions in state mental institutions, most notably Alfred Deutsch's *The Shame of the States,*[23] increased public awareness of the widespread abuse and neglect that plagued large institutions and sparked efforts to find smaller alternatives in the community. At the same time, passage of the Community Mental Health Centers Act in 1963 offered funding for outpatient mental health services, premised on the idea that community facilities could provide an effective, humane, and less costly alternative to institutions. In the field of mental retardation, the theory of normalization challenged the use of large, congregate-care institutions, based on the belief that the integration of people with mental retardation into small, home-like residences in the community would better promote their growth and development.

Deinstitutionalization was given a boost in the 1970s when the federal government made Medicaid available to states and Supplemental Security Income to individuals to pay for a significant part of the costs of community care. Finally, in the 1970s a wave of civil liberties reforms narrowed the standards for commitment and emphasized the creation of less-restrictive alternatives.

The tightening of commitment standards played a far less important role in emptying state institutions than is widely believed. It was not until the late 1960s, when the principle of normalization had already taken hold in the field of mental retardation and the release of individuals from psychiatric hospitals was well underway, that courts finally began to consider whether the federal Constitution placed any restrictions on the state's power to deprive a person of liberty for the purpose of treatment.

In fact, the population of public mental institutions began to drop long before the first major court rulings that imposed a dangerousness requirement on commitment. As Reisner and Slobogin found, "a number of studies . . . concluded that the 'libertarian' reforms of the 1970's had only a minimal impact on the number or type of people hospitalized, largely because the new statutory language is still broad enough to be flexibly applied. This research suggests that factors other than legal reform were responsible for much of the change in the hospital population and the admission rate."[24]

Meanwhile, major changes were taking place in the types of hospitals used in treating people with psychiatric disabilities and in the length of involuntary hospitalization. In the past, virtually all involuntary hospitalizations involved placement in long-term state facilities. Now state psychiatric hospitals are no longer the only location for civil commitment. By 1980 about 40 percent of people civilly committed for psychiatric treatment were brought to facilities other than state psychiatric hospitals.[25] Since the total number of people admitted to all inpatient facilities for psychiatric treatment is now more than two million people annually,[26] these hospitals are involuntarily treating close to a million people a year.

Although a small number of people continue to be hospitalized for long periods of time, involuntary civil commitment is now used primarily for short-term hospitalization. By 1980 more than half of all people involuntarily committed to a state hospital stayed twenty-five days or less and those committed to a psychiatric unit of a general hospital had a median length of stay of ten days or less.[27] The median length of stay continues to fall.

The shortcomings of the deinstitutionalization of people with psychiatric disabilities can be attributed in large part to problems of execution. The basic premise that community treatment, if properly funded, can be effective, more humane, and ultimately less costly than institutionalization remains valid. Although there continue to be people who require some period of hospitalization to stabilize their condition, the majority of people with psychiatric disabilities can live safely in their communities and do not need inpatient confinement. However, a number of problems have arisen over the years from the failure of mental health funds to follow patients into the community and of mental health systems to use available funds to provide services responsive to the needs and preferences of the individuals they serve.

The deinstitutionalization of people with mental retardation began somewhat later than the discharge of people with psychiatric disabilities. Its progress was slower but ultimately more successful. Since 1967 a total of ninety-four mental retardation institutions in thirty states have closed, and others are scheduled to close shortly, replaced by community-based services. Eleven states have fewer than 250 people with developmental disabilities living in institutions, and New Hampshire and the District of Columbia have none.[28] The decisive factor may be that a number of lawsuits against state mental retardation systems resulted in court-ordered deinstitutionalization plans. The continued monitoring and enforcement of state compliance with court decrees helped to ensure the availability of housing and treatment services to enable individuals to live successfully in the community. Federal courts presided over the deinstitutionalization of thousands of individuals with mental retardation in New York, Alabama, New Hampshire, Pennsylvania, Minnesota, and elsewhere—in some cases for over twenty years until community facilities were built and individuals properly housed.[29]

The existence of a court order provided a powerful inducement to governors and state legislators to allocate funds to mental disability needs that otherwise would have gone for other purposes. One study found, for example, that the ten states that have invested most heavily in community-based services for people with developmental disabilities have done so in large part because of litigation attacking the conditions in the states' institutions.[30] By contrast, there were relatively few court orders requiring the deinstitutionalization of psychiatric patients and the creation of community-based services.[31] Consequently, there was insufficient legal pressure to induce states to appropriate the funds needed to develop community mental health resources. The result was a nationwide shortage of outpatient services and housing for those who were discharged that is unlikely to be corrected in the foreseeable future.

What are the arguments made against civil commitment?

Opponents of civil commitment make the following arguments:

Civil commitment is a profound abridgement of individual liberties that has continuing consequences after release. In addition to the massive curtailment of liberty during confinement, commitment imparts a lasting stigma that can impair the ability to obtain employment, housing, an education, and other opportunities. Because commitment infringes so deeply on fundamental rights, the reach of state control should be restricted to situations where the state's police-power interest in curbing dangerous behavior clearly outweighs personal liberty.

Accordingly, no one should be committed in the absence of criminal behavior. To permit commitment on the sole basis of a diagnosis of mental illness and a prediction of future dangerousness is to authorize confinement for one's status rather than one's acts. Due process precludes criminal incarceration based on status,[32] and there is no principled justification for treating people with psychiatric disabilities more harshly. Whether the purpose of confinement is treatment or punishment, the consequences to the individual are equally serious and require equally stringent safeguards.

It is therefore unreasonable to single out mentally disordered people for preventive detention based simply on a prediction of future dangerousness, when other people cannot be confined without having violated the criminal law. First, there is no evidence that the vast majority of people with a mental disorder are any more dangerous than members of the general population. A consensus statement on violence and mental disorder summarizing research findings in the field reported that "the results of several large-scale research projects conclude that only a weak association between mental disorders and violence exists in the community" and that "mental disorders—in sharp contrast to alcohol and drug abuse—account for a minuscule portion of the violence that afflicts American society."[33] Although there may be a subgroup of people who are more dangerous, particularly alcohol and drug abusers,[34] research confirms that, even counting these individuals, the "absolute risk of violence among the mentally ill as a group is very small, and only a small proportion of the violence in our society can be attributed to persons who are mentally ill."[35]

Second, even if the scientific research did show a significant statistical relationship between serious mental illness and violent behavior as a general matter, psychiatric diagnoses and predictions of future dangerousness typically are not sufficiently reliable in individual cases to form the basis for confinement. In fact, psychiatrists tend to overpredict dangerousness because of the low base rate of frequency of the predicted dangerous behavior, which means that for every dangerous person that is committed, a number of harmless people are confined. Livermore explained the matter thus:

Assume that one person out of a thousand will kill. Assume that an exceptionally accurate test is created which differentiates with 95 percent effectiveness those who will kill from those who will not. If 100,000 people were tested, out of the 100 who would kill, 95 would be isolated. Unfortunately, out of the 99,900 who would not kill, 4,994 people would also be isolated as potential killers. In these circumstances, it is clear that we could not justify incarcerating all 5,090 people. If, in the criminal law, it is better that ten guilty men go free than that one innocent man suffer, how can we say in the civil commitment area that it is better that 54 harmless people be incarcerated lest one dangerous man be free?[36]

Opposition to *parens patriae* commitment is even more intense. In part this is because the standards governing when the state should intervene to help an individual tend to be vague. A more fundamental objection is that treatment may be either impossible or unacceptably compromised when accompanied by the use of force. In psychiatry, the doctor-patient relationship is of utmost importance, and the use of force disrupts that relationship or impedes its formation. Researchers have questioned the argument that in retrospect patients feel positively about having been committed,[37] and people who have been committed report feelings of humiliation, dehumanization, loss of control, and stigma.[38] A survey conducted in California reported that 47 percent of the former patients interviewed declined traditional mental health services after an experience with involuntary commitment.[39] To the extent it alienates people from the mental health system, involuntary commitment may prevent people from receiving treatment when they need it.

Although the essential purpose of commitment is to treat and improve the subject's mental condition, it is by no means certain that involuntary institutionalization accomplishes this goal. First, many large public institutions are overcrowded and understaffed and unable to provide a satisfactory level of care. Too often their history has been one of abuse at worst and indifferent care at best. Second, there is no convincing evidence that involuntary hospitalization is a more effective form of treatment than less-restrictive community alternatives. As a survey of the studies comparing hospital and community treatment found:

It seems quite clear from these studies that for the vast majority of patients now being assigned to inpatient units in mental institutions, care of at least equal impact could be otherwise provided. There is not an instance in this array of studies in which hospitalization had any positive impact on the average patient care investigated in this study. In almost every case, alternative care had more positive outcomes. There were significant and powerful effects on such life-related variables as employment, school attendance, and the like. There were significant and important effects on the probability of subsequent readmission. Not only did the patients in the alternative care not undergo the initial hospitalization but they were less likely to undergo hospitalization as well.[40]

The same can be said for short-term as well as long-term involuntary commitments. With the advent of mobile crisis units, intensive peer support, and other alternatives to involuntary hospitalization, many individuals can receive even acute care services on an outpatient basis. In many cases, the problem is that these acute care alternatives are in too short supply, not that they are inferior to involuntary hospitalization.

Some opponents of commitment also argue that dangerousness to self is not a justification for commitment without a finding that the person lacks the capacity to make a decision whether to be institutionalized. A handful of states,[41] such as Utah[42] and New York,[43] have adopted this view. Others deny the existence of mental illness altogether.[44] A few even oppose *parens patriae* commitment on the ground that it violates the right to control one's own body. According to this theory, individuals should be allowed to do whatever they want to themselves, so long as they do not harm others.

What arguments are made by proponents of involuntary commitment?

As currently formulated, involuntary commitment is a last resort for mentally disordered people who are imminently dangerous to themselves or others and are acutely in need of stabilization. Although the law generally recognizes the right to bodily autonomy, society has a duty to step in and make treatment decisions for people who are so disturbed that they have no capacity to protect themselves from harm or resist harming others. Many proponents of commitment insist that confinement should be based on a simple need for treatment, without a dangerousness requirement at all. They contend that the *parens patriae* power enables society to help those with diminished mental capacity who are unable to seek the treatment they desperately need.

To be sure, they argue, commitment is a serious curtailment of liberty, but mental illness itself erodes the individual's capacity for self-determination. No one can seriously suggest that a delusional, schizophrenic person who carries out the command of voices ordering him to harm another is acting freely. As one proponent notes, "The freedom to be wandering the streets, psychotic, ill, deteriorating, and untreated, when there is a reasonable prospect of effective treatment, is not freedom; it is abandonment."[45] By providing essential treatment, commitment restores decisional capacity and individual liberty. After treatment is completed, most patients who refused hospitalization while psychotic will be thankful that they were committed. Moreover, although the stigma of involuntary hospitalization can be serious, the stigma of an untreated mental illness is far more damaging.

Proponents also contend that it is inappropriate to compare commitment to criminal incarceration. For one thing, the consequences of an adverse ruling are not the same. Once appellate remedies have been exhausted, a conviction is generally final, and the convict must serve a prescribed sentence. By contrast, a psychiatrist can release a patient at any time before or after a commitment hearing if the person is no longer dangerous to self or others. In addition, the vast majority of hospitalizations today are short-term affairs, with the goal of returning the individual to the community as quickly as possible. The intrusion on personal liberty is thereby minimized as it is limited only to the period during which the individual cannot survive safely in the community.

Although many psychiatric predictions of future dangerousness may be unreliable, some are not. It would be cruel and senseless to require society to wait until a dangerous act has occurred before it intervenes to protect a mentally disabled person who is suicidal, assaultive, or dying of self-neglect. Moreover, John Monahan, who once discerned no significant relationship between mental disorder and violence, now acknowledges such a relationship and concedes that there are categories of people with psychiatric disabilities who are more prone to violence than the general population as a whole.[46] Although it is still difficult to identify who these people are, this finding underscores the need to try to find them and then commit them for involuntary treatment to prevent foreseeable harm. At least for these individuals, predictions of future dangerousness are thoroughly supportable.

Finally, however low the quality of treatment may be at some public institutions, they at least offer a measure of safety to people who might not otherwise survive in freedom. For many people with mental disabilities, the alternative to commitment is jail—a harsh, punitive environment, ill equipped to offer even minimal treatment.

How are these arguments to be sorted out?

We begin with the simple proposition that if civil commitment laws are to exist at all, they must be understandable and subject to definite legal standards. That criterion alone knocks out most *parens patriae* laws, since despite countless efforts, it has proven impossible to draft a paternalistic civil commitment law that does not amount to a vague rule that the person is in "need" of treatment. And aside from vagueness, it is inappropriate to have a standard that permits physicians, whether capable and caring or incompetent and overworked, to determine when an individual needs treatment. A standard that leaves commitment rules to the discretion of physicians means that people subject to these laws have almost no protection at all against unwanted hospitalization, no matter how many procedural safeguards are in place. Further, the benefits of involuntary treatment are far from being so well established as to warrant so thoroughgoing a deprivation of liberty.

That leaves commitments where the person is dangerous and there is no less-restrictive alternative to hospitalization. It is possible to write narrow standards for defining dangerousness to self or others, including the inability to survive safely in the community—but only if commitment is based on actual conduct, not speculation as to what a person might do in the future on the basis of a diagnosis or other demographic characteristics. Indeed, many states adopted such requirements in the 1970s. Even these narrowly drawn laws, it turns out, are frequently used in "need for treatment" situations.[47] While based on the modest goals of protecting society from danger and preventing the inappropriate imprisonment of people with mental disorders in jails, involuntary treatment laws based on the police power are hard to confine to such situations.

STANDARDS FOR INVOLUNTARY COMMITMENT

What is the constitutional standard for involuntary civil commitment?

Since the early 1970s many courts and legislatures have established stringent standards for commitment, requiring proof of a mental disability that poses a substantial threat of serious harm to oneself or to others. As a general rule, the threat of harm must be real and present[48] and the proof of dangerousness clear and convincing.[49] We note at the outset that *dangerousness* has a special, though elusive, meaning in the context of involuntary commitment. It refers not only to the likelihood of violence to oneself or to others but also to severe self-neglect, to the point where the individual is unable to survive safely in the community, as the Supreme Court was careful to explain in its landmark decision in *O'Connor v. Donaldson.*[50]

Although civil commitment had been practiced in the United States for over two hundred years, *O'Connor* was the first case in which the Supreme Court considered the constitutional boundaries of the commitment process. The case involved a fifty-five-year-old man who was committed to the Florida State Hospital at Chattahoochee in 1957 and kept there for nearly fifteen years without treatment,[51] although he had never been dangerous to himself or others, was capable of earning a living outside the hospital, and had received offers to live in a supportive halfway house or with a former college classmate who was willing and able to provide for his welfare. The superintendent rejected each of these offers, insisting that Donaldson could only be released to his parents, who, as the superintendent knew, were "too elderly and infirm"[52] to care for him and in fact had never been informed of the availability of the halfway house. Upon his release, Donaldson immediately obtained a responsible job in hotel administration.[53]

The Supreme Court ruled that "a State cannot constitutionally confine without more a nondangerous individual who is capable of surviving safely in freedom by himself or with the help of willing and responsible family members or friends."[54] Due process precludes the commitment of harmless, mentally ill people simply because they are dirty or unattractive, they have a diminished quality of life, or their presence at large is objectionable to some members of society. In tones that presaged the homelessness crisis a decade later, the Court admonished:

May the State confine the mentally ill merely to ensure them a living standard superior to that they enjoy in the private community? That the State has a proper interest in providing care and assistance to the unfortunate goes without saying. But the mere presence of mental illness does not disqualify a person from preferring his home to the comforts of an institution. Moreover, while the State may arguably confine a person to save him from harm, incarceration is rarely if ever a necessary condition for raising the living standards of those capable of surviving safely in freedom, on their own or with the help of family or friends.

May the State fence in the harmless mentally ill solely to save its citizens from exposure to those whose ways are different? One might as well ask if the State, to avoid public unease, could incarcerate all who are physically unattractive or socially eccentric. Mere public intolerance or animosity cannot constitutionally justify the deprivation of a person's physical liberty.[55]

The Supreme Court has reaffirmed the dangerousness standard in subsequent decisions.[56]

What is the meaning of *mental disability* for purposes of commitment?

Mental disability includes mental illness and developmental disabilities such as mental retardation and autism. Some states also provide for the civil commitment of alcohol and drug abusers, although substance abuse is not considered a mental disability in the traditional sense and is beyond the scope of this book. People with a mental illness or a developmental disability who also have a substance abuse problem can be involuntarily committed if they are dangerous to themselves or others as a result of their mental disability. Such people are said to have a "dual diagnosis" and made up an increasingly large percentage of psychiatric emergency room admissions in large urban areas during the 1980s and early 1990s.

There is relatively little controversy over the mental disability component of the commitment standard, apart from some grumbling about the definition of *mental illness* in various state statutes, which often tend to be vague[57] or circular. The seriousness of the disability must be such that it renders the individual dangerous to self or others and requires treatment in a confined setting. In the case of mental illness, the existence of a diagnosable condition is generally not enough. The "vast majority of today's statutes emphasize that only persons with severe, significant, gross, or substantial impairments are proper subjects for extended commitment."[58] This typically means a psychosis or other seriously disabling condition.

A few states add the additional requirement that the person be incapable of making a rational decision whether to accept treatment, on the theory that *parens patriae* commitments require a finding of incapacity to decide whether to seek hospitalization.[59] But such a finding typically does not constitute either a general determination of incompetency or a specific declaration of incapacity to make decisions about other forms of treatment (than involuntary hospitalization) during the period of commitment, such as the decision whether to take psychotropic medication.[60] In fact, many states have statutes that explicitly state that involuntary commitment does not, by itself, constitute a finding of incompetency.

What is the meaning of *dangerousness?*

Dangerousness is among the most elusive concepts in mental disability law. Most statutes provide minimal definitions and leave it to clinicians and the courts to fill in the details. In many states, there is relatively little case law on point because decisions at commitment hearings tend to be oral. Moreover, when an appeal is taken, the amount of time necessary to have the case heard and decided is frequently so great that most patients have already been discharged and their appeals dismissed as moot before a decision is rendered. Recently, however, an increasing number of courts have ruled on the issue, rendering decisions even after the release of the patient.

Dangerousness is a prediction about a person's future behavior. Alexander Brooks has written that the term can be broken down into at least four component parts: (1) the magnitude of harm; (2) the probability that the harm will occur; (3) the frequency with which the harm will occur; and (4) the imminence of the harm.[61] By weighing the various factors, he suggests, one can make a judgment whether an individual is dangerous. For example, a trivial harm that is unlikely to take place would not constitute dangerousness, whereas a serious harm that is highly likely to occur imminently would.

Most states require a finding of some substantial likelihood of serious physical harm to self or others.[62] Although a few states permit confinement for dangerousness to property, it is doubtful that the state's interest in protecting property alone, without risk to people, is an appropriate justification for such a serious deprivation of liberty. While leaving this ultimate question open, the highest federal court to consider the issue struck down a Hawaii statute that authorized commitment for danger to any property, regardless of its value or significance, noting that it would improperly allow commitment for threatening to shoot a trespassing dog.[63] It did not say what, if any, property interest might be significant enough to warrant commitment.

Dangerousness to self or others is generally demonstrated through prior acts, attempts, or threats of physical harm, or expert predictions of future harmful conduct. The danger to self need not be self-inflicted or violent but also encompasses the inability to survive safely outside of an institution, even with the help of others.[64] In some states, such as California, Colorado, and Virginia, people who cannot meet their basic survival needs because of a mental disability are called "gravely disabled." However, as the Supreme Court cautioned in *O'Connor*, mere self-neglect is not enough. Thus, a person who cannot provide for her basic needs for food, clothing, shelter, or medical care outside an institution because of a mental illness can be committed only if her inability to care for herself places her in real physical danger. Due process precludes the commitment of people who, albeit poor, illclothed, or disturbed, are nevertheless able to obtain the bare essentials to enable them to survive in the community.[65] By contrast, a delusional man who refuses to accept treatment for a gangrenous leg because he thinks that all doctors are part of a conspiracy to kill him directed by the C.I.A., would clearly present a danger to himself, as would a homeless person living on the street in sub-zero weather, shoeless and dressed only in shorts and a tee-shirt, because she is under the delusion that she is in the tropics.

The anticipated harm must be imminent, not remote or speculative.[66] For example, it is improper for a psychiatric outreach team to commit a homeless woman with a psychiatric disability who is surviving safely on the streets, simply because it fears that she will deteriorate in the coming months and become unable to care for herself. Although most state statutes contain an imminent harm requirement, they do not provide a precise definition of the term, leaving it to clinicians and the courts to decide whether the proper period is a matter of hours, days, or even weeks.

How reliable are psychiatric predictions of future violence?

"When it comes to predicting violence, our crystal balls are terribly cloudy," reports Dr. John Monahan, one of the leading experts on the prediction of future violent behavior. "The research indicates that clinicians are better than chance at predicting who will be violent, but they are far from perfect. The problem is there is no standard procedure and the field lacks a solid research base for knowing which factors to rely on."[67]

There is a substantial body of research documenting the inability of psychiatrists to make reliable predictions of future violent behavior.[68] The American Psychiatric Association has recognized some of the limitations of psychiatric expertise in this area, stating that the "unreliability of psychiatric predictions of long-term future dangerousness is by now an established fact within the profession."[69] In a review of the scientific research that has become a classic in its field,[70] Monahan concluded that two out of three clinical predictions of future dangerousness are wrong,[71] that is, "of every three people predicted to be violent, only one is discovered to be violent over the ensuing five years."[72]

Despite the unreliability of psychiatric expertise in this area, courts have been reluctant to increase due process safeguards to reduce the risk of error. Instead, they "have been willing to accept remarkably low levels of predictive accuracy"[73] to justify involuntary confinement and even execution. The most egregious example was a death penalty case in which the Supreme Court held that, even if clinical predictions are inaccurate two-thirds of the time, psychiatrists may nonetheless testify as expert witnesses before a jury for the purpose of offering predictions of the future dangerousness of the defendant.[74] The American Psychiatric Association, among others, had urged the court to vacate the death sentence and preclude psychiatrists from testifying as experts on dangerousness in death penalty cases because their testimony is so unreliable and prejudicial to a jury as to violate due process.[75]

In a related case, the Supreme Court relied in part on the "lack of certainty and the fallibility of psychiatric diagnosis" in rejecting a "proof beyond a reasonable doubt" standard at civil commitment hearings because it found "there is a serious question as to whether a state could ever prove beyond a reasonable doubt that an individual is both mentally ill and likely to be dangerous."[76] The Court observed that it is very difficult for an expert psychiatrist to "offer definite conclusions about any particular patient."[77] Ironically, it was precisely because of the uncertainty of psychiatric opinions, and the serious deprivation of liberty that could result from them, that the Court was asked to strengthen the safeguards at commitment hearings to protect against erroneous confinement. The Court, however, viewed the fallibility of psychiatric predictions as justification for lowering—not raising—due process protections.

Must there be an overt act demonstrating dangerousness?

There is a split among courts whether commitment can rest upon a mere prediction of future harm, without evidence of an actual act, attempt, or threat of dangerous behavior. Proponents of an "overt act" requirement argue that, standing alone, psychiatric predictions of future dangerousness are too arbitrary and unreliable to justify confinement. They insist that, in order to avoid erroneous commitments, recent evidence of dangerous threats or conduct should be required. Such evidence could include, for example, a threat to commit suicide, an attempt to throw a child in front of a car, or the mere act of sleeping uncovered on the sidewalk in sub-zero weather wearing only shorts and a tee-shirt. They further contend that it is unreasonable to forbid the confinement of a mentally typical person who has not committed a criminal act, while allowing the incarceration of a person with a mental disability for the same conduct.

A number of courts have ruled that state commitment statutes were overly broad or unconstitutionally vague without such an overt act requirement.[78] More recent decisions, however, have declined to require this standard.[79] For example, while conceding that "in most cases a somewhat more reliable prediction [of future dangerous behavior] can be made if there is a history of a recent overt act," one court found that there are some instances where a psychiatrist can determine from a clinical examination that a person is reasonably likely to harm herself or others. Although these cases "may be relatively few," the court reasoned, "they are not insignificant," and to adopt an overt act requirement would render the state "powerless to protect the mentally ill person and society in these cases."[80]

The existence of such a dual standard for criminal and mental health police power commitments betrays society's failure to accord people with mental disabilities the rights we take for granted in the criminal justice system when detaining individuals who threaten society. It also rests on the mistaken notion that people with mental disabilities, on the whole, tend to be significantly more dangerous than other, similarly situated members of society. At present, fewer than one-half of the states have commitment statutes that include an overt act requirement.

Does the doctrine of the least restrictive alternative apply to civil commitment?

Yes. The doctrine of the least restrictive alternative is based on the constitutional principle that, in pursuing legitimate state interests, the government must use means that least restrict fundamental personal liberties.[81] In the context of civil commitment, this means that the state may not involuntarily institutionalize an individual if less restrictive settings will suffice. For example, if release to the care of family or friends, the provision of outpatient services, or even a period of residence in a supervised community facility were sufficient to enable a person to survive safely in the community without endangering others, then commitment would be unconstitutional.

Virtually every state has incorporated this doctrine into its commitment laws,[82] and numerous courts have mandated it as a matter of constitutional due process.[83] The Supreme Court relied on it in *O'Connor v. Donaldson* in formulating its ruling that it is unconstitutional to confine, without more, nondangerous individuals who are "capable of surviving safely in freedom, on their own or *with the help of family or friends*"[84] and explicitly referred to *Shelton v. Tucker*, the Court's first modern decision setting forth this doctrine.[85] As a federal appeals court noted, "the principle of the least restrictive alternative consistent with the legitimate purposes of a commitment inheres in the very nature of civil commitment, which entails an extraordinary deprivation of liberty."[86] The doctrine of the least restrictive alternative also extends to other aspects of commitment, such as transfers from open to secure units within an institution[87] and decisions about forced treatment.[88] While there is disagreement whether a commitment is valid if a less restrictive setting is appropriate but unavailable, virtually every court that has considered the issue has ruled that the doctrine applies only where a less restrictive alternative is actually available.[89]

What has been the impact of state laws imposing more stringent criteria for commitment?

Almost from the beginning, many psychiatrists resisted the new, carefully defined and limited standards for involuntary civil commitment of the 1970s as countertherapeutic and even life threatening to people with psychiatric disabilities. Opponents filled the professional and popular literature with arguments that the commitment laws prevented them from intervening with desperately needed treatments until a person had deteriorated so far as to become violent or homeless. Therapists claimed they were helpless to offer assistance to people too delusional to act in their own interests. Very occasional, but highly publicized instances of violent or aggressive acts by people who had not been committed led to the belief that it is "impossible" to commit people with mental disorders, no matter what their behavior. Anecdotes circulated suggesting that even violent individuals could not be hospitalized under the new standards.

In 1973 one of these opponents, Doctor Darold Treffert, wrote a letter to a professional journal describing civil commitment reform as encouraging "dying with your rights on."[90]

The phrase so well captured the views of the opponents of the constitutionally based legal criteria for involuntary hospitalization that it stuck. Treffert and others proposed commitment standards based principally on the "need for treatment," in short, a return to the paternalistic approach of the past. The American Psychiatric Association proposed a law that permitted involuntary hospitalization if a person is likely to "substantially deteriorate" without treatment and if certain other requirements are met.[91]

We no longer need to rely on anecdotes. During the past decade social scientists have conducted studies to determine the real impact of the civil commitment reforms of the 1970s. These studies found that the new laws did not significantly restrict involuntary hospitalization. Moreover, they uncovered no evidence that there is a significant number of people who psychiatrists believe "need" hospitalization but who cannot be committed under the new standards. As Paul Appelbaum, a psychiatrist who undertook a comprehensive review of the literature[92] notes, "It has been remarkably difficult for researchers to demonstrate any of the presumed consequences of the new statutes. To the extent that consistent findings are available, they tend to show that the statutes have had less impact than expected (and in some cases minimal effect) on overall rates of commitment and on the nature of the committed populations. Nor has it been possible to identify individual patients who are 'dying with their rights on' in the very small number of carefully performed studies."[93]

The research suggests one of the principal reasons for the paradox that different standards for involuntary commitment seem to have little impact on the real world: they are not respected or followed. Many lawyers do not advocate that existing legal standards be applied to their clients, and judges frequently do not enforce them. This finding is consistent with the observations of other scholars that legal representation at civil commitment hearings, when measured by the usual expectations for a lawyer representing a client, is often grossly inadequate.[94]

What do we conclude from these data? Appelbaum argues that lawyers, judges, and clinicians have replaced legal standards with a "commonsense" approach to civil commitment, by which he means a standard based on a need for treatment. He argues that to restore legitimacy to the law, consideration should be given to a return to standards that rely on therapeutic need. Unfortunately, this approach yields to the very vagueness and lack of due process that led to civil commitment reform in the first place. Worse, as Michael Perlin has shown, the "ordinary common sense" Appelbaum relies upon, as concerns people with mental disabilities, is itself often infused with prejudice, stereotypical attitudes, and in some cases hostility toward them.[95] The "common sense" that results in hospitalizing people with psychiatric disabilities too often consists of their devaluation, lack of attention to their real medical and mental health needs, and willingness to use commitment as a substitute for meeting their requirements for housing and support.

What is the commitment standard for people with developmental disabilities?

There has been relatively little litigation around the commitment standard for people with developmental disabilities. Because the liberty interests of mentally ill and mentally retarded people are virtually identical, as are the state interests in providing them treatment and preventing harm, we think there is little principled justification for adopting different commitment standards for either of these two groups. Thus, if an individual can live safely in freedom and is not dangerous to self or others, involuntary commitment is unconstitutional, regardless whether the person suffers from mental illness or mental retardation.

The Supreme Court's decision in *Heller v. Doe*[96] does not change this analysis. In *Heller*, the Court upheld a Kentucky statute that authorized a lower standard of proof at commitment hearings for people with mental retardation than for people with mental illness. The statute also permitted family members and guardians to participate as parties at commitment hearings for people with mental retardation but not for people with mental illness. The Court found that, in contrast to mental illness, mental retardation tends to be a lifelong, relatively static condition with an early onset that is easier to diagnose than mental illness. As a result, future dangerousness is more predictable and the input of family members more relevant than with commitments for mental illness. Although the Court concluded that in this case the special nature of mental retardation justifies different procedural safeguards for determining which people with mental retardation need commitment, the Court did not suggest that different standards for commitment are appropriate or that anything less than dangerousness would suffice for the confinement of people with mental retardation.

At least two courts have reinterpreted broad state commitment laws for people with developmental disabilities to bring them into harmony with the standard enunciated in *O'Connor v. Donaldson* and other cases involving mental illness. They permit commitment only if a person has a developmental disability and is dangerous to self or others.[97] Although some states have adopted a dangerousness standard, others still authorize confinement upon the mere finding of a need for treatment, in contradiction of *O'Connor.*[98] These statutes will likely be the subject of future litigation.

Many states also institutionalize adults with developmental disabilities as voluntary or "non-objecting" patients without a finding of dangerousness to self or others. In fact, no real standard is used at all. A significant number of these people are severely or profoundly retarded and have no capacity to consent to their placement in large, congregate care institutions. This practice has aroused controversy. As James Ellis writes, "In reality, the states are using the fiction of 'voluntariness' for most institutionalized persons with mental retardation to avoid judicial scrutiny of individual placement decisions."[99] The result, according to Ellis, is that people can "get 'lost' and 'forgotten' in mental retardation institutions."[100] Ellis suggests that the Supreme Court's decision in *Zinermon v. Burch*,[101] could alter this practice. In *Zinermon*, the Court held that a mental hospital could be held liable for confining as a voluntary patient a man who lacked the capacity to give informed consent. Similarly, a California court held that a "nonobjecting" adult with developmental disabilities who was incompetent to consent to institutionalization could not continue to be confined without a hearing to determine whether she was dangerous to herself or others and required placement in a state institution.[102]

CIVIL COMMITMENT AND HOMELESSNESS

What are the rights of mentally ill homeless people?

The same standard for commitment applies to homeless people as to everyone else. The mere fact that a person has no home is not a sufficient basis for commitment, unless the person has a mental disability and is dangerous to self or others.

During the 1980s, there was an explosion in the number of homeless people in the United States, fueled by a scarcity of affordable housing and the destruction of existing low-income housing;[103] a drop in the real value of wages and welfare benefits compared to inflation;[104] a reduction in government benefits;[105] chronic unemployment in the inner cities, particularly among minority youths;[106] and the failure to develop community mental health services and housing for people discharged from public institutions.[107]

Efforts to determine the demographics of homelessness have been fraught with uncertainty, often relying on small samples and anecdotal reports. Estimates of the homeless population nationwide have ranged from a low of 250,000 to 350,000, put forward by the U.S. Department of Housing and Urban Development under the Reagan administration in 1984, to 2.2 million, suggested by the Community for Creative Nonviolence, a Washington advocacy group, in 1982.[108] In 1990 the Census Bureau conducted what has been termed "the largest and most ambitious" survey of its kind,[109] counting homeless people in the nation's two hundred largest cities. It found 230,000 homeless people living in shelters, on streets or in other nonresidential locations—a figure that has been attacked from all sides for overlooking many street homeless and even entire shelters.[110] A more recent study examined records of shelter admissions during a recent five-year period in New York City and found that 239,425 people, or 3.3 percent of the entire population of New York City had spent some time in city shelters during that period.[111]

Despite the general belief that a majority of homeless people suffer from serious mental illness, studies suggest that it is families with children that make up the largest subgroup of the homeless. A report issued by the United States Conference of Mayors in December 1993 concluded that families with children comprise approximately 43 percent of the homeless population nationwide and a staggering 75 percent of homeless people in New York City.[112]

Generalizations about homeless mentally ill people are frequently misleading because they often rely on surveys that focus on the streets and shelters, locations where homeless families are less likely to be.[113] The best estimates of the prevalence of major mental illness among the total homeless population range from 15 to 40 percent, depending on the definition of mental illness and the nature of the group sampled.[114]

Many homeless people live on the streets. Some fear going to shelters, which they see, with some justification, as unsafe, overcrowded, and as potential breeding grounds for communicable diseases such as tuberculosis. Others prefer more privacy than a shelter can offer, while still others are too disordered to seek assistance on their own. In the 1980s the presence of homeless people living in public places began to arouse strong public reactions, from compassion to outrage and disgust. Street homelessness became a quality of life issue for both the homeless, who suffered serious privations, and for a significant segment of the public, who watched with dismay the transformation of their sidewalks and parks into what they viewed as unsightly and unsanitary encampments.

Most city and state governments have been unable or unwilling to allocate enough of their scarce resources to provide adequate food, shelter, or permanent housing for the homeless. Faced with pressure to help the homeless and protect the quality of life of its more fortunate citizenry, some localities have begun to focus their efforts on the homeless mentally ill. In many quarters this group had become the focal point of compassion and distaste as the most visible example of a problem that had hitherto appeared insoluble.

One recurring suggestion has been the easing of commitment standards, on the theory that current laws are so stringent that they prevent the treatment of mentally ill homeless people who pose a threat to themselves or others or are unable to survive safely in the community. After a review of the empirical studies, the Federal Task Force on Homelessness and Severe Mental Illness concluded in its 1992 report *Outcasts on Main Street,* "Although changes in commitment standards have been suggested as a remedy to these problems, there is no empirical evidence to support the belief that changes in civil commitment laws would provide a solution to the problems of homeless mentally ill persons. In fact, current laws are much less restrictive than is commonly believed."[115]

The report noted that "other factors than the law," such as the availability of resources, may influence commitment decisions.[116] In a number of cities, for example, the lack of sufficient community resources for people with psychiatric disabilities ready for discharge from hospitals has caused unnecessarily extended hospital stays and a resulting shortage in inpatient psychiatric beds. In New York, where the crisis struck first and with the greatest severity, many people with serious mental disorders were turned away from municipal psychiatric emergency rooms and others were confined in waiting rooms for days on end, sometimes strapped to wheelchairs or stretchers, often without appropriate treatment or even a bed in which to sleep.[117]

At the height of this crisis, perhaps the most publicized initiative in the country to involuntarily commit homeless people began in New York City, when, in October 1987, Mayor Edward I. Koch ordered psychiatric outreach teams to comb the streets in search of mentally disordered individuals. At the same time, New York created a twenty-eight-bed unit at Bellevue Hospital to provide special care for the homeless people brought in by these teams. Although New York State law prohibited involuntary confinement without a finding of mental illness and imminent dangerousness, the city issued a directive authorizing the detention of homeless people who, although not imminently dangerous, were deemed by a psychiatrist to be likely to become so at an unspecified future date.

One of the first people to be confined was a homeless woman who called herself Billie Boggs.[118] Although she had survived safely on the street for more than a year, eating regularly, maintaining good health, and keeping warm next to a hot-air vent, Boggs was forcibly removed from the sidewalk on Manhattan's Upper East Side where she lived, injected with Haldol, and involuntarily confined in the special locked ward for homeless people. Calling herself a political prisoner, Boggs challenged her confinement.

Boggs argued that she was not imminently dangerous to herself or others and, although her lifestyle was neither aesthetically pleasing nor socially acceptable, she had demonstrated over a year and a half that she could survive safely in freedom and therefore must be released. Relying upon the Supreme Court's warning in *O'Connor* that the state could not confine the harmless mentally ill to improve their standard of living or shield the public from eccentric or objectionable behavior,[119] she claimed that her continued detention violated due process. She conceded that she had urinated and defecated on the sidewalk because there were no accessible toilets but asserted that this was not a proper basis for commitment. Any violation of criminal or public health laws, she urged, should be addressed in another setting.

The city countered that Boggs's mental condition was steadily deteriorating. It noted that she had burned money, tossed a sandwich and a milk carton at a psychiatrist, yelled epithets at delivery men, and once walked into Second Avenue against a red light. Although she had survived on the street until then, city psychiatrists predicted that she was likely to be dangerous to herself in the foreseeable future. To the city, the "most fundamental issue in the case"[120] was whether Boggs was mentally ill, because it was "less likely" that a mentally ill person could survive on the street.[121]

The hearing judge ruled that Boggs's confinement was unconstitutional.

Freedom, constitutionally guaranteed, is the right of all, no less of those who are mentally ill. . . . Whether [Billie Boggs] is or is not mentally ill, it is my finding . . . that she is not unable to care for her essential needs. I am aware that her mode of existence does not conform to conventional standards, that it is an offense to aesthetic senses. It is my hope that the plight she represents will also offend moral conscience and rouse it to action. There must be some civilized alternatives other than involuntary hospitalization or the street.

[T]he mayor's program is a first step in the right direction towards helping the homeless mentally ill. [Billie Boggs], however, does not fall within the ambit of that program.[122]

A split intermediate appeals court reversed in a 3–2 decision,[123] and the New York Court of Appeals dismissed the case as moot after the city released Boggs when a lower court denied the hospital's request to medicate her against her will.[124] Despite the prediction of her Bellevue psychiatrist that she would deteriorate and become suicidal within three days of her release, Billie Boggs moved into a specialized hotel for homeless women in Manhattan, where she remained for more than five years.

The Boggs case reflects the deep divisions in our society concerning the proper treatment of homeless people with psychiatric disabilities. It also illustrates the role that involuntary commitment has increasingly been asked to play in addressing the consequences of unresolved social issues, such as the lack of affordable housing and the dearth of community mental health services. In many ways, civil commitment in the age of homelessness has become a modern-day surrogate for the criminal vagrancy laws that the Supreme Court ruled were unconstitutional in the early 1970s.[125]

OUTPATIENT COMMITMENT

What is outpatient commitment?

Outpatient commitment is a court order for an individual with a mental disability to comply with a treatment plan on an outpatient basis.

The order may require the person to attend therapy sessions, comply with a medication regime, or participate in mental health programs. Outpatient commitment is increasingly popular among state legislators and some psychiatrists and families as a way of compelling people with mental disorders to take medication while they are living in the community. It is touted as an alternative to inpatient hospitalization, but raises serious concerns about whether the state ought to compel a person, otherwise free, to take medication that deeply affects his or her body.

What is the origin of outpatient commitment and how has the concept evolved?

Outpatient commitment occupies a paradoxical place in mental health law because it began as an expression of liberty and has been transformed into an expansion of state power over individuals. It originated as an expression of the principle that inpatient commitment could be ordered only if no less restrictive placement is available. In the seminal case of *Lake v. Cameron*,[126] the court held that the District of Columbia's civil commitment law must be interpreted to mean that an individual who met the legal criteria for involuntary hospitalization could not be confined in a psychiatric facility if she could live safely in the community. Instead, the court could order such a person to attend an outpatient program rather than confining her in a hospital. As another court reasoned, "Even if the standards for an adjudication of mental illness and potential dangerousness are satisfied, a court should order full-time involuntary hospitalization only as a last resort."[127] Many state laws continue to authorize this form of outpatient commitment.

From the concept of a more humane and less restrictive alternative to hospitalization, however, outpatient commitment has been transformed to a means by which people with psychiatric disabilities may be compelled to take antipsychotic medication or ordered into programs even if they do not meet the criteria for involuntary hospitalization. Supporters argue that people with serious mental disorders are more likely to remain stable if they continue to take medication but will decompensate if they do not. "Preventive" outpatient commitment is necessary, they contend, to stop the "revolving door" of hospitalization, release, noncompliance with treatment, deterioration, and rehospitalization. The proponents of outpatient commitment are vocal, prolific, and unapologetic in their advocacy of coercive solutions to individual mental health problems.[128]

In response to these arguments, some states have enacted laws permitting compulsory medication in the community under very loose standards, such as that the person's condition is likely to "deteriorate" in the absence of treatment, the treatment is available, and the person will not consent to it.[129] North Carolina's law, for example, allows outpatient commitment in order to prevent, among other things, "further disability or deterioration."[130] Only a handful of states have laws like North Carolina's, which permits compulsion in the absence of a finding of dangerousness, but many more are considering them.

Even devoted adherents of preventive outpatient commitment have expressed concern about the vast expansion of government authority over individual liberty it entails. Some psychiatrists have attempted to develop "clinical" guidelines to limit the group of individuals to whom outpatient commitment laws are applied.[131] Such guidelines, however, cannot erase the enormous expansion of state authority that this form of outpatient commitment represents.

The press for state control over psychiatric patients living in their own homes has spawned some stinging critiques. One ground of criticism is based on its deprivation of the liberty of people who are not dangerous. Permitting judges to order people who do not meet the criteria for involuntary hospitalization to submit to a regime of medication in the community, critics argue, expands state control over people beyond limits the constitution tolerates.[132] As one commentator has observed, "The predicted deterioration standard could easily create a class of patients who never escape the state's control because their dangerousness is always just around the corner."[133] Surprisingly, the constitutionality of these outpatient commitment laws remains largely untested.

A second critique focuses on the clinical claims made on behalf of outpatient commitment. Supporters argue that people remain stable, comply with treatment expectations, avoid hospitalization (or rehospitalization), and live better lives under an outpatient commitment order. In a thorough review of empirical studies purporting to support these contentions, Kathleen Maloy demonstrated that many of the studies are methodologically flawed and their conclusions vastly overstated, thus providing "almost no valid empirical evidence in support of the effectiveness of [involuntary outpatient commitment] laws vis-à-vis treatment compliance, success in the community for people with severe and persistent mental illness, or amelioration of the problems associated with 'revolving door' patients."[134]

Thus, despite the known infringement of liberty outpatient commitment in its present form represents, the current evidence provides scant basis for believing it substantially improves patient outcomes.

Third, as Maloy points out, the "revolving door" problem outpatient commitment is designed to solve is as likely to be a product of deficiencies in community mental health services as of lack of legal authority over patients. Even to the extent outpatient commitment lowers rehospitalization rates, it is not at all clear that the reason is court-ordered treatment rather than the availability of the treatment resources that accompany the law. Outpatient commitment may offer yet another illustration of society's use of compulsion over people with psychiatric disabilities as a substitute for providing appropriate services.

PLACEMENT IN A NURSING HOME

What protections do people with mental disabilities have against placement in a nursing home?

Although substantial procedural and substantive protections were introduced in the 1970s to prevent the inappropriate institutionalization of people with mental disabilities, one type of institution escaped attention altogether: nursing homes. Amidst all the ferment of reform of involuntary civil commitment laws, safeguards against unwarranted transfers of people with mental disabilities to nursing homes were never put in place. Indeed, the tightening of commitment standards contributed to a phenomenon some have called *transinstitutionalization,* or movement from psychiatric or mental retardation facilities to nursing homes. It is estimated that between 40 and 60 percent of the residents of state psychiatric hospitals who were discharged between 1963 and 1980 were sent to nursing homes,[135] including many who were relatively young.

Whatever differences exist between nursing homes and institutions for people with mental disabilities, the commonalities predominate: regimented institutional living, significant use of antipsychotic medications and physical restraints, a fostering of dependence, and a loss of initiative and control of everyday life among their residents.

In 1987, Congress finally enacted a law to address this problem and encouraged the development of community-based alternatives to institutions for people with mental disabilities who would otherwise have been sent to nursing homes.[136] It established a procedure to review admitting and retaining people with mental disabilities in nursing homes that receive Medicaid funds known as preadmission screening and annual resident review, or PASARR.[137] *As this book goes to press, though, Congress is considering repeal of PASARR.*

What is PASARR and how does it operate?

PASARR prohibits the admission or retention of any person with a mental disability in a nursing home unless that person has a condition that warrants the twenty-four-hour professional nursing care that these facilities offer.[138] Its goal is to force the development of alternatives to nursing homes.

PASARR establishes a "preadmission screen" and an "annual resident review." They consist of two steps or levels. The first level is a determination whether a person proposed for nursing home admission or retention has a serious mental illness, mental retardation, or other developmental disability that affects a person's cognitive abilities and functioning. The screen seeks to identify only mental disorders that are serious enough to interfere with a person's ability to carry on the usual activities of life. The Level I screen is conducted by a state mental health or mental retardation authority or may be delegated by that authority to another agency, such as a hospital or nursing home.

If the screen identifies one of these conditions, the reviewer then moves to the Level II screen, a determination whether the person needs health-related services beyond room and board that can only be provided in an institution. The Level II screen also identifies the need for "specialized services," which are discussed in chapter 6. The state mental retardation authority may conduct the screen itself or delegate this review to an independent agency that is not a nursing home or affiliated with one. However, the mental health authority must base its determination on Level II screens conducted by an independent entity.

If either screen results in a negative finding, *the nursing home may not admit the individual.* A person who is already living in the nursing home at the time this determination is made may continue to live there unless he or she has been a resident for less than thirty months. In that event, the person must be discharged according to a plan and a discharge process that involves the person, the family, and other relevant participants. If it is proposed that a person be admitted, the state agency must notify the person along with the person's legal representative (if any), of its decision.

Does this mean that a nursing home may refuse to admit a person with a mental disability?

No. It only means that certain individuals with mental illness or mental retardation who do not require twenty-four-hour nursing care will not be admitted. People who do have these needs have a right to be admitted and may not be discriminated against because they have a mental disability.

Does a person subject to a screen have the right to appeal?

Yes, but only if the person is found not to be appropriate for nursing home placement or not to need specialized services. There is no right to appeal a finding that a person should be placed in a nursing home.

What alternatives are there for a person found to be inappropriate for nursing home placement?

In theory, the state is supposed to make arrangements to provide alternatives for people who are found ineligible for nursing home placements. To date, however, there has been little evidence of such activity in most states.

What has been the impact of PASARR on limiting nursing home placements of people with mental disabilities?

Since its enactment, PASARR has had little impact on the admission and retention of people with mental disabilities in nursing homes.

First, congressional amendments and administrative interpretations have limited the group of people to whom it applies. The original version of PASARR applied to all residents with mental illness. The 1990 amendment limited its application to people with "serious mental illness." The Health Care Financing Administration's 1992 PASARR regulations define *serious mental illness* narrowly, to mean a major disorder that results in limitations in major life activities in the past three to six months and that has also resulted in partial or inpatient hospitalization within the past two years. Alternatively, a person must have experienced a significant disruption of his or her normal living situation due to the mental disorder that required supportive services or residential treatment, or resulted in intervention by housing or law enforcement officials.[139] These definitions severely constrict the number of people for whom a screen is necessary. Further, no screen is required for a person whose primary diagnosis is dementia, such as Alzheimer's Disease.[140]

Second, states have interpreted *serious mental illness* narrowly and have tended to overuse the diagnosis of dementia, which avoids the need for a screen.

Third, PASARR imposes no obligation to serve rejected nursing home candidates and creates no right to alternative, community-based care for people who otherwise would be placed in nursing homes and paid for by Medicaid. Congress intended to press states to make arrangements for people who would leave nursing homes under PASARR and specified that states develop alternative disposition plans, but the requirements it imposed were weak to begin with and were narrowed further by administrative regulations.

Fourth, PASARR was not accompanied by any mandate to use Medicaid funds to finance alternatives to nursing homes. Nursing home care may be fully funded by Medicaid, but community-based care has no source of Medicaid funding at all.

Finally, even to the extent PASARR creates legal obligations, enforcement has been so lackluster as to be virtually nonexistent.

The Commitment of Children

As a general rule, minors do not enjoy the full range of legal safeguards accorded to adults. Until the age of majority, minors are frequently presumed to lack the maturity and judgment necessary to make many basic decisions affecting their lives. For example, minors typically cannot marry, enter into contracts, file lawsuits, or make most medical decisions on their own. Instead, their parents or guardians generally exercise these rights for them, on the assumption that they are acting in the minors' best interests. Where there is no parent or guardian, the state may step in to make these decisions under certain circumstances, using its *parens patriae* power. This usually requires a court order.

In its deference to parental decision making, the law reflects traditional Western notions of the family unit, premised upon the twin beliefs that "parents possess what a child lacks in maturity, experience, and capacity for judgment required for making life's difficult decisions" and that "natural bonds of affection lead parents to act in the best interests of their children."[141] The theory is that the family—not the government—should be responsible for most childrearing decisions.

Within this concept of family privacy, however, there is a tension between the competing interests of parents and guardians to raise their children as they see fit and the right of minors to due process when state action threatens their liberty. On the one hand, a constitutional interest in family privacy insulates parental decision making from government review in all but extraordinary situations.[142] Thus, parents routinely decide where their children will attend school, how late they may come home at night, or whether they should have their tonsils removed. Unless parents are abusive or neglectful, the state may not intervene. At the same time, minors have a due process liberty interest in remaining free from confinement[143] and, if sufficiently mature to give informed consent, in making important health care decisions for themselves[144] without interference from the government or their parents. The tension is greatest where the parental decision restricts fundamental rights, such as personal liberty or reproductive privacy.

There are at least two situations where minors may be allowed to make their own medical decisions. The first is where they have the capacity to decide for themselves. Although there are obvious reasons why a seven-year-old should not be allowed to consent to surgery, older minors may have the maturity to make their own health care decisions. A "mature minor" rule has developed that permits older minors who are able to understand "the nature, extent and consequences of the medical treatment"[145] to make certain medical decisions without parental consent. Similarly, emancipated minors who are no longer under the care and control of their parents are free to make most medical decisions themselves. Although the procedures for emancipation vary from state to state and in some cases may require a court order a typical emancipated minor is one who is married, serving in the military, or living away from home and managing her own finances.[146]

How are minors admitted for inpatient treatment?

Minors, like adults, can be admitted as informal, voluntary, or involuntary patients. Many states, however, do not permit minors to apply for voluntary admission on their own, unless they are old enough to give informed consent. The precise age varies from state to state, ranging from fourteen to eighteen years of age.

As a general rule, it is the facility's duty to ensure that the prospective voluntary patient is capable of giving informed consent to be admitted. In *Zinermon v. Burch*,[147] the Supreme Court held that an incompetent person who was permitted to hospitalize himself as a voluntary patient could file a civil rights action for damages against state hospital officials who should have known that he lacked the capacity to apply for voluntary admission. If a minor is incompetent to give informed consent to admission, then a parent, relative, or guardian must apply for the child's admission.

What is a "minor voluntary" admission?

A minor voluntary admission is perhaps the most commonly used—and most controversial—means of institutionalizing a juvenile. Developed through state statutes passed in the late 1950s and 1960s in an effort to encourage voluntary admissions,[148] this procedure authorizes a parent, guardian, or the government (if the child is in state custody) to apply for the child's admission to a hospital or treatment center. A physician attached to the institution then examines the child to determine whether the admission is appropriate.

Although the admission is deemed "voluntary" because the parent or guardian has consented on the minor's behalf, from the child's perspective the process can be as voluntary as an attack of appendicitis. A few states require the consent of a minor who is over the age of twelve or thirteen. In most states, however, the child's wishes are legally irrelevant, and the child has no right to object to the confinement. In such cases, the admission is tantamount to an involuntary commitment. Yet, minor voluntary patients commonly have fewer rights than involuntary admittees. Minor voluntary patients can be confined against their will without notice, a judicial hearing, a lawyer, the right to present evidence and cross-examine witnesses, or the right to appeal. Frequently, only the person who "volunteered" the child can petition for discharge.

In addition, because the admission is technically voluntary, the constitutional standard for involuntary commitment does not apply. Minor voluntary patients can be confined against their will without a finding of dangerousness to themselves or others. The hospital need only find that they are mentally ill and can benefit from inpatient treatment. Indeed, they do not even have to have a serious mental illness.

Worse yet, there is usually no obligation to consider alternatives to confinement for minors who require treatment but would benefit from a less restrictive setting. This often results in unnecessary hospitalizations because parents may be unaware of appropriate alternatives or unable to afford them. For many parents, the decision to admit their child to an institution is a very stressful one, and stress tends to diminish the quality of the decision.

What are the consequences of the minor voluntary admission standard for children?

Because the minor voluntary admission standard is so lax, many minors are admitted against their will, even when they do not have a serious mental disorder. Studies of psychiatric hospitalization statistics suggest fewer than one-third of the children admitted for inpatient mental health treatment have major mental disorders, such as psychosis or major depression. The remaining two-thirds have such diagnoses as conduct disorder, personality disorder, childhood adjustment, or "transitional" disorders.[149] One critic noted, "An examination of the various 'symptoms' that characterized each type of disorder reveals that, in general, these categories describe troublemakers, children with relatively mild psychological problems, and children who do not appear to suffer from anything more serious than normal developmental changes."[150] By contrast, one-half to two-thirds of adults admitted to psychiatric units had a severe mental disorder.[151]

Compounding this problem is the tremendous growth of private psychiatric facilities, many of which have profitable adolescent wards. In 1968 there were no for-profit hospital chains offering psychiatric care. By 1982 investor chains controlled 43 percent of private psychiatric hospitals.[152] One of the unique aspects of the hospitalization of minors is that it takes place mostly in private facilities. In 1980 private institutions accounted for over 60 percent of all juvenile psychiatric admissions, and the numbers have "increased substantially" since then.[153] Children in private facilities are likely to have longer stays and less serious disorders than children in public facilities.[154]

As a result, the institutionalization rates for children skyrocketed during the 1980s.[155] The average daily census of minors in psychiatric hospitals and residential treatment centers increased 60 percent between 1983 and 1986, from 34,000 to 54,700.[156] To attract patients, many private hospitals "have enlisted a range of strategies, including professional marketing techniques, to help keep admissions rates high."[157] Some have placed advertise-

ments playing on parental fears of suicide and suggesting that hospitalization was the solution for a host of problems, from difficulties at school
to drug use, premarital sex, or unmanageable behavior.[158] In the early
1990s, growing allegations of abuse led to congressional hearings into
profit-making health care at which witnesses testified that "thousands of
people, mostly adolescents, were unnecessarily admitted to psychiatric
hospitals during the last decade as a part of money-making schemes that
milked insurance companies but offered little in the way of treatment."[159]

Although hospitals can help stabilize certain children who truly need
it, the consequences of commitment can be particularly harsh for many
minors. They are uprooted from their homes, separated from their peers,
subjected to an institutional regimen that severely restricts their freedom,
and are often provided substandard schooling. Many children find the
experience isolating and frightening. In addition, minors tend to remain
confined longer than adults. One source found that the average length
of stay for a child in a psychiatric hospital is approximately double that
of an adult.[160]

What has the Supreme Court said about the commitment of minors?

The Supreme Court's failure to accord minors the basic due process
right to challenge their psychiatric hospitalization in many cases has no
doubt played a large role in perpetuating this system. In *Parham v. J. R.,*[161]
the Supreme Court rejected a challenge brought by institutionalized minors to a Georgia statute authorizing the "voluntary" admission of unwilling minors without even the minimum procedural safeguard of a court
hearing. The minors argued that involuntary confinement in a mental
institution was so serious an infringement of their fundamental rights
to liberty and personal autonomy as to justify limiting the traditional
prerogatives of parents and guardians. Just as the Court had struck down
a Missouri statute authorizing the parental veto of a minor's decision to
have an abortion, they argued, the Court should at least require judicial
review of a parent's decision to confine a minor in an institution.

In a serious setback to the rights of juveniles, the Supreme Court held
that minors have no right to seek judicial review of their confinement,
finding that the admission and retention decisions of mental health professionals at the institutions provide all of the independent review that is
needed. In the Court's view, a judicial hearing is a "time-consuming

procedural minuet"[162] that would cause needless friction between parent and child, divert valuable state resources that should be devoted to providing treatment, and ultimately serve little useful purpose because courts are no better qualified than psychiatrists to render psychiatric judgments. The Court, however, did not consider whether physicians at profit-making hospitals were sufficiently free from financial interests and possible conflicts of interest to be the neutral decision makers it envisioned in the opinion.

The decision also failed to consider whether the confinement of minors under the legal fiction that they are "voluntary" patients—and therefore without a finding of dangerousness or any consideration of less restrictive alternatives—was unconstitutional because it dispensed with the safeguards required for involuntary commitment. In a subsequent case, the Supreme Court ruled that the voluntary admission of an adult who was incompetent to give consent violated due process, precisely because it did not afford him the protections mandated for involuntary admissions.[163] Although minors present a more complicated problem, the seriousness of the potential consequences of confinement and the importance of their liberty interest argue strongly for a similar result. At the very least, the standards for commitment should govern the admission of an objecting minor, and there should be a showing that there is no available, less restrictive alternative to institutionalization.

How does parental health insurance coverage affect the decision to institutionalize a child?

In many instances a parent's decision to admit a child for residential mental health treatment is influenced by the terms of the family's insurance coverage. Because of the high cost of mental health care, the availability of insurance reimbursement may be a family's only means of affording treatment. Currently, most health insurance plans set an unrealistically low ceiling on reimbursement for outpatient mental health treatment, while covering the cost of most inpatient treatment for the same mental illness.[164] Faced with the relentless pressure of unreimbursed outpatient treatment, many parents who seek help for their children may feel that they have no other recourse than to admit their children to an institution.

What are the rights of children in foster care regarding hospitalization?

One of the most powerful justifications for allowing parents to commit their children without due process safeguards is the presumption that parents generally act in the best interests of their children. Adversary hearings, it is argued, do little good and are likely to cause considerable damage to the parent-child relationship.[165] These assertions are unpersuasive in view of the serious deprivation of liberty that results from commitment, the large number of children who are unnecessarily committed, and the fact that many family relationships have been ruptured at the time the minor is institutionalized. But these rationales have no relevance whatsoever to children who are wards of the state and live in foster care.

When a child is in foster care, it is the state itself that effects the commitment. There is no parent to act in the child's best interests, and an adversary hearing poses no threat to family ties. However well-intentioned state social workers may be, the attention they can devote to a single child is often limited by high caseloads and their decisions dictated by a dearth of placement options. Children with mental disabilities are among the most difficult to place in the foster care system. Many foster families are loath to accept children with a psychiatric history, while others will not allow children they have cared for back into their homes once they have been hospitalized for a mental illness. Most child care residences and residential treatment centers are reluctant to admit children who have been institutionalized, and even fewer will consider those with "dual diagnoses," such as mental illness and mental retardation.

As a consequence, children in state custody may be forced to remain in an institution even after they have been declared clinically ready for discharge because there is no other place for them to go. In an especially egregious case, children at one psychiatric institution were confined for up to twenty-two months after their doctors had pronounced them ready for discharge because the local services agency could not provide appropriate places for them to live.[166]

In *Parham*, the Supreme Court found that wards of the state are not entitled to greater due process safeguards than children admitted by their parents. Pointing to a Georgia statute that presumed that the state acts in the best interests of its wards, the Court found that there was no reason why the state of Georgia would act so differently from a natural parent in seeking help for a child. However, experience shows that, whether through indifference, incompetence, red tape, or a lack of placement resources, it is not uncommon for children in foster care to languish in an institution substantially longer than those who have natural families to care for them.

How does a minor voluntary patient petition for discharge?

Adults admitted on voluntary status can request their discharge at any time. If the facility refuses to release them, it must file a motion with a court to convert them to involuntary status. The situation with minors is more complex because the minor did not consent to the admission in the first place. Instead, it is the parent or guardian who sought the initial admission—not the child—who can petition for the minor's discharge at any time. Some states have created statutory exceptions based on the child's age or maturity and allow minors who have attained competence or are over the age of sixteen to petition for their own release.

NOTES

1. Humphrey v. Cady, 405 U.S. 504, 509 (1972).

2. *Black's Law Dictionary* (5th ed. 1979).

3. Rothman, *The Discovery of the Asylum: Social Order and Disorder in the New Republic* 130 (1971).

4. *Id.* at 133.

5. Schloendorff v. Society of N.Y. Hosp., 211 N.Y. 125, 129, 105 N.E. 92 (1914).

6. *See, e.g.*, Jacobson v. Massachusetts, 197 U.S. 11 (1905).

7. A contemporaneous example of the exercise of this authority is the detention of people with multiple drug-resistant tuberculosis. The involuntary confinement of people with communicable diseases is subject to all of the due process safeguards applicable to the commitment of people with mental disabilities, including the requirement that there be no equally effective, less restrictive alternative to protect the public health. *See, e.g.*, Greene v. Edwards, 263 S.E.2d 661 (W. Va. 1980); New York City Public Health Code, § 11.47 (adopted March 1993).

8. This discussion of the history of involuntary institutionalization draws upon the works of Herr, *Rights and Advocacy for Retarded People* (1983) and Rothman, *supra.*

9. Brakel, Parry & Weiner, *The Mentally Disabled and the Law* 13 (3d ed. 1985).

10. Herr, *supra*, at 19.

11. *Id.* at 17.

12. Lessard v. Schmidt, 349 F. Supp. 1078, 1086 (E.D. Wis. 1972), *vacated and remanded on other grounds*, 421 U.S. 957 (1975).

13. Herr, *supra*, at 16. Herr writes that it was not until 1827 that New York State forbade the confinement of people with mental illness in jails, prisons, or houses of correction. *Id.* at 17.

14. Rothman, *supra*, at 138.

15. *Id.* at 112, quoting Isaac Ray, one of the leading medical superintendents of the pre–Civil War period in America.

16. *Id.* at 286.

17. *Id.*

18. *Id.* at 283.

19. Herr, *supra*, at 22.

20. Moore, *The Feeble-Minded in New York* 3, 89–92 (1911), cited in Herr, *supra*, at 23.

21. There is a vast amount of literature on deinstitutionalization. With respect to people with psychiatric disabilities, good starting points are Johnson, *Out of Bedlam: The Truth About Deinstitutionalization* (1990) and the more academic Rochefort, *From Poorhouses to Homelessness; Policy Analysis and Mental Health Care* (1993). For mental retardation, see *Deinstitutionalization and Community Adjustment of Mentally Retarded People* (Bruininks, Meyers, Sigford & Lakin eds., American Association on Mental Deficiency 1981). *See generally* Arnold v. Sarn, 775 P.2d 521 (Ariz. 1989).

22. Herr, *supra*, at 46 (citations omitted). Drawing upon data from the National Institute for Mental Health, Brakel et al. report that the average daily census in public mental institutions dropped from 551,390 in 1956 to 153,544 in 1978. Brakel et al., *supra*, at 47.

23. Deutsch, *The Shame of the States* (1948).

24. Reisner & Slobogin, *Law and the Mental Health System* (2d ed. 1990) at 601–2 (citations omitted).

25. National Institute of Mental Health, *Mental Health United States 1987*, Table 3.21.

26. National Institute of Mental Health, *Mental Health 1992*.

27. National Institute of Mental Health, *Mental Health United States 1987*, Table 3.24.

28. Braddock, Hemp, Bachelder & Fujiura, *The State of the States in Developmental Disabilities*, Institute on Disability and Human Development, University of Illinois at Chicago (March 1994).

29. For example, a federal court supervised the deinstitutionalization of some 5,400 people from the Willowbrook State School in New York during a period lasting more than twenty years. See New York State Association for Retarded Children v. Cuomo, No. 356, 357/72 (E.D.N.Y. 1993) (permanent injunction issued ending twenty-one years of active litigation and guaranteeing plaintiffs' rights to appropriate residences and individualized services in the community for the rest of their lives).

30. Braddock et al., *supra*.

31. There were, however, a few influential such cases in the 1970s. See, *e.g.*, Dixon v. Weinberger, 405 F. Supp. 974 (D.D.C. 1975); Brewster v. Dukakis, No. 76-4423-F (D. Mass. 1978)(consent decree).

32. Robinson v. California, 370 U.S. 660 (1962).

33. *Consensus Statement, Violence and Mental Disorder: Public Perceptions vs. Research Findings*, drafted jointly by the National Stigma Clearinghouse and the John D. and Catherine T. MacArthur Foundation Research Network on Mental Health and the Law, September 16, 1994. The statement is available from the Clearinghouse at 275 Seventh Ave., 16th Floor, New York, N.Y. 10001. 212-633-4349.

34. *Id. See also* Mulvey, *Assessing the Evidence of a Link Between Mental Illness and Violence*, 45 Hospital and Community Psychiatry 661 (1994).

The studies of the association between violent behavior and mental disorder and the conclusions to be drawn from them are still the subject of considerable debate. Although Mulvey, for example, has concluded that there is "an increased relative risk for violence among individuals with mental illness compared with the general population," he stresses that "the current state of the research provides very few leads about exactly what should be made of this association." *Id.* at 667. Mulvey further notes that there is "no clear indication of causality" between mental illness and violence, *id.* at 667, and observes that it "may well be that mental illness does not consistently increase the likelihood of violence within an individual." *Id.* at 664. ("The presence of mental illness might be the first link in a chain of events resulting in violence. It is also possible that frequent violent encounters exacerbate a mental illness. Alternatively these two phenomena could simply coexist." *Id.* at 664.)

35. Mulvey, *supra*, at 664.

36. Livermore, Malmquist, Meehl, *On the Justifications for Civil Commitment*, 117 University of Pennsylvania Law Review 75, 84 (1968). As Monahan noted, "knowledge of the appropriate base rate is the most important single piece of information necessary to make an accurate prediction." Monahan, *The Clinical Prediction of Violent Behavior* (National Institute of Mental Health, 1981) at 34. Unfortunately, clinicians are often unaware of the base rate when making predictions.

37. Hiday, *Civil Commitment: A Review of the Empirical Research*, 6 Behavioral Sciences and the Law 15 (1989).

38. *See* Parrish, *Involuntary Use of Interventions: Pros and Cons.* 2 Innovations & Research 15 (1993).

39. Campbell & Schraiber, *The Well-Being Project*, California Department of Mental Health and California Network of Mental Health Clients (1989).

40. Kiesler, *Mental Hospitals and Alternative Care: Noninstitutionalization as Potential Public Policy for Mental Patients*, 37 American Psychologist 349, 350 (1982), in Reisner and Slobogin, *supra*, at 686–87. However, as Reisner & Slobogin point out, and Kiesler himself acknowledged in a later study, the research data did not appear to cover people considered imminently dangerous to self or others. *Id.* at 687; Kiesler & Sibulkin, *Mental Hospitalization* 177 (1987).

41. According to a chart of state commitment criteria that appeared in the Mental and Physical Disability Law Reporter, ten state statutes contain some requirement that the individual be unable to make treatment decisions. Parry, *Survey of Standards for Extended Involuntary Commitment*, 18 Mental and Physical Disability Law Reporter 330 (May–June 1994).

42. *See* Colyar v. Third Judicial Court, 469 F. Supp. 424 (D. Utah 1979).

43. *See* Mental Hygiene Law § 9.01.

44. This view, popularized by R. D. Laing and Thomas Szasz in the 1960s and 1970s, has few adherents today.

45. Treffert, M.D., *The Obviously Ill Patient in Need of Treatment: A Fourth Standard for Civil Commitment*, 36 Hospital and Community Psychiatry 264 (1985).

46. *See, e.g.*, Monahan, *supra*, at 77–82 and Monahan, *Mental Disorder and Violent Behavior*, 47 American Psychologist, 511–21 (1992).

47. *See* discussion of impact of reform of civil commitment laws below.

48. *See, e.g.*, Lessard v. Schmidt, *supra*, at 1094; Scopes v. Shah, 398 N.Y.S.2d 911, 913 (3d Dept. 1977) (due process requires finding that person to be committed poses "a real and present threat of substantial harm to himself or others").

49. Addington v. Texas, 441 U.S. 418 (1979).

50. 422 U.S. 563 (1975).

51. The superintendent testified at trial that Donaldson received "milieu therapy" while at the hospital. Members of the hospital staff admitted that this was really a euphemism for confinement in the "milieu" of a psychiatric hospital. *Id.* at 568–69.

52. *Id.* at 569.

53. *Id.* at 568.

54. *Id.* at 576.

55. *Id.* at 575 (citations omitted).

56. *See* Zinermon v. Burch, 110 S. Ct. 975, 987 (1990). ("The involuntary placement process serves to guard against the confinement of a person who, though mentally ill, is harmless and can live safely outside an institution. Confinement of such a person . . . is unconstitutional.")

57. Challenges to the imprecision of the definition of *mental illness* in state statutes are generally unsuccessful. For example, in rejecting the claim that the definition of mental illness in Utah's commitment statute was unconstitutionally vague and overly broad, a Utah federal court noted that "the field of mental health is not one that lends itself to extremely precise definitions. To require a degree of precision that the current science cannot afford would be futile." Colyar v. Third Judicial District Court, 469 F. Supp. 424, 434 (D. Utah 1979).

58. John Parry, *Survey of Standards for Extended Involuntary Commitment*, and accompanying Table, 18 Mental and Physical Disability Law Reporter 330 (May–June 1994).

59. *Id.* (approximately ten states have such a requirement in one form or another). *See also Colyar v. Third Judicial Court, supra*, at 431–32.

60. *See, e.g.*, Rivers v. Katz, 495 N.E.2d 337 (NY 1986).

61. Brooks, *Law, Psychiatry & Mental Health Systems* 680 (1974).

62. Courts as well have required such a finding, as a matter of due process. *See, e.g.*, State v. Krol, 344 A.2d 289 (N.J. 1975); Matter of Harry M., 468 N.Y.S.2d 359, 364 (2d Dept. 1983)("the danger must be a substantial threat to his physical wellbeing to justify commitment").

63. Suzuki v. Yuen, 617 F.2d 173, 176 (9th Cir. 1980). *But see* State v. Krol, 344 A.2d 289, 301 (N.J. 1975), a New Jersey Supreme Court decision recognized "substantial destruction of property" as a component of dangerous behavior.

64. *See, e.g.*, O'Connor v. Donaldson, supra.

65. *See, e.g.*, the Supreme Court's admonition in *O'Connor, supra*, at 535, that the Constitution prohibits the use of institutionalization to raise an individual's standard of living or to protect the public from eccentric or unattractive behavior, if the individual has the capacity to survive safely in the community.

66. *See, e.g., Lessard v. Schmidt, supra*, at 1094.

67. Quoted in Rosenthal, *Who Will Turn Violent? Hospitals Have to Guess*, N. Y. Times, April 7, 1993 at C1.

68. *See, e.g.*, Monahan, *The Clinical Prediction of Violent Behavior, supra*; Ennis & Litwack, *Psychiatry and the Presumption of Expertise: Flipping Coins in the Courtroom*, 62 California Law Review 693 (1974).

69. Brief *amicus curiae* of the American Psychiatric Association in Barefoot v. Estelle, 463 U.S. 880 (1983), at 12.

70. Monahan, *supra*, at 49.

71. *Id.* at 13, quoting Monahan, *supra*.

72. *The Clinical Prediction of Dangerousness: An Interview with John Monahan, Ph.D.*, 10 Currents in Affective Illness No. 6, at 7 (June 1991).

73. *Interview with John Monahan, Ph. D.*, *supra* at 7.

74. Barefoot v. Estelle, 463 U.S. 880 (1983).

75. Brief *amicus curiae* of American Psychiatric Association, *supra*, which argued that this testimony was all the more pernicious because it came cloaked in a mantle of expertise that a jury would find difficult to dismiss.

76. Addington v. Texas, 441 U.S. 418, 429 (1979).

77. *Id.*

78. *See, e.g.*, Lessard v. Schmidt, *supra*, 349 F. Supp. at 1093; Lynch v. Baxley, 386 F. Supp. 378, 391 (M.D. Ala. 1974); Doremus v. Farrell, 407 F. Supp. 509, 514–15 (D. Neb. 1975); and Stamus v. Leonhardt, 414 F. Supp. 439, 451 (S.D. Iowa 1976).

79. *See, e.g.*, Project Release v. Prevost, 722 F.2d 960, 973 (2d Cir. 1983); *Colyar v. Third Justice District Court, supra*, at 434.

80. United States *ex rel.* Mathew v. Nelson, 461 F. Supp. 707, 711 (N.D. Ill. 1978) (three-judge court).

81. *See, e.g.*, Shelton v. Tucker, 364 U.S. 479 (1960) (Arkansas statute requiring public school teachers to list all organizations to which they belonged or contributed was unconstitutional because state had less drastic means for pursuing its interest in monitoring fitness of teachers).

82. Reisner & Slobogin, *supra*, at 683 ("As of 1985, at least forty-seven states required that involuntary patients be committed to treatment in the least restrictive setting. Keilitz, Conn & Giampetro, *Least Restrictive Treatment of Involuntary Patients: translating Concepts into Practice*, 29 St. Louis University Law Review 691, 708 (1985)).

83. *See, e.g.*, *Lessard v. Schmidt, supra* at 1095–96; Kesselbrenner v. Anonymous, 305 N.E.2d 903 (N.Y. 1973) (federal and state constitutional grounds); Lynch v. Baxley, *supra*, 386 F. Supp. at 392; and Suzuki v. Quisenberry, 411 F. Supp. 1113, 1132–33 (D. Hawaii 1976).

84. O'Connor v. Donaldson, *supra*, 422 U.S. at 576 (emphasis added).

85. *Id.* at 575.

86. Lynch v. Baxley, 744 F.2d 1452 (11th Cir. 1984).

87. *See* Covington v. Harris, 419 F.2d 617 (D.C. Cir. 1969); *Kesselbrenner v. Anonymous, supra*.

88. *See, e.g.*, Rivers v. Katz, 67 N.Y.2d 485, 495 N.E.2d 337 (1986).

89. Similarly, as discussed in chapter 6, courts have been reluctant to interpret the least restrictive alternative doctrine to require an array of community-based services for people who are involuntarily committed.

90. Treffert, *Dying with Their Rights On*, 130 American Journal of Psychiatry 1041 (1973).

91. The proposal is set forth, with analysis, in Stromberg & Strone, *A Model State Law on Civil Commitment for the Mentally Ill*, 20 Harvard Journal of Legislation 275 (1983).

92. Appelbaum, *Almost a Revolution; Mental Health Law and the Limits of Change* (1994).

93. Appelbaum, *supra*, at 40.

94. Perlin, *Fatal Assumption: A Critical Evaluation of the Role of Counsel in Mental Disability Cases*, 16 Law and Human Behavior 39 (1991).

95. Perlin, *On Sanism*, 16 Southern Methodist University Law Review 373 (1992).

96. 113 S. Ct. 2637 (1993).

97. *See, e.g.*, Matter of Harry M., 468 N.Y.S.2d 359 (2d Dept. 1983) (due process permits involuntary commitment of mentally retarded persons only upon showing of danger to self or others and lack of less restrictive alternatives); Kinner v. State, 382 So. 2d 756 (Fla. App. 1980) (commitment only appropriate for persons who are dangerous to self or others or lack the capacity to evaluate for themselves the risks of freedom and the benefits of institutionalization). *But see* Matter of Vandenberg, 617 P.2d 675 (Or. 1980) (upholding statute authorizing commitment of "mentally deficient" persons provided that they meet the American Association of Mental Deficiency's definition of mental retardation and that institutionalization "is the optimal available plan" and "in the best interest of the person and the community").

98. Brakel et al., *supra*, at 37–39.

99. Ellis, *Decisions by and for People with Mental Retardation: Balancing Considerations of Autonomy and Protection*, 37 Villanova Law Review 1779, 1809 (1992).

100. *Id.* at n. 124, citing Clark v. Cohen, 794 F.2d 79 (3d Cir. 1986), *cert. denied* 409 U.S. 962 (1986) (woman confined thirty years despite requests for release).

101. 494 U.S. 113 (1990).

102. *In re* Hop, 623 P.2d 282 (Cal. 1981).

103. *See generally*, Levy, *Should the Homeless Have a Right to Counsel?*, The Brief, Summer, 1989, at 7, 8. *See also* U.S. General Accounting Office, *Homelessness: A Complex Problem and the Federal Response* (1985) (30 percent of all Americans earning half or less of the median income paid 70 percent of their income in rent in 1983).

104. *See, e.g.*, Dugger, *Study Says Shelter Turnover Hides Scope of Homelessness*, N.Y. Times, Nov. 16, 1993, A1 (the value of the monthly rental subsidy to families on welfare has declined by 42 percent since 1972, while the real cost of housing has risen). *See also* Levy, *supra*; More of Homeless Are Now Families, N.Y. Times, Dec. 22, 1993, A18. (Unveiling a report on hunger and homelessness in American cities, the cochairman of the United States Conference of Mayors reported in 1993 that there was "a significant number of working poor among the homeless," and noted that 30 percent of adults requesting food assistance in 1993 were employed); and Wicker, *Always with Us*, N.Y. Times, Nov. 19, 1987, at A31 (Figures from a 1986 Census Bureau Report showed that 41.5 percent of the poor in America had a job in 1985 and that the working poor were the fastest growing segment of the poverty population: 18.9 million—up 33 percent from 1979.)

105. In 1981 the federal government adopted procedures that caused over 350,000 people to lose their Supplemental Security Income (SSI) benefits. Many of these people had mental disabilities. Perlin writes, "While these cutbacks have diminished in the face of public outrage and congressional response, there is no question that the reduction of disability benefits was a significant factor in the increase in the number of homeless persons." Perlin, *Mental Disability Law* § 7.25 at 686 (1989).

106. *See*, Wicker, *supra*.

107. Johnson, *Out of Bedlam, supra*; Culhane, Dejowski, Ibanez, Needham & Mac-

chia, *Public Shelter Admission Rates in Philadelphia and New York City: The Implications of Turnover for Sheltered Population Counts* (Fannie Mae Office of Housing Research 1993), citing Burt, *Over the Edge: The Growth of Homelessness in the 1980s* (Russell Sage Foundation 1992); Rossi, *Down and Out in America: The Origins of Homelessness* (Chicago: University of Chicago Press, 1989); and Hopper & Hamberg, *The Making of America's Homeless,* in *Critical Perspectives on Housing* (Bratt et al. eds. 1986).

108. Culhane et al., *supra,* at 2.

109. *Id.* at 3.

110. *Id.*

111. Dugger, *Study Says Shelter Turnover Hides Scope of Homelessness,* N.Y. Times, Nov. 16, 1993, A1. A similar study of Philadelphia shelter admissions found that 3 percent of that city's population had spent time in its shelters during the same period. *Id.* The authors of the study estimated that more than two million Americans may become homeless at one time or another during a given year. *Id.*

112. *More of Homeless Are Now Families,* N.Y. Times, Dec. 22, 1993, A18.

113. The public is also generally less aware of homeless families because they are less visible than single homeless people with mental illness or substance abuse problems, who are more often in evidence on the streets and in public places.

114. *See, e.g.,* N.Y. State Dept. of Social Services, *Homelessness in New York State: A Report to the Governor and the Legislature* (1988); *Fear and Dependency Rub Shoulders in the Shelters,* N.Y. Times, Nov. 4, 1991, A1, B2 (survey of 202 New York City shelter residents in 1990 found 21.5 percent had received counseling services for an emotional problem or nervous condition); Lamb & Talbott, *The Homeless Mentally Ill: The Perspective of the American Psychiatric Association,* 256 Journal of the American Medical Association 498 (1986) (voicing the opinion that the most sound studies indicate prevalence of major mental illness of about 40 percent among total homeless population); Jencks, *The Homeless* (1994) (about one-third of homeless have a psychiatric disorder).

115. *Outcasts on Main Street,* Federal Task Force on Homelessness and Severe Mental Illness (1992) at 50.

116. *Id.*

117. *See, e.g., Lizotte v. HHC, supra,* a federal class action lawsuit brought on behalf of patients confined in municipal psychiatric emergency rooms in New York City challenging their extended confinement in psychiatric emergency rooms because no inpatient beds were available. A consent order was issued in July 1992.

118. Although her real name was Joyce Brown, she preferred to be called Billie Boggs, after the television personality Bill Boggs, maintaining that she used a pseudonym to elude the efforts of her family to locate and commit her.

119. *O'Connor v. Donaldson, supra,* at 575.

120. Respondents' Brief to the New York Court of Appeals, Jan. 5, 1988 at 24.

121. *Id.* at 11.

122. Matter of Boggs, 522 N.Y.S.2d 407, 412–13 (Sup. Ct. N.Y. Co. 1987).

123. 523 N.Y.S.2d 71 (1st Dept. 1987).

124. 520 N.E.2d 515 (N.Y. 1988), *rearg. den.* 524 N.E.2d 879, *appeal dismissed* 70 N.Y.2d 981.

125. *See, e.g.,* Papachristou v. City of Jacksonville, 405 U.S. 156 (1972).

126. Lake v. Cameron, 364 f. 2d 657 (D.C. Cir. 1966).

127. *Lessard v. Schmidt, supra,* at 1078.

128. *See, e.g.,* Mulvey, Geller & Roth, *The Promise and Peril of Involuntary Outpatient Commitment,* 42 American Psychologist 571 (1987); Geller, *Rights, Wrongs, and the Dilemma of Coerced Community Treatment,* 143 American Journal of Psychiatry 1259 (1986).

129. For a compendium of these laws, see McCafferty & Dooley, *Involuntary Outpatient Commitment: An Update,* 14 Mental and Physical Disability Law Reporter 277 (1990).

130. N.C. Gen. Stat. §§ 122C–263(d)(1989).

131. Geller, *Clinical Guidelines for the Use of Involuntary Outpatient Treatment,* 41 Hospital and Community Psychiatry 749 (1990).

132. *See, e.g.,* Schwartz & Costanzo, *Compelling Treatment in the Community: Distorted Doctrines and Violated Values,* 20 Loyola of Los Angeles Law Review 1329 (1987); Stefan, *Preventive Commitment: The Concept and Its Pitfalls,* 11 Mental and Physical Disability Law Review 288 (1987). *See* discussion of the constitutional basis for civil commitment above.

133. Slogobin, *Involuntary Community Treatment of People Who are Violent and Mentally Ill: A Legal Analysis,* 45 Hospital and Community Psychiatry 685, 867 (1994).

134. Maloy, *Analysis: Critiquing the Empirical Evidence: Does Involuntary Outpatient Commitment Work?* Mental Health Policy Resource Center (1992).

135. Liptzin, *Major Medical Disorders/Problems in Nursing Homes: Implications for Research and Public Policy* in *Mental Illness in Nursing Homes: Agenda for Research* (Harper & Lebowitz eds. 1986).

136. Elderly people with mental illness benefit as much from community living as younger people do. *See* Bernstein and Rose, *Psychosocial Programming for the Elderly Who are Mentally Ill,* 14 Psychosocial Rehabilitation Journal 4 (1991); Mosher-Ashley & Guild, *When Older People with Chronic Mental Illness Move: From a State Institution to a Share Apartment.* Aging 22 (1991).

137. The PASARR process is contained in the Medicaid statute at 42 U.S.C. § 1396r(e)(7). It is governed by regulations appearing at 42 C.F.R. 483. The Omnibus Budget Reconciliation Act has a second feature as well, obligating the nursing home and the state each to provide certain mental health and habilitation services to nursing home residents with mental disabilities. These are discussed in chapter 6.

138. For an overview of the legislation and the PASARR process, *see* Pepper & Rubenstein, *What Preadmission Screening and Annual Resident Review Means for Older People with Mental Disabilities,* 27 Clearinghouse Review 1447 (1994).

139. 42 C.F.R. § 483.102(b). Advocates have criticized the amendment as limiting the screens to too small a group of people at risk of inappropriate nursing home admission. *See* Pepper & Rubenstein, *supra.*

140. 42 U.S.C. § 1396r(e)(7)(G)(i).

141. Parham v. J.R., 442 U.S. 584 (1979) (citations omitted).

142. *See, e.g.,* Pierce v. Society of Sisters, 268 U.S. 510, 535 (1925) (state law forcing parents and guardians to accept schooling for their children from public teachers only violates due process right to direct the upbringing and education of children under their control and is inconsistent with "the fundamental theory of liberty upon which all governments in this Union repose").

143. *See, e.g., In re* Gault, 387 U.S. 1 (1967) (minors charged with juvenile delinquency have right to basic due process rights, including notice, counsel, the privilege against self-incrimination, and the right to confront and cross-examine witnesses); *In re* Winship, 397 U.S. 358 (1970) (charges in juvenile delinquency proceedings must be proved beyond a reasonable doubt); *but see* McKeiver v. Pennsylvania, 403 U.S. 528 (1971) (due process does not require jury trials in juvenile delinquency proceedings).

144. *See, e.g.,* Planned Parenthood of Central Missouri v. Danforth, 428 U.S. 52 (1976) (mature minors may obtain abortions without parental consent); Hodgson v. Minnesota, 497 U.S. 417 (1990) (statute requiring two parent notification before minor undergoes abortion is unconstitutional without judicial bypass provision authorizing abortion without consent of one or both parents if judge finds (a) has maturity to consent to abortion or (b) abortion without parental notification is in minor's best interests).

145. Annas, *The Rights of Patients* 111 (1989).

146. *Id.* at 110–11.

147. 494 U.S. 113 (1990).

148. Brakel et al., *supra,* at 44.

149. Lock & Strauss, *Psychiatric Hospitalization of Adolescents for Conduct Disorder,* 45 Hospital and Community Psychiatry 925 (1994) (between 30 and 70 percent of adolescents admitted for psychiatric hospitalization have conduct disorder); Weithorn, *Mental Hospitalization of Troublesome Youth: An Analysis of Skyrocketing Admission Rates,* 40 Stanford Law Review 773, 778–92 (1988), citing Lerman, *Deinstitutionalization and the Welfare State* 135 (1982) (1975 national study showed severe disorders constituted less than 21 percent of admissions of minors to mental hospitals); National Institute of Mental Health, *Use of Inpatient Psychiatric Services by Children and Youth Under Age 18, United States, 1980* at 15 (1986) (serious mental disorders constituted approximately 20 percent of minor psychiatric admissions); Warren & Guttridge, *Adolescent Psychiatric Hospitalization and Social Control,* in Mental Health and Criminal Justice 119, 123 (Teplin ed. 1984) (severe mental disorders comprised approximately 20 percent of children admitted to psychiatric hospitals).

150. Weithorn, *supra* at 789.

151. *Id.,* citing Lerman, *supra,* at 135 (1975 national study indicated that between 51.6 percent and 67.8 percent of adults admitted to psychiatric units suffered from psychotic, depressive, or organic disorders).

152. Weithorn, *supra,* at 816 (citations omitted).

153. *Id.* at 817 (citations omitted).

154. *Id.,* citing Warren & Guttridge, *supra,* at 122–23, 131–33. The authors attribute this phenomenon in part to the greater availability of private insurance coverage for juvenile admissions to private hospitals.

155. *Id.* at 817–18 (citations omitted).

156. House Select Committee on Children, Youth, and Families, *No Place to Call Home: Discarded Children in America,* H. Rep. 101-395, 101st Cong., 2d Sess.

157. Weithorn, *supra,* at 819 (citation omitted).

158. *Id.*

159. Brown, *Mental Health System Abuses Cited in Care of Adolescents,* Washington Post, April 28, 1992.

160. *Id.*, citing Schwartz, Jackson-Beeck & Anderson, *The "Hidden" System of Juvenile Control,* 30 Crime and Delinquency 371, 375–76 (1984).

161. 442 U.S. 584 (1979).

162. *Id.* at 605.

163. Zinermon v. Burch, 494 U.S. 113 (1990).

164. Koocher, *Different Lenses: Psycho-Legal Perspectives on Children's Rights,* 16 Nova Law Review 711, 722 (1992).

165. *See* Parham, *supra.*

166. Sesto v. Prevost, 78 Civ. 3533 (E.D.N.Y.).

III

Procedures for Admission and Release

Procedural safeguards are designed to ensure that a decision is made fairly and accurately. They reflect the value society places on the individual interests at issue in a given proceeding. Traditionally, the Constitution has afforded the most comprehensive safeguards when personal liberty is at stake. Thus, criminal defendants typically enjoy the broadest array of procedural protections, while litigants in commercial cases have the fewest.

Advocacy for procedural safeguards in the civil commitment process dates back more than a century. Post–Civil War reformers demanded fair hearings after witnessing civil commitment proceedings that appeared structured to assume the very outcome they were supposed to decide: that the person had a mental disability and needed treatment. Their agitation led some states to adopt procedures borrowed from criminal prosecutions, including jury trials. Ever since, the level of scrupulousness of the fact-finding procedures in civil commitment has been the subject of debate.

That debate parallels the arguments about the standards for civil commitment. Advocates of strong procedural safeguards argue that commitment should be analogized to criminal confinement. In both situations, they urge, individuals are stripped of their freedom of movement, separated from family and friends, and subjected to an institutional regimen that controls virtually every aspect of their life. Moreover, unlike prisoners, these individuals may be forced to undergo intrusive treatment, such as electroconvulsive therapy and psychotropic medication,[1] administered in hospitals that are often overcrowded and understaffed and that may provide substandard and, in some cases, abusive care. That the purpose of commitment is said to be therapeutic rather than punitive makes little difference to the individual who is detained behind the locked doors of a psychiatric ward. Fundamentally, they submit, the consequences are the same: the loss of liberty and personal autonomy. Indeed, they may be worse, because psychiatric hospitalization can be even more stigmatizing than a criminal conviction.

In addition, clinical and legal standards for institutionalization differ. Experience has shown that even with elaborate procedural safeguards, it is difficult for courts to adhere to legal, rather than clinical standards for confinement. In the absence of these safeguards, they assert, the likelihood of following the law is scant indeed. Finally, the uncertainty of psychiatric diagnoses and the unreliability of predictions of future dangerousness necessitate heightened safeguards to prevent erroneous commitments. All told, loose, informal procedures impede accurate determination of the facts concerning a person's behavior, diagnosis, and prognosis. Before engaging in this extraordinary deprivation of liberty, they argue, we must be sure that the person really meets the standards the state has established for involuntary commitment.

Proponents of more relaxed procedures counter that commitment is designed to help, not punish, and that psychiatrists, who have no interest in unnecessarily confining an individual who does not need treatment, are the best check against improper confinement. Whereas prisoners cannot be released until they have served a fixed portion of their sentence, psychiatrists can discharge their patients whenever they no longer need hospitalization. Periodic review by an impartial treating psychiatrist, they argue, is a better safeguard than court hearings, lawyers, or the other trappings of the criminal justice system because judges and juries are untrained in psychiatry and less capable than physicians of evaluating the evidence supporting commitment. Importing criminal justice safeguards, such as *Miranda* warnings[2] and the privilege against self-incrimination, into the commitment process would undermine the therapeutic relationship between doctor and patient. Worse yet, requiring proof beyond a reasonable doubt would make commitments nearly impossible to obtain because of the relative uncertainty of psychiatric diagnoses and predictions of long-term future dangerousness.

We find the arguments for strong procedural safeguards more persuasive. However well intentioned an application for commitment, the decision to deprive an individual of liberty profoundly affects fundamental rights and is ultimately a legal, not a medical, decision that concerns mental illness and dangerousness and not merely an individual's "need for treatment." In making this decision, judges may be called upon to weigh the persuasiveness of complex psychiatric testimony, just as they must evaluate medical and scientific evidence in the criminal law and other fields. The fact that psychiatric conclusions may be less certain or reliable than other expert evidence, requires increased—not diminished—procedural safeguards to avoid subjecting individuals to a greater risk of wrongful confinement. Moreover, because people of means are less likely to be confined in public facilities and may be better able to secure less restrictive alternatives to commitment, the poor and homeless, who lack the resources to correct an erroneous commitment, are most likely to suffer the consequences of insufficient safeguards.

Courts and legislatures have generally agreed. Although the specific procedural rights they require vary, there is a general consensus that commitment is a substantial deprivation of liberty that requires heightened due process safeguards. The debate is over which criminal justice procedures should apply to commitment hearings. Thus, some states mandate a speedy probable cause hearing followed by a full adversary hearing to test the validity of a commitment,[3] while others provide hearings only upon request[4] or following days or even weeks of confinement.[5] Although most courts require proof of the need for commitment by clear and convincing evidence, some accept no less than proof beyond a reasonable doubt and recognize a Fifth Amendment privilege against self-incrimination in commitment proceedings.[6]

This chapter will describe the various ways in which people are admitted to institutions and examine some of the procedural protections for people on voluntary and involuntary status. Although virtually all of the case law developed out of litigation involving people with psychiatric disabilities, the decisions are almost universally applicable to people with mental retardation as well.

INFORMAL AND VOLUNTARY ADMISSION

How are people admitted to institutions?

Admission to an inpatient facility for the treatment of a mental disability is a legal rather than a medical procedure. There are three categories of patients: informal, voluntary, and involuntary. Each category is distinguished by the criteria for admission and the relative ease of securing one's release.

What is informal admission?

Informal admission is the only truly voluntary inpatient status. Informal patients can admit themselves without a formal or written application, subject to the approval of the facility and a finding that they are suitable for care and treatment. Above all, informal patients may leave the institution at any time. Unlike voluntary or involuntary patients, they "carry their own key"[7] because they cannot be converted to another status.[8] Few states offer this option,[9] and even when they do, most facilities are loath to utilize it, rendering this status all but meaningless.[10] The aversion to informal admissions stems largely from the reluctance of many institutions to admit residents who cannot be required to remain at the facility to complete treatment, as well as to the scarcity of beds at many urban institutions and the resulting need to admit people with the most serious problems.

What is voluntary admission?

Voluntary admission is designed to allow people who believe they need inpatient care to sign themselves into an institution for treatment. The decision to admit is at the discretion of the facility, which must determine whether an individual has a mental disability that requires inpatient care and treatment. Unlike informal patients, however, voluntary patients are not free to leave whenever they wish but typically must apply to the director for their release. In this sense, the term *voluntary* can be somewhat misleading. Most states require a voluntary patient to make a formal, written application for release and authorize their retention for up to seventy-two hours or more while the facility decides whether to institute involuntary commitment proceedings. An oral request for discharge frequently has no legal effect.

In addition, many people sign voluntary admission forms believing that they have no choice. Often they are already in police or hospital custody or have been told that they will be arrested or involuntarily committed if they refuse voluntary admission. Others have little understanding of the rights they have waived because the facility has failed to explain them or because they lack the mental capacity to understand the consequences of a voluntary admission.[11] From the individual's standpoint, the circumstances of voluntary hospitalization can often feel as coercive as civil commitment.[12]

What are the advantages of voluntary admission?

Voluntary patients frequently enjoy greater rights than those on involuntary status, such as increased grounds privileges, home visits, placement in unlocked wards, and most notably the right to refuse treatment. In some states they cannot be transferred to another facility without their consent.

However, in many states refusal of treatment can trigger conversion to involuntary status. Consequently, many voluntary patients feel compelled to accept treatment they do not want in order to avoid being converted to involuntary status and thereby suffering the loss of significant privileges or transfer to an inferior facility.

Must a person have capacity to give informed consent in order to be admitted voluntarily?

Yes, an individual applying for voluntary admission must be capable of giving knowing, understanding, and voluntary consent.[13] In *Zinermon v. Burch*,[14] the only Supreme Court case to consider voluntary commitment, the Court held that a Florida man could bring a federal civil rights claim against state hospital officials for depriving him of his liberty when it admitted him as a voluntary patient, even though he lacked the mental capacity to give informed consent to his admission. When Burch arrived at Chatahoochie State Hospital, he was confused, hallucinating, and psychotic and believed that he was in heaven. Although he clearly did not understand what he was doing, the hospital allowed him to sign voluntary admission forms and retained him for five months without court review.

After his release, Burch sued the hospital for violating his right to due process of law. The court reasoned that if he could not give valid consent, Burch's confinement was involuntary and must meet the requirements for involuntary commitment. In such a case, he would have been entitled to the procedural safeguards accorded to involuntary patients, including a hearing and proof by clear and convincing evidence that he was dangerous to himself or others. Without these safeguards, incompetent patients who do not meet the criteria for commitment could be held indefinitely as "voluntary patients" without their consent.

For a similar reason the New York Court of Appeals decided more than twenty years earlier that the Constitution required a judicial hearing and a review of change in status whenever an involuntary patient was converted to voluntary status.[15] The court ruled that "although the benefits which attach to voluntary admission may be valuable, a withholding from those converted to such a status of the procedural safeguards surrounding their involuntary admission would serve to deny them the equal protection of the laws and, perhaps, due process of law as well."[16]

Zinermon created a furor among clinicians who read it as undercutting voluntary admissions. Yet, despite its profound implications for admissions practices, the requirements of *Zinermon* are relatively easy to satisfy. Staff need only assure that, before admitting a person, they take reasonable steps to assure that the individual has the capacity to make the decision. As Alan Stone has explained, this is not a great burden, but it requires "more safeguards than a consent form, a pen and a witness."[17] Despite the possibility of liability, many facilities have been slow to implement these procedures.

INVOLUNTARY ADMISSION

What is involuntary admission?

As described in chapter 2, a person can be involuntarily committed if she has a mental disability that poses a danger to herself or others and there is no less restrictive alternative. A person has a right to release when one or more of these conditions no longer exists.[18] Although some states provide for various types of inpatient commitment, such as emergency detention, confinement for evaluation and observation, and long-term commitment, all must comply with this minimum constitutional standard. The standards and procedures for involuntary outpatient commitment are discussed in chapter 2.

How does the process for involuntary admission begin?

Generally, someone must apply to admit a person involuntarily to a mental health facility. The authority to make such a request varies from state to state. In most jurisdictions, the list includes police officers, psychiatrists, or other designated mental health professionals, designated family members, and certain public health officials. Some states permit any adult to make such an application. Most states also require a medical certification or other corroborating evidence that the person meets the standard for commitment.[19]

Many people are admitted through streamlined emergency commitment procedures, which authorize the police, psychiatrists, and others to detain an individual for relatively short periods of time, ranging from twenty-four hours to fifteen days, upon a finding of dangerousness to self or others. These emergency commitments may take place without any opportunity to be heard and typically require only a certification by a physician that the individual meets the criteria for involuntary hospitalization. If judicial involvement is required at all, it usually consists of a paper review without the presence of the person to be committed or a lawyer. In some jurisdictions, rights to notice, appointment of a lawyer, and a hearing before a judge are triggered only after the expiration of the period of emergency hospitalization. In others, a person may be admitted under an emergency standard, then converted to long-term involuntary status, which allows extended confinement, often under a less stringent standard.

Emergency hospitalization has been increasingly used in many states as a means of providing immediate medication to people in psychotic states. Once hospitalized, the staff seeks to stabilize the person's condition, usually through psychotropic medication, and then releases the person before any hearing or even the appointment of a lawyer takes place. In recent years, municipalities have increasingly used this form of admission to hospitalize homeless people alleged to have serious mental disorders.

How are people with mental retardation admitted to institutions?

Admission of a mentally retarded person to an inpatient facility is generally for a long period of time. People with mental retardation are admitted on voluntary, involuntary, or *non-objecting* status—a hybrid of voluntary and involuntary status, whereby neither the mentally retarded person nor a guardian, if any, has sought admission and the individual typically lacks the capacity to make such a decision. Voluntary and involuntary status generally resemble their counterparts for people with psychiatric disabilities. Non-objecting status is a kind of procedural limbo that neither affords the safeguards accorded involuntary residents nor requires informed consent, as mandated for voluntary admission.[20] At present no court has declared this practice unconstitutional; however, it may be vulnerable to challenge under *Zinermon*.

RIGHTS TO NOTICE AND A HEARING

Is there a right to a judicial hearing before involuntary admission?

No. Although some statutes provide for court-ordered detention, most involuntary commitments do not initially involve a judge. Typically, the confinement is based on the certification of one or more doctors that the individual meets the legal prerequisites for involuntary admission. As long as there is an opportunity for a hearing a reasonable time after admission, the Constitution does not require a hearing prior to confinement. Unfortunately, this often leaves people confined from five to ten days or more without independent judicial review of their need for hospitalization;[21] if released before that time, of course, they will never have had an opportunity for a hearing. In addition, there are often extended delays when an individual asks the court to appoint an expert witness to assist at the commitment hearing.

Is there a right to judicial review after involuntary admission?

The right to a judicial hearing to contest involuntary confinement is well established. The timing of the hearing varies from state to state. Some states provide automatic commitment hearings, while others provide a hearing only upon request.

There are two kinds of commitment hearings: a preliminary or probable cause hearing and a full hearing. The purpose of a preliminary hearing is to determine whether there is sufficient evidence to justify bringing commitment proceedings and continuing the individual's confinement. If not, the person must be released and the petition dismissed.

Preliminary hearings are often shorter and less formal than full hearings and generally require less proof. Typically, the facility need only show that there is reasonable cause to believe that the individual meets the commitment standard. The major advantage of a preliminary hearing is that it can be held shortly after admission and can provide a prompt judicial safeguard against improper confinement. A finding of probable cause at the preliminary hearing does not constitute a decision that commitment is appropriate but merely a ruling that there is substantial evidence in favor of commitment. Unlike a final hearing, there is no requirement at this stage that the proof in support of commitment be clear and convincing.[22]

It is often to an individual's advantage to have a hearing as soon as possible. A great deal happens during the initial period of confinement. Individuals are typically held on a locked ward, deprived of fresh air and exercise, or given drugs or other treatment against their will. In addition, institutionalization may cause them to lose their job, home, friends, property, or even the custody of their children.

Many states do not provide for a preliminary hearing, and courts have disagreed whether the Constitution requires one. One court mandated a preliminary hearing within forty-eight hours of confinement because "even a short detention in a mental facility may have long lasting effects on the individual's ability to function in the outside world."[23] Other courts have allowed slightly longer periods of confinement before a preliminary hearing.[24] Mandating a probable cause hearing within seventy-two hours of confinement, the Minnesota Supreme Court observed: "There is no consensus in the courts as to the maximum time limits between initial confinement and a probable cause hearing that will not violate due process. The tendency, however, has been to shorten the delay before a preliminary hearing."[25]

Some courts have rejected the need for a preliminary hearing on the ground that the objective is treatment not punishment.[26] These courts reason that the assertedly benevolent purpose of commitment justifies a relaxation of certain due process safeguards that attend the deprivation of liberty in criminal proceedings.[27]

The Supreme Court has not yet decided whether preliminary hearings are constitutionally required. The Court's decision in *Addington v. Texas*[28] and its summary affirmance in *French v. Blackburn*[29] suggest that they may not be. In *Addington,* the Court declined to require the stringent "beyond a reasonable doubt" standard of proof at commitment hearings, suggesting that criminal justice safeguards do not necessarily apply to the commitment process. The *French* decision summarily affirmed a lower court ruling that upheld a North Carolina statute that did not require a full hearing until ten days after confinement. Plaintiff had sought a probable cause hearing within forty-eight hours of admission.[30]

At the final hearing, the individual is guaranteed a full complement of procedural safeguards, as described below, and the need for commitment must be proved by clear and convincing evidence.[31] The timing of these hearings is a matter of much debate. Every court that has considered this issue has held that due process requires that a full hearing be held "within a reasonable time after confinement or custody."[32] What this means can vary from state to state, e.g., from five days after a person files a request for a hearing[33] to ten days after confinement.[34]

Most states provide hearings automatically, with strict safeguards to ensure that any waiver of the right to a hearing is informed and voluntary. Others offer hearings upon the request of the confined person, her family, friends or representatives. Courts disagree whether the failure to provide automatic hearings violates due process. A federal court of appeals ruled that automatic hearings are necessary because people facing commitment may be unable or reluctant to seek judicial review. The court noted that they may be under heavy sedation, inhibited by the surroundings, afraid of courts and attorneys, anxious to cooperate with the staff, "the people who will control nearly every aspect of [their] life for some period of time."[35] Another court of appeals took the opposite tack, rejecting the need for automatic hearings and finding it sufficient that assigned counsel, family, or friends can request a hearing in the event the individual does not.[36]

Who is the prosecutor at a commitment hearing?

Typically it is an institution—a public or private hospital or developmental center—that seeks the order to confine an individual. It may be represented by counsel and generally sends a clinician to attempt to convince the court of the need for commitment. In some cases, however, no lawyer appears on behalf of the party petitioning for commitment.

Do families have a right to participate at a commitment hearing?

The general rule is that family members may be witnesses but not parties to commitment hearings. This means that they may be called upon to give testimony but cannot prosecute, call witnesses, conduct cross-examination, make objections, or appeal the court's decision.

States may, however, make a limited exception to this rule for people with mental retardation. Although family members do not have a constitutional right to prosecute commitment hearings, the Supreme Court has said that it is not unconstitutional for a state law to allow close relatives to participate as parties in a commitment hearing for a person with a developmental disability.

In *Heller v. Doe*,[37] the Court considered a Kentucky law that allowed guardians and immediate family members to participate at commitment hearings for people with mental retardation but excluded similar participation at hearings for people with mental illness. Under the statute, close relatives and guardians of people with mental retardation could act as parties to the proceedings and, among other things, cross-examine witnesses and appeal any decision not to institutionalize. In rejecting the claim that the disparate treatment of people with mental illness and those with mental retardation violated the Constitution's equal protection clause, the Court ruled that it was both constitutional and reasonable to allow guardians and close family members to participate because of the special nature of mental retardation. Reasoning that mental retardation begins early in life and is a permanent, relatively static condition, the Court concluded that family members acquire valuable experience that could be useful at a commitment hearing.

The Court found that mental illness is more transient, may strike later in life, and is more difficult to diagnose. Consequently, it believed that the input of family members carries less weight. In a dissenting opinion, Justice Souter denounced the formal participation of families and guardians as unfairly providing a second prosecutor and saw no justification for affording diminished safeguards to people with mental retardation at these hearings.

Three points bear noting when considering *Heller*. First, this was an exceptional statute; Kentucky is the only state we know of that authorizes families to participate as parties at commitment hearings. Second, the decision does not allow guardians or close relatives of people with psychiatric disabilities to participate as parties at commitment hearings. Third, family members may always participate at hearings as witnesses.

Is there a right to notice before a commitment hearing?

Yes. One of the basic elements of due process is the right to timely and sufficient information to enable an individual to prepare for a commitment hearing. Before the reforms of the 1970s, many prospective patients were given little or no notice that a hearing was about to take place, often receiving only a terse announcement just hours, or even minutes, before the hearing began. The rationale offered for this practice was the paternalistic claim, made with little or no supporting evidence, that prior specific notice would traumatize a person with a mental disability. That claim presupposed that the person had a mental disability, a fact not yet proven, and assumed that notice would aggravate any mental disorder that did exist and outweigh the trauma of confinement without notice and the opportunity to present an adequate defense.

During the last twenty years, courts have made clear that the Constitution requires meaningful notice well in advance of any judicial hearings. Although the precise timing and content of the required notice may vary from state to state, the following points seem clear. At least one day prior to a probable cause hearing and several days prior to a final hearing, the person facing commitment should be given written notice in a language the individual understands specifying the time and place of the hearing; the name, address, and telephone number of the attorney who will represent the individual; and the basis for detention. How detailed the notice should be varies from state to state. More than one court has required notice of the statutory standard under which the person may be committed, the reasons and specific facts that are alleged to justify commitment, the names of every person who will testify in favor of hospitalization, and the substance of their testimony.[38]

THE COMMITMENT HEARING

Is there a right to counsel at commitment hearings?

The right to counsel is in many respects the key to all other safeguards in the civil commitment process. Attorneys help people facing commitment understand their rights, provide legal advice in exercising them, and guide their clients through a thicket of laws and procedures to enforce them. Without a lawyer, most of the constitutional protections discussed in this section—the right to a hearing, to cross-examine adverse witnesses, indeed to have one's "day in court"—would be illusory.

Until the early 1970s, few states required hearings or provided counsel to people facing involuntary commitment.[39]

Although the Supreme Court has yet to rule on this issue, its decisions in related areas leave no doubt that such a right exists. Historically, the right to counsel existed only in criminal cases; however, recent case law has established a presumption that parties to civil lawsuits are entitled to appointed counsel where "the litigant may lose his physical liberty if he loses the litigation."[40] Civil commitment clearly fits this description. In an analogous decision, four of the five Supreme Court Justices who reached the merits found that an indigent prisoner is entitled to appointed counsel before being transferred to a mental hospital for treatment.[41] Virtually every court that has considered the matter has found a federal constitutional right to counsel at civil commitment hearings.[42] Today, every state makes some provision for the appointment of counsel, particularly where an individual is indigent and unrepresented.[43]

How well do lawyers perform at commitment hearings?

The answer, of course, depends on the quality of the individual lawyer and of the program offered in each state. Although many skilled and conscientious lawyers represent individuals at commitment hearings, there has been considerable criticism of the overall quality of legal representation at these proceedings. The problems range from a lack of training in the complexities of mental disability law to inadequate compensation for the work performed, insufficient time to prepare for hearings, insensitivity to the needs of people with mental disabilities, and a lack of zeal and imagination. In all too many cases, lawyers unilaterally decide what is in the best interests of competent clients and improperly take positions that their clients actively oppose.[44]

A key factor is the mechanism for appointing counsel. As one observer lamented:

While scholars and critics are virtually unanimous that advocacy services to the mentally disabled should be provided through organized regular mechanisms . . . the vast majority of lawyers who represent the disabled on individual matters are appointed on individual bases such as specialized rather than random, individual appointments. Such appointments almost never measure up to the appropriate ethical or constitutional standards for such representation; . . . full-time, structured counsel is inevitably more effective.[45]

One solution is the use of organizations that specialize in representing people with mental disabilities, combined with training of all regular participants in commitment hearings, from attorneys to judges.[46] Although it provides no guarantee of optimal representation in every case, with the proper training, leadership, and internal controls, such a system has a better chance of success than one relying on occasional advocates drawn from private practice who have little experience or expertise in this complex field of law.

Is there a right to counsel at a prehearing psychiatric interview?

At least one court has ruled that there is a constitutional right to the presence of counsel at prehearing psychiatric examinations, in order to gather information needed to mount an effective cross-examination of the psychiatrist at the commitment hearing and to preserve the individual's right to a fair trial.[47] The decision limits counsel's role to that of an unintrusive observer. Counsel may not participate or provide assistance during the examination.

Is there a right to a court-appointed expert at a commitment hearing?

Expert opinion is central to the outcome of virtually every commitment hearing. Some advocates argue that the right to an expert witness is even more important than the right to counsel.[48] Typically, the case for commitment rests on the testimony of a psychiatrist or psychologist who interviews the person, interprets the individual's medical records, offers a diagnosis, and concludes that she will present a danger to herself or others unless she is committed. Often this clinician is the only witness at the hearing. To mount a proper defense, the person facing commitment will almost invariably need her own expert to provide an independent diagnosis, rebut the prediction of future dangerousness, and, if appropriate, propose less restrictive alternatives to confinement. Because attorneys defending commitment hearings may lack the training to evaluate portions of the evidence themselves, an expert can also play an invaluable advisory role in formulating the defense and preparing for the cross-examination of the opposing experts.

Frequently, however, the defense has no expert witness to rebut the testimony of the facility doctor, simply because it cannot afford to hire one. In such cases, the odds in favor of commitment can be nearly insurmountable.

In an attempt to level the playing field and decrease the risk of erroneous commitments, some advocates have sought to establish a right to expert assistance at commitment proceedings. Few courts have considered this issue. One federal appeals court, however, recently ruled that, although due process does not require states to provide an indigent patient a consulting psychiatrist in every instance, there may be such a right in specific cases where an attorney demonstrates a need to be educated by an expert or where the judge finds that independent expert testimony is necessary to make a reliable assessment of the individual.[49]

Some state statutes provide for the appointment of independent experts to advise courts at commitment hearings. Although these experts are not selected by the person facing commitment or intended to offer only testimony favorable to release, they can provide a counterweight to the testimony of the facility's expert. In some jurisdictions, however, the caliber of the experts has been compromised by the low rate of compensation for this task and the resulting small number of individuals willing to serve in this capacity.[50]

Some practitioners further question whether such an examination can ever be truly impartial because virtually every expert brings personal and professional values to each proceeding, often depending on the kind of practice the expert has. For example, a psychiatrist who works with community mental health programs may be more likely to find less restrictive alternatives appropriate than one who works almost exclusively in an inpatient facility. Because psychiatry is such a subjective field, these practitioners argue, the choice of an expert can determine the outcome of the proceeding.

Who bears the burden of proof at a commitment hearing and by what standard?

The Supreme Court has ruled that the party seeking commitment must prove by no less than "clear and convincing evidence" that commitment is warranted.[51] By instructing judges and juries about the degree of confidence they should have in the correctness of their decision, the standard of proof apportions the risk of error between the state and the individual at a commitment hearing and reflects the value society places on the individual liberty interests at stake.[52]

The Court found the consequences of commitment too serious to permit confinement upon proof by a "mere preponderance of the evidence," the measure used in ordinary civil cases. To do so placed a substantial risk of error on the shoulders of the person facing commitment, since the state needed to show only that it is more likely than not that the individual is mentally disabled and dangerous to self or others.

At the same time, the Court was unwilling to require the state to prove its case "beyond a reasonable doubt," the exacting standard of proof used in criminal and juvenile delinquency cases, "designed to exclude as nearly as possible the likelihood of an erroneous judgment."[53] Because the consequences of a conviction are so great, society historically "imposes almost the entire risk of error upon itself" in criminal proceedings.[54] In rejecting the analogy to criminal confinement, the Court suggested that an erroneous commitment, although deplorable, is more acceptable than an erroneous conviction and can be more easily corrected, in this case through periodic review by psychiatrists. In the Court's view, the old adage that it is better to set ten guilty people free than to confine one innocent person does not apply to commitment. "One who is suffering from a debilitating mental illness and in need of treatment is neither wholly at liberty nor free of stigma. It cannot be said . . . that it is much better for a mentally ill person to 'go free' than for a mentally normal person to be committed."[55] What's more, the Court warned, so strict a standard could prove unworkable in the field of mental health. "Given the lack of certainty and the fallibility of psychiatric diagnosis, there is a serious question as to whether a state could ever prove beyond a reasonable doubt that an individual is both mentally ill and likely to be dangerous."[56]

The Court settled instead on the intermediate "clear and convincing evidence standard." In so doing, it appears to have placed excessive confidence in the ability of doctors to prevent erroneous commitments and overestimated the difference in stigma and loss of liberty between commitment and conviction. Equally puzzling is the Court's insistence that the uncertainty of psychiatric diagnoses and predictions of future dangerousness justify lowered—not increased—due process protections to guard against errors.

What these standards mean[57] and whether factfinders actually make a distinction between evidence that is "clear and convincing" or merely "more likely than not to be correct" is a matter of some debate. Regardless, all states must and do use at least the clear and convincing evidence standard; a few states require proof beyond a reasonable doubt.[58]

Do people facing commitment have the right to see their medical records in order to prepare for a commitment hearing?

In many cases, an individual's medical or psychiatric records contain the bulk of the evidence supporting commitment. Typically, these records are placed before the court at the commitment hearing and form the basis for an expert's opinion that commitment is necessary. Because they are often voluminous, detailed, and technical and may require the assistance of an expert to evaluate, access to medical records must be granted a reasonable time before the hearing in order to enable the individual to prepare an adequate defense.

Some states permit only counsel—not the person facing commitment—to see the medical records, on the grounds that full access to hospital records could result in harm to the person or that disclosure might reveal information supplied by family members in confidence, thereby compromising an important source of information. Denying individuals the right to examine evidence that will be used against them at a commitment hearing raises serious due process concerns. Although the general rule is that psychiatric patients do not have a constitutional right of access to their medical records,[59] the interests in access to records are far more substantial when the records are sought as preparation for a commitment hearing. They include the interest in a fair hearing, in preventing an erroneous confinement, in avoiding the stigma associated with institutionalization, and in refusing potentially intrusive treatment. The records are often voluminous and may contain unreliable or inaccurate information that only the individual can identify and understand. Although attorneys representing patients at commitment hearings are entitled to review their clients' records, providing them exclusively to counsel does not protect these interests adequately.

The general practice in most states is to deny individuals access to their records at commitment hearings. Courts have written little on this subject. For example, in a terse footnote, a federal appeals court denied a challenge to a New York statute that permitted the release of patients' records to their attorneys but not to the individuals themselves, saying simply that "due process does not require more."[60]

Is there a right to remain silent in civil commitment proceedings?

Generally not. Most states have not extended the Fifth Amendment privilege against self-incrimination to civil commitment proceedings. Historically, the Fifth Amendment has shielded individuals from governmental coercion to provide incriminating evidence against themselves. This right has been applied to criminal and juvenile delinquency proceedings. Thus, criminal and juvenile defendants cannot be forced to testify at trial. Similarly, admissions obtained from suspects in police custody cannot be used against them in juvenile or criminal proceedings unless they had received prior notice of their right to remain silent, of the possibility that their statements could be used against them, and of their right to consult with an attorney.[61]

Because involuntary hospitalization, like criminal and juvenile detention, constitutes a massive deprivation of liberty, and a patient's statements may form the basis for confinement, a handful of courts have applied the privilege against self-incrimination to commitment proceedings.[62] In these jurisdictions patients must be notified of their right to remain silent during psychiatric interviews and informed that any statements they make may be the basis for involuntary confinement. Only voluntary statements made after these warnings have been given are admissible at a commitment hearing.[63]

Most courts, however, have declined to apply the privilege against self-incrimination to civil commitment proceedings because the purpose of confinement is treatment not punishment.[64] The underlying theory is that confinement alone does not trigger the privilege; there must be a punitive objective. Notice of the right to remain silent, it is argued, would restrict a psychiatrist's access to information and interfere with the therapeutic goals of the commitment process. Although the Supreme Court has not directly addressed this issue, it has refused to apply the privilege to civilly confined "sexually dangerous persons" on the ground that the proceeding was not criminal in nature.[65] However, it is not clear why labeling the motives of the committing party as benevolent lessens the deprivation of individual liberty or justifies a diminished vigilance of the rights of individuals facing detention.

Frequently overlooked in this debate is the potential for confusion about the physician's role in the commitment process. In the typical medical setting, doctors develop a treatment plan with the patient and work toward a common goal of restoring or maintaining the patient's health. As part of this process, patients are encouraged to disclose all relevant information to their physicians in exchange for a promise of confidentiality. The decision to seek the involuntary hospitalization of an unconsenting patient disrupts this relationship and creates a conflict between the psychiatrist's roles as partner in medical decisions and enforcer of involuntary detention laws. In addition, otherwise confidential doctor-patient communications are generally admissible in commitment proceedings. The better rule would be that patients facing commitment must be advised that any statement they make to a psychiatrist is not protected by the usual rules of confidentiality and could become the basis of an involuntary commitment. At the very least, such a rule would protect unsuspecting people who mistakenly believe that the usual rules of medical confidentiality operate in the commitment process. A truthful description of the psychiatrist's role might also reduce misunderstandings and increase the possibility of establishing a therapeutic relationship with the proposed patient.

Does a person facing commitment have a right to be present at the commitment hearing?

Like any other party to a legal proceeding, whether civil or criminal, a person who faces commitment has a due process right to attend and participate in the hearing. The person also has a right to be present at all conferences, either in open court or in chambers, where discussions take place that concern his or her case. This right has been widely recognized through state statutes and state and federal court decisions.[66]

The individual's presence is critical to preserve and implement other legal rights, including the effective assistance of counsel and the right to confront adverse witnesses. For example, new allegations of fact may appear for the first time during courtroom testimony. The person facing commitment may be the only one who can recognize and correct false allegations or place true allegations in their proper perspective.

Commitment decisions will be more informed if the judge or jury has an opportunity to observe the individual's demeanor in the courtroom. The central issue at a commitment hearing is mental status. Typically, expert and lay testimony about the individual's speech, thought patterns, behavior, or appearance is introduced to support or contest a diagnosis of mental illness or a prediction of future dangerousness. More often than not, there is conflicting testimony, leaving the factfinder to choose which version of the prospective patient is the more accurate. In such situations the individual's presence at the hearing is crucial, for it allows the judge or jury to measure the person's actual demeanor against the varying descriptions they have heard, as well as to overcome any stereotypes about people with mental disabilities that judges or juries might have.

Two cases illustrate how a trial judge found an individual's behavior in court to be decisive in resolving disputes about civil commitment. One involved the homeless woman whose case was discussed in chapter 2. She had been living on the streets of New York and was brought to a city hospital against her will by a psychiatric outreach team. At the commitment hearing, hospital psychiatrists described the woman as illogical, incoherent, agitated, and irrational. Her expert witnesses sharply disagreed. After observing the woman's testimony under direct and cross-examination as well as her conduct and demeanor throughout a lengthy public trial, the judge found that she was rational, logical, and coherent and had conducted herself appropriately in the courtroom. Based on these findings, the judge concluded that the woman's expert psychiatrists had presented a more accurate picture of her mental state than the city's experts.[67]

A sharply divided appeals court reversed, holding that the judge should have relied on the experts and refrained from drawing his own conclusions from the woman's actual behavior in court. Although the case was appealed to the New York Court of Appeals, this question was never resolved, since the woman was released before a decision was issued, and the appeal was dismissed as moot. The appellate ruling, however, was misguided to the extent it could be read to discourage judges from drawing their own conclusions from the mental state and demeanor of patients at commitment hearings. The trier of fact traditionally has the responsibility of evaluating the evidence and determining which version of the facts is most likely to be correct. The factfinder's role is especially critical in mental health cases, where expert opinions are frequently in conflict, stereotypes are pervasive, and the accuracy of psychiatric diagnoses and predictions of dangerousness has been called into serious question. Where an individual's mental state is at issue, his or her words and conduct will constitute part of the evidence that the court must evaluate in making its decision. If one side believes that the individual's conduct at the hearing is atypical, it can present evidence to that effect and urge the factfinder to give little weight to the individual's behavior in court. However, to prohibit the factfinder from considering the individual's mental state during the hearing would prevent patients from presenting what may be their best evidence at the proceeding and in effect deny them their day in court.

Another example of the impact of a person's presence at a commitment hearing is the case of Helen Morgan, a woman who spent more than forty-five years in a public psychiatric hospital in Washington, D.C., and was granted a commitment hearing after a judge found that she and others had been confined under procedures that did not meet constitutional standards. At the hearing, hospital clinicians painted an exaggerated picture of a woman whose mental incapacity, inappropriate social behavior, and incontinence rendered her too impaired to live in a supervised residence in the community. Experts testifying for Ms. Morgan disagreed. In the judge's view, the opportunity to hear her testimony and observe her behavior in the courtroom over the course of a long hearing proved critical.

Finding that continued commitment was unwarranted, the judge contrasted the opinions of the hospital staff with his own observations. For example, although the hospital claimed that Ms. Morgan, who had undergone a frontal lobotomy, was incapable of learning, the judge saw her behavior in the courtroom and concluded otherwise.[68] "She's certainly acted in accordance with the court's directions, that if for any reason she wanted a recess to go the bathroom, she should either ask the court or mention it to her counsel so that she could be taken care of, and we never had a problem at all during the entire three days or thereabouts of trial of Ms. Morgan being incontinent at all. So I think Ms. Morgan is a person who can learn." As to her mental capacity, the judge found that "she testified more directly on the witness stand, [was] more aware of the questions than many, many witnesses who have appeared before me."[69]

Most states allow a prospective patient to waive the right to be present at the commitment hearing, while some require the individual's presence as a safeguard against possible abuses.[70] In rare instances, a court has the power to order an individual excluded from the courtroom. Because the meaningful exercise of other legal rights discussed in this chapter often depends on the person's presence, exclusion from the courtroom should be the last resort, implemented only after other less drastic measures such as short delays or warnings have been tried and the removal of the person from the courtroom is absolutely necessary for the hearing to continue.[71] A decision to exclude should not be made before a hearing or based solely on the certificate of a psychiatrist.[72] If exclusion is ordered, the court should do everything it can to permit as much participation as possible by the excluded individual, including the continued assistance of counsel and, where available, access by microphone and videotape to the hearing.

Individuals have a right to appear at hearings in street clothes, not hospital gowns, and generally to be free from conditions that might stigmatize them or prejudice the judge or jury. As one advocate quipped when the director of a large municipal hospital refused to allow his patients to wear their own clothing at commitment hearings, "The equal protection provision of the Fourteenth Amendment requires that if the patient has to appear in court in a hospital gown, the psychiatrist has to testify in his pajamas."[73] Other stigmatizing practices still persist in some courts, such as permitting psychiatrists to testify from the witness stand but requiring prospective patients to testify from their seats or conducting hearings in rooms where people are constantly interrupting with other business.

Do the rules of evidence apply at civil commitment hearings?

Yes. Judicial hearings are typically conducted according to rules of evidence that govern the use of documents and the admissibility of testimony. The purpose of these rules is to assure that only reliable, accurate, and trustworthy evidence is the basis for judicial decisions. Because of the importance of the liberty interests at stake in commitment decisions, most states have applied the rules of evidence to civil commitment hearings.[74]

In practice, however, these rules are often ignored. In many cases courts admit all evidence because they want to hear all potentially relevant information, and in others lawyers simply neglect to make the proper objections. The most common abuse of the rules of evidence is the routine admission of hearsay evidence, which consists of statements purportedly made by individuals who are not present in court and thus not available for cross-examination. Hearsay is inadmissible in part because it is unreliable but also because it unfairly deprives the opposing party of the right to cross-examine the person who made the statement. Despite strict limitations on the use of statements made outside the courtroom that are not subject to cross-examination, doctors and nurses are frequently permitted to testify about statements made by third parties outside of their presence. Hospital records are often admitted into evidence containing the hearsay statements of police officers, neighbors, or relatives. Statements on a ward chart, for example, that a neighbor said the prospective patient "threatened dangerous acts" or "was aggressive" will likely influence a judge or jury even though there may be no opportunity to show through cross-examination that the neighbor had overreacted to idle talk and boisterous behavior or, indeed, was speaking of someone else. Once admitted into evidence, the problem is compounded as the hearsay becomes a part of the record and can be considered in any appeal.

Does a person facing commitment have the right to present evidence and cross-examine witnesses at the commitment hearing?

Yes. Implicit in the right to be present at a hearing is the right to confront adverse witnesses and present evidence in one's own defense. This is so basic to the notion of due process that virtually every court that has considered the issue has agreed.[75]

There are particularly compelling reasons why cross-examination is important in civil commitment hearings. Frequently the evidence supporting commitment consists of the opinion testimony of a psychiatrist or hearsay statements contained in a medical record made by third parties not present in court. Cross-examination can help clarify the basis of these opinions and reveal any discrepancies in the statements on which the expert relied.

Psychiatric testimony can also be problematic when a prediction of dangerousness is based exclusively on a mental status examination rather than direct observations of actual conduct. As the American Psychiatric Association argued in a brief to the Supreme Court in another context, psychiatric testimony can carry undue weight because it is cloaked "in a mantle of expertise."[76] Cross-examination, then, plays a critical role in evaluating the soundness of a psychiatrist's testimony and in helping the judge or jury separate well-founded conclusions from mere speculation.

A similar mystique surrounds medical records. Because the information they contain has been recorded in a written document, many judges and juries tend to believe that hospital charts are more trustworthy than oral testimony. In this regard, hospitalized people are frequently placed at a disadvantage because the chart is typically written from the perspective of the psychiatric staff that is seeking commitment; excerpts from the records are often selectively introduced at the hearing to highlight the need for commitment; and most of the people who make entries in the records are usually not present at the hearing.[77] Rarely will the chart contain statements from staff members who disagree with the official position of the hospital. Without the opportunity to cross-examine the people who made the records or whose statements are recorded in them or to present additional witnesses, it may be difficult to put the record in its proper perspective.

In one interesting case, the treating psychiatrist testified that a man should be committed because he was impulsive and uncooperative and, if released, would not take the medication he needed to function in the community.[78] An important part of the doctor's assessment was based on notes contained in the hospital records. To challenge the doctor's conclusions, the patient called as a witness a nurse who worked on the ward where he was confined. She testified that the patient was cooperative, was not impulsive, and took his medication regularly, seeking her out when she was late distributing it. Although the nurse had spent considerable time observing the patient, more time in fact than the doctor, her observations did not appear in the patient's hospital chart.

Can a patient require nurses and other staff members to testify at a commitment hearing?

Yes. A patient can subpoena reluctant witnesses and compel them to testify at a commitment hearing. This may occasionally be necessary with nurses and other staff members who often fear that they will be disciplined or fired if their testimony conflicts with the testimony of another staff member or with the official position of the hospital.

Does a staff member have the right to testify at a commitment hearing, even if the testimony is at odds with the official position of the hospital?

Yes, if the hospital is owned or operated by the government. Employees of public facilities have a First Amendment right to testify at court hearings without fear of retaliation, as long as their testimony is truthful. Government may not restrict its employees' freedom to speak about matters of public concern when they are compelled to testify at a judicial proceeding.

For example, in the *Vaughn* case described above, the municipal hospital fired the nurse whom it had long employed on a per diem basis because she testified on behalf of the patient the hospital was attempting to commit. The nurse filed a federal lawsuit, claiming that her dismissal violated her First Amendment right to freedom of speech. She argued that she had not volunteered to testify, but once called as a witness she had no choice but to tell the truth. In a court-ordered settlement, the hospital agreed to pay the nurse back pay and damages and circulated a policy statement to all of its employees reassuring them that they could testify freely at any court proceeding without fear of reprisal, even if their testimony conflicts with the official position of the hospital or the testimony of other employees.[79]

Appeal

Is there a right to appeal an order of commitment?

Yes. Appeal is the usual remedy for a dissatisfied party to a legal proceeding. Because commitments can be lengthy and have lasting legal and practical consequences even after release, the right to an appeal is an important remedy. However, this right is often more illusory than real because most people are released before their appeal is ever heard or decided.

In an appeal, an appellate court reviews the record of the proceedings at the trial level to determine whether the lower court's decision is legally and factually justified. Typically, many months pass before the appeal is decided. A complete transcript of the entire commitment hearing must be prepared, legal briefs drafted, and oral argument heard. Even after oral argument, it may take several months before a decision is issued. By then, most people have already been discharged and, more often than not, the appeal is dismissed as moot. In exceptional circumstances, a court may agree to an expedited appeal, which may shorten the process to three or four months.

The lack of a meaningful right to appeal has serious consequences both for people facing commitment and for the legal process. Some people are illegally confined because they have no real opportunity to correct an erroneous commitment. Many carry the stigma of a wrongful commitment for years because some appellate courts are reluctant to decide appeals after an individual has been released. As a result, they have no opportunity to clear their records and erase the stigma.

The legal system suffers as well. First, without timely appellate review there is no effective mechanism to correct lower court errors and deter arbitrary decisions. In addition, in some jurisdictions it has become virtually impossible to develop a coherent and consistent body of caselaw to guide judicial decision making. As discussed in the preceding chapter, in 1987, New York City began picking up and involuntarily hospitalizing a number of homeless people who lived on the streets. When a homeless woman named Joyce Brown challenged her commitment, there were few cases in New York defining the meaning of dangerousness to self or others, particularly in the context of homeless people. Shortly after the case was argued before New York's highest court, the city released Ms. Brown, and the court dismissed the case as moot.[80] Although they differed among themselves over the outcome, many of the intermediate appellate judges who had decided the case were disappointed and privately agreed that a decision from the state's highest court was necessary to provide guidance in an area where there was little.[81]

In a few states, a different appeal procedure is used. In these states, the initial hearing does not take place before a court of record but before a lawyer, a panel of lawyers and mental health professionals, or a court of limited jurisdiction where the rules of evidence are not applied and the right to a jury does not exist. In these states, if committed, the individual has a right to an entirely new hearing before a court where all the safeguards required by law apply. After this second hearing, the individual may seek review by an appellate court.

RELEASE AND TRANSFER

Are individuals automatically released if they win their commitment hearings?

No. The party seeking commitment may appeal the decision and ask for a stay, or delay, of the release. In most cases, the stay is granted only if the party can show a likelihood of winning the appeal and of irreparable harm if the individual is discharged before the appeal has been decided.

At least one state law provides for an indefinite automatic stay of lower court orders against the government, if the government files an appeal. In commitment cases, this means that individuals in public hospitals who win their hearings automatically remain in custody until either the government's appeal is decided or the hospital chooses to release them.[82] Because the appellate process is so slow, most individuals remain confined as long as they would if they had lost their hearing. In such cases, an automatic stay provision renders the right to a commitment hearing virtually meaningless and violates the constitutional right to due process of law.[83]

Is there a right to a writ of habeas corpus in commitment proceedings?

Yes. A writ of habeas corpus, from the Latin meaning "you have the body," is a traditional legal remedy for people seeking release from confinement by the state. It is available at any point during the commitment process and offers the quickest way to challenge an unfair or unconstitutional confinement.

Habeas corpus has two principal drawbacks. Known as an "extraordinary writ," habeas corpus requires a showing that no other remedy, such as a commitment hearing or an appeal, is meaningfully available. In states that provide speedy commitment hearings or the right to appeal, judges often tend to dismiss these writs or adjourn them until the hearing or appeal is completed.

To make matters more difficult, the burden of proof is reversed in habeas corpus proceedings. Whereas at commitment hearings the party seeking commitment must prove the need for commitment by clear and convincing evidence,[84] it is the detainee who bears the burden of proof in a habeas corpus petition. As a result, habeas corpus is rarely the remedy of choice in most commitment proceedings.

How long can a person be involuntarily confined?

Most state statutes authorize commitment only for specified periods of time and require judicial reauthorization and a new hearing, with a full array of procedural safeguards, if the commitment is to be extended.

A few states provide for unlimited commitment, although the denial of periodic judicial review likely violates due process.[85] Virtually every state, however, requires some form of periodic review of the need for commitment and imposes a duty on the facility to release an individual who no longer meets the criteria for involuntary confinement.[86] The typical commitment order is for up to six months. Orders for emergency detention or temporary observation are generally for twenty-four hours to two weeks.

How are involuntarily committed individuals released?

Involuntary confinement is authorized only as long as a person meets the standards for commitment. The Supreme Court has ruled that due process requires the release of any person who does not both have a mental disability and present a danger to self or others.[87] Thus, facilities have a constitutional obligation to conduct frequent reviews of every involuntary patient and discharge those who can survive safely in a less restrictive setting. This is true even after a court has authorized a commitment, where the conditions that justified confinement no longer exist. Unlike jails and prisons, institutions for people with a mental disability are generally free to release a civilly committed person at any point during confinement, without the permission of a court. In some cases, facilities may be required to provide notice to a court, law enforcement officials, or private parties.

There are various ways to seek release when a facility refuses to grant it. One way, of course, is to seek judicial review through a commitment hearing or a writ of habeas corpus. If a court finds that a person does not meet the criteria for commitment, it must issue an order of release. Sometimes, merely requesting a hearing will accelerate a discharge. Such a request may force a reevaluation of the justification for commitment, and the clinician or the facility's lawyer may conclude that there are insufficient grounds to continue the confinement or that a less restrictive setting will do. In close cases, the facility may opt for release, simply to avoid the inconvenience and expense of a hearing.

What is conditional release?

Some state statutes provide for conditional release, which authorizes administrative discharge to a community setting in exchange for an agreement to comply with certain conditions. The theory is that many people with mental disabilities who would be a danger to themselves or others on their own can survive safely in the community under supervision. Conditional release ends confinement without cutting the ties to the institution. Ordinarily, the conditions involve some form of outpatient treatment, such as taking medication, seeing a clinician or attending a day treatment program. Conditional release cannot be imposed on informal patients nor on voluntary patients without their consent or, in the case of minor voluntary patients, without the consent of their parent, legal guardian, or next-of-kin.

If properly used, conditional release statutes can offer voluntary, less restrictive alternatives to commitment for those who wish to remain in the community and do not object to the terms of release. Conditional release, however, is not appropriate for individuals who can survive safely outside an institution without court-imposed conditions. Nor should the term of the conditions be unreasonably long. Some states limit conditional release to the period for which the person was committed.[88] Others prescribe periods of from ninety days to one year.[89] Elsewhere, conditional release can continue for years, sometimes so long that everyone involved forgets the existence of a court order. Individuals can seek discharge from conditional release status on the ground that they are no longer suitable for commitment. Some states also provide for court hearings to challenge the appropriateness of the conditions of release.[90]

Can a person be reconfined simply for violating a condition of release?

There is some disagreement whether the violation of a condition of release can itself justify reconfinement, without a contemporaneous finding that the person meets the standards for involuntary commitment.[91] Such a result, however, would violate the Supreme Court's holding in *O'Connor v. Donaldson*,[92] which prohibited the continued confinement of a man who was not mentally ill and dangerous to himself or others. It would also conflict with the purpose of civil commitment, which is to treat a dangerous mental disability, not to punish the failure to adhere to a prescribed form of treatment. Unlike parole, where a convicted prisoner remains in legal custody for a defined period of time after release from incarceration, the state's authority to confine a person with a mental disability ceases once an individual no longer meets the criteria for commitment, whether or not the conditions of release were satisfied. For example, it would violate due process to reconfine an individual who failed to comply with a condition requiring the use of medication, if the individual is no longer mentally ill or does not present a danger to self or others.

Similarly, many,[93] but not all,[94] courts have held that due process requires a hearing before a neutral body and other safeguards before a conditional release can be revoked. Finding that reconfinement is an infringement of personal liberty, these courts have reasoned that conditionally discharged people with mental disabilities are entitled to at least the same rights as convicted prisoners charged with violating parole and have applied many of the safeguards that the Supreme Court found applicable to parolees.[95]

Is there a right to a hearing before an individual can be transferred from one facility to another?

Most states provide for the opportunity for some sort of review before an individual can be transferred from one facility to another or to a more restrictive ward within a facility. Some statutes establish a right to a court hearing,[96] while others allow only an appeal to medical personnel within the institution.[97] Typically, the standard for evaluating a transfer is whether the move would be "medically appropriate" or in the individual's "best interests."

There are many reasons why transfers take place. Some facilities are designed only for acute, i.e., short-term, care and routinely transfer patients who need intermediate or long-term confinement to institutions created for that purpose. Other transfers are intended to provide specialized care not available at the current facility, such as intensive psychological services for people with challenging behaviors; twenty-four hour nursing care; fire safety equipment for people deemed incapable of "self-preservation" in the event of a fire; or a less restrictive, more normalized environment. In such cases, the transfer is generally upheld. However, not all transfers are strictly for medical, safety, or treatment reasons. Some people are transferred because a facility is closing or is overcrowded. Although one could argue that a new setting is in the individual's best interests in both cases, hearings before impartial decision makers are particularly important in these instances because of the potential for subordinating the individual's needs to the institution's interests. In other cases the reasons may be subject to challenge. Examples include when a transfer is to a more restrictive ward or facility, when questions arise as to whether the motive for transfer was to punish an individual or his or her relatives or advocates for asserting their rights, and when an individual's behavior is difficult and staff members would prefer not to deal with him or her.

The few courts that have considered the issue have split as to whether an individual has a constitutional right to a judicial hearing prior to being transferred from one institution to another. In one case, a federal court found that a judicial hearing is necessary when the transfer is from a less restrictive to a more restrictive setting[98] because of the significant infringement on personal liberty. In another, a state court refused to mandate a judicial hearing, viewing the decision to transfer as within the discretion of the clinicians involved and "reflect[ing] primarily a medical judgment about the kind of facility that would best serve the patient's therapeutic needs."[99]

As a general rule, individuals on informal or voluntary status cannot be transferred without their consent, unless they are converted to involuntary status.

To date the Supreme Court has not considered a case involving the right of civilly committed persons to a hearing before transfer to another institution. However, the Court has ruled that a convicted felon serving a prison term has a right to a hearing prior to being transferred to a psychiatric hospital, because of the stigma of psychiatric commitment and the possibility of forced treatment.[100] The hearing must be held before an impartial body, but need not be before a judge.

PROCEDURES FOR OUTPATIENT COMMITMENT

What are the procedures for outpatient commitment?

In some cases, an order for outpatient commitment after a commitment hearing is issued as a less restrictive alternative to hospitalization. The procedures for this form of outpatient commitment are identical to those for inpatient hospitalization with the exception that in some states, after a finding that a person meets the standards for involuntary hospitalization, the court holds an additional hearing to determine whether a less restrictive placement is possible.

Preventive outpatient commitment, which is discussed in chapter 2, follows different procedures. State laws vary in both the safeguards they afford and the specificity of the findings they require before a judge can authorize commitment.[101] The statutes always provide for notice and a hearing, but some do not provide for the automatic appointment of counsel.

Preventive outpatient commitment typically will not be ordered unless the judge finds that an available community-based program will provide treatment that will likely prevent the person from deteriorating and becoming a danger to self or others in the community. Often the court itself must approve the treatment plan, which then becomes an order of the court. These orders can remain in place for many years.

Like the substantive standard, the truncated procedures often used in preventive outpatient commitment remain largely unchallenged. The same considerations that apply to inpatient hospitalization, however, should apply because of the importance of the individual liberty interests that are at stake, including the right to bodily autonomy and the right to make basic decisions about one's health care. Moreover, because the standards for outpatient commitment are generally so vague, enhanced procedural safeguards are necessary to minimize erroneous commitments.

Is there a difference between outpatient commitment and conditional release?

Generally there is very little difference, except for the time and the manner in which the order is entered. Typically, outpatient commitment is ordered by a court, often without ever hospitalizing the individual. Conditional release, by contrast, amounts to a form of hospital discharge and, except in a few states or in cases involving forensic patients, involves an administrative—not a judicial—decision that is generally made by a clinician.

How is outpatient commitment enforced?

The enforcement of outpatient commitment in any of its forms is problematic. The usual consequence of violating a court order is a finding of contempt, which is punishable by fines or imprisonment. This obviously makes no sense in a case where compulsion is invoked for therapeutic ends.[102] However, other methods of enforcing orders requiring individuals to undergo treatment are often inappropriate and impractical outside the controlled setting of a hospital. Thus, it is improper to restrain and inject an individual with neuroleptic medication on the street, in a train station, or in other unsupervised environments, even if the person has violated an order to take medication.

Many proponents of outpatient commitment therefore urge that the consequences of violating the order should be inpatient hospitalization, and that is the typical consequence of a violation,[103] just as it is for conditional release. As in the case of a violation of the rules of conditional release, confinement is illogical, because inpatient hospitalization should never be used as a *penalty* for noncompliance; it is warranted only if the person otherwise meets the criteria for compulsory inpatient care, including mental illness and dangerousness.[104] Nevertheless, inpatient treatment is often the consequence of violating an order for outpatient commitment even if the individual does not meet these criteria.[105] In our view such a result is unconstitutional.

Revocation of outpatient status is considered a further deprivation of liberty and may not be accomplished without due process of law. For example, a court in the District of Columbia required that the hospital superintendent file an affidavit within twenty-four hours of hospitalization showing the patient's failure to comply with treatment requirements or a deterioration in his condition. It further required service of the affidavit on the patient's attorney and notification of the patient. Within five days, the hospital must either release the patient or hold a judicial hearing to determine whether outpatient status should be revoked.[106] At that hearing, the hospital must show why inpatient treatment is required and that it is the least restrictive appropriate treatment available.[107] While the person's behavior on outpatient status may be taken into account in this hearing, the mere failure to take prescribed medication or otherwise to comply with a treatment program is insufficient, standing alone, to order rehospitalization.[108]

NOTES

1. After surveying the scientific literature regarding psychotropic medication, the Supreme Court concluded: "It is not disputed that such drugs are 'mind-altering.' Their effectiveness resides in their capacity to achieve such results." Rogers v. Mills, 457 U.S. 291, 293, n. 1 (1982).

2. Miranda v. Arizona, 384 U.S. 436 (1966) (Constitution requires, *inter alia,* police to warn criminal suspect of right to remain silent and right to have counsel present during interrogation).

3. *See, e.g.* Doe v. Gallinot, 486 F. Supp. 983, 994 C.D. Cal. 1979), *aff'd,* 657 F.2d 1017, 1023–24 (9th Cir. 1981).

4. *See, e.g.,* Project Release v. Prevost, 766 F.2d 960, 975 (2d Cir. 1982).

5. *See, e.g.,* French v. Blackburn, 428 F. Supp. 1351 (M.D.N.C. 1977), *aff'd,* 443 U.S. 901 (1977) (full hearing ten days after confinement); Logan v. Arafeh, 346 F. Supp. 1265 (D. Conn. 1972), *aff'd sub nom.* Briggs v. Arafeh, 411 U.S. 911 (1973) (forty-five-day confinement prior to hearing).

6. Lessard v. Schmidt, 349 F. Supp. 1078, 1095, 1102 (E.D. Wis. 1972), *vacated and remanded on other grounds*, 421 U.S. 957 (1975).

7. Interview with Clifford Carr, Deputy Director, Mental Hygiene Legal Service, First Department, New York, New York (Mar. 29, 1993).

8. Because informal patients cannot be converted to voluntary or involuntary status, some facilities occasionally have resorted to subterfuge in dealing with an informal patient whose mental condition has deteriorated but who still seeks to leave the institution. As the individual departs, the facility places a call to the police, and the person is picked up and taken to the emergency room of another facility and is subsequently admitted involuntarily. *Id.*

9. According to Brakel, Parry & Weiner, *The Mentally Disabled and the Law* 180 (3d ed. 1985), only ten states offer the possibility of informal admissions.

10. *See id.* at 180–81.

11. *See, e.g.*, Appelbaum, Mirkin & Bateman, *Empirical Assessment of Competency to Consent to Psychiatric Hospitalization*, 138 American Journal of Psychiatry 1170 (1981) (study of fifty voluntary patients showed that a "large percentage" lacked capacity to consent to admission).

12. Hoge et al., *Patient, Family and Staff Perceptions of Coercion in Mental Hospital Admission: An Exploratory Study*, 11 Behavioral Science and the Law 281 (1993).

13. Under certain conditions, minors and people who are legally incompetent may be admitted on voluntary status by third parties. The special issues relating to minor voluntary admissions are discussed in chapter 2.

14. 494 U.S. 113 (1990).

15. *In re* Buttonow, 297 N.Y.S.2d 108 (Ct. of Appeals 1968).

16. *Id.* at 102.

17. Stone, Answer to *Ask the Experts*, 15 AAPL Newsletter 95 (1990).

18. *See* O'Connor v. Donaldson, 422 U.S. 563 (1975); Colyar v. Third Judicial District Court, 469 F. Supp 424 (D. Utah 1979).

19. For a survey of precommitment procedures, *see* Brakel et al., *supra*, Table 2.6.

20. *See* Zinermon v. Burch, *supra*.

21. In such a case, of course, an individual can file a writ of habeas corpus. However, because the time between the filing of a writ and the scheduled date of a commitment hearing is often only a matter of days, courts frequently adjourn the hearing on a writ to the date of the commitment hearing, without ruling on the need for commitment.

22. *See* discussion of standard of proof, below.

23. Lessard v. Schmidt, *supra*, 349 F. Supp. at 1092. *See also* Matter of Elkow, 167 Ill. Ap. 3d 187, 521 N.E.2d 290 (1988) (one day); Matter of De Loatch, 532 A.2d 1343 (D.C. 1987) (one day).

24. *See, e.g.*, Luna v. Van Zandt, 554 F. Supp. 68, 77 (S.D. Tex. 1982) (three days); Doe v. Gallinot, 486 F. Supp. 983, 994 (C.D. Cal. 1979), *aff'd*, 657 F.2d 1017, 1023–24 (9th Cir. 1981) (three days unless holidays and weekends intervene, but in no case longer than seven days after initial detention); Doremus v. Farell, 407 F. Supp. 509, 515 (D. Neb. 1975) (five days); Bell v. Wayne County Gen. Hosp., 384 F. Supp. 1085, 1098 (E.D. Mich. 1974) (five days); Lynch v. Baxley, 386 F. Supp. 378 (M.D. Ala. 1974) (seven days).

25. State *ex rel.* Doe v. Madonna, 295 N.W.2d 356, 365 (Minn. 1980).

26. *See, e.g.*, Logan v. Arafeh, 346 F. Supp. 1265, 1269 (D. Conn. 1972), *aff'd sub nom.*, Briggs v. Arafeh, 411 U.S. 911 (1973). Rejecting the claim that a forty-five-day confinement without a hearing was too long, the court cautioned: "It must be remembered that commitment has not been undertaken for the sake of penal detention. The patient is committed for treatment and care and some knowledge of his mental condition can be gained by visual observation and diagnostic tests. This takes time." *Id.*

27. *See, e.g., Project Release v. Prevost, supra.*

28. Addington v. Texas, 441 U.S. 418 (1979).

29. French v. Blackburn, 428 F. Supp. 1351 (M.D.N.C. 1977), *aff'd*, 443 U.S. 901 (1977).

30. *Addington* may be distinguishable because the requirement of proof beyond a reasonable doubt is traditionally reserved only for criminal cases, and the Court feared that so exacting a standard might result in errors and quite possibly make commitment all but impossible in a field where professional diagnoses and predictions of future dangerousness can be so uncertain. By contrast, preliminary hearings have a less stringent standard of proof, have not historically been reserved exclusively for criminal cases, and are all the more necessary precisely because of the uncertainties of psychiatric diagnoses and predictions of dangerousness. As a summary affirmance, *French* has less precedential weight than a full Supreme Court decision. *French* also relied in part on the Supreme Court's summary affirmance in Logan v. Arafeh, 346 F. Supp. 1265 (D. Conn. 1972), *aff'd sub nom.*, Briggs v. Arafeh, 411 U.S. 911 (1973) upholding a forty-five-day confinement prior to a hearing. *Logan*, however, was decided before O'Connor v. Donaldson, 422 U.S. 563 (1975), in which the Supreme Court first limited the power to commit and established a requirement of dangerousness before an individual could be confined under the *parens patriae* power. As a result, there is some question about the precedential value of *Logan*, hence of *French* as well.

31. *See Addington v. Texas, supra.*

32. *See, e.g., French v. Blackburn, supra,* at 1355.

33. N.Y. Mental Hyg. Law § 9.27 (McKinney 1988 & Supp. 1993).

34. *See, e.g.,* French v. Blackburn, *supra*, 428 F. Supp. at 1355 (ten-day confinement prior to full hearing not unconstitutional where patient receives treatment during this time). *See also*, Lessard v. Schmidt, *supra*, 349 F. Supp. at 1091–92 (ten to fourteen days, after confinement, where probable cause hearing held within forty-eight days of confinement).

35. Doe v. Gallinot, 657 F.2d 1017, 1023 n. 7 (9th Cir. 1979) (fourteen-day confinement without mandatory hearings is too long).

36. Project Release v. Prevost, 722 F.2d 960 (2d Cir. 1982).

37. 113 S. Ct. 2637 (1993).

38. Lessard v. Schmidt, *supra*, 349 F. Supp. at 1092. ("Notice of date, time and place is not satisfactory. The patient should be informed of the basis for his detention . . . the standard upon which he may be detained, the names of examining physicians and all other persons who may testify in favor of his continued detention, and the substance of their proposed testimony.") *See also*, Suzuki v. Quisenberry, *supra*, 411 F. Supp. at 1127; Lynch v. Baxley, *supra*, 386 F. Supp. at 388; Bell v. Wayne County General Hospital, *supra*, 384 F. Supp. at 1092; Wessel v. Pryor, 461 F. Supp. 1144, 1146 (E.D. Ark. 1978).

39. Perlin, *Fatal Assumption: A Critical Evaluation of the Role of Counsel in Mental Disability Cases,* 16 Law & Human Behavior 39, 43 (1991). This article provides an excellent discussion of the importance of counsel in the civil commitment process and of the inadequacy of legal advocacy in many jurisdictions today.

40. Lassiter v. Dept. of Social Services, 452 U.S. 18, 25 (1981). *See also In re* Gault, 387 U.S. 1, 41 (1967) (although juvenile delinquency proceedings are not per se criminal in nature, due process requires the right to appointed counsel because the juvenile's freedom might be curtailed).

41. Vitek v. Jones, 445 U.S. 480 (1980).

42. *See, e.g.,* Lessard v. Schmidt, *supra,* 349 F. Supp. 1078; Bell v. Wayne County Gen. Hosp., 384 F. Supp. 1085, 1092–93 (E.D. Mich. 1974); Stamus v. Leonhardt, 414 F. Supp. 439, 448 (S.D. Iowa 1976); State *ex rel.* Hawks v. Lozaro, 202 S.E.2d 109, 124 (W. Va. 1974).

43. Brakel et al., *supra,* at 69 and Table 2.15.

44. Empirical studies have reached the same conclusion. *See* Miller, Ionescu-Pioggia & Fiddleman, *The Effect of Witnesses, Attorneys and Judges on Civil Commitment in North Carolina: A Prospective Study,* 28 Journal of Forensic Sciences 829 (1983); Hiday, *The Attorney's Role in Involuntary Civil Commitment,* 60 North Carolina Law Review 1027 (1982).

45. Perlin, *supra,* at 44 (citation omitted).

46. *See id.* at 58–59 for a list of suggestions on the matter.

47. Ughetto v. Acrish, 518 N.Y.S. 2d 398 (2d Dep't. 1987), *appeal dismissed,* 523 N.Y.S.2d 497 (right to presence of counsel at preretention psychiatric examinations required by state statute and U.S. Constitution in order to enable counsel to cross-examine state's expert at hearing; but counsel may only observe, not participate or assist at interview).

48. *E.g.,* Professor William Brooks, telephone interview Sept. 30, 1994.

49. Goetz v. Crosson, 967 F.2d 29 (2d Cir. 1992).

50. *Id.*

51. *Addington v. Texas, supra.*

52. *Id.* at 423, 425 (1979).

53. *Id.* at 423 (citations omitted).

54. *Id.*

55. *Id.* at 429 (citations omitted).

56. *Id.* (citations omitted).

57. Although the differences between these standards are difficult to calibrate, the popular wisdom holds that proof beyond a reasonable doubt requires 95% certainty, clear and convincing evidence between 60 and 70% certainty, and a preponderance of the evidence 51% certainty.

58. *E.g.,* Kentucky.

59. *See, e.g.,* Gotkin v. Miller, 379 F. Supp. 859 (E.D.N.Y. 1974), *aff'd,* 514 F.2d 125 (2d Cir. 1975).

60. Project Release v. Prevost, 722 F.2d 960, 976, n. 16 (2d Cir. 1982); *see also* French v. Blackburn, 428 F.Supp. 1351 (M.D.N.C. 1977), *aff'd mem.,* 443 U.S. 901 (1979) (although not discussing access to clinical records, the court denied patients' requests for copies of the petitions for their commitment on the grounds that they might have been submitted by family members).

61. Miranda v. Arizona, 384 U.S. 436 (1966).

62. *See, e.g.*, Lessard v. Schmidt, 349 F. Supp. 1078, 1102 (E.D. Wis. 1972), *vacated and remanded on other grounds*, 421 U.S. 957 (1975); Lynch v. Baxley, 386 F. Supp. 378, 394 (M.D. Ala. 1974).

63. *Lessard v. Schmidt, supra*, at 1102.

64. *See, e.g.*, French v. Blackburn, 428 F. Supp. 1351, 1358–59 (M.D.N.C. 1977), *aff'd mem.* 443 U.S. 901 (1979); Project Release v. Prevost, 551 F. Supp. 1298, 1308 (E.D.N.Y 1982) *aff'd on other grounds*, 722 F.2d 960 (2d Cir. 1983); State *ex rel.* Hawks v. Lazaro, 202 S.E.2d 109, 126 (W. Va. 1974); Ughetto v. Acrish, 130 Misc. 2d 74, 494 N.Y.S.2d 943, 947 (Sup. Ct. 1985), *aff'd* 518 N.Y.S.2d 398 (2d Dep't. 1987).

65. Allen v. Illinois, 478 U.S. 366 (1986).

66. *See, e.g., Lessard v. Schmidt, supra*, at 1091 (prospective patient's attendance at hearing is mandatory); Kendall v. True, 391 F. Supp. 413, 419 (W.D. Ky. 1975); Bell v. Wayne County General Hospital, 384 F. Supp. 1085 (E.D. Mich. 1974).

67. Matter of Anonymous (Billie Boggs) v. NYC Health and Hospitals Corporation, 522 NYS 2d 407 (Sup. Ct., N.Y. County, 1987), *rev'd*, 523 NYS 2d 71 (1st Dep't. 1987), *dismissed as moot*, 525 NYS 2d 792 (Ct. App. 1988).

68. "I find watching Ms. Morgan throughout this trial, that she was a person who can exercise some control and who can learn things." In the Matter of Helen Morgan, M.H. No. 83–89 (Superior Court of District of Columbia, Family Division), transcript of findings of fact and conclusions of law July 13, 1989.

69. *Id.*

70. *See, e.g.*, Lessard v. Schmidt, *supra* 341 F. Supp. at 1091. *See also* cases cited in Perlin, *Fatal Assumption, supra*, n. 175–76.

71. *See, e.g.*, Kendall v. True, 391 F. Supp. 413, 419 (W.D. Ky. 1975); Suzuki v. Quisenberry, 411 F. Supp. 1113, 1129–30 (D. Hawaii 1976) (exclusion permissible where the individual's "presence makes it impossible to conduct the hearing in a reasonable manner"); Toliver v. State, 638 S.W.2d 122 (Tex. Ct. App. 1982). *But see* Coll v. Hyland, 411 F. Supp. 905, 912–13 (D.N.J. 1976) (upholding constitutionality of New Jersey rule permitting exclusion of individual for "good cause").

72. *Suzuki v. Quisenberry, supra*, at 1130.

73. Harvard Hollenberg, Letter to the Editor, New York Law Journal, Aug. 7, 1992, 2 (describing the advocacy of Simon Rosenzweig at Bellevue Hospital in New York City in the 1970s).

74. *See, e.g.*, Lessard v. Schmidt, 349 F. Supp. 1078, 1103 (E.D. Wis. 1972), *vacated and remanded*, 414 U.S. 473, *on remand*, 379 F. Supp. 1376 (E.D. Wis. 1974), *vacated and remanded*, 421 U.S. 957 (1975), *reinstated*, 413 F. Supp. 1318 (E.D. Wis. 1976); Lynch V. Baxley, 386 F. Supp. 378, 394 (M.D. Ala. 1974); Doremus v. Farrell, 407 F. Supp. 509, 517 (D. Neb. 1975); Suzuki v. Quisenberry, 411 F. Supp. 1113, 1130, (D. Hawaii 1976).

75. *See, e.g.*, Lynch v. Baxley, 386 F. Supp. 378, 394 (M.D. Ala. 1974).

76. Brief amicus curiae for the American Psychiatric Association in Barefoot v. Estelle, 460 U.S. 880 (1983), at 16. The association argued, *inter alia,* that psychiatrists should not be permitted to present expert testimony at the sentencing phase of a death penalty proceeding concerning the risk of future dangerousness because a jury is likely to give

undue weight to their testimony "because it is, or purports to be, a statement of professional opinion." The association went on to argue that such testimony is often unreliable. The reliability of psychiatric predictions of dangerousness is discussed in chapter 2.

77. Medical records are admissible at court hearings under the business records exception to the hearsay rule as long as they were made in the ordinary course of business, but the statements of third parties contained in them are generally not. For example, nurses' notes of their observations of an individual's behavior are admissible, but a policeman's statements to a nurse generally are not.

78. Vaughn v. Harlem Hospital Center (91 Civ. 3050, S.D.N.Y.).

79. *Id.* The directive read: "As hospital personnel, you may be asked to testify at a commitment hearing or other court proceeding involving the hospital or a patient at the hospital. You are free to testify truthfully on behalf of a patient, the hospital or any other person or entity, and without fear of retaliation, job disciplinary action or dismissal, even if your testimony conflicts with that of other hospital personnel or the official position of the hospital."

80. At the time it was dismissed, the Court of Appeals could still have decided the appeal, on the grounds that the issue was capable of repetition and likely to evade review and that the fact of her commitment could be used against her in future proceedings.

81. Author's interview with one of the judges on the intermediate appellate panel, February 1988.

82. Although less common than appeals by individuals, appeals by the government of commitment decisions often occur in cases of public importance. *See, e.g., Matter of Boggs, supra* (case challenging New York City's policy of confining mentally ill homeless people who were not imminently dangerous to themselves or others); Matter of Seltzer, New York Law Journal, Mar. 3, 1993 (2d Dep't) (state's appeal of release of so-called Wild Man of 96th Street, who, according to widely publicized press accounts, had terrorized residents of Manhattan's Upper West Side with violent behavior resulting from combination drug use and mental illness).

83. A mental health consumer group challenged the application of New York's automatic stay provision to commitment proceedings as unconstitutional. The state agreed to a court-ordered stipulation limiting the automatic stay to five days and requiring the government to file a motion demonstrating the need for an extension beyond that period. Project Release v. Surles, 90 Civ. 4912 (S.D.N.Y. 1992).

84. *Addington v. Texas, supra.*

85. Wyatt v. King, 773 F. Supp. 1508 (M.D. Ala. 1991); Fasulo v. Arafeh, 173 Conn 473, 378 A.2d 553 (1977); State v. Fields, 77 N.J. 282, 390 A.2d 574 (1978).

86. As described below, it violates due process to continue to confine a person who is no longer mentally ill and dangerous to others or who can survive safely in freedom with the help of family or friends. *See, e.g., O'Connor v. Donaldson, supra.*

87. *O'Connor v. Donaldson, supra.*

88. *See, e.g.,* N.Y. Mental Hyg. Law § 29.15(b)(1) (McKinney 1988 & Supp. 1993).

89. For a chart of state conditional release provisions, see Brakel et al., *supra,* Table 4.3. The authors report that some forty states provide for the conditional release of people with mental illness and twenty-five have provisions for people with developmental disabilities or mental retardation.

90. *See, e.g.,* N.Y. Mental Hyg. Law § 29.15(d)(2) (McKinney 1988 & Supp. 1993).

91. *See, e.g.,* Birl v. Wallis, 633 F. Supp. 707, 711 (M.D. Ala. 1986) ("[H]ospital could not . . . reconfine a fully discharged patient without going through initial commitment proceedings once again; nor may it do so with a patient released on trial visit."); *In re* Richardson, 481 A.2d 473 (D.C. 1984) (before conditional release can be revoked, patient entitled to due process hearing at which inpatient confinement must be shown to be the least restrictive alternative available). *But see* Matter of Roberds, 473 N.W.2d 378 (Minn. App. 1991) (least restrictive alternatives need not be considered).

92. *See also* Foucha v. Louisiana, 111 S. Ct 1412 (1991) (involuntary civil confinement not permissible unless individual is both mentally ill and dangerous).

93. *See, e.g.,* Birl v. Wallis, 619 F. Supp. 481, 489–91 (M.D. Ala. 1985); *In re* Richardson, *supra,* 481 A.2d at 478–79; Lewis v. Donahue, 437 F. Supp. 112 (W.D. Okla. 1977); Meisel v. Kremens, 405 F. Supp. 1253 (E.D. Pa. 1975); G.T. v. Stone, 622 A.2d 491 (Vt. 1992).

94. *See, e.g.,* Dietrich v. Brooks, 27 Or. App. 821, 558 P.2d 357 (1976) (hearing not required for revocation of convalescent leave program because consequence is therapeutic not punitive).

95. *See* Morrissey v. Brewer, 408 U.S. 471 (1972) (parolees accused of violating conditions of parole entitled to prerevocation hearing before neutral decision maker).

96. *See,* S.C. Code Ann. § 44-23-210 (4) (1976 § 1993 Supp.); Pa. Stat. Ann. tit. 50, § 7306 (c) (1983 & 1994 Supp.); Ohio Rev. Code Ann. §§ 5122.20, 5123.21 (1980 and 1994 Supp.).

97. *See, e.g.,* Ihler v. Chisholm, No. ADV-88-383 (Montana First Judicial District 1991); N.Y. Mental Hyg. Law § 29.11 (McKinney 1984 & 1995 Supp.), 14 N.Y. Comp. Codes R. & Regs. tit. 517.4. (criteria that must be considered in evaluating a proposed transfer include, *inter alia,* the need for continued inpatient treatment, the appropriateness of services at the receiving facility, overcrowding at the sending and receiving facilities, and the proximity of the institutions to friends and family).

98. Eubanks v. Clarke, 434 F. Supp. 1022 (E.D. Pa. 1977) (transfer from minimum security facility to maximum security facility requires judicial hearing).

99. Savastano v. Nurnberg, 567 N.Y.S.2d 618. 77 N.Y.2d 300 (Ct. App. 1990) (administrative review process, but no hearing, required for transfer from acute-care to state intermediate and long-term care facility). In determining whether to transfer a patient from an acute-care facility to a state institution, the following are some of the criteria that must be considered under New York State regulations: (1) the proximity of the sending and receiving facilities to the individual's significant others; (2) the ability of the sending and receiving hospitals to provide adequate overall treatment to the individual, as affected by overcrowding, the availability of services the person needs, and bed capacity; and (3) the individual's need for services that are more readily available at the receiving facility. *See also* Ihler v. Chisholm, *supra.*

100. Vitek v. Jones, 445 U.S. 480 (1980).

101. Schwartz & Costanzo, *Compelling Treatment in the Community: Distorted Doctrines and Violated Values,* 20 Loyola of Los Angeles Law Review 1329, 1369–72 (1987).

102. Matter of Tarpley, 581 N.E. 2d 1251 (Ind. 1991).

103. *In re* McPherson, 176 Cal. App. 3d 332, 222 Cal. Rptr. 416 (1985); *In re*

Richardson, 481 A.2d 473 (D.C. 1983); *In re* Cross, 99 Wash. 2d 373, 662 P.2d 828 (1983).

104. Birl v. Wallace, 633 F. Supp. 707 (M.D. Ala. 1986) (revocation of conditional release); *In re* Crainshaw, 54 N.C. App. 429, 283 S.E. 2d 553 (1981).

105. *See, e.g., In re* Bryant, 127 Or. App. 68, 871 P.2d 129 (1994) (no finding of mental illness required for revocation of outpatient commitment).

106. *In re* Feenster, 561 A.2d 997 (D.C. 1989).

107. *In re* James, 507 A.2d 155 (D.C. 1986); *In re* Mills, 467 A.2d 971 (D.C. 1983).

108. *In re* James, 507 A.2d 155 (D.C. 1986); *In re* Richardson, 481 A.2d at 479 n. 5.

IV

Personal Autonomy, Informed Consent, and the Right to Refuse Treatment

There is perhaps no right more basic than the right to control what happens to one's own body. Variously referred to as the right to bodily integrity, the right to privacy, the right to personal autonomy, and the right to determine the course of one's own medical treatment, this right is at the heart of our society's concept of personal liberty. As one court has observed, "In our system of a free government, where notions of individual autonomy and free choice are cherished, it is the individual who must have the final say in respect to decisions regarding his medical treatment in order to ensure that the greatest possible protection is accorded his autonomy and freedom from unwanted interference with the furtherance of his own desires."[1]

It is a well-established principle of the common law that any unwanted bodily intrusion or physical contact is considered an assault or a battery. Justice Benjamin Cardozo's famous articulation of this right holds as true today as when it was first enunciated in the early part of this century. "Every human being of adult years and sound mind has a right to determine what shall be done with his own body."[2]

Although every adult is presumed to be competent unless there is a judicial determination to the contrary,[3] people with mental disabilities do not always enjoy the benefit of this presumption. In addition, there are complex questions about the way decisions should be made for people who are incompetent, and particularly serious concerns about the potential for coercion. This chapter examines the doctrine of informed consent and the right to refuse treatment as they relate to decisions regarding medical treatment, psychotropic medication, electroconvulsive therapy, psycho-surgery, behavior modification, aversive treatment, and experimental treatment. It concludes with a consideration of methods of making treatment decisions for people who lack the capacity to make them for themselves, including advance directives and guardianship proceedings.

INFORMED CONSENT

What is the doctrine of informed consent?

In *The Rights of Patients*, George Annas observes that the doctrine of informed consent exists for two basic reasons: "(1) to promote self-determination and (2) to promote rational decision making."[4] The doctrine requires that patients be provided sufficient information before consenting to a test, treatment, or procedure, in order to make a competent, informed, voluntary, and understanding decision whether or not to consent. At a minimum this means that patients must be told of (1) the risks and benefits of the proposed treatment or procedure; (2) any side effects or complications; (3) the likelihood of improvement with and without the treatment, including an explanation of the kinds of improvement that should be expected; and (4) any alternative treatment methods. As a prerequisite to giving informed consent, a patient must have the capacity to make a reasoned decision whether to accept or refuse the proposed procedure.[5]

The doctrine of informed consent applies whenever a medical procedure poses an inherent risk of injury or death that the patient might not be aware of, when there are alternative procedures, or when the probability of its success is low.[6] It applies to a broad range of medical procedures, including the administration of medication, diagnostic tests, and major or minor surgery.[7]

The physician has a duty to convey the information necessary to make an informed decision in language the patient can understand. As long as the patient has the capacity to make such a decision, it is the patient, and not family members or other third parties, who has the right to receive the information and make the final decision.

Does the doctrine of informed consent apply to people with mental disabilities?

Yes. The doctrine of informed consent applies to every competent adult. The existence of a mental disability, by itself, does not disqualify an otherwise competent person from exercising this right. All adults are presumed competent and remain so unless a court makes a finding of incompetency or partial incompetency. As one court observed with regard to mental illness: "Indeed, it is well accepted that mental illness often strikes only limited areas of functioning, leaving other areas unimpaired, and consequently, that many mentally ill persons retain the capacity to function in a competent manner."[8]

Although some states have treated an involuntary commitment order as a finding of a lack of capacity to refuse mental health treatment such as psychotropic drugs, as explained in chapter 2, most states have rejected this approach and require a separate judicial finding of incapacity before an involuntary patient can be treated without consent.[9]

What is a competent decision?

To give competent consent, a person must be able to make a reasoned decision whether to accept or refuse a proposed procedure. It is the patient's ability to weigh the relevant factors, not the patient's final decision, that determines competency. Because one of the purposes of informed consent is to enhance individual autonomy, people have broad latitude to make choices that reflect their personal values. A person is not incompetent merely because her treatment decision deviates from what the majority of patients would do, appears irrational, is not in her best interests, or contradicts a doctor's advice. For example, a competent patient diagnosed with cancer of the larynx may reject life-prolonging surgery because it removes the voice box, decline radiation treatment because of its painful side effects, or choose no treatment at all because, despite a hastened death, this course offers what the patient considers to be a better quality of life.

Those familiar with facilities for people with mental disabilities know that an individual's decision is rarely questioned as long as it agrees with the doctor's. A psychiatrist recommending psychotropic drugs, such as Haldol or Thorazine, generally accepts a patient's consent without further question, but is likely to challenge the competency of a patient who refuses treatment. Inmates who disagree with the recommendations of their psychiatrist are often said to lack "insight" into their condition and, consequently, the capacity to make treatment decisions. Such a conclusion is legally unsound, since disagreement cannot be equated with lack of capacity without a finding that the individual is incapable of making a reasoned decision about treatment. This principle has been applied in states that recognize a right of medical autonomy, built upon the common-law principles of informed consent, that includes the right of competent, involuntarily committed persons to refuse antipsychotic medications.[10] By the same token, it is also improper to presume the competency of people who raise no objection to treatment if they do not have the capacity to understand the consequences of their decision, and clinicians who do so may subject themselves to liability.[11]

Although clinicians have written extensively on the subject, there is no standard test for determining competency. The key question is whether the person understands the nature of the proposed treatment and its risks and benefits, alternative forms of treatment, and the prognosis with and without the recommended treatment.

Can people with mental retardation give informed consent?

Yes. The answer depends on the nature of the decision and the person's level of functioning. The vast majority of people with mental retardation, those identified as "mildly retarded" or "moderately retarded" under the old but still commonly used system of classification,[12] are capable of living independently and making a broad range of decisions for themselves. Since the capacity to make decisions can vary from person to person and decision to decision, a careful, individualized assessment of capacity should be made. Even people formerly classified as "profoundly retarded,"[13] who function at a much lower intellectual level and generally require guardians to help them make most of their decisions, may have the capacity to make certain decisions affecting their lives.

Indeed, the assumptions that governed thinking about decisional capacity have proven largely unfounded as people with mental retardation make decisions about where and with whom they live, where they work and whether they want a particular medical procedure. These assumptions have broken down because of a change in our understanding of capacity and its assessment. The ability to absorb and process information, for example, is a product not just of skills in abstract reasoning but of the manner in which information is communicated. Moreover, "capacity" is a relative concept and may vary depending on the type of decision to be made. A person may have the capacity to choose a residence or apply for a job but be unable to make complex financial decisions. Where the decision involves intrusive or potentially risky medical treatment, great care should be taken to determine whether the person is capable of giving informed consent. If there are doubts, a court should make the determination at a hearing that affords the individual due process safeguards and provides for the appointment of a surrogate decision maker in the event of incapacity. These principles apply to people who lack the capacity to consent to all forms of treatment for a mental disability, such as medication or behavior modification.

It should be noted that clinicians who provide intrusive treatment to non-objecting individuals who lack the capacity to consent may be exposing themselves to liability under the Supreme Court's decision in *Zinermon v. Burch*, which was discussed in chapter 2. *Zinermon* held that a hospital violated due process by admitting as a voluntary patient a person who lacked the capacity to consent to his admission.[14] *Zinermon* has potential application to people with developmental disabilities who do not have decision-making capacity but nonetheless receive intrusive treatment without the consent of a guardian or other authorized surrogate.

Most of the choices facing people with mental retardation have little to do with treatment but concern other fundamental aspects of their lives such as their residence, work, education, or sexuality. As a general rule, much less attention is paid to the decision-making process outside the medical arena. Many individuals with mental retardation are capable of choosing where to live, selecting a job, or consenting to sexual relationships. Others are able to take some part in these decisions with the assistance of a relative or guardian. Yet they are frequently not allowed to participate in decision making to the extent of their abilities. In addition, many people who lack capacity do not have family or guardians to act on their behalf and ensure that proper decisions are made for them.

Some states have established advocacy groups to enhance individual decision making or, where necessary, make basic decisions when no family or friend is available. Perhaps the most successful of these is the Consumer Advisory Board (CAB), which was created by the Willowbrook Consent Decree to provide an advocate for Willowbrook residents who need assistance but have no relative actively looking after their interests. CAB consists of a board made up largely of parents and advocates, along with a paid professional staff. Board and staff members keep in regular contact with the individuals they represent, inspect residences, attend treatment team conferences, screen transfers to new facilities, monitor programs and advocate for proper services. As family members age or move away and can no longer advocate for their relatives, CAB steps in to fill their role. The board is authorized to act as a surrogate for people who are not competent to make decisions on their own and to assist those who can in making the decisions they desire. Under the March 1993 Willowbrook permanent injunction, the state of New York is required to provide sufficient funding for the Consumer Advisory Board as long as any member of the Willowbrook plaintiff class is alive.[15]

Who makes treatment decisions for people who lack the capacity to consent?

The answer to this question is still evolving as states experiment with new procedures designed to protect the welfare of people who cannot make decisions for themselves, while minimizing the intrusions on their personal liberty. In the past, states relied heavily on guardianship proceedings in which, after declaring an individual incompetent, a court appointed a guardian or a committee with the authority to make decisions about virtually every aspect of the person's life. Typically, guardians controlled the personal finances of their wards, determined their living arrangements—including admission to institutions or nursing homes—and gave or withheld consent to medical treatment. Among its many shortcomings, this system unnecessarily stripped individuals of the power to make most decisions for themselves, even if they had the capacity to make decisions in all but one limited area, such as medical treatment, on their own.

In response to growing dissatisfaction with traditional guardianship laws, states have begun to develop less intrusive alternatives, such as limited guardianships, to meet the needs of people with mental disabilities. In other cases, states have sought to bypass the judicial system altogether in the hope of obtaining quicker, better, and less costly decisions. One of these alternatives, New York State's Surrogate Decision-Making Committee (SDMC) program, rules on requests for major medical treatment[16] for people with mental disabilities who live in facilities operated or licensed by the state and who allegedly lack the capacity to give informed consent. Enacted in 1985 "to maximize patient autonomy and to reduce delays in obtaining judicial authorization for treatment,"[17] the program operates through panels of four volunteers, each consisting of a health care professional; a consumer, relative, or advocate of a person with a disability; an attorney; and another person with knowledge or interest in the treatment of people with mental disabilities. After receiving an application to authorize treatment, the panel must decide (1) whether there is clear and convincing evidence that the person lacks capacity to make the decision; and (2) if so, whether a preponderance of the evidence demonstrates that the treatment proposed is in the individual's best interests. Throughout this process, the panel must take the preferences of the individual into consideration.

Although hailed by supporters as hastening treatment, promoting personal autonomy, and improving decision making,[18] there have been several reports of delays in obtaining necessary diagnostic tests and treatment.[19] SDMC represents an important effort to devise techniques for surrogate decision making that enhance respect for individual choices and values while at the same time ensuring that the surrogate acts in a principled and accountable manner.

When is consent not voluntary?

To be valid, consent must be freely given, without threats, intimidation, or coercion. Pressure to consent can be direct, such as a threat to initiate commitment proceedings if the patient does not agree to a particular treatment. A patient on a psychiatric unit in a voluntary hospital in New York City once consented to electroshock therapy after being told that if she refused, she would be transferred to a state hospital. Her physician knew that she had found a previous confinement at a state hospital to be one of the most terrifying experiences of her life and would do almost anything to avoid returning there.[20]

The pressure can also be more subtle, especially in a setting where individuals are dependent on staff for their basic needs and privileges can be granted or withheld at the staff's discretion. In *The Willowbrook Wars*,[21] an insightful study of the efforts to reform a notorious institution for people with mental retardation that Senator Robert Kennedy once called a "snakepit," David and Sheila Rothman described how, in 1958, some parents were apparently coerced into consenting to have their children admitted to a special research unit where many children were injected with live hepatitis virus in an effort to develop a vaccine against the disease.

Many parents of children accepted at Willowbrook but still awaiting actual admission—a wait that could last for several years . . . receive[d] [a] letter from . . . Willowbrook's director. . . . Almost every phrase in this particular letter encourages parents to commit their children to the unit. . . .

To send such a letter over the signature of Willowbrook's director appeared coercive. These parents wanted to please the man who would be in charge of their child. Moreover, an especially raw form of coercion may have occasionally intruded. When overcrowding at Willowbrook forced a close in regular admissions, an escape hatch was left—admission via [the hepatitis] unit. A parent wanting to institutionalize a retarded child had a choice: Sign the form or forgo the placement.[22]

In a thoughtful analysis of an extreme procedure, a Michigan court held that involuntary commitment was in itself so inherently coercive that a person could not voluntarily consent to participate in experimental brain surgery, which might result in death or possible injury to the brain.[23] The court concluded that the "fact of institutional confinement has special force in undermining the capacity of the mental patient to make a competent decision" about irreversible experimental psychosurgery.[24] "The involuntarily detained mental patient is in an inherently coercive atmosphere even though no direct pressures may be placed upon him. He finds himself stripped of customary amenities and defenses. Free movement is restricted. He becomes a part of communal living subject to the control of the institutional authorities."[25]

No court has extended this analysis to nonexperimental treatment, such as medication. Thus, the general rule is that, absent evidence of actual coercion, competent, involuntary patients are free to give informed consent to procedures that are not experimental or dangerous and irreversible.

Finally, it should be noted that many doctors use heavy persuasion to gain the consent of patients to forms of treatment they recommend. Although it may feel coercive to the individual, as a legal matter this form of persuasion generally will not void an individual's otherwise informed consent, on the theory that patients often rely on the expertise of their physician. Without evidence of duress, a consent obtained by a silver-tongued doctor is considered voluntary.

THE RIGHT TO REFUSE MEDICATION

What are psychotropic drugs?

Drugs are the most common form of treatment in psychiatric facilities and are often prescribed as well for people with mental retardation who have aggressive or self-abusive behaviors. *Psychotropic drugs,* or drugs that act on the brain, include antipsychotic drugs; antidepressant drugs; lithium, for treatment of manic depression, now called bipolar disorder; and minor tranquilizers, such as Valium.[26]

Antipsychotic drugs, also known as neuroleptics or major tranquilizers, and lithium are the medications most frequently used to treat major mental disorders. Commonly prescribed antipsychotic drugs include Thorazine, Haldol, Prolixin, Navane, Mellaril and Compazine. Introduced into psychiatry in the early 1950s, neuroleptics have been hailed as shortening hospital stays, reducing symptoms, and enabling individuals who would otherwise have spent much of their lives in institutions to live in less restrictive community settings. As the Supreme Court has explained, their purpose is to "alter the chemical balance in a patient's brain, leading to changes, intended to be beneficial, in his or her brain processes."[27] They are widely used to treat psychoses, particularly schizophrenia. Generally, these drugs can be administered by pill, by liquid, or by injection—which permits staff members to administer medication over a person's objection.

For all their usefulness, antipsychotic drugs are far from being the antibiotics of mental illness. Unlike antibiotics, these drugs do not cure mental illness—they control symptoms. They are most effective at reducing psychotic thinking, hallucinations, delusions, and paranoia. Antipsychotics are also used as heavy duty tranquilizers to reduce hyperactivity, agitation, and aggressiveness. Although many physicians believe that antipsychotics are at their best in treating schizophrenia, where they can help decrease both the florid symptomatology and the rate of relapse, the former Chief of the Center for Studies of Schizophrenia at the National Institute of Mental Health has cautioned that "symptom reduction by itself is not synonymous with successful treatment" and has suggested that the most disabling aspects of schizophrenia may be beyond the reach of treatment with drugs.[28] In addition, the drugs are not effective at all for a substantial number of individuals.[29]

Recognizing the limitations of traditional psychotropic drugs, a number of clinicians have urged the use of Clozapine, which "appears to offer some advantage in refractory patients"[30] although not necessarily for those in which "negative or deficit symptoms predominate."[31] One disadvantage of this drug is the increased risk of agranulocytosis, a diminution of white blood cells that fight infection, but this risk can be reduced by regular monitoring of blood levels.[32]

There has been considerable debate over the efficacy of antipsychotic drugs, as well as over the care with which they are prescribed. Although there is general agreement that certain neuroleptics can help control the symptoms of schizophrenia and that lithium can help manage manic depression, there is not universal agreement as to the effectiveness of these drugs in treating other conditions. The dispute over the uncertainty of psychiatric diagnoses also affects decisions about medication.[33] For example, one court found that "even the value of psychotropic drugs as a means of controlling symptoms of mental illness (as opposed to their use as a cure for such disorders) often depends upon the accuracy of the diagnosis as to what disorder the patient suffers from, and there is wide recognition that such diagnosis is a less than precise art."[34]

Even where drug treatment is statistically most effective, as in the treatment of schizophrenia, and the diagnosis is properly made, it may be difficult to predict with any certainty whether a particular individual will respond positively, negatively, or not at all to a given drug. It may not be easy to determine which drug is best for a given set of symptoms[35] or which dosage should be prescribed for a particular patient.[36] Further compounding this difficulty, doctors in large institutions as well as private settings may not have access to the patient's prior history or the time to study it carefully and may be unaware of past diagnoses, the effectiveness of prior treatments, or any side effects that were experienced.

In *Is There No Place on Earth for Me?*[37] Susan Sheehan chronicled the life of the pseudonymous Sylvia Frumkin, a woman with a chronic psychiatric disability, and her attempts to obtain treatment in and outside of mental institutions. At the book's conclusion, an expert in pharmacology evaluated the various psychiatrists who treated her and the medications they prescribed. "One of the most striking things about Sylvia Frumkin's case history is that many psychiatrists—those she encountered, at least, and I don't think her case is uncommon in this respect—don't take the time and trouble to study case histories. No treatment she received over a period of thirteen years bore any logical relationship to a previous treatment."[38]

What are the side effects of psychotropic drugs?

Despite their therapeutic benefits, antipsychotic drugs also have an undeniable dark side, for they can produce severe, painful, and at times debilitating side effects that in some respects are potentially as disabling as the conditions they are prescribed to treat. The toxic effects of these drugs are well documented in the scientific and legal literature[39] and run the gamut from minor irritations to irreversible damage to the central nervous system and even death from neuroleptic malignant syndrome.

The mild side effects include dry mouth, dizziness, blurred vision, constipation, and muscle stiffness. Even a relatively modest side effect such as drowsiness can be a source of acute distress to patients who are struggling to feel wide awake and think more clearly.

More severe reactions include muscular side effects known as extrapyramidal symptoms, such as akathesia (motor restlessness and agitation); akinesia (physical immobility and lack of spontaneity); dystonic reactions (muscle spasms, irregular flexing, writhing, or grimacing movements); and pseudo-Parkinsonian symptoms (tremors, muscle stiffness, drooling, shuffling gait). Most extrapyramidal symptoms cease when the drugs are discontinued and can be controlled by the administration of additional drugs such as Cogentin. However, one study found that tardive dystonia[40] is not treatable with these medications and may continue even after the use of neuroleptics has been stopped. There is also evidence that in some cases parkinsonian symptoms go unrecognized for substantial periods of time among both adults and children, are resistant to anti-parkinsonian medication, and can linger for months after the discontinuation of neuroleptics.[41]

One of the most serious side effects of antipsychotic drugs is *tardive dyskinesia*, a neurological syndrome characterized by involuntary, rhythmic, and often grotesque movements of the face, lips, tongue, fingers, hands, legs, and pelvis. Although most cases of tardive dyskinesia appear after at least six months of drug use,[42] some people have developed this syndrome after only a few months on antipsychotics.[43] Once discovered, tardive dyskinesia is considered irreversible in two of every three cases, even after the person ceases taking the medication.[44] There is no proven cure for persistent tardive dyskinesia at this time. Early cases, however, frequently go undetected, partly because antipsychotics tend to mask the symptoms and partly through inattention. Many people do not demonstrate symptoms until they have discontinued the medication and it is too late to halt the disorder.[45] Even when symptoms are apparent, psychiatrists may overlook them. In two disturbing studies, psychiatrists failed to notice signs of tardive dyskinesia in some 75 percent[46] and 90 percent[47] of the cases, respectively.

The prevalence of tardive dyskinesia is staggering. After surveying the scientific literature, the Supreme Court, for example, concluded that between 10 and 25 percent of all patients treated with antipsychotic drugs display the symptoms of tardive dyskinesia.[48] Estimates of tardive dyskinesia among chronic or institutionalized patients run even higher.[49]

Finally, there is increasing concern about neuroleptic malignant syndrome, which has been described as "one of the most devastating side effects of antipsychotic medication."[50] Characterized by fever, tachycardia, high blood pressure, and delirium or coma, this usually strikes suddenly and swiftly and can cause permanent neurological damage or death.[51] Although the prevalence of neuroleptic malignant syndrome has been difficult to estimate, studies have suggested a rate of between 1 and a little over 2 percent of patients using neuroleptic drugs.[52] One commentator concluded:[53]

Despite the seriousness and prevalence of [neuroleptic malignant syndrome], most authoritative texts fail to even mention the syndrome.[54] This disorder continues to be underdiagnosed by clinicians, even in sophisticated hospital settings.[55] Due to the explosive course of this condition, lack of early recognition can prove fatal. And even when recognized, treatment remains problematic. Other than the obvious measure of immediate discontinuation of antipsychotic agents, specific treatment recommendations have been impeded by a lack of controlled studies.[56]

The potential benefits and risks of the use of neuroleptic medications illustrate the importance of the doctrine of informed consent. Despite the side effects of these drugs, the vast majority of people in psychiatric hospitals are on a drug regimen that they are encouraged to maintain after they leave the institution. In many cases, however, they are not adequately informed of the potential risks and benefits of neuroleptic medications. Despite their risks, there is nothing inherently objectionable about taking neuroleptics. There are sound reasons why a competent person with a mental disorder might choose or reject treatment with these drugs, just as a cancer patient might elect chemotherapy, radiation treatment, surgery, or no treatment at all for a malignancy. Ultimately, weighing the risks and benefits of a proposed treatment is a matter of personal values. As Alexander Brooks aptly observed: "The decision whether or not to accept drugs is for many patients a difficult one in which the patient is often between Scylla and Charybdis. It is difficult for some patients to know which is worse, the illness itself or the side effects of medication."[57]

The critical question is whether the individual has been fully informed of the risks and benefits of the drugs, and of any alternative treatments, and is permitted to exercise informed consent. In too many cases, the answer is no.

The process of informed consent about these medications, like all discussions for the purpose of informed consent, should, wherever possible, include a dialogue between doctor and patient in which the physician explains the advantages and disadvantages of the proposed treatment in language the individual can understand, answers questions, and takes pains to lay out all of the information necessary to make a knowledgeable decision. Doctors are free to give advice, describe the prognosis with and without the treatment, explain what other patients have done, and suggest what he or she would do if the roles were reversed. Ideally, the doctor should distinguish between his or her medical expertise, which provides such information as a diagnosis, prognosis, and explanation of the risks and benefits of a given procedure, and the personal decision the individual must make, based on values unique to that person. That decision ultimately rests with the individual.

The process of obtaining informed consent involves more than a physician's recitation of the possible adverse side effects of the medications or treatment, followed by the reasons for recommending the procedure anyway. In many cases truly informed consent requires that doctors make an effort to understand an individual's concerns about treatment by discussing them with the patient, allowing sufficient time for reflection and, if necessary, renewing the dialogue later. Such a discussion, for example, might elicit information about a patient's prior bad experience with a particular medication and lead to the selection of a different medication or an alternative form of treatment altogether.

Is there a right to refuse antipsychotic drugs?

Yes, but the extent of that right depends on the individual's admission status and can vary from one state to another. Outpatients generally have a right to refuse medication unless a court has declared them incompetent or has imposed an outpatient commitment order. Most states extend this right to voluntary and informal patients, who have the additional option of leaving the institution[58] unless the facility takes steps to have them committed.

The rights of involuntary patients, however, are more complicated. For years proponents of forced medication argued that involuntary commitment constitutes a judicial determination of incapacity to make decisions about treatment.[59] However, as discussed in chapter 3, almost every state has now enacted civil rights laws declaring that involuntary commitment does not suspend individual rights or render individuals incompetent to exercise them. Without a specific adjudication of incompetency, involuntary patients generally have the right to vote, marry, enter into contracts, and make wills and to execute advance health care directives. One of the most basic of these rights is the "fundamental right to make decisions concerning one's own body."[60]

Coupled with this greater respect for individual rights is what one court has termed "the nearly unanimous modern trend in the courts, and among psychiatric and legal commentators, to recognize that there is no significant relationship between the need for hospitalization of people with psychiatric disabilities and their ability to make treatment decisions."[61] The fact that a person has a psychiatric disability does not necessarily mean that she cannot make a reasoned decision whether to take medication. For example, the decision to refuse medication may be a rational one, based on personal experience of the side effects of the drugs.[62] It is well established that mental illness can impair one area of functioning while leaving others intact.[63] Nor does an involuntarily committed person's inability to survive safely outside an institution or her propensity for violence to others necessarily affect her capacity to make treatment decisions inside a hospital.[64] Unless a court makes a specific finding at the commitment hearing that an individual lacks the capacity to make treatment decisions inside the institution, an order of commitment should not constitute such a finding.

Virtually every court that has considered this issue has found that confined persons have a protected interest in refusing treatment, based on either the common-law doctrine of informed consent or state or federal constitutional law.[65] Most often, the source of the constitutional right is the liberty interest in the due process clause of the Constitution, triggered by both the drugs' potential for altering thought processes and hampering physical mobility, and the infringement on the individual's ability to make treatment decisions that affect his or her body.[66] It is no coincidence that these drugs can also be used as "chemical restraints."[67] Because antipsychotic drugs can affect the will and the mind of the subject,[68] the First Amendment right of free speech,[69] including the right to generate thoughts, as well as the constitutional right of privacy are also implicated. Former Supreme Court Justice Louis Brandeis expressed in 1928 the principles underlying these rights as eloquently as anyone before or since.

> The makers of our Constitution undertook to secure conditions favorable to the pursuit of happiness. They recognized the significance of man's spiritual nature, of his feelings and of his intellect. They knew that only a part of the pain, pleasure and satisfactions of life are to be found in material things. They sought to protect Americans in their beliefs, their thoughts, their emotions and their sensations. They conferred, as against the Government, the right to be let alone— the most comprehensive of rights and the right most valued by civilized men.[70]

The key elements that make up the right to refuse medication are (1) the standard for determining whether a person may be medicated involuntarily; and (2) the process for deciding whether that standard has been met. Although some of the details may vary from one jurisdiction to another, there are essentially two models for making these decisions: a "medical" model and a "legal" or "informed consent" model.

What is the "medical" model for evaluating objections to treatment?

Under the medical model, the decision whether an involuntary patient can be forced to take antipsychotic drugs is a question of professional expertise rather than personal autonomy. The inquiry involves whether medication is clinically appropriate to treat and control a mental illness that has caused the person to be dangerous to self or others and thereby to require involuntary confinement. In other words, doctor knows best— unless the doctor's opinion is well beyond the pale of psychiatric standards and practice.

Although the Supreme Court has not directly ruled in a case prescribing the standards and procedures for the forced treatment of civilly committed individuals,[71] virtually every court that has considered the federal constitutional right to refuse treatment has applied the test outlined by the Court in *Youngberg v. Romeo*,[72] which set forth a medical model analysis.[73] By contrast, many state constitutional decisions have adopted an informed consent analysis.[74]

The medical model analysis is illustrated by the decision of the Second Circuit Court of Appeals in *Project Release v. Prevost*,[75] which applied

Youngberg in upholding New York's involuntary treatment regulations against a constitutional challenge. The New York rules allowed doctors almost complete discretion to medicate involuntary patients. A person who disagreed with the doctor's decision could "object to" and "appeal" but not refuse treatment with antipsychotic drugs. The ultimate decision whether to medicate by force lay with doctors and administrators at the hospital or the State Office of Mental Health. The regulations did not provide a single standard for making this decision but gave carte blanche to hospital employees to "review" the individual's objection, "consider the appeal and make a decision."[76] It was not even necessary to find that the medication was needed to prevent the person from endangering herself or others, that the person lacked the capacity to make a treatment decision, or that there was no less intrusive alternative to the drugs. There was also no requirement that the drug be administered at the lowest effective dosage.

Applying the *Youngberg* test, the federal court of appeals found that the individual's "interest in being free from bodily restraint" is satisfied if "professional judgment was in fact exercised."[77] In other words, a doctor's decision to medicate an unwilling patient is presumed correct unless it is "such a substantial departure from accepted professional judgment, practice, or standards as to demonstrate that the person responsible actually did not base the decision on such a judgment."[78] There is little room in this equation for personal choice, no matter how competent the individual, how well reasoned the individual's objections, how serious the potential side effects, or how appropriate other, less intrusive therapies may be.

As for procedures, the court concluded that there should be an opportunity for a "hearing" to review the individual's objections to treatment. However this need only consist of the opportunity to voice objections to supervising hospital personnel.[79] In the court's view, due process requires no more. Other courts adopting the medical model approach have demanded more thorough reviews by psychiatrists or panels of psychiatrists independent of the treating physician.[80] Even so, without independent decision makers or a strict legal standard, these nonjudicial procedures run the risk of rubber stamping the treating physician's decision, as was often the case in New York. Although in some instances reviewers have proven surprisingly willing to uphold the individual's wishes,[81] most hospital reviewers are generally unlikely to conclude that a colleague's decision to administer antipsychotic medication was so erroneous as to warrant reversal. Thus, the results can vary from state to state, and even from hospital to hospital, depending upon the willingness of the state or an individual facility to scrutinize the decisions of its own doctors.

What is the "legal" or "informed consent" model for evaluating objections to treatment?

Under the legal or informed consent model only a court can authorize a doctor to override an involuntary patient's refusal of medication. The mere fact of involuntary commitment does not strip a person of the capacity to make this decision;[82] a judicial finding of incapacity is a prerequisite to overruling individual choice.

This model relies on state constitutional law and the common-law doctrine of informed consent and entails a two-step process. First, in order to outweigh the individual's fundamental liberty interest in bodily autonomy, the state must demonstrate a compelling[83] or "overwhelming"[84] state interest. This generally requires either an emergency, where forced medication is necessary to prevent a danger to self or others within the institution, or a judicial declaration of incapacity to make the treatment decision at issue. Because there is a general presumption that involuntary patients are competent to make treatment decisions,[85] this model bars forced drugging without a court order, except in emergencies.

Second, if the court finds that an individual lacks the capacity to refuse medication, in most cases the court, not the doctor, makes the final decision whether the person can be involuntarily medicated. Some courts apply a "substituted judgment" analysis, in which they attempt to put themselves in the incompetent person's shoes and determine what the individual would have decided, if competent.[86] Others attempt to determine what would be in the person's best interests and weigh such factors as the risks and benefits of the proposed treatment, the prognosis, and the individual's expressed wishes. Under both analyses, courts pay careful attention to alternative treatments. Even when ordering forced medication, judges have the power to scrutinize the number and type of medications to be administered, and their dosage, to ensure that the treatment is narrowly tailored to the individual's needs. Using a substituted judgment analysis, the Massachusetts Supreme Judicial Court has even extended the right to refuse treatment to legally incompetent people whose guardians seek an order to administer medication.[87]

Finally, the legal model provides a full panoply of procedural protections, including a hearing, the right to counsel, and the right to have the need for involuntary medication proved by clear and convincing evidence.[88]

The New York Court of Appeals's decision in *Rivers v. Katz*[89] best illustrates the difference between the medical and legal models. Applying a strict legal analysis, *Rivers* struck down on state constitutional grounds the same New York regulations that the federal court of appeals sitting in New York had upheld under a federal constitutional, medical model analysis.

The legal model has several advantages over the medical model. First, it adheres to the general rule of law that, except in emergencies, competent individuals—not doctors—have the right to weigh the therapeutic benefits of the drugs against their serious and potentially irreversible side effects. The mere fact that an individual may arrive at a different conclusion from the treating psychiatrist does not make that decision any less competent. After all, it is the individual who will live with the consequences long after the clinician has left the scene.

Second, the legal model establishes clear standards and procedures for overriding an individual's treatment decision, rather than leaving it to the unfettered discretion of a psychiatrist. This is particularly important in view of the historic overuse of these drugs and their potential for abuse. As one psychiatrist has written: "Placing unbridled discretion in the hands of a single clinician has often led to unskillful and at times unfortunate use of medications. This is particularly true in some of our public facilities, which historically have had difficulties recruiting and supporting competent clinicians."[90]

Courts adopting the legal model have recognized that antipsychotic medications have been overprescribed,[91] prescribed as punishment,[92] and administered for the convenience of staff.[93] Without the strong safeguards of the legal model, the individual has little protection against such abuses.

Finally, the legal model affirms that people with mental disabilities are entitled to the same judicial safeguards of their medical autonomy as other individuals, regardless of their diagnosis.

Can a person be medicated involuntarily prior to a commitment hearing?

There is little legal justification for forcibly drugging a legally competent person who is awaiting a commitment hearing. Prior to the hearing, there has been no adjudication of incapacity to make treatment decisions.

Thus, in the absence of an emergency where the person presents an imminent danger to self or others inside the institution that can only be quelled by medication, there is no principled justification for dispensing with the doctrine of informed consent.

Medication may impair an individual's ability to prepare for and function at the commitment hearing, thus interfering with the right to a meaningful opportunity to challenge the appropriateness of confinement. At least four courts have recognized a right to be free of intrusive[94] or potentially debilitating treatment prior to a hearing.[95] Despite the possibility of therapeutic benefits for some patients, the neurological and muscular effects of the drugs, such as restlessness, twitching, grimacing, shuffling, or sedation, can have adverse effects on a person's demeanor and mental functioning and create a strong impression that the person is not "normal." This can have a prejudicial effect on the trier of fact: "Often it is the drugs themselves which are responsible for 'crazy' behavior. Tranquilizers often give people a blank, starey look and make them slow in responding to questions."[96]

In a related context, the Supreme Court ruled that a criminal defendant has a right to be free of psychotropic medication during his criminal trial, unless the state can show that drugs are medically appropriate and essential for his safety or the safety of others or that there was no less intrusive means of obtaining a verdict at trial.[97] The defendant in this case had argued that the medication interfered with his ability to consult with his lawyer at trial, prevented him from taking part fully in the proceedings, and presented a distorted picture of his mental state that undermined the credibility of his assertion of the insanity defense to the jury.

Has the existence of a right to refuse drugs significantly increased the number of involuntarily confined persons who refuse medication?

Despite the fears of many institutions that a right to refuse drugs would create chaos and harm patients, studies of facilities that have implemented such a right have generally found that drug refusals were relatively rare and easily handled. Not only does such a right not impair patients' overall treatment, but one study of drug refusals at a Massachusetts hospital observed that in some cases it actually yielded positive advantages, and "the feared epidemic of refusals did not materialize."[98] A more recent study of drug refusal in Massachusetts found that "fewer than 8% of patients refused medication, over half of those reaccepted medication voluntarily, just under a quarter had their refusals respected by clinicians, and the remainder had their refusals overturned in court."[99]

The empirical research conducted in the wake of the right-to-refuse treatment litigation also suggests that an individual's treatment may improve as a result of the opportunity to be heard on medication issues. After reviewing every study of the impact of the establishment of a right to have objections to treatment reviewed in some form, Paul Appelbaum, a proponent of involuntary medication, concluded that: "Allowing patients to object to treatment, forcing reappraisal of their situation by the treating physician or by outside reviewers, often results in a decision to alter treatment, and sometimes in a decision to suspend it altogether. This suggests that the process has some utility—a conclusion that, on reflection, should not be surprising."[100]

Researchers have also looked at the grounds for refusing treatment. Although clinicians have often contended that only people who are delusional or in denial refuse medication, the studies show otherwise: a significant percentage of people who refuse psychotropic medication do so on perfectly rational grounds.[101] The largest study of this kind found that 35 percent of people who refused medication cited adverse side effects as the reason.[102]

How often do courts grant requests to refuse medication?

Studies, observations of judicial hearings, and interviews with practitioners suggest that courts deny most patients' objections to medication, even in states like Massachusetts, Minnesota, and New York, which have a clearly articulated right to refuse treatment based on a strong legal model.[103] The explanation appears to be a combination of judicial reluctance to override professional judgment and the informal, prehearing resolution of a percentage of clear cases where patients obviously have the capacity to withhold consent to the medication.

Is there a right to refuse drugs in Medicaid-funded ICF/MRs?

People with mental retardation who live in facilities funded by Medicaid, called intermediate care facilities for the mentally retarded (ICF/MRs), discussed in chapter 6, enjoy extensive rights under regulations issued by the U.S. Department of Health and Human Services. As a condition of participation in the ICF/MR program, each facility must ensure the basic rights of its residents. These rights incorporate the doctrine of informed consent and include a right to refuse treatment. Thus, facilities must inform their residents or their legal guardians of the individuals' "medical condition and behavioral status, attendant risks of treatment, and of the right to refuse treatment."[104]

Even where the individual or her guardian has consented to treatment, the ICF/MR regulations further require facilities to ensure that their residents are free from any unnecessary drugs and are provided active treatment to reduce their dependency on medication.[105] The regulations warn that drugs must not be given in doses that "interfere with the individual client's daily living activities."[106] Finally, the use of medication to control "inappropriate behaviors" is prohibited unless approved by the interdisciplinary team and there is a finding that "the harmful effects of the behavior clearly outweigh the potentially harmful effects of the drugs."[107]

ADVANCE DIRECTIVES

One promising model for enhancing the autonomy of competent people and avoiding the potential quagmire of forced treatment is the advance directive. *Advance directives* enable individuals, while still competent, to leave instructions about the treatments they wish to receive or avoid if they become incompetent or to designate someone else to make health care decisions in their stead.

Advance directives hold particular promise for people with mental disabilities, offering them the possibility of exercising increased control over their lives by planning for their own health care in the event that they become incapacitated by their disability. Both proponents and opponents of a right to refuse psychotropic medication have welcomed the use of advance directives in appropriate circumstances as an alternative to forced psychiatric treatment.

What are advance directives for medical care?

An advance directive is a legal document that provides guidelines for any health care decisions that need to be made if and when an individual loses the capacity to make those decisions. There are two principal forms of advance directives used in health care: living wills and durable powers of attorney.

A *living will* is a directive that instructs health care providers to provide or withhold certain kinds of treatment under designated circumstances. Its most typical use is to enable a person to decide in advance whether life-sustaining treatment should be continued if an individual has a terminal medical condition or is in a persistent vegetative state. Almost all states have living will statutes that enable people to make these choices while still healthy.

A *durable power of attorney*, also known as a health care proxy, is a legal document permitting an individual to designate another person, called a "proxy" or "agent," to make decisions affecting his or her affairs in the event the person becomes incapacitated. The label *durable* is used to distinguish this document from the usual power of attorney, which is not valid when the person who executes it loses decision-making capacity. A "durable" power of attorney is still valid—indeed, it may only come into play—after the person loses capacity.

The durable power of attorney has existed for many years and is available in every state, but has only recently been adapted to health care decisions. Like a living will, it enables individuals to specify in advance whether they wish to receive a particular treatment in the event they are unable to make such a decision for themselves. A durable power of attorney offers the additional advantage of designating a proxy to make those treatment decisions that the now incapacitated person did not anticipate when drafting the advance directive. Typically, the proxy is a spouse, a close relative, or a friend who understands the individual's values and can be trusted to apply them to any unanticipated treatment decision that may arise. In the past decade, virtually every state has enacted legislation encouraging the use of durable powers of attorney for health care decisions. A proxy must obey the health care directives contained in the durable power of attorney.[108] The person creating the durable power of attorney can make these instructions as broad or as narrow as desired.

Do durable powers of attorney or other advance directives apply to psychiatric treatment?

Generally yes. Most laws enacted to permit advance directives apply to all types of treatment, whether for a medical condition or a mental disability.[109] A few state laws explicitly include mental health or psychiatric care as one of the forms of health care covered by the durable power of attorney.[110] As a result, these laws can effectuate a person's wishes with respect to antipsychotic medication in the same way as other medical procedures. While competent, the person may include directives in the durable power of attorney regarding medication, electroconvulsive therapy,[111] and other forms of treatment for a mental disability.

For example, an advance directive can specify:

• Whether, in the event of a psychotic episode or other serious mental disorder, the agent should consent to psychotropic medication.

• The type and dosage of medication and whether it should be administered orally or by injection.

• Whether and under what circumstances electroconvulsive therapy may be used.

Take the example of Rosa M., a thirty-three-year-old woman involuntarily hospitalized in a psychiatric facility. While confined, she underwent three courses of electroconvulsive therapy. Thereafter, and at a time when she had the capacity to make such a decision, she signed a consent form authorizing her psychiatrist to administer ECT. Three weeks later, while still competent, Ms. M. changed her mind and signed a document withdrawing her consent to ECT and another document stating that she did not want to discuss ECT without her lawyer present. When she subsequently lost the mental capacity to make treatment decisions, the hospital sought a court order authorizing the administration of ECT. Treating the documents withdrawing her consent to ECT as advance directives and finding that Rosa M. had capacity at the time she signed them, the court ruled that the hospital could not override her wishes and administer ECT.[112]

Advance directives generally are not binding in an emergency, e.g., when an individual presents a danger to self or others and a physician orders medication, seclusion, or restraint to protect the individual or third parties from harm. In an emergency, the state's interest in preventing harm under its police and *parens patriae* powers may outweigh the individual's interest in personal autonomy. Even in such circumstances, though, an advance directive can still play an important role in alerting clinicians to the individual's choice of treatment—e.g., a medication rather than a restraint—particularly where there is more than one effective option for addressing the emergency.

Do durable powers of attorney or advance directives apply to admission to a psychiatric hospital?

Most likely not. In some states, the advance directive law prohibits the proxy from admitting an incapacitated person to a psychiatric hospital.[113] Other states have no provision at all regarding hospital admission, but because of the special considerations involved in admission to a psychiatric hospital and the safeguards required even for voluntary admission, it is virtually certain that a proxy does not have the power to admit a person to a psychiatric hospital—particularly without specific authorization in the advance directive.

What if the advance directive instructs the agent, under specified circumstances, to admit the individual to a psychiatric hospital, regardless of any objections the individual might have at the time of admission? This is the *Ulysses contract*, named after the legendary hero who ordered that he be tied to the mast of his ship to prevent him from succumbing to the call of the sirens. The Ulysses contract has been advocated as a means for individuals to plan for their own admission while they are still capable of making a rational decision. It is, however, a contract of dubious validity. Constitutional requirements make it highly doubtful that a person's contemporaneous objections to psychiatric hospitalization can be put aside through an advance directive.[114] It is more likely that the admission will still have to be approved by a judge after a hearing under the state's involuntary admission law.

How is a durable power of attorney created?

Most state laws include a form that meets the statutory requirements for executing a valid durable power of attorney. The form typically describes the nature and possible consequences of the instrument so that the person drafting it fully understands its effect. Most statutes require the power of attorney:

1. To identify a proxy, or agent, to make decisions when the person executing the document loses decisionmaking capacity. The proxy must be an adult and, to avoid possible conflicts of interest, should not be associated with the health care facility where the person is receiving treatment.

2. To describe the authority granted the agent to make health care decisions when the person writing it lacks capacity, including any limitations or specific instructions about particular decisions the agent is to make, such as the withholding of food or water or the administration of medication.

3. To be signed.

4. To be witnessed, generally by at least two adults not associated with a person providing health care to the individual.

Can a person with a mental disability execute a durable power of attorney, living will, or other advance directive?

Yes, as long as the individual has capacity. An advance directive must be signed by a person who has the capacity to make treatment decisions. The law presumes that every adult has capacity. As explained above, neither involuntary civil commitment nor placement in a developmental center takes away that capacity. Typically, the only way a person loses the capacity to sign an advance directive is through a court determination of incompetency or incapacity to make treatment decisions. Courts may also be asked to determine retrospectively whether a person who has not been declared incompetent nevertheless lacked decisionmaking capacity at the time the advance directive was executed.[115]

When does a durable power of attorney or advance directive go into effect?

When a person loses the capacity to make health care decisions. This determination is usually made informally by a physician or, in some states, two physicians. If the physician subsequently concludes that the person has regained capacity, the person's authority to make health care decisions is restored and the agent's authority is revoked.

Can a durable power of attorney be revoked?

Yes, at any time. The law presumes that a person has the capacity to revoke a durable power of attorney. If the person's capacity at the time of revocation is challenged, only a court can overturn the person's decision.

What responsibilities do health care facilities have to facilitate the use of advance directives?

A great many. In 1991, Congress enacted the Patient Self-Determination Act[116] to foster education and awareness about advance directives among facilities providing medical care financed in part by Medicaid and Medicare and to assure that these facilities inform individuals admitted to their care about opportunities under their state's law to write an advance directive.

The law applies to inpatient facilities such as hospitals, nursing homes, and hospices. It requires a health care facility to provide information *in writing* to every adult admitted about the right to make health care decisions, including the right to refuse treatment and to create an advance directive. The law also requires a facility to have written information about its policies to implement advance directives and to educate the community about decision-making rights in health care.

The facility has one final, but critical, obligation: it must record the existence of an advance directive in the chart, so that everyone treating the individual is aware of it.

CONSENT TO PHYSICAL INTERVENTIONS

The fields of psychiatry and mental retardation have long had a fascination with physical treatments. Insulin coma therapy; the use of cold, wet sheet packs; electrical shocks for behavior modification; psychosurgery; and sterilization have all been popular interventions at some time in this century.[117] Today few intrusive physical interventions remain in common use: electroconvulsive therapy and physical behavior modification techniques are used as therapies, and sterilization is used as a permanent form of birth control. Because of the irreversibility of sterilization and the risks posed by certain of these interventions to the body and the brain, stringent safeguards are essential to ensure informed consent.

Is there a right to refuse psychosurgery?

Psychosurgery is surgery performed on the brain for the purpose of treating mental illness. Unlike traditional brain surgery, its goal is to change people's behavior.[118] It is undoubtedly the most invasive and controversial form of mental health treatment performed in this century. Its first known use was by the Incas, who "perforated" the skull to relieve mental illness by releasing evil spirits inside the brain.[119] Between 1936 and 1961 approximately 40,000 to 50,000 people in the United States underwent an early and notorious form of psychosurgery known as prefrontal lobotomy,[120] which involved interrupting some of the connections between the frontal lobes and other parts of the brain.[121] Despite some reported successes, many of the results were harrowing, featuring blunted emotions, pain, stupor, and, in from 1 percent to 4 percent of cases, death.[122] In one study of 134 men who underwent this procedure, 50 percent of the subjects had seizure disorders, 25 percent had severe intellectual disabilities, and only 10 percent had been released from a hospital.[123]

Lobotomies went out of favor in the 1950s with the advent of psychotropic drugs and the discrediting of its adherents' claims for success.

Because psychosurgery is highly invasive, has a long history of abuse, and is still considered by many to be experimental and dangerous, many states prohibit this procedure altogether and others have imposed stringent consent requirements. The combination of clinical disfavor and legal restrictions have led to the virtual disappearance of psychosurgery in psychiatry.

Is there a right to refuse electroconvulsive therapy?

Electroconvulsive therapy (ECT), also called electroshock therapy, is primarily a treatment for severe depression whereby a current of from 70 to 130 volts of electricity is introduced into the brain to induce a convulsion similar to an epileptic seizure.[124] ECT is most often used to treat severe episodes of depression.

This treatment was first developed by an Italian psychiatrist named Cerletti who theorized that administering a shock to the brain could have a beneficial effect on people with mental illness. From the beginning, however, this procedure has swirled in controversy. Plotkin describes the moment during Cerletti's first experiment on a human subject when, after producing a seizure on his first attempt, Cerletti paused to consider whether to begin a second treatment.[125] Unexpectedly, the patient spoke up and said clearly, "Not another one! It's deadly." Disregarding his patient's directive,[126] Cerletti proceeded with the second treatment and later wrote this account of his reasoning. "I confess that such explicit admonition under such circumstances, and so emphatic and commanding, coming from a person whose enigmatic jargon had until then been very difficult to understand, shook my determination to carry on with the experiment. But it was just this fear of yielding to a superstitious notion that caused me to make up my mind."[127] Plotkin commented: "Thus [ECT] was born—appropriately enough in complete disregard of the subject's 'superstitious' refusal."[128]

In fact, ECT did prove deadly in a small but significant number of cases, although the initial subject was not one of them. During its first few decades of use, the mortality rate from ECT was approximately 1 per every 1,000 patients.[129] With the development of improved safety techniques, the risk today is substantially lower. The consent form used by the American Psychiatric Association estimates the number of deaths caused by ECT at 1 per 10,000 patients.[130] The more frequent side effects are disorientation and short and long term memory loss.[131]

Today, many clinicians continue to support ECT as an effective treatment for severe depression, and a number of people have reported that ECT markedly relieved their depression after medication and other treatments had failed. Nevertheless, ECT remains a controversial therapy whose effects are not well understood and whose merits are hotly debated. Many people who have undergone this treatment have complained bitterly of memory loss, and a number of consumer and psychiatric survivor organizations have sought to outlaw its use.

As with other intrusive treatments with significant potential risks and benefits, many states have enacted special informed consent rules for ECT, especially in public facilities. The few courts that have considered the issue have generally required strict informed consent rules and imposed severe restrictions on the involuntary administration of ECT.[132] In 1992 the ECT standard in the *Wyatt* case,[133] which is discussed at length in the next two chapters, was revised to require that specific information about ECT be conveyed to the patient and that consent for ECT be put in writing. For individuals who have been judicially declared incompetent or whose competency is in question, only a court or court-appointed guardian may give consent. The consent of the guardian must be in writing.[134]

Is there a right to refuse behavior modification techniques?

As the name implies, behavior modification consists of a range of techniques designed to alter a person's behavior. This form of treatment frequently operates on a system of rewards or punishments to reinforce desirable and minimize unacceptable behaviors. Behavior modification techniques can be relatively benign, such as token economies, where behaviors earn or lose tokens that can be exchanged for essential items as well as privileges. Many clinicians view behavior modification as a particularly effective alternative to psychotropic medications that can enable people with mental retardation to overcome inappropriate behaviors without the side effects of drugs. Consent is generally not required for unintrusive forms of behavior modification.

Behavior modification techniques can also be highly intrusive and even painful, as in the use of powerful electrical shocks or drugs that make people feel that they cannot breathe. Intrusive behavior modification programs require informed consent, as do programs that inhibit the exercise of basic constitutional rights, such as communication, privacy, association, or liberty. In a particularly memorable example of involuntary behavior modification, psychiatric inmates were injected with a drug that induced vomiting for up to an hour. The drug was used to punish patients for "not getting up, for giving cigarettes against orders, for talking, for swearing, or for lying."[135] A federal appeals court ruled that subjecting inmates to this treatment without their consent constituted cruel and unusual punishment and was prohibited by the federal Constitution.[136]

The regulation of potentially abusive behavior modification programs was an important part of the early institutional reform lawsuits[137] and continues to be an issue even in the 1990s. For example, the Basic Research Institute in Rhode Island and Massachusetts has been the focus of a controversy spanning more than two decades for its use of aversives such as the SIBIS helmet and the Graduated Electronic Device (GED) in combination with food deprivation and physical restraints to alter the behavior of children with mental disabilities. The SIBIS is a modified hockey helmet equipped with, among other things, a hose that blows ammonia up the child's nose upon command. In 1990 it gave way to the GED, a device through which a staff member administers electric shocks by remote control to five or more body parts (both arms, both legs, the stomach, and sometimes the bottom of the feet) to discourage bad behavior.[138] Two organizations have filed complaints with the Food and Drug Administration seeking to ban the use of the GED.[139]

The use of behavior modification is regulated by a number of state statutes, as well as the regulations governing Medicaid-funded intermediate care facilities for mentally retarded people. Some jurisdictions have outlawed the use of aversives altogether. Others require consent. The Medicaid rules take no firm stance on the use of aversive techniques. Rather, they state only that the facility must have a policy about the use of "painful or noxious stimuli," procedures for implementing and supervising their use, and a monitoring protocol for these interventions. Whenever a facility proposes to use aversive techniques, its staff must discuss and implement them through the individual program plan process.[140] These safeguards are entirely procedural in nature. A facility may use aversives as long as it follows these procedures.

What are the rights of people with mental disabilities regarding sterilization?

Sterilization was one of the most egregious abuses promoted by the now-discredited eugenics movement, which dominated thinking about mental retardation in America during the latter part of the nineteenth century and the first three decades of the twentieth.[141] Eugenicists sought to raise the quality of the nation's gene pool by preventing the propagation of categories of people they deemed to be hereditarily inferior, such as people with mental disabilities and certain felons, who they erroneously believed passed on their traits to the next generation. Echoing these thoughts, Oliver Wendell Holmes wrote, "It is better for all the world, if instead of waiting to execute degenerate offspring for crime, or to let them starve for their imbecility, society can prevent those who are manifestly unfit from continuing their kind."[142]

To carry out their program, eugenicists secured the enactment of compulsory sterilization laws throughout the country, based on a model statute that was designed "to prevent the procreation of persons socially inadequate from defective inheritance, by authorizing and providing for eugenical sterilization of certain potential parents carrying degenerate hereditary qualities."[143] The legal highwater mark of the eugenics movement came in 1927, when the Supreme Court upheld the constitutionality of a Virginia compulsory sterilization law in *Buck v. Bell*,[144] concluding that "Three generations of imbeciles are enough." Subsequent research by Stephen Jay Gould and others has revealed, however, that neither Carrie Buck, whose sterilization the Court authorized, nor her daughter, nor, in all likelihood, her mother had mental retardation. Rather, Gould reports, Buck was an illegitimate child who was committed by her foster parents to the State Colony for Epileptics and Feeble Minded at the age of eighteen after she had been raped by a relative of the foster family and became pregnant. "Almost surely, she was (as they used to say) committed to hide her shame (and her rapist's identity), not because enlightened science had just discovered her true mental status."[145]

Although the Buck decision has never been overruled, it is highly unlikely that the forced eugenic sterilization of people with mental disabilities would again be tolerated, much less legally sanctioned. Scientific research has largely discredited the eugenicists' hypothesis that the majority of mental retardation is inherited,[146] and most eugenic sterilization laws have been repealed. A body of constitutional doctrine has since developed under the right of privacy, affording individuals substantial freedom from governmental interference with their right to reproductive freedom.[147] In *Wyatt v. Stickney*,[148] the court held that the involuntary sterilization of institutional residents at the discretion of facility administrators violated the due process clause of the Constitution. That decision and many others led states either to repeal their sterilization laws[149] or rewrite them to provide detailed procedures to assure that sterilization was only accomplished after proper notice and the opportunity to be heard by a judge. The law now stands that involuntary sterilization is only permissible by judicial order under very stringent standards.

Competent individuals have a constitutional and common-law right to decide whether or not to bear a child. This includes the right to be sterilized as well as the right to procreate. The difficult issues surrounding sterilization today involve people who lack the capacity to exercise this right. If a woman is incompetent to decide whether or not to be sterilized, does she then have a "right" to be sterilized or a "right" to bear a child? If the decision is to sterilize, isn't this just involuntary sterilization under another name? If the opposite decision is made, isn't this a denial of the woman's right to sterilization?[150]

These questions typically arise when a family member requests sterilization on the grounds that the mentally incompetent person is unable to use contraceptives easily and argues that the woman would either not be a fit parent or would suffer medical harm if she gave birth. In deciding between the individual's twin rights of procreation and sterilization, as with other substitute decision making, the critical question is who can make such a decision and under what circumstances.

State statutes concerning sterilization can vary significantly in the protections they afford, but a small body of caselaw is slowly developing in this area. Courts have by and large recognized a "right" to "voluntary" sterilization for incompetent women, exercised through a substitute decision maker and approved by a judge after a hearing.[151] Because sterilization is considered intrusive and irreversible, the caselaw generally establishes the following guidelines for authorizing the procedure: (1) the decision must be made by a court; (2) the individual must lack the capacity to give informed consent to sterilization now and in the foreseeable future; (3) there must be proof by clear and convincing evidence that contraception is necessary because the person is capable of procreation, is sexually active, and is permanently incapable of caring for a child, even with reasonable help; (4) there must be a finding that sterilization is in the individual's best interests;[152] and (5) all less drastic means of contraception must be unworkable and sterilization must be the least intrusive available method.[153]

Despite the development of stricter legal standards and procedures, decisions to sterilize incompetent women can be problematic. Theoretically such decisions should be made in a way that enhances a woman's reproductive choices, but it is often difficult to ascertain precisely what an incompetent person would choose in such a situation. Instead, as Susan Stefan notes, these decisions are often governed by benevolent plans for the woman that were made by others and based on factors that have little or nothing to do with reproductive choice, such as finding an appropriate community program or fears about the woman's experience with childbirth.[154]

EXPERIMENTATION ON PEOPLE WITH MENTAL DISABILITIES

What rules govern human experimentation and research?

Experimentation on human subjects has played a central role in the development of modern medicine.[155] Countless medications, vaccines, and medical procedures owe their genesis to clinical trials involving human beings. Yet, for all its contributions to the advancement of science, human experimentation has also been prone to serious abuse. The history of science is replete with medical experiments that were conducted on unwitting or unwilling individuals who were exposed to great risks without their informed consent. Many, but by no means all, of these experiments involved poor or institutionalized people, minorities, or children. Examples include the Tuskegee study, in which researchers withheld proper treatment from black men with syphilis for decades without their consent, in order to learn more about the disease;[156] the injection of live cancer cells into unconsenting, terminally ill patients at the Jewish Chronic Disease Hospital in Brooklyn, New York, to test their immune response;[157] and the transmission of hepatitis virus to institutionalized children with mental retardation at the Willowbrook State School without proper consent, to hasten the development of a hepatitis vaccine.[158]

One of the most bizarre and disturbing experiments was financed by the CIA in the 1950s and conducted by a renowned psychiatrist and president of the American Psychiatric Association, Ewen Cameron, whose research sought to discover ways in which psychiatry could help prevent destructive human conduct in the wake of the Holocaust. His subjects were people who came to him for treatment of anxiety, depression, and other mental disorders.[159] Without ever seeking his patients' consent or explaining what he was doing, Cameron subjected them to "psychic driving" and "depatterning" experiments designed to alter conventional brain patterns and introduce new ones intended to create new modes of behavior and thought.[160] Cameron compared the effects of his experiments to psychiatric firestorms raging within his subjects and administered dangerous and addictive drugs without their knowledge as well. He freely admitted ignoring patients' pleas to stop and conceded that his research had caused serious harm to at least one of his subjects who ran away, became violent to her family, and required hospitalization. Major journals published his paper, and no objections were raised to the lack of consent.

In December 1993, newspaper accounts of secret research involving the use of radioactive materials on unconsenting subjects prompted U.S. Secretary of Energy Hazel R. O'Leary to announce the declassification of cold war records of human experimentation and call for compensation of the victims. In one experiment conducted during the 1940s and 1950s by researchers from Harvard University and the Massachusetts Institute of Technology, nineteen boys with mental retardation who thought they were taking part in a science club were given radioactive milk as part of a study of the body's ability to digest minerals. The institution never informed the children's parents of the experiment or suggested that the boys would be exposed to radiation. Instead it sent a letter to the boys' parents with this description of the program: "We are considering the selection of a group of our brighter patients, including your son, to receive a special diet." This experiment was kept secret for over forty-five years.[161]

Even today, experimentation is still conducted on people with mental disabilities without their consent. In 1994 the Federal Office of Protection from Research Risks censured researchers from the University of California at Los Angeles for their long-term study of the effects of taking people with schizophrenia off their medication after one year. The authors of the study allegedly did not fully inform their patients of the severity of the possible consequences of withdrawing medication, or of the availability of care if they did not take part in the study. Indeed, some people appear to have been affirmatively misled. Over 70 percent of the participants suffered "at least minor relapses," one committed suicide after the project ended, and another left college and threatened to kill his parents.[162] The institutional review board created to oversee the experiments failed to step in to alter the experiments or protect the patients.[163]

Such abuses highlight the need for strict guidelines and more careful monitoring of human subject research. The legal basis for regulating medical experimentation in the United States derives from the common-law doctrine of informed consent, statutory law and the constitutional rights of privacy and personal autonomy,[164] free speech,[165] and freedom from cruel and unusual punishment.[166]

This authority also stems from principles of international law. In 1947 the Nuremberg Code established the first comprehensive standards for human experimentation after the trial of Nazi doctors for war crimes committed in the name of science. At the heart of the Code is the doctrine of informed consent. It states that human subjects must have the legal capacity to consent, and requires voluntary, fully informed, and under-standing consent as "absolutely essential" in all research. The Code sets minimum standards for human research that have been recognized throughout much of the world.[167] State statutes, federal regulations, court decisions,[168] and international accords have since drawn upon the Code in setting guidelines for experimentation.

The federal government now requires all hospitals that receive federal funding to establish institutional review boards (IRB) to evaluate experi-mental research proposals before subjects are asked to participate. It is the IRB's job to protect the safety of research subjects by ensuring, among other things, that the risks are minimized and proper procedures are in place for obtaining informed consent.[169] However, an IRB did not protect the subjects of the UCLA experiments, and there has been general criticism of the IRB process from experts who argue that it is not working and should be revamped.[170]

The UCLA experiments and the revelations from the Energy Depart-ment have focused attention on the shortcomings in state and federal law. Many states have no laws governing experimentation, and those that do generally provide insufficient protection.[171] Federal regulations afford somewhat greater safeguards but do not cover most state or privately funded research and are subject to the criticisms just described.[172]

At times courts have adopted special safeguards for people with mental disabilities because of the possibility that they may lack the capacity to consent or may be confined in institutions where the voluntariness of their decisions is in question. For example, because of the history of experimentation at the Willowbrook State School, an institution for people with mental retardation, the Willowbrook Consent Judgment prohibited "physically intrusive, chemical or bio-medical research or experimentation . . . at Willowbrook or upon members of the plaintiff class."[173] All other experimentation or behavioral research required the informed consent of the individual or guardian and the approval of a special committee.[174]

The court order in *Wyatt v. Stickney*, another institutional reform case, was less restrictive. It did not ban broad categories of research but required the informed consent of an individual or a proxy and established a human rights committee to review and approve each experiment before consent could be sought.[175]

In one of the most interesting cases involving human experimentation, *Kaimowitz v. Department of Mental Health*,[176] a Michigan court invalidated an involuntary patient's consent to experimental brain surgery that could have destroyed part of the limbic system, as part of a research project to discover whether such a procedure could control aggression. The project had already received funding, but only John Doe, who had been involuntarily confined for seventeen years after killing a nurse while committed to a mental hospital, was considered to be a suitable subject. The court ruled that involuntary patients could never give voluntary consent to experimental psychosurgery where the risks were great and the potential benefits low. Mental institutions, the court reasoned, are inherently coercive environments where inmates are unused to making decisions on their own and depend on the goodwill of the staff for every privilege and their eventual release. In making its decision, the court relied in part on the Nuremberg code, the First Amendment right to generate ideas, and the Constitutional right of privacy and personal autonomy.

An unusually thoughtful decision, the case nevertheless raises the difficult question whether some alternative safeguards could have been devised to protect John Doe while still allowing him the opportunity to make the final decision. Reasonably or not, some people may prefer the risk of bodily harm to the prospect of remaining institutionalized the rest of their lives. If the right of personal autonomy includes the right to consent to experimental treatment, and if adequate safeguards were put in place to ensure that the consent obtained was truly informed and uncoerced, an absolute prohibition against involuntary patients making such a decision would sweep too broadly at the expense of individual liberty.[177]

Where a person is not capable of giving informed consent to take part in experimental research, a legal guardian may do so if the therapeutic benefits to the individual outweigh the risks; if the person had consented to be part of the specific research program while competent; or, "in unusual cases, where there is minimal risk, but the knowledge to be gained is important to the group of patients to which the subject belongs and cannot be obtained any other way."[178]

GUARDIANSHIP

What are incompetency or guardianship proceedings?

Incompetency is a legal determination that an individual lacks the capacity to make rational decisions about his or her person.[179] The law presumes all adults to be competent unless a judge makes a finding of incompetency and appoints a guardian with the legal authority to make decisions on their behalf. The laws surrounding guardianship are in a state of transition. For many years, guardianship was an all or nothing proposition, with surrogate decision makers appointed to make a broad range of decisions about the incompetent's person or assets. Some states are beginning to incorporate the doctrine of the least restrictive alternative into their statutes and to move toward systems of limited, partial, or temporary guardianship to assist individuals in making decisions in those areas where they lack capacity. For example, the preamble to New York's recently revised guardianship law[180] describes its goals in the following way:

The legislature finds that it is desirable for and beneficial to persons with incapacities to make available to them the least restrictive form of intervention which assists them in meeting their needs but, at the same time, permits them to exercise the independence and self-determination of which they are capable. . . . [I]t is the purpose of this act to promote the public welfare by establishing a guardianship system which is appropriate to satisfy either personal or property management needs of an incapacitated person in a manner tailored to the individual needs of that person, which takes in account the personal wishes, preferences and desires of the person, and which affords the person the greatest amount of independence and self-determination and participation in all the decisions affecting such person's life.[181]

In order to minimize intrusions into personal liberty, guardianship statutes speak increasingly of "capacity" rather than "competence." Capacity is a much narrower concept, focusing on specific problems an individual has in a particular area of decision making, such as managing money or making treatment decisions. A person may have the capacity to make a reasoned decision whether to take Thorazine but may require a guardian to ensure that the rent is paid on time. Incompetence, by contrast, is a legal finding that a person lacks capacity in every respect. A finding of incompetence should be a measure of last resort, used only when less restrictive alternatives, such as limited guardianships, are inappropriate.[182]

The standard for appointing a guardian varies from state to state. The basic element is incapacity to make responsible decisions about one's person or property. Some states also require a finding of a physical or mental disability, and a growing number include a least restrictive alternative requirement. Once a court has made a finding of incapacity, its overriding concern is determining what is in the best interests of the individual. Although some courts merge the two inquiries, a court should not consider the individual's best interests unless it has first established incapacity. Most states provide for a right to notice and a hearing. There is no national consensus as to the standard of proof; however, some states have imported the clear and convincing evidence standard from the involuntary commitment cases.

Is there a right to notice and a hearing before a guardian is appointed?

Yes. However, many states do not provide a right to counsel at guardianship hearings. Instead, in these states courts appoint a guardian *ad litem* whose job is to act in the individual's best interests—not to represent the individual's wishes. In effect, a guardian *ad litem* becomes another judge, at times urging the court to make a finding of incapacity, even though the individual might vehemently oppose it. As a result, the individual is deprived of the basic right to representation. If the court doubts the individual's capacity, it should appoint a guardian *ad litem* in addition to counsel for the alleged incapacitated person.

What are the powers of a guardian?

The powers of guardians depend to a large extent on whether they are primarily guardians of the person or of property. As one would expect, conservators or guardians of the property deal solely with the person's finances. By contrast, many states grant guardians of the person broad authority over the ward's daily life, including housing and medical care.[183]

In most states, however, a guardian's authority is not unlimited. Modern guardianship laws limit the guardian's powers to the specific areas where the individual lacks capacity. Thus, a guardianship order for a person who is incapable of managing money would not authorize a guardian to consent to medical treatment or to admit the individual to a nursing home.

In addition, a majority of states require court approval before a guardian can authorize highly intrusive measures such as admission to a psychiatric hospital, electroconvulsive treatment, abortion, or sterilization.[184] In the first case of its kind in the country, for example, the highest court in Massachusetts ruled that a guardian could not impose psychotropic medication on an incompetent ward without the determination of a court applying a substituted judgment test.[185]

How does a guardianship end?

Whenever a person regains the capacity to make decisions independently, the guardian, the ward, or another interested party can petition the court for a hearing to remove the guardian and restore the person's legal capacity. However, many states do not provide full due process protections at restoration hearings, including such essential safeguards as the right to be present at the hearing.

NOTES

1. Rivers v. Katz, 504 N.Y.S. 2d 74, 78, 435 N.E. 2d 337 (1986).
2. Schloendorff v. Society of N.Y. Hosp., 211 N.Y.125, 129, 105 N.E. 92 (1914).
3. *See, e.g.*, Annas, *The Rights of Patients* 89 (1989). *See also* Jarvis v. Levine, 418 N.W. 2d 139, 148 (Minn. 1988); Winters v. Miller, 446 F.2d 65, 68 (2d Cir. 1971).
4. Annas, *supra*, at 87.
5. *Id.*
6. *Id.* at 87–88.
7. *Id.* at 88.
8. *Rivers v. Katz, supra.* A recent study found that almost half of people with schizophrenia and more than 75 percent of people with serious depression could make decisions in a wide range of matters affecting them. When one of the legal tests of competence was used, 75 percent of people with schizophrenia and 90 percent of people with depression were found competent. Grisso and Appelbaum, *Abilities of Patients to Consent to Psychiatric and Medical Treatments*, 19 Law and Human Behavior 149 (1995).
9. *See, e.g.*, Rogers v. Commissioner, Dep't. of Mental Health, 458 N.E.2d 308 (Mass. 1983); Rivers v. Katz, *supra*, 504 N.Y.S.2d at 79 ("the nearly unanimous trend in the courts and among psychiatric and legal commentators is to recognize that there is

no significant relationship between the need for hospitalization of mentally ill patients and their ability to make treatment decisions.") (citations omitted).

10. *See, e.g., Rivers v. Katz, supra; Jarvis v. Levine, supra.*

11. *See* Zinermon v. Burch, 494 U.S. 113 (1990).

12. Roos, *Basic Facts about Mental Retardation,* in *Legal Rights of Mentally Disabled Persons,* 127, 134 (Practicing Law Institute, 1979). Roos estimated that 89 percent of all mentally retarded people are mildly retarded (Revised Stanford Binet I.Q. 67–52), 6 percent are moderately retarded (I.Q. 51–36), and only 5 percent are severely (I.Q. 35–20) or profoundly (I.Q. less than 20) retarded. More recently, however, the American Association on Mental Retardation has changed the definition of mental retardation, moving away from classification by IQ toward a functional and cognitive definition. *See* Luckasson et al., *Mental Retardation: Definition, Classification, and Systems Support* (9th ed.) (American Association on Mental Retardation 1992), discussed at greater length in chapter 1.

13. *See id.*

14. 494 U.S. 113 (1990).

15. At the time the permanent injunction was issued, approximately 3,800 of the original 5,400 member plaintiff class were still alive.

16. N.Y. Mental Hyg. Law § 80.03(a) defines major medical treatment as a "medical, surgical or diagnostic intervention or procedure where a general anesthetic is used or which involves significant risk or any significant invasion of bodily integrity requiring an incision or producing substantial pain, discomfort, debilitation, or having a significant recovery period." The statute, however, does not give SDMCs jurisdiction over issues involving abortion, sterilization, emergency treatment, or the refusal of life-sustaining treatment.

17. Herr & Hopkins, *Health Care Decision Making for Persons with Disabilities,* 271 JAMA 13, 1017, 1018 (1994). For readers interested in pursuing this issue further, this article provides an interesting and detailed look at the SDMC process.

18. *Herr & Hopkins, supra,* at 1021.

19. For example, the Willowbrook Consumer Advisory Board has documented several examples of what it believed to be unreasonably lengthy delays in obtaining authorization for treatment. Interview with Rita L. Martin, Executive Director, Consumer Advisory Board, Aug. 4, 1994.

20. It is improper for physicians, however, or any government officials to condition privileges, such as remaining at a particular hospital, on an individual's agreement to forfeit a constitutional right. *See* Sherbert v. Verner, 374 U.S. 398, 404 (1968); Thomas v. Review Bd. of Indiana Employment Sec., 450 U.S. 707, 716–17 (1981).

21. Rothman & Rothman, *The Willowbrook Wars* (1984).

22. *Id.* at 265–66.

23. Kaimowitz v. Department of Mental Health, No. 73-19434-AW, 1 Mental Disability Law Reporter 147 (Cir. Ct. of Wayne County, Mich, July 10, 1973).

24. *Id.* at 150.

25. *Id.* at 151.

26. Brakel, Parry & Weiner, *The Mentally Disabled and the Law* 328–29 (3d ed. 1985).

27. Washington v. Harper, 494 U.S. 210, 229 (1990).

28. Keith, *Drugs: Not the Only Treatment*, 33 Hospital and Community Psychiatry 793 (1982). ("The deficit state that characterizes the disorder [schizophrenia]—lack of goal-directed behavior, the profound asociality, the absence of affectual drive—is even more significant for prognosis and over-all outcome. These negative symptoms are not now, and do not seem likely to become, amenable to a pharmacologic approach.")

29. One commentator concluded, "A substantial number of patients receive no benefit from antipsychotic medication." Cichon, *The Right to "Just Say No" : A History and Analysis of the Right to Refuse Antipsychotic Drugs*, 53 Louisiana Law Review 283, 295 (1992), citing Baldessarini & Frankenburg, *Clozapine: A Novel Antipsychotic Agent*, 324 New England Journal of Medicine 746 (1991) (20 percent of schizophrenic patients receive no benefit from psychotropic medication); Brown & Herz, *Response to Neuroleptic Drugs as a Device for Classifying Schizophrenia*, 15 Schizophrenia Bulletin 123, 126 (1989) (some 20 percent of schizophrenics are clearly resistant to high doses of psychotropic medication).

30. Kaplan & Sadock, *Comprehensive Textbook of Psychiatry* I 778 (5th ed. 1989). *See also* Honigfeld et al., *Clozapine: Antipsychotic Activity in Treatment-Resistant Schizophrenics*, 1 Advances in Therapy 2, 77, 84 (1984) (Clozapine provides more rapid antipsychotic activity covering the full spectrum of psychotic symptomatology, including thought disturbance and hostility); Marder, Van Putten, *Who Should Receive Clozapine?* 45 Archives of General Psychiatry 865, 867 (1988) (review of controlled clinical trials revealed that "the advantage of clozapine over currently available drugs is most apparent in the more severely ill, treatment-refractory patient" and 30 percent of patients treated with Clozapine improved significantly within six weeks of treatment, as compared with only 4 percent of chlorpromazine/benztropine mesylate recipients).

31. *Marder & Van Putten, supra*, at 867.

32. According to one study, the cumulative incidence of agranulocytosis is 2 percent, a finding which Marder and Van Putten found "sobering," despite the fact that all ten patients in one study recovered after the drug was discontinued. *Id.* at 865.

33. *See* chapter 2 and, as to racial and gender problems in diagnosis, chapter 5.

34. Davis v. Hubbard, 506 F. Supp. 915, 937 (N.D. Ohio 1980) (citations omitted).

35. *See, e.g.*, Ayd, *Pre-Treatment Prediction of Responsiveness to Chlorpromazine: Is it Possible?* 10 International Drug Therapy Newsletter 4 (1975).

36. *See, e.g.* May et al., *Predicting Individual Responses to Drug Treatment in Schizophrenia: A Test Dosage Model*, 162 Journal of Nervous & Mental Disease 177, 178 (1976).

37. Sheehan, *Is There No Place on Earth for Me?* (1983).

38. *Id.* at 282.

39. *See Kaplan & Sadock, supra*; American Psychiatric Association, *Tardive Dyskinesia: A Task Force Report of the American Psychiatric Association* (1992); *Physician's Desk Reference*; Pearlman, *Neuroleptic Malignant Syndrome: A Review of the Literature*, 6 Journal of Clinical Psychopharmacology 257 (1986); Goldstone et al., *Effects of Trifluoperazine, Chlorpromazine and Haloperidal upon Temporal Information Processing by Schizophrenic Patients*, 65 Psychopharmacology 119 (1979); Cichon, *supra*; Plotkin, *Limiting the Therapeutic Orgy: Mental Patients' Right to Refuse Treatment*, 72 Northwestern University Law Review 461 (1977).

40. Wojcik et al., *A Review of 32 Cases of Tardive Dystonia*, 145 American Journal of Psychiatry 513 (1988).

41. *See, e.g.*, Weiden et al., *Clinical Nonrecognition of Neuroleptic-Induced Movement Disorders: A Cautionary Study*, 144 American Journal of Psychiatry 118, 1150 (1987) (symptoms not recognized in 42 percent of cases); Richardson et al., *Tardive Dyskinesia and Associated Factors in Child and Adolescent Psychiatric Patients*, 148 American Journal of Psychiatry 1322 (1988) (parkinsonian symptoms did not abate with use of anti-parkinsonian drugs).

42. Salzberger, *Tardive Dyskinesia: A Risk in Long-Term Neuroleptic Therapy*, 31 Medical Trial Technology Quarterly 203 (1984) Crane, *A Classification of the Neurologic Effects of Neuroleptic Drugs*, in *Tardive Dyskinesia* 188 (Fann ed., 1980).

43. *See* Gardos & Cole, *Overview: Public Health Issues in Tardive Dyskinesia*, 137 American Journal of Psychiatry 776 (1980); Gualtieri et al., *Tardive Dyskinesia Litigation and the Dilemmas of Neuroleptic Treatment*, 14 Journal of Psychiatry & Law 187, 201, 204 (1987). *See also, Early Onset of Tardive Dyskinesia: A Case Report*, 136 American Journal of Psychiatry 1323 (1979) (patient developed tardive dyskinesia after only one month of drug exposure).

44. Jeste, Iager & Wyatt, *The Biology and Experimental Treatment of Tardive Dyskinesia and Other Related Movement Disorders*, in 8 *American Handbook of Psychiatry* 536 (Berger & Brodie eds. 2d ed. 1986).

45. *See* Jeste et al., *supra*, at 560; Chouinard, *supra*, at 1323.

46. Hansen, Casey & Weigel, *TD Prevalence: Research and Clinical Differences*, New *Research Abstracts*, 139th Annual Meeting of the American Psychiatric Association (1986), cited in Brief Amicus Curiae of American Psychological Association, n. 20, submitted in support of respondent in Washington v. Harper, *supra*.

47. Weiden et al., *Clinical Nonrecognition of Neuroleptic-Induced Disorders: A Cautionary Study*, 144 American Journal of Psychiatry 1148, 1150 (1987).

48. Washington v. Harper, *supra*, 494 U.S., at 230.

49. Jeste et al., *supra*, at 539 (25.6 percent of chronic psychiatric inpatients treated with neuroleptics have tardive dyskinesia); Crane, *Neuroleptics and Their Long-Term Effects on the Central Nervous System*, in *Tardive Dyskinesia and Related Involuntary Movement Disorders* (DeVeaugh-Geiss ed., 1982) ("50% of patients in long-term drug therapy show evidence of long-lasting neurotoxicity"). *See also* Schatzberg & Cole, *Manual of Clinical Psychopharmacology* 99 (1986) (over 50 percent prevalence); Barnes et al., *Tardive Dyskinesia: A 3-Year Follow-up Study*, 13 Psychological Medicine 71, 80 (1983); *Davis v. Hubbard, supra* (citing Sooner et al., *Tardive Dyskinesia and Informed Consent*, Mar. 1978 Psychosomatics 173); Rennie v. Klein, 476 F. Supp. 1294, 1306 (expert evidence indicated that 25 to 50 percent of institutionalized patients have tardive dyskinesia).

50. Cichon, *supra*, at 307.

51. Addonizio et al., *Symptoms of Neuroleptic Malignant Syndrome in 82 Consecutive Inpatients*, 143 American Journal of Psychiatry 1587, 1588 (1986); Guze & Baxter, *Neuroleptic Malignant Syndrome*, 313 New England Journal of Medicine 163 (1985). *See generally* Cichon, *supra*, at 307–10.

52. *See* Addonizio, *supra*, at 1588 (annual prevalency rate of 2.4 percent); Pope et al., *Frequency and Presentation of Neuroleptic Malignant Syndrome in a Large Psychiatric*

Hospital, 143 American Journal of Psychiatry 1227, 1231 (annual prevalency rate of 1.4 percent).

53. Cichon, *supra,* at 309–10.

54. Sternberg, *Neuroleptic Malignant Syndrome: The Pendulum Swings,* 143 American Journal of Psychiatry 1273, 1273 (1986); Pope et al., *supra,* at 1232.

55. Pope et al., *supra,* at 1231–32; Addonizio et al., *supra* at 1587; Sternberg, *supra,* at 1274.

56. Addonizio et al., *supra,* at 1589; Sternberg, *supra,* at 1274.

57. Brooks, *Constitutional Right to Refuse Antipsychotic Medications,* 8 Bulletin of the American Academy of Psychiatry & Law 179, 191 (1980).

58. In many states, there is a waiting period of one to several days before a voluntary patient can leave the hospital while the facility evaluates whether to initiate commitment proceedings. *See* chapter 3.

59. For an interesting discussion of this point, *see* Plotkin, *supra,* at 474–79.

60. Rivers v. Katz, *supra,* 504 N.Y.S.2d at 79.

61. *Id.*

62. *See, e.g.,* Marder et al., *A Comparison of Patients Who Refuse and Consent to Neuroleptic Treatment,* 140 American Journal of Psychiatry 470, 472 (1983).

63. *See, e.g.,* Brooks, *supra,* at 191.

64. *See id.*

65. *See, e.g.,* Riggins v. Nevada, 112 S. Ct. 1810 (1992) (criminal defendant has significant liberty interest in refusing psychotropic medication at criminal trial); Washington v. Harper, *supra,* 494 U.S. at 221–22 (prisoner possesses significant due process liberty interest under federal constitution in avoiding unwanted administration of antipsychotic drugs, citing, *inter alia,* Youngberg v. Romeo, 457 U.S. 307, 316 (1982)); *In re* K.K.B., 609 P.2d 747, 752 (Okla. 1980); Rivers v. Katz, *supra,* 504 N.Y.S.2d at 78, 435 N.E.2d 485 (common-law right and state constitutional liberty interest to refuse medical treatment); Rogers v. Comm. of Dept. of Mental Health, 458 N.E.2d 308, 314 (Mass. 1983) (common-law right and state constitutional interest in being free from "nonconsensual invasion of bodily integrity") (citation omitted).

66. *Washington v. Harper, supra; Rivers v. Katz, supra. See* Cruzan v. Director, Mo. Dep't of Health, 497 U.S. 261 (1990).

67. *See, e.g., Rogers v. Comm. of Dept. of Mental Health, supra,* at 321. *See* discussion of chemical restraints in chapter 7.

68. Washington v. Harper, *supra,* 494 U.S. at 238 (Stevens, J. dissenting).

69. For a detailed analysis of a First Amendment theory of the right to refuse medication, see Winick, *The Right to Refuse Mental Health Treatment: A First Amendment Perspective,* 44 University of Miami Law Review 1 (1989).

70. Olmstead v. United States, 277 U.S. 438, 478 (1928) (Brandeis, J., dissenting).

71. In Washington v. Harper, 494 U.S. 210 (1990), the Supreme Court adopted a medical model analysis in ruling that a prisoner's liberty interest in refusing antipsychotic drugs can be overridden by a showing that the prisoner has a serious mental illness, is dangerous to self or to others, and the treatment is in the prisoner's medical interests. The Court also ruled that the prison need only prove its case by the minimal "preponderance of the evidence" standard and that due process required no more than an "independent"

decision maker consisting of physicians on the staff of the institution—not a judicial hearing. Because *Harper* involved a convicted prisoner, who had lesser rights than a civilly committed patient, it can be distinguished from a civil commitment case. Nonetheless, it has had a significant influence on state and federal cases decided since 1990.

72. 458 U.S. 1119 (1982). *Youngberg,* a right to treatment case based on the finding of a due process liberty interest in avoiding unreasonable restraints, held that treatment decisions are presumptively valid as long as they were made by a professional and are not a substantial departure from accepted professional judgment, standards, and practice. Under the *Youngberg* standard, an involuntarily confined person has a right to refuse psychotropic medications only if the doctor has substantially departed from acceptable professional standards in the field. *Youngberg* is discussed in greater detail in chapter 6.

73. In Rennie v. Klein, 653 F.2d 836 (3d Cir. 1981) (en banc), *cert. granted and judgment vacated and remanded in light of* Youngberg v. Romeo, 458 U.S. 1119 (1982), the Supreme Court vacated a Third Circuit Court of Appeals decision in a case challenging the authority of a psychiatric institution to override an involuntarily hospitalized person's objections to psychotropic medication and directed the appeals court to consider its ruling in *Youngberg.*

Since then, a number of state and federal courts have applied *Youngberg* to right to refuse medication claims, ruling that a decision to order medication is presumptively valid if it was made by a professional and is not a substantial departure from professionally accepted judgment, standards, and practices. *See, e.g.,* United States v. Charters, 863 F. 2d 302 (4th Cir. 1988); Dautremont v. Broadlawns Hospital, 827 F.2d 291 (8th Cir. 1987); Johnson v. Silvers, 742 F.2d 823 (4th Cir. 1984); *Project Release v. Prevost, supra,* at 980–81; Stensvad v. Reivitz, 601 F. Supp. 128 (W.D. Wis.1985); R.A.J. v. Miller, 590 F. Supp. 1319 (N.D. Tex. 1984).

74. *See, e.g., Rivers v. Katz, supra; Jarvis v. Levine, supra; Rogers v. Comm. of Dep't. of Mental Health, supra.*

75. *Supra,* at 980–81.

76. These provisions were codified at 14 N.Y.C.R.R. 27.8(b)(d).

77. Project Release, *supra,* at 989 (citations and emphasis omitted).

78. *Youngberg v. Romeo, supra,* at 322–23.

79. New York's regulations allowed the patient to object to the treating psychiatrist, the chief of service, and the director of the hospital. There was no impartial hearing, right to present evidence or confront witnesses, or right to be present at the deliberations. Where a state facility was involved, there was a further right to object to the regional commissioner of mental health.

80. These procedures may include reviews by panels of outside psychiatrists, the facility's medical director, state agency officials or some combination of the above. *See, e.g., Washington v. Harper, supra; Rennie v. Klein, supra; R.A.J. v. Miller, supra.*

81. *See* studies cited in Appelbaum, *Almost a Revolution* (1994) at 144.

82. *See, e.g.,* Rivers v. Katz, *supra,* 495 N.E.2d at 492; Rogers v. Comm. of Dep't. of Mental Health, *supra,* 458 N.E.2d at 314; State *ex rel.* Jones v. Gerhardstein, 416 N.W.2d 883, 896 (Wis. 1987); *In re* K.K.B., 609 P.2d 747, 749 (Okla. 1980); Jarvis v. Levine, *supra,* 418 N.W.2d at 148–49; People v. Medina, 705 P.2d 961, 973 (Colo. 1985); *In re* Milton, 505 N.E.2d 255, 257–58 (Ohio 1987); Goedecke v. State, 603 P.2d 123, 125 (Colo. 1979).

83. *See, e.g., Rivers v. Katz, supra.*

84. *Rogers v. Comm. of Department of Mental Health, supra.*

85. *See, e.g., Jarvis v. Levine, supra; Rivers v. Katz, supra. But see* A.E. v. Mitchell, No. C.78-466 (D. Utah 1980), *aff'd,* 724 F.2d 864, 867 (10th Cir. 1983) (rejecting request for order barring forcible administration of drugs to involuntary patients without a declaration of incompetency on grounds that Utah's commitment law specifically requires finding of incompetency to consent to treatment). This case, however, turned on the unique provisions of Utah's commitment statute. Most state statutes do not contain such a provision.

86. *See, e.g.,* Rogers v. Comm. of Department of Mental Health, *supra.*

87. Matter of Guardianship of Richard Roe III, 421 N.E.2d (1981).

88. *See, e.g., Rivers v. Katz, supra.*

89. 504 N.Y.S. 2d 74 (Ct. App. 1986).

90. Appelbaum, *The Right to Refuse Treatment with Antipsychotic Medications: Retrospect and Prospect,* 147 American Journal of Psychiatry 413, 418 (1988).

91. *See, e.g., Davis v. Hubbard, supra.*

92. *See, e.g.,* Nelson v. Heyne, 355 F. Supp. 451, 455 (N.D. Ind. 1972), *aff'd* 491 F.2d 352 (7th Cir.), *cert. denied,* 417 U.S. 976 (1974); Mackey v. Procunier, 477 F.2d 877 (9th Cir. 1973); Pena v. New York State Div. for Youth, 419 F. Supp. 203, 207 (S.D.N.Y. 1976); Bee v. Greaves, 744 F.2d 1387, 1390 (10th Cir. 1984) (jail inmate forcibly injected with medication "for the express purpose of intimidating him so he wouldn't refuse the oral medication anymore"), *cert. denied,* 469 U.S. 1214 (1985).

93. *See, e.g.,* the Willowbrook consent decree, NYSARC v. Carey, 393 F. Supp. 715 (E.D.N.Y. 1975), appendix A, (Q) (4) (to remedy past abusive medication practices at an institution for people with mental retardation, the decree mandated: "Medication shall not be used as punishment, *for the convenience of staff,* as a substitute for program, or in quantities that interfere with the resident's program.") (emphasis added).

94. Bell v. Wayne County Hospital, 384 F. Supp. 1085 (E.D. Mich 1974) (Michigan prehearing detention and temporary commitment statutes violated constitutional right of privacy to the extent they permitted involuntary treatment of a physically intrusive nature).

95. *See* Lessard v. Schmidt, *supra,* 349 F. Supp. at 1092; Doremus v. Farrell, 407 F. Supp. 509, 515 (D. Neb. 1975); Suzuki v. Quisenberry, 411 F. Supp. 1113, 1129 (D. Haw. 1976); and Lynch v. Baxley, 386 F. Supp. 378 (M.D. Ala. 1974). The broader question of the propriety of prehearing medication was also briefed and argued in *Project Release v. Prevost, supra,* but the Court of Appeals did not rule on the issue.

96. *Lessard v. Schmidt, supra,* at 1092, n. 19, citing Hearings before the Senate Subcommittee on Constitutional Rights, 91st Congress, 1st and 2nd Session, 426 (1970).

97. Riggins v. Nevada, 112 S. Ct. 1810 (1992). In an interesting analysis of the opinion, Michael Perlin suggests that the Court's use of a "less intrusive alternatives" analysis might open the door to a "recalibration of the *Youngberg* doctrines" and stimulate the filing of innovative right to refuse treatment lawsuits in the federal courts. Perlin, *Mental Disability Law, supra,* at § 5.65A, pp. 90–91.

98. Appelbaum & Gutheil, *Drug Refusal: A Study of Psychiatric Inpatients,* 137 American Journal of Psychiatry 340, 344 (1980). *See also* Brooks, *supra,* at 213 (no adverse effects resulting from right-to-refuse-drugs decision in *Rennie v. Klein, supra*); Davis v. Hubbard, *supra,* 506 F. Supp. at 937, n. 31 (experts testified that, in institutions where

the right to refuse drugs had been recognized, there were no adverse effects on the operation of the institution or on its treatment goals); Rogers v. Okin, 478 F. Supp. 1342, 1370 (D. Mass. 1978). (Only 12 of 1,000 involuntary patients refused drugs for extended periods during the two years the temporary restraining order was in effect. The court found that "the great majority of patients have not declined their psychotropic medication during the pendency of the T.R.O. [establishing the right of involuntary patients to refuse drugs]. Most of those who did changed their minds within a few days.")

99. Appelbaum, *Legal Issues Relevant to Homelessness and the Severely Mentally Ill Population,* 20 Bulletin American Academy Psychiatry & Law 455 (1992) citing Hoge, Appelbaum, Lawlor, et al., *A Prospective, Multicenter Study of Patients' Refusal of Antipsychotic Medication,* 47 Archives of General Psychiatry 949 (1990).

100. Appelbaum, *supra,* at 149.

101. *Id.* at 141.

102. *Id.,* citing Hoge et al., *A Prospective, Multicenter Study of Patients' Refusal of Antipsychotic Medication, supra.*

103. *See, e.g.,* Ciccone, Tokoli, Clements et al., *Right to Refuse Treatment: Impact of Rivers v. Katz,* 18 Bulletin of the American Academy Psychiatry & Law 203 (1990); Cournos, McKinnon & Stanley, *Outcome of Involuntary Medication in a State Hospital System,* 148 American Journal of Psychiatry 489 (1991); Deland & Borenstein, *Medicine Court, II: Rivers in Practice,* 147 American Journal of Psychiatry 38 (1990); Hoge, Gutheil & Kaplan, *The Right to Refuse Treatment under Rogers v. Commissioner: Preliminary Empirical Findings and Comparisons,* 15 Bulletin American Academy Psychiatry & Law 163 (1987); Farnsworth, *The Impact of Judicial Review of Patients' Refusal to Accept Antipsychotic Medications at the Minnesota Security Hospital,* 19 Bulletin American Academy Psychiatry & Law 33 (1991).

104. 42 C.F.R. § 483.20(a) (2).

105. 42 C.F.R. § 483.20(a) (6).

106. 42 C.F.R. § 483.450 (e) (1).

107. 42 C.F.R. §§ 483.450 (e) (2), (3), (4).

108. In California, for example, the statute authorizing durable powers of attorney requires the decisions of health care proxies to be consistent with the instructions set forth in the durable power of attorney. Cal. Civil Code § 2330 et seq.

109. *See* Appelbaum, *Advance Directives for Psychiatric Treatment,* 42 Hospital and Community Psychiatry 983 (1991). In one decision of questionable reasoning, the Court of Appeals of the District of Columbia, however, has interpreted a durable power of attorney statute not to apply to decisions concerning psychiatric care and medication. Khiem v. United States, 612 A. 2d 160 (1992). This case arose, however, in the context of a criminal commitment, where special circumstances may apply.

110. Massachusetts's law includes, within the concept of "health care," services or procedures to treat a "physical or mental condition of a patient." Massachusetts General Law ch. 201D § 1. Similarly, New York's law covers treatment of "an individual's physical or mental condition." New York Public Health Law § 2980(4).

111. California, however, does not allow the proxy to authorize particularly controversial procedures, including psychosurgery, electroconvulsive therapy, and sterilization. Cal. Civil Code § 2345(b), (c) and (d).

112. *In re* Rosa M., No. 96965/89 (New York Supreme Court 1991).

113. *E.g.*, California. Cal. Welf. & Inst. Code 2345(a).

114. For discussions of the Ulysses contract, see Sales, *The Health Care Proxy for Mental Illness: Can It Work and Should We Want It To?* 21 Bulletin of the American Academy of Psychiatry and Law 161, 172–74 (1993); R. Dresser, *Bound to Treatment: The Ulysses Contract*, 14 Hastings Center Report 6 (1984); M. Winston and S. Winston, *Can a Subject Consent to a "Ulysses Contract"?* 12 Hastings Center Report 8 (1982).

115. *See Matter of Rosa M., supra.*

116. Pub. L. No. 101-508 §§ 4206 and 4751, 42 U.S.C. § 1395cc(a)(1)(Q) (Medicare) and 1396a(a)(57) (Medicaid).

117. Sociologist Elliot Valenstein has documented the unwarranted, unscientific, and harmful use of many such treatments, including insulin coma therapy, all popular in their time, that did far more harm than good. Valenstein, *Great and Desperate Cures: The Rise and Decline of Psychosurgery and Other Radical Treatments for Mental Illness* (1986).

118. Plotkin, *supra*, at 466. In this well-written and researched article, Plotkin provides an excellent summary of a number of psychiatric treatment procedures and an insightful analysis of the right to refuse treatment.

119. *Id.*

120. Culliton, *Psychosurgery: National Commission Issues Surprisingly Favorable Report*, 194 Science 299 (1976), in Reisner & Slobogin, *Law and the Mental Health System*, at 873–74.

121. *Id.*

122. Plotkin, *supra*, at 470.

123. *Id.* at 469, citing Moser, *A 10-Year Follow-Up of Lobotomy Patients*, 20 Hospital and Community Psychiatry 381 (1969).

124. Lojuk v. Quandt, 706 F.2d 1456, 1465 (7th Cir. 1983) (citation omitted).

125. Plotkin, *supra*, at 471–72.

126. Ten years later, Cerletti's actions would have violated the Nuremberg code, promulgated in 1948, which set forth "basic principles" that "must be observed in order to satisfy moral, ethical and legal concepts" relating to experimentation on human subjects. The ninth principle provides that the subject of the experiment "should be at liberty to bring the experiment to an end if he has reached the physical or mental state where continuation of the experiment seems to him to be impossible." *See* Judgment of the court in United States v. Karl Brandt, Trial of War Criminals before the Nuremburg Military Tribunals, vols. 1 and 2, "The Medical Case," (Washington D.C., U.S. Government Printing Office 1948), cited in Kaimowitz, *supra*, 1 Mental Disability Law Reporter 150. The Nuremburg Code is discussed at greater length later in this section.

127. *Id.* at 472, quoting Cerletti, *Electroshock Therapy*, in *The Great Physiodynamic Therapies in Psychiatry: A Historical Reappraisal*, 91–92 (Sackler, Sackler, Marti-Ibaner eds. 1956).

128. Plotkin, *supra* at 472.

129. *Electroconvulsive Therapy Consensus Development Conference Statement*, vol. 5, no. 11, 1985 (U.S. Dept. of Health and Human Services, Public Health Service, National Institutes of Health, Office of Medical Applications of Research), reprinted in Reisner & Slobogin, *supra*, at 871.

130. American Psychiatric Association, *The Practice of Electroconvulsive Therapy: Recommendations for Treatment, Training and Privileging* (1990).

131. Lojuk v. Quandt, 706 F.2d 1456, 1465 (7th Cir. 1983); Plotkin, *supra,* at 473. *See also* Note, *Regulation of Electroconvulsive Therapy,* 75 Michigan Law Review 363 (1976). One court read the literature as raising the possibility of permanent brain damage and a slowing of brain waves, Lojuk v. Quandt, 706 F.2d 1456, 1466 (7th Cir. 1983), citing Aden v. Younger, 57 Cal. App. 3d 662, 129 Cal. Rptr. at 541. This has not been proven.

132. *See e.g.,* Price v. Sheppard, 239 N.W.2d 905 (Minn. 1976) (although rejecting parents' claim that hospital's subjecting their minor child to ECT without their consent violated the Eighth Amendment prohibition against cruel and unusual treatment, court prohibited further administration of ECT without parental consent); Gundy v. Pauley, No. 80-DA-1737-MR, 5 Mental Disability Law Reporter 321 (Ky. Ct. App. Aug. 21, 1981) (prohibiting involuntary administration of ECT absent an emergency or the patient's incompetence). *But see Lojuk v. Quandt, supra,* at 1467–68 (applying *Youngberg v. Romeo* to claim that involuntary administration of ECT violated due process rights of incompetent, voluntary patient, court held that standard is whether decision to administer ECT "departed from accepted professional practice"). In a significant decision extending the doctrine of informed consent to psychiatric living wills, a lower court in New York refused to impose ECT on a woman who had consented to three courses of ECT but signed a statement withdrawing her consent to a fourth. There was no dispute that she was competent at the time of signing and that she later became incompetent. Matter of Rosa M., 595 N.Y.S.2d 544 (N.Y. Sup. Ct. 1991). This case is discussed in greater detail in the section on advance directives earlier in this chapter.

133. Wyatt v. King, 793 F. Supp. 1058 (M.D. Ala. 1992). This is the same case previously known as *Wyatt v. Stickney.*

134. The standards are contained in appendix § 1 9(3).

135. Knecht v. Gillman, 488 F.2d 1136 (8th Cir. 1973).

136. *Id.*

137. *See, e.g.,* New York State Assn. for Retarded Children v. Carey, 393 F. Supp. 715 (E.D.N.Y. 1975) (the *Willowbrook* case) at appendix A (P). *See also* appendix A of this book for behavior modification standards in Wyatt v. Stickney. For a discussion of the legal issues, which remain as compelling today as twenty years ago, see Paul Friedman, *Legal Regulation of Applied Behavior Analysis in Mental Institutions and Prisons,* 17 Arizona Law Review 39 (1974).

138. Interview with Steven Schwartz, Director, Center for Public Representation, Northampton, Massachusetts, an attorney who has worked for many years on behalf of children confined at BRI.

139. The Institute for Public Representation and the National Association of Protection and Advocacy Services.

140. 42 C.F.R. 483.40(d)(2), (3), (4).

141. For a brief discussion of the eugenics movement, see chapter 2.

142. Buck v. Bell, 274 U.S. 200, 207 (1927).

143. Gould, "Carrie Buck's Daughter" in *The Flamingo's Smile* 309 (1985), quoting a "model sterilization" law proposed in 1922 by Harry Laughlin, superintendent of the Eugenics Record Office.

144. 247 U.S. 200 (1927).

145. Gould, *supra*, at 314. Gould notes that the records of the trial "reek with the contempt of the well-off and well-bred for poor people of 'loose morals.' Who really cared whether [Carrie Buck's daughter] was a baby of normal intelligence? She was the illegitimate child of an illegitimate woman. Two generations of bastards are enough. Harry Laughlin began his 'family history' of the Bucks by writing: 'These people belong to the shiftless, ignorant and worthless class of anti-social whites of the South.'" *Id.*

146. Modern research has found that the majority of mental disabilities are by no means hereditary. As Stephen Jay Gould has written: "Some forms of mental deficiency are passed by inheritance in family lines, but most are not—a scarcely surprising conclusion when we consider the thousand shocks that beset us all during our lives, from abnormalities in embryonic growth to traumas of birth, malnourishment, rejection, and poverty." Gould, *supra*, at 386. Researchers have reached similar conclusions about the inheritance of a propensity toward criminality.

147. *See, e.g.*, Skinner v. Oklahoma, 316 U.S. 535 (1942) (calling the right to procreate "one of the basic civil rights of man," the Court struck down a statute authorizing sterilization of people convicted two or more times of "felonies involving moral turpitude"); Griswold v. Connecticut, 381 U.S. 479 (1965) (right of privacy forbids state from criminalizing use of contraceptives by married people or punishing persons who provide them with contraceptives or information about their use).

148. 386 F. Supp. 1382 (M.D. Ala. 1972), discussed in chapters 6 and 7.

149. Some of these laws survive, though, and remain subject to constitutional challenge. As recently as 1991, Arkansas had a law permitting involuntary sterilization by medical decision and without provision for either due process or judicial oversight. The law was determined to be unconstitutional. McKinney v. McKinney, 805 W.S. 2d 66 (Ark. 1991).

150. For an analysis of the complex relationship between mental disability rights and reproductive choice, see Stefan, *Whose Egg Is It Anyway: Reproductive Rights of Incarcerated, Institutionalized and Incompetent Women*, 13 Nova Law Review 405 (1989).

151. *In re* C.D.M., 627 607 (Alaska 1981); Conservatorship of Valerie N., 40 Cal. 3d 143, 707 P.2d 760, 219 Cal. Rptr. 387 (1985) (*en banc*); *In re* A.W., 637 P. 2d 366 (Colo. 1981) (*en banc*); *In re* P.S., 452 N.E. 2d 969 (Ind. 1983); *In re* Matejski, 419 N.W. 2d 576 (Iowa 1988); *In re* Moe, 385 Mass. 555, 432 N.E. 2d 712 (1982); *In re* Grady, 426 A. 2d 467 (N.J. 1981); *In re* Guardianship of Ebehardy, 102 Wis. 2d 539, 307 N.W. 2d 881 (1981).

152. Some courts apply a "substituted judgment" rather than a "best interests" test in making surrogate decisions for incapacitated persons. *E.g.*, *In re* Moe, 385 Mass. 555, 432 N.E.2d 712 (1982). Unlike the best interests analysis, in which a court frankly decides what it thinks is best for the incompetent individual, the substituted judgment test requires a court to determine what the woman herself would decide if she had capacity.

153. *In re* Guardianship of Hayes, 608 P.2d 635 (Wash. 1980). These guidelines have served as a model for other court decisions. *See, e.g.*, *In re* Grady, 426 A.2d 467 (N.J. 1981). *See also* Matter of Sallmaier, 378 N.Y.S.2d 989 (Sup. Ct. N.Y. Co. 1976) (application of parent of severely retarded woman granted because of, *inter alia*, substantial likelihood of psychotic reaction from pregnancy).

154. Stefan, *supra*.

155. *See* Annas, *supra*, at 141–59, for a crisp and informative discussion of human experimentation.

156. *See* Jones, *Bad Blood: the Tuskegree Syphilis Experiments—a Tragedy of Race and Medicine* (1981); Brandt, *Racism, Research and the Tuskegee Syphilis Study*, 8 Hastings Center Report 21 (Dec. 1978).

157. Katz, *Experimentation with Human Beings* 10–65 (1972).

158. Rothman & Rothman, *The Willowbrook Wars, supra.*

159. Rubenstein, *Psychiatric Experimentation: The Lessons of History*, 5 Journal of the California Alliance for the Mentally Ill at 22 (1994). For an account of the experiments and the litigation they spawned, told from the perspective of one of the victims' sons, himself a psychiatrist, see Weinstein's *Psychiatry and the CIA: Victims of Mind Control* (1990).

160. *Id.*

161. "Paper says experiment exposed 19 retarded youths to radiation," N.Y. Times, Dec. 27, 1993 at A. 19.

162. "Medical Ethics in the Dock," N.Y. Times, Mar. 1, 1994.

163. *Id.* For a legal and ethical analysis of the UCLA experiments, see Katz, *Human Rights and Human Experimentation*, 38 St. Louis University Law Review 7 (1993).

164. *See, e.g.*, Cruzan v. Director, Missouri Dep't of Health, 497 U.S. 261 (1990).

165. *Id.*

166. *See, e.g.*, Mackey v. Procunier, 477 F.2d 877 (9th Cir. 1973).

167. Note, however, that the Supreme Court has held the Nuremberg Code inapplicable to the United States military in a case against the army by a former serviceman who had been an involuntary subject of an experiment involving LSD. *See* United States v. Stanley, 483 U.S. 669 (1987).

168. *See, e.g., Kaimowitz v. Department of Mental Health, supra.*

169. 45 C.F.R. § 46.111.

170. *See* Katz, *supra*; Testimony of Cliff Zucker, Executive Director, Disability Advocates, Inc., before Advisory Committee on Human Radiation Experiments, July 13, 1994.

171. *Id.*

172. *Id. See* 45 C.F.R. § 46.101 (federal research regulations cover federally supported research and research "otherwise subject to regulation by any federal department or agency," such as new drugs).

173. New York State Association for Retarded Children, *supra*, at appendix A (P) (4).

174. New York State Association for Retarded Children, *supra*, at appendix A (P) (3).

175. Wyatt v. Stickney, 344 F. Supp. 387, 401–2 (M.D. Ala. 1972).

176. *Kaimowitz v. Department of Mental Health, supra.*

177. Although it was one of the first cases to grapple with the complex and difficult issues surrounding informed consent, the *Kaimowitz* case has aroused more interest among scholars than jurists and has had relatively little impact on the development of the law.

178. Annas, *supra*, at 153.

179. Brakel et al., *supra*, at 372. Much of the material for this section is drawn from their excellent discussion of incompetency and guardianship.

180. N.Y. Mental Hyg. Law, Article 81 (McKinney 1993).

181. *Id.* at § 81.01.

182. The American Bar Association Commission on Mental and Physical Disability Law has published two interesting publications on guardianship reform: *Guardianship: An Agenda for Reform* and *Steps to Enhance Guardianship Monitoring.*

183. Brakel et al., *supra,* at 384.

184. *Id.*

185. *In re* Guardianship of Roe, 421 N.E.2d 40 (Mass. 1981).

V

The Right to Be Free
from Discrimination

Of all the wrongs committed against people with mental disabilities, the most common and pervasive is discrimination. Many employers refuse to hire or retain employees who have had psychiatric treatment rather than judge them by ability. Others assign people with mental retardation to menial positions without opportunities for promotion. Landlords frequently refuse to rent to prospective tenants who have been hospitalized for psychiatric treatment. The federal government used to deny security clearances to job applicants who were treated for depression. Indeed, people with mental disabilities are frequently denied the opportunity to manage their own money or to make basic decisions about health care, sexuality, and other critical aspects of their lives, even when they are clearly capable of doing so. Some of these discriminatory practices have been authorized by law through statutes that unreasonably restrict the right to raise children, drive a car, and even vote, solely on the basis of mental disability. The prejudice is so deeply rooted that such forms of discrimination have long been accepted without question and as a matter of "common sense"[1]—in stark contrast with the values of equality otherwise so central to American life and law.

Indeed, the mere disclosure that a person has been hospitalized or treated for a psychiatric disorder may arouse shock or disapproval. Here's how one man learned the consequences of disclosure even in a supposedly safe environment.

While strolling down a corridor on pass during my first hospitalization, I met a surgeon who was a colleague of my father's and whom I had known since childhood. He asked me what brought me to the hospital. When I told him I was a patient on the psychiatric unit, a look of horror gripped his face momentarily. The expression was too quickly replaced by forced humor. "That's a good one, Danny," he laughed loudly and briskly walked on. I knew from that time on I was branded and should not lightly share information about my hospitalization.[2]

Such attitudes may be difficult to change, but a society governed by principles of fairness and equality should afford them no legal recognition. As long as an applicant meets the qualifications for employment, housing, a service, or a benefit, the presence of a mental disability should play no role in any decision making. Thus, the mere fact that a prospective tenant had a prior psychiatric hospitalization is not relevant to her ability to pay rent on time or to obey the rules of the lease. Only actual conduct that directly reflects on the person's ability to be a satisfactory tenant can reasonably be considered in predicting whether she will adhere to these obligations. Similarly, if an applicant is otherwise qualified in every respect to perform the duties of a particular job, an employer cannot justifiably refuse to hire him simply because he has Down's syndrome or a psychiatric diagnosis.

One of the most important recent developments in mental disability law has been the enactment of federal legislation prohibiting discrimination in housing, employment, public accommodations, and benefits and programs run by federal, state, and local government. These laws are as important to people with mental disabilities as the Civil Rights Act of 1964 and the Fair Housing Act of 1968 have been to people of color.

The first of these laws, Title V of the Rehabilitation Act,[3] was enacted two decades ago and laid the groundwork for what was to follow. It prohibits discrimination against people with disabilities by the federal government, recipients of federal financial assistance, and federal contractors. Equally important are the regulations that federal agencies issued to implement the Rehabilitation Act, which introduced the concept of "reasonable accommodation" for people with disabilities. Recognizing that there may be differences between people who have disabilities and those who do not, the doctrine of reasonable accommodation requires that social institutions make practical adjustments to their rules, policies, and physical facilities so that people with disabilities can gain access or participate equally with other citizens.

Although enforcement of the Rehabilitation Act and its implementing regulations was lackluster and complicated by many legal questions about its scope, meaning, and enforceability, it paved the way for the 1988 Amendments to the Fair Housing Act[4] and the Americans with Disabilities Act[5] of 1990 (ADA), which together have opened the door to equal participation in American life for people with mental disabilities.

THE AMERICANS WITH DISABILITIES ACT

The Americans with Disabilities Act is the most comprehensive civil rights law in a generation and affects every aspect of civic life. The ADA outlaws discrimination in public and private employment, public services, transportation, communication technology, and in what are known as public accommodations, which consist mainly of private businesses open to the public.

The sweep of the ADA is broad and its meaning subject to varying interpretations. Because the law was enacted so recently, there are still unanswered questions about its scope and application that courts are just beginning to address. This chapter discusses the key provisions of the statute and significant judicial decisions. Where the meaning of the law is unclear, it suggests interpretations we believe are consistent with the language, history, and purposes of the ADA. Although a discussion of the physical access, transportation, and communication provisions of the law is beyond the scope of this book, there are resources regarding the rights of people with physical disabilities included in appendix B.

What are the key goals of the ADA?

The two primary goals of the ADA are to "provide a clear and comprehensive national mandate for the elimination of discrimination against individuals with disabilities"[6]. . . [and] for the integration of persons with disabilities into the economic and social mainstream of American life."[7] The second requires a few words of explanation. In describing the findings and purposes underlying the ADA, Congress wrote that "historically, society has tended to isolate and segregate people with disabilities and, despite some improvements, such forms of discrimination against individuals with disabilities continue to be a serious and pervasive social problem."[8] Segregation can take the form of using separate schools for children with disabilities who are capable of being mainstreamed in regular schools; relying on institutions to house people with mental disabilities who can live in the community; and operating social programs categorized by disability. As the Department of Justice, which is charged with the enforcement of much of the Act, states in the introduction to its ADA regulations, "Integration is fundamental to the purposes of the Americans with Disabilities Act. Provision of segregated accommodations and services relegates people with disabilities to second-class status."[9]

Who has rights under the ADA?

The simple answer is any person with a disability. But what did Congress mean by a person with a disability? In fact, Congress meant three different groups of people. The first consists of people with a current disability, which Congress defined as a physical or mental impairment that significantly limits one or more major life activities.[10] The impairment can be a disease, such as cancer, a condition, such as mental retardation, or a mental disorder, such as depression or schizophrenia. The impairment must limit a person's ability to engage in a major life activity like walking, working, communication, or social interaction.

The second group consists of people who had a disability in the past, but no longer have one. For example, a person who has a diagnosis of manic depression but whose condition no longer limits major life activities still has rights under the ADA.

The third group is the largest: people who have no disability but are nonetheless regarded by others as having one. For example, a person with mental retardation who can engage in the usual activities of life but is discriminated against because of mental retardation is protected under the ADA because others regard her as having a disability. Similarly, a person who is denied a security clearance because of participation in psychotherapy for family problems should have rights under the ADA, despite having no impairment or limitations in major life activities, because the agency regards him as having a disability.

Controversy about the ADA's coverage of people with psychiatric disabilities led Congress to deny protection to people with certain mental disorders associated with antisocial behavior. These conditions include kleptomania, pyromania, compulsive gambling, sexual behavior disorders (including gender identity disorders not resulting from physical impairment), and psychoactive substance resulting from the current use of illegal drugs.[11] In addition, current users of illegal drugs are not covered by the law. This exclusion, however, does not apply to individuals who participate in or have completed a supervised drug rehabilitation program and are no longer engaged in the illegal use of drugs.[12]

What aspects of life does the ADA cover?
Virtually any aspect of civic life one can think of. The ADA is organized in four key parts or "titles":

Title I: Private employment.
Title II: Services by public entities—in other words, government and government-sponsored or -operated agencies, including public transportation. Title II also covers employment in the public sector.
Title III: Public accommodations, which typically means private businesses open to the public, including privately owned transportation systems such as intercity bus lines.
Title IV: Telecommunications.

The ADA does not cover the activities of the federal government, which fall within the jurisdiction of the Rehabilitation Act. Section 501 of that law prohibits discrimination on the basis of disability in federal employment and Section 504 outlaws discrimination in other activities conducted by the federal government.

Employment

Work is the central activity in the lives of most adults, a basis for economic independence and, for many, a critical element of self-worth. So it is not surprising that employment has been a focal point for the civil rights struggles of the last quarter-century. Tens of thousands of cases of employment discrimination have been filed under the Civil Rights Act of 1964, and controversies over burdens of proof and other seemingly arcane issues in employment discrimination law have led to political struggles at the highest levels of government.

Until the enactment of the ADA, people with mental disabilities had not benefited from this explosion of concern about discrimination in the workplace. To be sure, some state antidiscrimination laws protected people with mental disabilities. In addition, Sections 503 and 504 of the Rehabilitation Act of 1973 prohibit disability-based employment discrimination by federal contractors and recipients of federal financial assistance.[13] But the vast majority of people with mental disabilities had no protection from discrimination.

The costs of this omission appear to have been quite high.[14] Researchers have estimated that almost 70 percent of Americans of working age who have a severe mental disorder are not employed.[15] Because no comprehensive studies have been conducted, no one knows how much of this unemployment is attributable to discrimination on the basis of psychiatric disability or a history of psychiatric treatment, but existing research as well as accounts of personal experiences suggest that discrimination is pervasive. People with psychiatric disabilities report that disclosure of treatment for a mental health condition often results in rejection from a job.[16] In addition, studies of employer attitudes have shown that bias against people with psychiatric disabilities is greater than against any other disability group, especially among employers who have not had experience with people with mental disabilities.[17]

The research also demonstrates that despite their capacity to engage in competitive work, many people with mental retardation are relegated to jobs in sheltered workshops or other noncompetitive positions. The data from one comprehensive study in Oklahoma, for example, show that the adaptive skills of people with mental retardation in competitive employment differed little from those engaged in supported employment,[18] suggesting that people capable of competitive employment are afforded the opportunity to participate.

There is evidence that exposure to people with mental disabilities in the workplace results in decreased employer prejudice. Employers who have hired people with psychiatric disabilities or people with mental retardation subsequently show less bias toward them than employers who have not.[19] The ADA, which prohibits discrimination by employers with fifteen or more employees, provides a vehicle to increase that exposure. People who are qualified for jobs are protected from discrimination on account of their current or past disability, or an employer's erroneous notion that they have a disability. This focus on an individual's qualifications is central to all civil rights law and is understandably the centerpiece of the ADA. As the Supreme Court emphasized in interpreting analogous provisions of the Rehabilitation Act, an "individualized inquiry" into a person's qualifications is essential if it is to "achieve its goal of protecting handicapped individuals from deprivations based on prejudice, stereotypes, or unfounded fears."[20]

In determining a person's qualifications, the ADA also requires employers to make a "reasonable accommodation" for a person's disability if that accommodation will enable the person to engage in productive work.[21] These concepts are described more fully in the pages that follow.

What employment rights do people with disabilities have?
Employers may not discriminate against a qualified person with a disability in any aspect of employment. These include:

- Hiring and firing
- Classifying employees, such as placement into temporary or permanent positions
- Promotion
- Compensation
- Terms and conditions of employment (like work hours, vacation, fringe benefits)
- Participation in health, life, or disability insurance plan

The right to be free of such discriminatory employment practices applies regardless of the manner of hiring and includes employees hired through special affirmative action programs for people with disabilities.[22]

Who is a qualified individual with a disability?
Like other civil rights laws, the ADA is designed to promote equality, not to enable unqualified people to gain preference in employment over qualified people. Therefore, the ADA requires candidates to possess the skills, experience, and other attributes that are essential to the performance of the job. Note, however, that the qualifications must be essential, not simply desirable, for the job. It is generally up to the employer to determine what those essential functions are, such as the ability to lift a certain weight, concentrate for extended periods of time, or engage in extensive social interaction. These determinations, however, can be challenged.

At the same time, Congress recognized that employers may be required to make certain adjustments in the work place, in the form of physical changes, scheduling, and other policies, in order to enable people with disabilities to engage in competitive work. Accordingly, Congress defined a qualified person with a disability as one who is able to perform the essential functions of the job *with or without reasonable accommodation.*

In other words, a person is considered qualified if a reasonable accommodation would enable the him or her to do the job.[23]

What is a reasonable accommodation?

A reasonable accommodation is an alteration in the work environment that will enable the employee to perform the essential functions of the job. The accommodation must be practicable and reasonable in terms of cost to the employer and ease of accomplishment; in the words of the ADA, it cannot be an "undue hardship" to the employer. The accommodation can be physical, such as a ramp up a few steps or an amplification device on a telephone. For people with mental disabilities, the core of reasonable accommodation is an adjustment in the work environment that will enable the person to perform at a productive level. These can include such changes as:

- Flexible scheduling
- Reassignment to a different job
- Changes in the physical location of the work
- Alterations in supervision
- Unpaid leave for therapy
- Sensitizing coworkers

There are many other kinds of accommodations that can be developed jointly by the employer and the employee and tailored to fit individual circumstances.[24] Indeed, the ADA *requires* that reasonable accommodations be developed together in an "informal, interactive process."[25] The employer can neither impose an accommodation ("Go to therapy or be fired") or demand that the employee devise one. The process of developing an accommodation is crucial, involving, among other things, the identification of relevant facts, consultation and negotiation, an assessment of costs, and the establishment of a plan, preferably in writing.[26]

How can a person with a mental disability be sure that the fact of the disability is not used to discriminate?

Discrimination on the basis of disability can be insidious and difficult to detect. In an effort to make it harder for employers to discriminate, Congress limited their opportunity to delve into questions about a person's disability. It accomplished this by changing the hiring procedures for every employer covered by the ADA.

In the initial phase of the hiring process, employers may not ask applicants whether they have a disability or inquire about the nature or extent of an apparent disability.[27] This means, for example, that an employer may not inquire, either on an application form or during an interview, whether an applicant has had a psychiatric condition, undergone therapy, or been hospitalized. If the disability is obvious or the prospective employee volunteers information about a disability, the employer cannot ask about its nature or extent. The employer *can* ask questions about a person's ability to perform the essential functions of the job.

The employer can then make a conditional offer of employment. At that point, the applicant can be required to undergo a medical examination. The employer may only ask questions about disability or the individual's medical conditions if the questions are asked of all people conditionally offered employment and the results are kept confidential.[28] Once an employee is on the job, an employer can require periodic medical examinations, but only if the inquiry is job-related and consistent with business necessity.[29]

How does keeping one's condition private square with the duty of reasonable accommodation?

The two are necessarily inconsistent and present one of the most difficult practical problems for an employee with a disability. A prospective employee can insist on the right to be protected from inquiry about medical condition or disability in the initial stage of the hiring process and, to a lesser extent, while on the job. But whenever someone seeks a reasonable accommodation to meet qualification standards, the disability must be disclosed, since reasonable accommodations are only mandated for people with disabilities, and the employer must be aware of the disability before an accommodation can be designed.

For people with psychiatric disorders the obligation to disclose as a prerequisite for a reasonable accommodation can be one of the most troubling and problematic aspects of the ADA, since disclosure can jeopardize the opportunity to get a job. The fact that discrimination at this point is unlawful is of small comfort to an applicant witnessing a hostile or dismissive reaction to a request for reasonable accommodation. Laura Mancuso has offered suggestions for gaining support and adequately preparing for the fact of disclosure,[30] but unfortunately there is no satisfactory solution to the problem. The trade-off between reasonable accommodation and privacy under the ADA is real.

Can an employer who learns about prior institutionalization or treatment use that information in the hiring process?

No. Many employers are reluctant to hire a person who has been hospitalized or treated for a mental disability, especially for an extended period. However, they may not use an applicant's history of receiving treatment, or even the underlying condition that required treatment, as a basis for denying a person a job. In some circumstances, an employer may consider whether gaps in work experience occasioned by institutionalization affect job qualifications, but only if continuous experience is essential for the job.

Can an employer use standardized tests in the hiring process?

Yes, but only as long as they test the skills and abilities required to perform the job and are necessary to determine whether the applicant in fact possesses them.[31] Further, they may not screen out, or tend to screen out, people with disabilities. Psychological tests are permissible if the employer is able to meet these requirements. The tests must be administered in a way that ensures that the test measures the skill or aptitude required for the job rather than an impairment that impedes good test performance.[32] This means, for example, that people with learning disabilities who need extra time to complete a standardized test must be offered that additional time.

What if the employer believes that a job applicant will be a threat to self or others in the workplace?

The ADA provides that no employer must hire or retain a person with a disability who poses a direct threat to the health and safety of other individuals that cannot be eliminated through reasonable accommodation.[33] In enacting this common-sense provision, Congress sought to ensure that the threat was direct and real, not the product of prejudice and unwarranted stereotypes about violent behavior among persons with mental disabilities. As a result, the conclusion that a person presents a direct threat to others must be predicated on an individualized assessment based on recent, credible, and objective evidence.[34]

Harm to self is a somewhat different story. There is no provision in the ADA that allows employers to terminate or refuse to hire qualified individuals solely out of a concern that, because of the disability, the job would be too stressful or otherwise not in the person's best interests. The ADA says nothing about such paternalistic concerns and indeed one of the law's purposes is to eliminate "overprotective rules and policies."[35] Thus the ADA only permits rejection based on threats to others, not to self. Nevertheless, the Equal Employment Opportunity Commission, the agency responsible for enforcing the private employment provisions of the ADA, has adopted a rule that permits employers to deny employment to people who may cause harm to themselves at the workplace.[36] Because it appears contrary to the ADA, the rule is likely to be challenged in the courts.

Does the ADA permit an employer to deny a person with a mental disability the right to participate in the employer's health plan or to refuse to hire the individual to avoid higher health costs?

No. A health insurance plan is a term or condition of employment under the ADA, and it prohibits an employer from

* Denying employment to a potential employee because of the existence of a particular health condition that the employer fears will increase health insurance premiums
* Denying employment to a potential employee because the employer's health insurance plan does not cover a particular condition
* Excluding a person with a disability from the employer's health insurance plan

These rights extend to dependents of employees because the ADA protects the rights of those associated with people with disabilities. Thus, for example, an employer could not deny health insurance to an employee who has a child with mental retardation.

Must the health benefit plan offered by the employer cover mental health treatment to the same extent that it covers other health conditions?

This is the crucial employee benefits question under the ADA, and the answer is not yet known. Cases brought under the Rehabilitation Act challenging discriminatory mental health coverage in federal health benefit plans were rejected,[37] but it can be argued that the ADA's specific prohibition against discrimination in terms and conditions of employment should apply to the coverage provided in a health plan.

The question is complicated by the fact that the ADA contains a provision that prohibits challenges to employers' health benefit plans that are consistent with state law, as long as they are not a "subterfuge" to "evade" the purposes of the ADA. The exact meaning of this exception remains unclear and subject to dispute. Most people reading the law agree that the ADA does not prohibit an employer's health plan from excluding or limiting coverage of preexisting conditions of new participants in the plan. But what about imposing higher copayments, arbitrary limitations on coverage, and dollar annual or lifetime ceilings on reimbursement for mental health benefits, as is common in health plans? Employers have taken the position that in virtually all cases, the content of health benefit plans cannot be attacked under the ADA.

The federal Equal Employment Opportunity Commission has taken a different position: employers may not, without a compelling justification, exclude or limit coverage of a particular disability (e.g., AIDS), a group of disabilities, or disability generally unless the exclusion can be justified on the basis of actuarial data or is required to assure that the health plan is fiscally sound and affordable with adequate coverage. However, they may exclude or limit coverage of groups of conditions (such as mental health conditions) that include some conditions considered disabilities under the ADA and some that are not.[38] Advocates for people with mental disabilities dispute this interpretation, contending that an employer cannot discriminate against people with psychiatric disabilities simply because the health coverage category they are in also includes conditions that are not disabilities.

According to these advocates, an employer's health plan may not deny employees with psychiatric disabilities (and dependents, if otherwise covered by the plan) coverage for their disability equal to the coverage employees with other conditions receive. Thus, for example, if the employer covers rehabilitation services for physical conditions, it cannot deny psychiatric rehabilitation services to a person with a serious mental illness whose major life activities are significantly limited. In the absence of a satisfactory justification (e.g., maintaining fiscal soundness of the plan) this differential treatment would amount to unlawful discrimination on the basis of psychiatric disability.

On the other hand, the employer would not have to make mental services equal in scope to physical health benefits available to all participants in the plan. That is because the ADA does not require changes in health or any other benefits to people without disabilities.

The courts have yet to rule on the scope of the nondiscrimination mandate as applied to employers-provided health coverage. If they agree with the interpretation presented here, the ADA has the potential to enable people with psychiatric disabilities to gain greater access to employer-provided mental health benefits. But it cannot bring about equality in mental health coverage for others who do not have a disability.

How are employment rights under the ADA enforced?

They are enforced in the same way as other federal employment laws, through the Equal Employment Opportunity Commission and the courts. Before filing a case in court, the victim must first file a complaint with the United States Equal Employment Opportunity Commission (EEOC) within 180 days of the discriminatory act, unless the individual lives in a state that has its own civil rights agency that accepts complaints of employment discrimination based on disability. In that case, the complainant may file with the state agency and wait 300 days before filing with the EEOC. These filing requirements are very important, for unlike housing discrimination cases, the failure to file on time with the EEOC will preclude ever having the opportunity to bring the case to court.

The EEOC or state agency will investigate the complaint and may try to resolve it with the employer. In rare instances it may file a lawsuit on the complainant's behalf. If the EEOC does not file suit and the complainant is not satisfied with any proposed resolution, or if, after 180 days the EEOC's work on the case is not completed, the complainant may bring a lawsuit in federal court for back pay, damages, and, in some circumstances, an order to hire or reinstate her in the position.

Services by Public Entities

For almost two decades, the federal Rehabilitation Act has prohibited discrimination against people with disabilities by recipients of federal financial assistance, which includes just about every state and local government in the United States. So when Congress enacted the ADA, it decided once again to prohibit discrimination on the basis of disability in all public programs and services, regardless whether they receive federal financial assistance. These programs and services range from public libraries to public universities, from police departments to prisons, from Medicaid programs to community mental health centers. The ADA even affects local and state laws that discriminate against people with disabilities and the practices of courts that enforce these laws.

Title II of the ADA provides that no qualified individual with a disability may, because of a disability, be excluded from participation or be denied the benefits of services, programs, or activities of a public entity, nor be subjected to discrimination by the public entity.[39] A qualified person with a disability is someone who "with or without reasonable modification of rules, policies or practices, the removal of architectural, communication or transportation barriers, or the provision of auxiliary aids or services, meets the essential eligibility requirements for the receipt of services or the participation in programs or activities provided by a public entity."[40] In other words, as in employment, the determination of whether the person is qualified to participate includes figuring out what the essential eligibility requirements are and whether obstacles to meeting those requirements can be removed at a reasonable cost. Thus, Title II has the same approach to discrimination as the employment provisions of Title I, except that in place of the phrase "reasonable accommodation" it uses the term "reasonable modification," which has essentially the same meaning as reasonable accommodation but encompasses rules as well as practices.

The statute also covers discrimination by private individuals or organizations that are engaged in activities through contracts or licenses issued by a governmental body.

What activities of public entities are covered by the ADA?
Virtually all of them:

- Programs and services of agencies operated for the public (or a segment of it), including social services, income maintenance programs, health and welfare programs, recreation and cultural programs, education, and many more
  - Programs and services offered through contractors
  - Employment by the public entity
  - Public transportation systems operated by state or local government

- The judicial system, including courthouses and actions taken by the judiciary in administering the law
- Voting and access to the ballot

What forms of discrimination by public entities are prohibited by the ADA?

Just about anything one could think of. Here are eight examples.[41]

1. *Denying a qualified person with a disability the opportunity to participate in a service or benefit.* This prohibition includes not only outright denials of benefits but obstacles put in the way of people with disabilities. For example, the ADA prevents a child welfare agency from offering counseling and support to troubled families while requiring parents with psychiatric disabilities to seek such help elsewhere. Similarly, a school cannot prevent students from taking part in recreational activities solely because they have a disability if they are otherwise qualified to participate. The statute also generally prohibits an agency from excluding a particular group of people with disabilities from its programs; this is discussed later in the chapter.

2. *Denying a qualified individual with a disability the opportunity to participate in a service or benefit that is equal to the service or benefit available to others.* A striking example of the application of this rule occurred when the state of Oregon first sought federal approval to revise its Medicaid plan. The proposed change included the numerical ranking of medical conditions and treatments according to a set of criteria the state had developed. The state anticipated covering as many conditions on the list as there were funds available so that those conditions ranked very low were the least likely to be covered.

One of the criteria used for ranking was an individual's "quality of life." The drafters of the plan appeared to base their decisions on the "premise that the value of the life of a person with a disability is less than the value of a person without a disability."[42] The result was that in some instances the same treatment ranked lower if it was sought by a person with a disability. For example, liver transplants for alcoholic cirrhosis of the liver were ranked lower than the same procedures for nonalcoholic cirrhosis of the liver. Thus, people with disabilities were afforded less access to a benefit—Medicaid—than individuals without disabilities. For this reason the Secretary of Health and Human Services determined that the plan violated the ADA: people with disabilities were permitted to participate in Medicaid but were not provided equal benefits.

3. *Providing a qualified individual with a disability a benefit or service that is not as effective in affording equal opportunity to obtain the same result or benefit or to reach the same level of achievement as provided to others.* This rule generally applies where the benefit or service offered to persons with disabilities is specialized for them, e.g., a special sports program for people with disabilities. The program must offer them the opportunity to gain the same benefit or level of achievement as mainstream sports programs. It would violate the ADA to provide people with disabilities in a special program a lower quality of uniform, field, or coaching than those available to people without disabilities in the mainstream program.

This provision can become a powerful tool to curb efforts by local governments to cut funding for programs serving people with disabilities if the effect of the cuts is to deny them an equal opportunity to reach the same level of benefit or to achieve the same results as people without disabilities. Thus, a court ruled that a municipality violated the ADA when it eliminated funding for recreation programs for people with mental disabilities but left other city-funded recreation programs intact because people with disabilities were left with programs that were less effective than those serving others.[43]

This does not mean that government cannot allocate funds consistent with its resources, only that it cannot fund programs in a discriminatory fashion. As the court said:

While Title II does not require any particular level of services for persons with disabilities in an absolute sense, it does require that any benefits provided to non-disabled persons must be equally made available for disabled persons. Therefore, had the City cut their entire budget for the Department of Leisure Services, effectively eliminating recreational programs for disabled and non-disabled alike, the ADA would not be implicated because both groups would be equally affected. However, if the City chooses to provide leisure services to non-disabled persons, the ADA requires that the City provide equal opportunity for persons with disabilities to receive comparable benefits.[44]

4. *Providing separate or different benefits or services to people with disabilities, unless separate or different benefits are necessary to provide qualified individuals benefits or services that are as effective as those provided to others.* As a general rule, the government may provide special services, such as vocational rehabilitation, training, or case management services, to people with mental disabilities or even a subset of them. But governments may not provide separate or different services unless they are needed to be effective.

In addition, the existence of specialized services does not permit the government to exclude people with disabilities from participating in programs available to all. For example, a recreation department may operate a program for people with special needs, but it may not deprive the people with disabilities for whom these programs were designed from also participating in recreation programs open to everyone else.

5. *Using criteria or methods of administration that either discriminate directly against people with disabilities or have the effect of defeating or substantially impairing the accomplishment of the objectives of the public entity's program with respect to people with disabilities.* This seemingly obscure right, about "criteria or methods of administration" is one of the most important features of the ADA. It means that the maze of bureaucratic procedures that, intentionally or not, so often deter people with mental disabilities from applying for or obtaining government services or benefits, may themselves be unlawful under the ADA. For example, long waits and complicated forms for general assistance benefits may have the effect of denying these benefits to people with psychiatric disabilities. This rule is discussed in greater detail later in this chapter.

6. *Discriminating in employment against people with disabilities.* The obligations of state and local government agencies are the same as employers in the private sector.

7. *Excluding people with disabilities from participation in programs or benefits because the facilities are physically inaccessible or unusable by individuals with disabilities.* This provision is particularly important to people who have physical as well as mental disabilities.

8. *Imposing eligibility requirements that tend to screen out people with disabilities or classes of individuals with disabilities from fully and equally enjoying services, programs, or activities unless the rules are necessary for the service, program, or activity being offered.* This rule means that, unless a requirement is essential to the operation of a program, people with disabilities, or a category of people with disabilities, cannot be barred from participation because of an eligibility requirement they cannot meet (e.g., prohibiting individuals from riding in an airplane unless they can walk). This rule is particularly important because governments frequently impose eligibility rules that deny people with accompanying mental disabilities the opportunity to participate in programs offered to people with physical disabilities.

The rule can be difficult to apply, though, because the essential nature of a program is not always clear, or a state may recharacterize the program for the very purpose of limiting access. In one case, a state offered attendant support services to people with physical disabilities living in their homes, but only if they were able to control and supervise the attendant and met certain other criteria. Two women with mental disabilities who were found not sufficiently "mentally alert" to meet the control and supervision rule challenged their exclusion from the program. The trial court found that the ability to control and supervise was not an essential feature of the attendant care program—the purpose, it found, was to enable people to live outside institutions—and, even if it was, the court said the rule should be reasonably modified to allow the two women to participate.[45]

The court of appeals reversed because it disagreed with the lower court's characterization of the program. Instead of seeing the essential nature of the program as providing community living as an alternative to institutionalization for people with disabilities, it found that the attendant care program was designed to enable people with disabilities to live independently. The capacity to exert personal control and supervision was, in its view, critical to the capacity to be independent and hence to the program.[46] For the same reason, reasonable modification was not possible because modification would change the nature of the program. The case shows both the potential of the ADA and the degree to which its qualifications and limitations can defeat its larger purposes.

Do government agencies have an obligation to modify or change their rules, practices, programs, and services to meet the needs of people with disabilities?

Yes, as long as it does not fundamentally alter the essential nature of the service, activity, or program. The duty of reasonable modification requires two kinds of changes:

1. *Modifications in policies, practices, or procedures when these modifications are necessary to avoid discrimination unless the changes would fundamentally alter the nature of the program.* These modifications usually involve creating an exception to a rule in order to allow people with disabilities to participate in a program. Modest changes in an agency's day-to-day rules and practices can mean the difference between participation and exclusion. In one early ADA case, for example, a group of people with psychiatric disabilities requested that a local mental health and mental retardation board change its meeting time from 7 A.M. to later in the day

because the sedative effects of the psychotropic medications they took rendered it impossible for them to attend meetings so early in the morning. Since rescheduling the time of the meetings would occasion no disruption of the board's functions, the ADA compelled the change.[47]

2. *Physical or structural changes to make the program physically accessible.* The government does not have to make every facility accessible, as long as the program as a whole is accessible. For example, every group home for people with mental retardation operated by a housing provider does not have to be accessible as long as people with mental retardation and physical disabilities have access to a group home, and the changes do not result in a fundamental alteration of the program or cause undue financial or administrative burdens. Structural changes must have been in place by 26 January 1995 and are subject to a transition plan setting out a schedule of proposed structural changes that was to have been established in 1992.

Does the ADA require government agencies to integrate people with mental disabilities into mainstream programs?

Yes. As emphasized earlier in the chapter, the ADA is concerned not only with preventing discrimination but with affirmatively integrating people with disabilities into social and economic life. This emphasis on integration led the Department of Justice to issue a regulation under Title II requiring public entities to "administer services, programs, and activities in the most integrated setting appropriate to the needs of qualified individuals with disabilities."[48] Given the history of separate programs, separate services and even separate housing for people with disabilities, the integration mandate can have a profound impact on their lives and, indeed, on society as a whole.

Take the case of a woman identified as Idell S., a forty-three-year-old woman who became paralyzed from the waist down after contracting meningitis. Although able to cook and care for own needs, she needed assistance with activities such as shopping, doing household chores, and getting out of bed. A state social services agency assessed her needs and found that its attendant care program, which provides help for people in their homes, could benefit her, but all the slots were taken. Ms. S. was placed on a waiting list for that program and remained in a nursing home for years, separated from her two children and her neighborhood. From the state's viewpoint, this was unfortunate, since she did not need to be in an institution, and financially irrational, since the nursing home cost more than an in-home attendant, but it claimed nothing could be done but continue to wait.

The lower court found no violation of the ADA. Taking a rather conventional approach to the question, it reasoned that she was not discriminated against not because she had a disability, but rather because the program simply ran out of funds. The court of appeals, though, took as its starting point the fact that Ms. S.'s exclusion from the program defeated the ADA's mandate of integrating people with disabilities into community life. The court interpreted the ADA to be "intended to insure that qualified individuals receive services in a manner consistent with basic human dignity rather than in a manner which shunts them aside, hides or ignores them."[49] Thus, even in the absence of international discrimination, the court of appeals found that keeping Ms. S. in the nursing home denied her the benefits of the attendant care program and the right to integration guaranteed by the ADA.

Further, the court decided that a modification of the program to pay for Ms. S.'s attendant was not unreasonable, since the payment would not change the nature of the program. The fact that the state would be required to shift its budget priorities did not fundamentally alter its program and thus did not affect its integration obligation under the ADA.

The ADA's "most integrated setting" rule represents a profound change in the way social services must be provided to people with disabilities, mental as well as physical. They no longer have to accept segregated services if existing integrated services would serve their purposes. The only limitation on this obligation is that public programs do not have to fundamentally alter their nature to accomplish integration.

Taken to its limits, the ADA's integration requirement can be interpreted to require the creation and development of integrated community programs as alternatives to institutionalization. This interpretation is discussed in the chapter on the right to treatment and services.

What must governments do to make sure they comply with the ADA?

They must engage in "self-evaluation" to determine whether they comply with their obligations under the ADA. The self-evaluation process must include input by people with disabilities. If necessary, states must make reasonable modifications in their programs so that people with disabilities are not subjected to discrimination.

How does Title II affect discrimination permitted by state or local laws?

State and local laws that discriminate against people with disabilities are not immune from the ADA. Indeed, the impact of the ADA on these laws may be significant. For example, some states have laws denying competent people with psychiatric disabilities the right to make decisions regarding certain medical treatments while allowing other competent people to make these decisions. This difference discriminates against people with psychiatric disabilities and probably violates the ADA.

What limitations are there on exclusion of people with mental disabilities from benefit or services programs?

Benefit programs are by their nature discriminatory: they select a particular group of people to assist and leave out others. For example, the fact that a community develops housing for people with mental retardation does not obligate it, by that gesture alone, to develop housing for people with AIDS or mental illness as well. The fact that a state or local government chooses to provide services or income benefits to one group of people with disabilities does not mean that it has to provide those benefits to all groups of people with disabilities. In a case brought under the Rehabilitation Act, the Supreme Court held that Congress may create a program to pay benefits to veterans with certain disabilities but not alcoholism.[50]

However, discrimination against certain categories of people with disabilities is not permissible in programs of general application. For example, institutions for mentally retarded people often provide vocational training programs only to people with moderate disabilities. This practice obviously discriminates against people with more severe disabilities in a program of general application and therefore violates the ADA and Section 504 of the Rehabilitation Act; the exclusion is based on discrimination, not on the essential nature of the program.[51]

What impact does the ADA have on public health care programs like Medicaid?

Medicaid is simply an example of a government-provided benefit program of general application, and is described more fully in chapter 6. Because Medicaid affects so many millions of people, however, the impact of the ADA already has gained a great deal of attention.

Earlier, we described how the U.S. Department of Health and Human Services rejected a state's revisions to its Medicaid plan because it found that the plan intentionally discriminated against people with disabilities in violation of the ADA. Recall that under the proposed Oregon plan, liver transplants for people with alcoholism-based cirrhosis of the liver were ranked lower than liver transplants for cirrhosis of the liver caused by factors other than alcoholism. The plan was rejected and sent back for rewriting to eliminate this discriminatory feature. Oregon did so.

The intentional exclusion or limitation of coverage of psychiatric disabilities in state-operated Medicaid programs may also violate the ADA. For here, too, in a program of general application—health coverage— the state would be making a decision to limit access to appropriate health care for a particular group of people based on their disability. As in the case of employer-provided health insurance, nondiscriminatory Medicaid coverage would only be available to people with mental disabilities (i.e., someone whose mental impairment substantially limited major life activities), not to all people with a desire for mental health treatment. Still, this rather straightforward application of the ADA can have profound effects on the availability of coverage, especially in the era when managed care plans may seek to limit the access of people with psychiatric disabilities to mental health services. Although yet untested in the courts, the argument has force.

In considering discriminatory features of state Medicaid or related programs, it is important to distinguish intentional exclusion of equal coverage of mental disabilities from other features of the plan which, though applicable to everyone, especially disadvantage people with disabilities. These discriminatory effects of an otherwise neutral plan are not so easily challengeable.

For example, in the 1980s, Tennessee lowered the number of hospital days Medicaid would reimburse from twenty to fourteen, an action that had a disproportionately harmful effect on people with disabilities. The cutback was challenged as a violation of the ADA's predecessor, Section 504 of the Rehabilitation Act. In *Alexander v. Choate*, the Supreme Court held that in the absence of intent to discriminate, no violation existed as long as people with disabilities have "meaningful access" to benefits under the program.[52] Here, the Court said that the reduction in the number of hospital days did not deny people with disabilities meaningful access to the Tennessee Medicaid program.

Many people mistakenly apply the reasoning of the Supreme Court in *Choate* to limitations on coverage of services for people with psychiatric disabilities. But those exclusions are not the product of a general rule not targeted at a particular group, like the cutback in hospital days. Rather, they are highly targeted, singling out a disfavored population for unequal treatment.

How does the ADA affect administration of benefit programs?
Benefit programs, especially those designed for low-income people, are often administered impersonally, imperiously, and arbitrarily. Applicants are frequently subjected to long waits in crowded rooms, asked to fill out multiple forms, told to return with different or additional information, treated rudely by staff, and expected to follow indecipherable directions.

Such practices may discourage people from applying for benefits. For people with mental disabilities, they can be tantamount to exclusion from the program. The duty to make reasonable accommodations under Section 504 and reasonable modifications of rules and practices under the ADA mandate that these methods of program administration be adjusted to meet the needs of people with disabilities. Some potential administrative modifications include:

- Training and sensitizing staff about people with disabilities, including hearing directly from consumers of agency services
- Scheduling appointments flexibly
- Granting additional time and assistance in filling out applications
- Assisting people to keep appointments, such as by placing timely reminder calls and making home visits
- Providing transportation to offices
- Providing interview and application areas that minimize distractions and ensure privacy[53]

These solutions represent more than good practice. They are among the possible ways agencies operating benefit programs may comply with their legal obligations under the ADA.

What rights do people with mental disabilities have in licensing and certification procedures?
States and local governments issue licenses of all kinds, from driver's

licenses to licenses to practice law, medicine, or dentistry. In order to obtain one, applicants are often asked whether they have been diagnosed or treated for a mental or emotional problem. Relying on stereotypes about people who have had mental health treatment, licensing agencies frequently invade applicants' privacy and draw unwarranted conclusions about their abilities instead of directing questions to the agency's legitimate area of concern—a person's conduct and competence. Even when the question does nothing more than trigger additional investigation, it remains discriminatory because it subjects individuals to special scrutiny because they have had mental health treatment. The Department of Justice and a number of courts have therefore concluded that blanket inquiries into a person's history of mental health treatment are unlawful under the ADA.[54]

Licensing is another instance where compliance with the ADA actually enables an agency to do its job better. Instead of focusing on prejudicial irrelevancies, the agency can target its questions to actual behavior, from which it can determine whether a person can exercise the responsibilities required for the licensed activity.

What reasonable accommodations must be available in taking examinations for licenses?

Licensing agencies must make accommodations to enable a person to be properly tested for the skill required for the license, rather than for success in the testing environment. For example, someone whose phobia prevents him from performing in a crowded room must be given access to a space that will enable him to demonstrate his capacity in the tested subject matter. The object of the examination, after all, is to test for knowledge and skill, not for the ability to function well in a crowd.[55]

Does the ADA apply to the criteria used to make decisions about marriage, child custody, termination of parental rights, and other decisions by the state about parenting?

Yes. The rights to marry and raise children have long been recognized as fundamental under the Constitution.[56] Many states nevertheless have kept marriage laws on their books that date back to the eugenics era and declare marriages of "lunatics," "idiots," and other stereotypical classifications of people with mental disabilities to be either void or subject to annulment. Even before the ADA, however, these laws were rarely enforced. Typically, marriage license forms do not even call for information relating to mental status.[57] Nonetheless, these laws almost certainly violate Title II of the ADA, since they deny qualified individuals with disabilities the opportunity to avail themselves of an important social institution in American society.

In theory, determinations in abuse and neglect proceedings, child custody disputes, and proceedings to terminate parental rights should be based on an evaluation of whether an individual has properly discharged the duty to care for a child. Frequently, however, the existence of a mental disability is a determining factor in these decisions, without regard to an individual's actual parenting skills.

In such cases people with mental disabilities who are in fact qualified to be parents are denied the fundamental right to raise children under laws and judicial practices that are based on unfounded stereotypes about people with mental disabilities.[58] Under the laws of many states, mental disability cannot be the sole factor in determining parental rights,[59] but statutes often permit courts to take the mere existence of such a disability into account in terminating parental rights or denying custody, and judges candidly acknowledge that they frequently do so.[60] Many judges, social service officials, and even experts called to testify in these cases appear to share the same prejudices as the rest of society against allowing qualified parents with mental disabilities to keep their children.[61]

Determinations of parental rights are typically made by courts and governmental agencies, which are public entities and are therefore covered by Title II of the ADA. Under the Act, decisions about parental fitness should be based on a person's conduct and parental capacity, not on a diagnosis of mental illness or mental retardation. Thus, a court should not deny a mother custody of her child solely because she has been diagnosed as having bipolar disorder. It must make an individualized evaluation of her actual behavior as a parent to determine fitness. That behavior may be associated with bipolar disorder, but a fair reading of the ADA requires that the behavior, not the diagnosis, be the basis of an individualized determination of parental rights.

What implications does the duty of reasonable modification have on parental rights?

A great many. The duty of reasonable modification in this context means that if the state is intervening in the parent-child relationship at least in part because of the parent's disability, it must take reasonable steps beyond those that are otherwise required by law to keep the family together and to provide supports for the parent. These modifications may include parent training, housekeeping assistance, and opportunities for counseling.

How can a person enforce the right to be free of discrimination in programs operated by public entities?

There are two options:

1. The person can sue the state or local government in federal court.

2. Within 180 days of the discriminatory act, the person can file a complaint with the Department of Justice or with the federal agency that appears to be most closely associated with the activity of the state or local government (e.g., for a university, the Department of Education). There is no penalty for filing with the wrong agency, and a complaint can always be filed with the Department of Justice, as long as it is within the 180-day period.

The federal agency has authority to investigate the complaint. It may attempt to resolve the problem informally. If informal resolution fails, but the federal agency determines that a discriminatory practice has occurred, it may issue a letter of findings. That letter of findings once again leads to efforts to secure voluntary compliance, but if those efforts fail, the Department of Justice has the authority to sue the state or local government for the violation.

Public Accommodations

The ADA also prohibits discrimination against qualified individuals with a disability in going about the business of everyday life in the community: at the local grocery store, the civic auditorium, the neighborhood restaurant, the doctor's office, and all other commercial businesses open to the public. And it requires these entities, collectively called "public accommodations," to make reasonable modifications in structures and in policies so that people with disabilities can take advantage of the services offered. These rules are contained in Title III of the ADA.

Like other titles of the ADA, Title III demands both nondiscrimination and inclusion. Goods and services must be afforded to an individual with a disability "in the most integrated setting" appropriate to the needs of the individual.[62]

What is a public accommodation under the ADA?

Public accommodations include almost every service or business a person is likely to encounter on a day-to-day basis.[63]

- Motels, hotels, inns, and similar lodgings[64]
- Restaurants, bars, and other places that serve food
- Places of entertainment, including theaters, concert halls, movie theaters, and stadiums
- Auditoriums, convention centers, lecture halls, and other places for large public gatherings
- Stores, including grocery stores, bakeries, shopping centers, and places where goods are sold
- Businesses that provide services, including banks, barber shops, gas stations, laundromats, medical, dental, and law offices, hospitals, and insurance offices
- Stations, depots, and terminals used in transportation
- Places of public display, including museums, libraries, and galleries
- Recreation facilities, including parks, zoos, and amusement parks
- Schools, including nursery, elementary, secondary, undergraduate, and graduate
- Social service centers, including day care centers, senior centers, food banks, homeless shelters, and adoption agencies
- Exercise facilities, including gymnasiums, bowling alleys, and golf courses
- Privately operated transportation facilities

What kinds of discrimination are prohibited?

Public accommodations cannot engage in conduct that denies people with disabilities the opportunity to take advantage of the facility or service. To illustrate the various forms of behavior the ADA prohibits, we use an example of rules or practices, now unlawful under the ADA, relating to an adult with mental retardation who wishes to swim in a community pool. The ADA prohibits the following.

- *Denial of participation*—people with mental retardation may not use the community pool.
- *Participation that is not equal to those afforded other individuals*—

people with mental retardation can swim in a community pool only in the afternoons, while everyone else can use the pool morning, afternoon, and evening.

• *Participation that is different or separate from people without disabilities*—people with mental retardation are sent to a special pool program. The ADA does not prohibit the provision of extra programs for people with disabilities, such as a swimming period for people with disabilities, but does outlaw restricting people with disabilities to those special programs. For example, the pool could offer special swim classes for people with mental retardation but cannot restrict people with mental retardation to those programs.

• *Use of standards or methods of administration that have the effect of discriminating on the basis of disability*—a required written test about pool rules.

Does a public accommodation have an obligation to change its policies and physical structures so that people with disabilities can use them?

Yes. The ADA requires places of public accommodation to make three kinds of changes to enable people with disabilities to use them.

• *Reasonable modifications in policies, practices, or procedures* when these modifications are necessary to enable people to take advantage of the goods or services offered, unless making the modifications would fundamentally alter the goods or services offered. To continue the community pool example, the pool would have to modify a rule against bringing metal equipment to the pool if a person with mental retardation who is not ambulatory cannot get to the pool except in a wheelchair.

• *Making available auxiliary aids and services*, such as supplying interpreters or readers or modifying equipment where these aids are necessary to enable the person with a disability to take advantage of the public accommodation, unless making these aids available would fundamentally alter the nature of the goods or services offered.

• *Removing architectural and communication barriers* where their removal is readily achievable, that is, they can be eliminated without much difficulty or expense.

How do these rules apply to medical care?

A health care professional cannot refuse to treat a qualified person with a mental disability. In this context, to be qualified probably means having a condition the specialist treats, maintaining eligibility for third-party payment if the provider generally demands it, and engaging in behavior appropriate for a medical office. In all cases, though, these qualifications are also subject to the rule that if a reasonable modification in rules is possible, e.g., that the person be accompanied by a friend in the examination room to assure appropriate behavior, it must be made available. Thus a dentist or a gynecologist cannot refuse to treat a person with a mental disability unless the person is not a qualified person with a disability. The duty of nondiscrimination would not require a health care professional to treat a person for a condition outside her specialty.

What if a business claims that its customers are upset by people who have disabilities, such as someone with Down's syndrome?

It is no excuse that other customers, such as patrons in a restaurant, do not want to be in the presence of a person with a disability. A public accommodation cannot exclude people because its customers are prejudiced.

Does the ADA apply to insurance practices that discriminate against people with disabilities?

Yes. One of the public accommodations listed in Title III is an insurance office, and the legislative history and Justice Department regulations confirm that the ADA applies to the insurance products sold in the office as well as the office itself.[65]

A basis to challenge discrimination in availability of insurance is particularly important to people with mental disabilities because the practice of discrimination against them is so pervasive. They are denied life insurance because they have a history of depression, denied automobile insurance because of psychiatric hospitalization, and discriminated against in long-term disability coverage. As discussed in the employee benefits section, the ADA permits insurance companies to make decisions that are consistent with state law and not a subterfuge to evade the purposes of the act.[66]

The ADA should not permit companies to deny coverage when they can simply adjust the premium consistent with actuarial data concerning the person's condition; when the risk associated with the disability is not covered by the policy anyway, e.g., suicide in an insurance policy; when arbitrary limitations on coverage are placed on people with mental disabilities, as is typical in long-term disability policies; and when the companies deny coverage based only on stereotypes about people with mental disabilities.

What rights do students with mental disabilities have in higher education?

The ADA applies to higher education, regardless whether the institution is public or private. The latter is covered by Title III and the former by Title II. The ADA, together with Section 504 of the Rehabilitation Act, prohibits colleges, universities, and other institutions of higher learning from discriminating on the basis of disability. The Individuals with Disabilities Education Act, discussed in chapter 6, does not apply to higher education.

The nondiscrimination and reasonable modification requirements of the ADA guarantee that students with mental disabilities have access to higher education as long as they can meet the essential requirements of the program, with or without reasonable modifications of the rules applicable to the institution. Two recent cases, albeit one involving secondary education, show how these obligations can be applied. Under Texas law, no student over the age of nineteen can participate in interscholastic sports. Two football players with learning disabilities who were delayed in reaching high school because they had to repeat grades in elementary school sought a reasonable modification of the over-nineteen rule that would enable them to play. The court evaluated the reasonableness of the requested modification, paying particular attention to athlete safety, and ultimately ruled that the failure to waive the over-nineteen rule constituted illegal discrimination under the ADA.[67]

In the other case, a college student with bipolar (manic depressive) disorder was suspended for disruptive behavior and, after a period of hospitalization and therapy during which her condition stabilized, applied for reinstatement. The college contended that, under its policies, her suspension eliminated her right to re-enroll. However the court found that the refusal to readmit her violated the ADA and issued a preliminary injunction ordering the college to take her back.[68]

Professional education presents more difficulties for people with disabilities. In a decision of questionable reasoning, the Supreme Court interpreted the term "qualified individual with a disability" under the Rehabilitation Act to apply not only to the ability to succeed in school but to succeed in the profession itself. It thus upheld the exclusion of a deaf woman from a nursing program not because she could not meet the academic requirements of the program but because the clinical component required training nurses to serve patients in the "customary" way.[69] Whether ADA cases will adopt this overly narrow interpretation of the right to nondiscrimination in professional education remains to be seen.

How does a person enforce the right to be free from discrimination by a public accommodation?

By bringing a lawsuit against the public accommodation or filing a complaint with the Department of Justice. The department has the authority to investigate the case and, if it sees fit, to file a lawsuit on the complainant's behalf.

THE FAIR HOUSING ACT

The responses to people with mental disabilities who seek to rent an apartment or to move as a group into a neighborhood have become virtual mantras of discrimination.

"Sorry, we don't rent to handicapped people."

"You've been in a psychiatric hospital—we just can't take a chance on leasing you an apartment."

"A home for the mentally retarded isn't really appropriate in a family neighborhood like this."

"Is this area of town really safe for you?"

"We have enough housing for people with disabilities already—we're saturated."

Statements like these occur everyday in communities throughout the United States. For many years, the struggle of people with mental disabilities to obtain housing, hard enough because of a lack of financial resources and, in many places, a tight housing market, was exacerbated by the failure of the federal Fair Housing Act to cover disability-based discrimination.

In 1985 the United States Supreme Court decided a case involving a town that sought to prevent the opening of a group home for people with mental retardation. The town rejected the home's application for a zoning permit under an ordinance that regulated "hospitals for the insane and feebleminded," asserting that it feared for the safety of children in a school across the street and was "concerned" for the well-being of the residents of the home, which was to be located on a five-hundred-year floodplain. The Supreme Court recognized these reasons for what they were, pretexts to discriminate, and held that the Constitution's equal protection clause prohibits localities from making land-use decisions regarding people with mental disabilities based on prejudice, stereotypes, or unwarranted concerns that the presence of people with mental disabilities would diminish the quality of life in a neighborhood.[70]

Three years later, Congress took a dramatic step. For the first time ever, it extended a general civil rights law to protect people with disabilities against discrimination. The Fair Housing Amendments Act of 1988 prohibits discrimination in housing against people with physical or mental disabilities in rental and private housing and covers as well the actions of zoning boards and other land-use regulators. And like the regulations of the Rehabilitation Act that preceded it, the amendments added provisions that require housing providers and government to make reasonable accommodations to enable people with disabilities to obtain and keep housing.[71]

The Fair Housing Act contains only minor exceptions to the general prohibition on discrimination on the basis of disability. That act exempts owners who sell a house without the use of a real estate agent and who do not own more than three other single-family houses. The Fair Housing Act also does not cover rental units in an owner-occupied building with four or fewer apartments. State laws or local ordinances, however, may prohibit discrimination in transactions in these situations. Overall, however, the Fair Housing Act has become the means to open the door to housing opportunities for people with mental disabilities.[72]

The right to be free from discrimination in housing, then, is generally protected by the Fair Housing Act rather than the Americans with Disabilities Act, although the latter applies in certain instances. For example, a homeless shelter is considered a place of public accommodation.

What rights do people with mental disabilities have to be protected from discrimination in housing?

Housing providers may not discriminate against a person on the basis of disability. Like the ADA, the Fair Housing Act protects people who have a mental disability now, had one in the past, or who are regarded by the other party to the transaction as having a disability.[73] It also protects people "associated with" a person with a disability, such as the parents of a child with a disability who are seeking to rent an apartment or a service provider seeking to develop housing for people with disabilities. Finally, the law protects individuals with disabilities against interference by third parties, such as unwelcoming neighbors, in exercising their right to live in housing of their choice.[74]

Discrimination on the basis of disability is prohibited with respect to:

- Buying a house, cooperative share, or condominium
- Obtaining financing for housing, such as a mortgage
- Renting an apartment
- Placing conditions in leases
- Evicting a person from housing
- Zoning and other land use decisions affecting housing
- Licensing, health, and safety regulations concerning housing

The practical effects of the law and its effect on conventional justifications for denying housing to people are enormous. For example, discrimination disguised as concern that a neighborhood is too dangerous for a person with a disability is illegal. Real estate agents may not refuse to show an apartment because the landlord is uncomfortable with people with mental disabilities, nor may they steer persons with mental disabilities to neighborhoods the agent thinks are most "appropriate." Nor may a person with a mental disability be denied housing because of a fear that property values will decline or that the person will not "fit" into the neighborhood. Instead, housing decisions must be based on reasonable criteria applied to all applicants. These typically include whether the person can afford the rent or mortgage payments, has a record of reliability, and is likely to comply with the terms of the lease or other tenancy or mortgage document. A history of hospitalization, psychiatric treatment, or mental disability alone is insufficient reason to deny housing.

May a landlord, seller, or other participant in a housing transaction inquire whether the person has a mental disability, has been hospitalized, or has received treatment for a mental disability?

No. Congress recognized that the right to fair housing could readily be circumvented if landlords or others could ask about the nature or extent of a person's disability. With that information, it is all too easy for a landlord, bank, or real estate agent to discriminate and find a pretext to hide their actions. So when Congress wrote the law, it prohibited landlords, sellers, agents, and financial institutions from asking a prospective buyer or renter about the existence or extent of a disability.[75] Thus, for example, questions on a rental application whether an applicant has a disability, has ever sought treatment for a mental condition, or has ever been hospitalized for psychiatric reasons are now prohibited.[76] Nor can a landlord ask whether the applicant is capable of living alone.[77]

A landlord or other party to a real estate transaction can, however, ask whether the applicant meets the requirements of tenancy or purchase, such as financial qualification standards, but only if all applicants are asked these questions. Similarly, applicants, prior landlords, or references may be asked whether the applicant's tenancy poses a direct threat to the health or safety of other individuals or would result in substantial physical damage to the property.[78] In doing so, however, very strict rules apply. All applicants must be asked these questions, not just people the landlord or seller knows to have a mental disability. Further, the inference that a person is a direct threat must be made only on the basis of the individual's prior recent conduct. Landlords are specifically prohibited from drawing conclusions about the possible antisocial behavior of a person with a mental disability from having the disability, having been hospitalized, or having been in a treatment program. In other words, unwarranted assumptions about the behavior of people with mental disabilities cannot justify denying an individual housing. There must be objective, reliable evidence that suggests that the person will not comply with the conditions of tenancy or ownership or will pose a threat to others.

What obligations do landlords have to accommodate a person's disability?

One of the most important features of the Fair Housing Act is the duty to make reasonable accommodations for a person's disability. This means that the operator or seller of housing, when aware of dealing with a person with a mental disability, must take practical and feasible steps to accommodate the person's needs.

The accommodations may be changes to the unit in order to make it accessible to a person with a physical disability. The Fair Housing Act contains extensive provisions permitting reasonable modifications of the premises—at the tenant's expense—to make the space physically usable.[79] Newly constructed multifamily dwellings of four or more units must include an accessible building entrance, accessible common use areas, doors that allow passage by a person in a wheelchair, an accessible route through the dwelling unit, light switches and other environmental controls in accessible locations, reinforcements in bathroom walls that will accommodate grab bars, and kitchens and bathrooms that allow a wheelchair to maneuver about.[80]

Not all accommodations are physical, though. Like the ADA, the Fair Housing Act requires reasonable modification of rules and policies that, while universally applicable, tend to impede the ability of certain people with disabilities to live on the premises. One example is the now widely accepted reservation of close-in parking spaces for people with physical disabilities. Another is a rule disallowing pets. Courts have held that, while a landlord may impose a no-pets rule, the duty of reasonable accommodation requires a landlord not to enforce the rule with respect to a guide dog for a blind person or a person with a mental disability who needs a pet as a support.[81] Other accommodations may meet the needs or consider the behavior of certain people with mental disabilities. In one case, a tenant with a psychiatric disability created minor damage to the apartment walls by beating on them. Before being evicted, though, the tenant had to be given time to obtain mental health services that might be effective in moderating her behavior. A landlord is not, however, required to *provide* mental health services.[82]

The duty of reasonable accommodation is on the landlord. To obtain an accommodation, though, the tenant or prospective tenant must ask for one.

Do people with mental disabilities have any rights to be free of discrimination in zoning and land-use decisions and in health and safety regulations?

Yes, very important ones, all designed to overcome the notorious NIMBY—not in my backyard—syndrome.

The housing crisis for people with mental disabilities has led local governments, nonprofit organizations, and private developers to develop housing to meet the overwhelming need for affordable dwellings. These efforts take many forms, including apartment units, group homes, single room occupancy buildings, and many others. But developers frequently face formidable and hostile opposition from neighbors, civic associations, and local zoning officials seeking to limit the presence of people with mental disabilities in their midst.

Opponents typically rely on local land-use rules, health and safety regulations, and other regulatory powers to keep the housing out. Zoning rules are used to restrict the districts in which "special needs" housing can be developed, the number of unrelated people who may live in a home, even the distance between the homes. Officials manipulate health, safety, building code, and licensing laws to restrict the availability of housing to people with mental disabilities by demanding burdensome and expensive physical changes to the premises or lot. They often erect procedural obstacles as well, such as onerous, expensive, and time-consuming procedures to obtain permits for the housing.

The Fair Housing Act has become a major tool for overturning many of these discriminatory restrictions. The law provides developers of housing for people with disabilities the same right to be protected from discriminatory housing practices as the people they serve, since the law prohibits discrimination against people "associated with" people with disabilities.

Courts have overturned land-use and other regulatory restrictions because they intentionally discriminate against people with mental disabilities, because they have the effect of discriminating against people with mental disabilities, or because they fail to reasonably accommodate the needs of people with mental disabilities. For example, the following types of restrictions have been found unlawful:

- *Distance requirements*, e.g., a rule that requires group homes for people with disabilities be located at least 1,000 feet (about one-fifth of a mile) from one another[83]
- *Occupancy limits*, e.g., rules that only four, five, or six unrelated people can live in a home[84]
- *Special procedural requirements*, e.g., conditional use permit, variance, certificate of occupancy, or building permit rules that impose special burdens on developers of housing for people with disabilities[85]
- *Compliance with onerous health and fire safety rules*, e.g., special sprinkler system, egress rules[86]
- *Neighborhood hearing or approval rules*, e.g., a rule requiring the operator of a residence for people with disabilities to provide advance notice to neighbors about the proposed home and to provide information about it[87]
- *Decisions based on neighborhood opposition*, e.g., refusal of a building permit because neighbors object to people with mental illness[88]

• *Restrictive covenants in deeds,* e.g., rules that only related people can live in the home[89]

Despite these decisions, localities, often at the behest of neighborhood associations, continue to discriminate against people with mental disabilities through land-use powers. Only concerted advocacy, together with information about rights, can overcome it.

Do people with mental disabilities have the right to be protected from self-help eviction in homes operated by mental health or mental retardation agencies?

In our view, yes, but this issue has not been fully resolved. Mental health agencies, board and care homes, and nonprofit housing providers dedicated to serving people with mental disabilities often believe that because they are regulated by state or local government and, in any event, have the best interests of people with mental disabilities in mind, eviction law should not apply. They argue, for example, that they have a responsibility to all residents and must be able to evict a disruptive or rule-breaking resident quickly, without a court hearing, to protect the integrity of the program. In addition, they contend, notice and the right to be heard are not so important because unlike private landlords, their goal is to serve the tenants.

The housing rights of people in this type of housing are especially fragile because they are often connected to a program of services. Operators of programs that also own or lease housing typically condition the right to live in the house on satisfactory participation in a program. The residence is not, in their view, housing, but rather the housing component of a program. If a person is dismissed from the program and thus loses a place to live, the provider still does not view that as "eviction."

These attitudes and the practices accompanying them—the denial of the right to remain in one's house unless a court decides otherwise—need to be changed dramatically. It is discriminatory for people with mental disabilities to remain constantly at risk of exclusion from their homes without a shred of due process. Further, most of the arguments that housing providers make to justify their eviction practices apply equally to ordinary housing. For example, any landlord has an interest in protecting law-abiding tenants from disruptive renters or drug dealers, but that does not mean that they may be denied due process of law.

Here again, the principles embodied in the Fair Housing Act should come into play. People with mental disabilities have the same right to remain in their homes as anyone else, and if a state establishes an eviction procedure, it should apply no matter who the tenant and the housing provider are. Relying on their interpretation of state landlord-tenant law without reference to the Fair Housing Act, several courts have so far adopted this view.

In one case, a court in New York held that the operators of a supervised, licensed community residence for people with psychiatric disabilities could not exclude a resident who had lived there for eighteen months without abiding by the procedures required generally for eviction from a rental unit.[90] The residence operator argued that it ran a "treatment program" governed by state regulations. The tenant was alleged to have engaged in repeated incidents of substance abuse, conduct that, under the program rules, represented grounds for exclusion as long as the residence operator had written and implemented a discharge plan. The provider claimed that as long as it followed these and certain other procedures, it could not be treated as a landlord subject to landlord-tenant law.

The court held otherwise, ruling that the fact that the facility also offered treatment and supervision did not mean it was not also a home. It said that if the operator wanted to oust the man, it would have to commence eviction proceedings, thus providing him with an opportunity for a hearing before a neutral judge on the allegations against him.

Given prevailing attitudes, additional litigation will likely be brought before the right to due process in exclusion from program-related housing is recognized. Providers of housing will have to alter their procedures and ways of thinking. But it is not too much to expect that the Fair Housing Act can be relied on to guarantee a right to a hearing before one's home is taken away, regardless who the provider of housing is.

Are there any exceptions to nondiscrimination rules?

Unfortunately yes. Fueled by hysteria about the increasing number of people with psychiatric disabilities living in public and assisted housing, Congress in 1992 enacted legislation permitting public housing authorities and operators of federally assisted housing to set aside units originally financed under programs to house elderly or disabled as available to elderly people only.[91] Under this law, current tenants of the units may not be evicted, but empty units—indeed entire floors or buildings—can be designated as "elderly only" or as "disabled only." Public housing authorities must conduct public hearings before they designate their buildings but private providers of subsidized housing need not and may also reject applicants with mental disabilities while admitting applicants with physical disabilities.[92]

Although certain procedural requirements must be met before public housing authorities engage in this process, these designations discriminate on the basis of disability. But the Fair Housing Act does not apply here. The draconian implications of the law began to be felt soon after its passage as the number of public and assisted housing units for people with mental disabilities began to diminish.[93]

How are fair housing rights enforced?

Victims of discrimination may file a complaint with the Department of Housing and Urban Development (HUD), which is charged with enforcing the law. In some localities, a state, city, or county has a fair housing law that HUD has determined to be substantially equivalent to federal fair housing law. In that case, the complaint may be filed with that agency or with HUD.

Either way, the complaint must be filed within one year of the discriminatory act. HUD has a toll free hotline. At this writing, the phone number is 1-800-669-9777.[94]

If HUD or the local investigative agency finds that a complaint has merit, it will try to conciliate the complaint; if it cannot, it can sue the violator on behalf of the victim. HUD may seek an order enjoining the discriminatory practices as well as civil penalties. In the case of a "pattern or practice" of discrimination or discriminatory zoning rules, HUD will forward the complaint to the Department of Justice, which will review the case and also has the authority to sue.

A person does not have to file a complaint with one of these agencies, but instead (or in addition) may file a lawsuit within two years of the discriminatory act. Individual enforcement can be a powerful tool, especially because the courts have the power to issue an injunction against housing providers who discriminate and order them to pay damages as well.

MEDICAL CARE FOR INFANTS WITH
SEVERE DISABILITIES

In 1982 the parents of an infant born with Down's syndrome, a form of mental retardation, refused to consent to routine corrective surgery on the child's esophagus. Instead, they chose to allow the infant to starve to death in the belief that its mental disability made its life not worth living. Although challenged by outside parties who sought to save the child, this decision was upheld by the Supreme Court of Indiana as within the province of the parents.[95] Baby Doe died six days later. This was not the first instance of parents refusing to consent to medical treatment for a baby with a disability, but in this case the withholding of a simple operation solely because of the child's disability sparked a national debate over the circumstances under which parents may choose to withhold medical care for newborns on account of their disabilities. The Baby Doe case spawned new statutes and regulations as well as increased enforcement of existing laws in order to prevent similar incidents from occurring.

Who generally decides to withhold treatment from an infant with severe disabilities?

As described in chapter 2, most minors lack the capacity to make medical decisions for themselves. As a general rule, their parents, who are presumed to be acting in their best interests, have the authority to make these decisions and are protected by a constitutional right of privacy from unwanted interference by the government. The state can override a parental decision only in exceptional circumstances, typically in cases of abuse, neglect, or abandonment, where parents have endangered the health or safety of their children. The issue in the Baby Doe case was whether the decision to withhold routine surgery that could have enabled an infant with disabilities to live a healthy life constituted such an exception and justified state intervention.[96]

Parental decisions, however, do not take place in a vacuum. In the first place, the baby is usually in a hospital, typically in a neonatal intensive care unit. The parents are grappling with a traumatic and usually unanticipated decision. In the hours and days after birth, their decisions are often heavily influenced by hospital physicians and other staff, and that special role may impose obligations on the physicians and hospital administrators in cases where denial of treatment places the child's life at risk.

Does antidiscrimination law affect the provision of medical care to infants with disabilities?

Yes. Even before enactment of the Americans with Disabilities Act, Section 504 of the Rehabilitation Act prohibited hospitals that received federal financial assistance—which virtually all hospitals do—from discriminating in the provision of medical treatment solely on the basis of disability. A hospital cannot deny access to clearly beneficial medical services because of the infant's disability.[97]

In the wake of the Baby Doe case, the federal government sought to use the Rehabilitation Act in a far more aggressive way. It sent a letter to thousands of hospitals reminding them about Section 504's requirements and then promulgated a special rule regarding infants with disabilities. It required hospitals to post notices in delivery rooms, maternity and pediatric wards, neonatal intensive care units, and nurseries stating that nourishment and medical treatment could not be denied an infant on account of handicap, listing the name and phone number of a child protective agency and alerting people to a toll-free hotline to report cases of suspected withholding of treatment or nourishment.

Although the Supreme Court decided a case challenging these and related rules,[98] it has never decided the underlying questions: (1) whether and under what circumstances parents may withhold medical treatment from infants with disabilities and (2) what are the obligations of physicians, hospitals, and other health care providers in these cases. The Oregon Medicaid decision by the Department of Health and Human Services, discussed earlier in this chapter, sheds some light on these unanswered questions, suggesting that a facility that discourages or restricts access to treatment based on an infant's disability or an assessment of its potential quality of life violates the ADA.

In 1984 Congress took another approach. It enacted amendments to the Child Abuse Prevention and Treatment Act (CAPTA), which represented another attempt to regulate practice in the neonatal unit.[99] These amendments require states that accept federal child abuse funds to prevent the withholding of "medically indicated treatment" from a disabled infant with a life threatening condition.[100] The amendments make exceptions to this rule when, in the "reasonable medical judgment" of a physician, the infant is irreversibly comatose or treatment would merely prolong dying, would not correct all of the life threatening conditions, or would be futile or "virtually futile."[101] In such cases, the hospital has no obligation to engage in heroic treatment but only to provide nutrition, hydration, and medication. However, even this rudimentary treatment may be withheld if, in the reasonable medical judgment of a physician, it is not appropriate.

These amendments and the regulations and guidelines implementing them have brought intense criticism on the ground that they limit physi-cians' ability to engage in the judgments central to the practice of medicine. But as George Annas has pointed out, the "virtually futile" provisions give physicians great latitude to make reasonable medical judgments.[102] Moreover, Annas notes, the regulations do little more than state the law as it has been for decades, that "withholding necessary medical treatment can be child neglect if treatment would be in the child's best interests."[103]

Robert Burt has brought another perspective to CAPTA and linked the immediate life-and-death decision to the broader context of support for families of children with disabilities. "The more basic question is whether the society offers support to all who are in need, or whether the dominant ethos is rigidly competitive and individualistic. . . . In such a society, parents know only that their abnormal child was unwelcome, but that no one would offer assistance to them in their efforts to meet the special needs of this child."[104] By making it more difficult to allow the child to die, Burt concludes, the 1984 legislation, although imperfect, was a "reaffirmation of our vision of ourselves as a nurturant, caretaking community."[105]

How does quality of life figure in the decision whether to treat a newborn with a disability?

Because the concept is so subjective, quality of life generally should not be a factor in decisions of this nature, unless the provision of treatment would be futile or cause the infant needless suffering. The use of a quality of life measure is also suspect because it tends to validate prejudices and stereotypes about the diminished value of the lives of people with disabili-ties and, indeed, allows people with disabilities to die.

The CAPTA guidelines seek to prevent the use of subjective quality of life factors and, to the extent possible, to tie the decision whether to withhold medical treatment from a disabled infant to a medical evaluation of the value of the proposed treatment in sustaining conscious life.[106]

How do emergency medical treatment laws affect obligations to treat infants for whom treatment is futile?

Emergency medical treatment laws generally require physicians to furnish treatment in an emergency, but allow them to decline to do so when they believe their intervention is futile or ethically inappropriate. As a result, these laws have had little impact on Baby Doe cases.

A federal emergency treatment law enacted for entirely different purposes, however, has been interpreted to require physicians to furnish stabilizing treatment to a newborn even when the physician believes treatment is futile or ethically inappropriate. The Emergency Medical Treatment and Active Labor Act was enacted by Congress principally to prevent hospitals from turning away uninsured patients in critical condition or active labor.[107]

Baby K was born with anacephaly, a congenital malformation in which a major portion of the brain, skull, and scalp is missing and which leaves the person permanently unconscious. After surviving for a month in the hospital, Baby K was transferred to a nursing home, but suffered periodic breathing difficulties which required emergency care. The Virginia hospital where Baby K was born and returned for emergency care sought a court order relieving it of the obligation to provide the care on the ground that its staff believed the treatment was futile and ethically inappropriate. The baby's mother insisted on the emergency interventions.

Although recognizing that the federal law was enacted for a different purpose, the federal court of appeals decided by a 2–1 vote that its specific terms required the hospital to provide stabilizing treatment to prevent deterioration of a person's condition. In the court of appeals' view, the statute provides no exception for care that "physicians may deem medically or ethically inappropriate."[108]

The *Baby K* case raises extraordinarily troublesome questions, upsetting the balance CAPTA sought to achieve between providing appropriate care and avoiding futile gestures. It remains to be seen whether the Baby K approach will itself survive.

DISCRIMINATION ON THE BASIS OF RACE, GENDER, AND ETHNICITY

In addition to discrimination on the basis of disability, people with mental disabilities have also suffered discrimination in the delivery of treatment and services because of their race, gender, or ethnic background. There are numerous reports of mental health and developmental disability agencies withholding service to people of color or of nonmajority cultures. As a result, legislation has been enacted mandating that traditionally underserved populations be represented in the planning and implementation process of mental health, mental retardation, vocational, education, and early intervention programs.

The problems go far beyond underserving some groups. Disturbingly differential treatment based on race, particularly in the mental health system, has been documented for many years. Both professional and general circulation publications have reported that African Americans, particularly men, are disproportionately institutionalized in state psychiatric hospitals and involuntarily hospitalized far more frequently than whites.[109] One recent study of a state's psychiatric services found that while Tennessee's African Americans compose 16% of the general population, they represent 30% of involuntarily committed patients in mental health facilities.[110]

The problems of racial differentials are not limited to excessive hospitalization. For years psychiatrists and sociologists have noted that African Americans are disproportionately diagnosed with schizophrenia, as compared to whites, and that these differentials are, in significant measure, a product of misdiagnosis.[111] In the Tennessee study, for example, 48 percent of all persons involuntarily institutionalized and 37 percent of all persons served in outpatient clinics carrying a diagnosis of schizophrenia were African American.[112] The consequences of misdiagnosis are considerable and harmful. To start with, it means that the correct treatment is not given. And, of course, the wrong medication, one that may be accompanied by many untoward side effects, is given. And since the person does not get better, the system becomes ever more involved with, and often punitive toward, the patient. One researcher explained these consequences for African Americans who are properly diagnosed as manic depressive but are instead labeled as suffering from schizophrenia. "Correct evaluations fail to occur and the patient does not get the benefit of lithium carbonate therapy, which leads to further psychotic break, increased recidivism, and unwanted neurological and other adverse effects of long-term neuroleptic therapy. When hospitalized again, the prior diagnosis plays a heavy role in arriving at the current diagnosis, thus repeating the cycle of misdiagnosis, improper management and an increase in iatrogenic morbidity."[113] The "iatrogenic morbidity"—harm caused by medical interventions themselves—referred to has been documented as well. African Americans suffer from tardive dyskinesia, the irreversible movement disorder caused by neuroleptic medications, at twice the rate of whites.[114]

Other disturbing, though not necessarily replicated, findings have been made as well: that African Americans receive higher doses and more high potency neuroleptic medications than whites,[115] that African Americans are more subject to "as needed" medications than whites,[116] and that black patients displaying the same behavior as white patients are physically restrained at four times the rate of whites.[117] As one of the leading researchers in the field has concluded, "The evidence of different treatment experiences can no longer be regarded as 'scanty, piecemeal, and inconclusive.'"[118]

The pattern of differential treatment of other ethnic groups is equally unmistakable, often complicated by language and cultural barriers, conscious and unconscious stereotypes, socioeconomic deprivation, and different patterns of use of social and medical services.[119]

There is strong evidence of mistreatment of women in the mental health system as well. Gender biases affect the diagnosis of women, and at the same time some of their real needs are not addressed. For example, until very recently, little attention was paid to special situations of mothers with chronic mental illness.[120] As one group of researchers put it bluntly, "the parenting status of these women appears to be largely ignored by mental health professionals."[121] Despite the intimate involvement of the mental health system in their lives, it is hardly uncommon for mental health professionals to ignore their role as mother, to view pregnancy exclusively as a medical condition rather than as a precursor to motherhood, and to fail to consider the needs of hospitalized mothers to maintain relationships with their children. When parenting is considered at all, it is sometimes in a negative light.[122]

In addition, the mental health system has paid scant attention to what, for an enormous number of women, is a central experience of their lives, physical or sexual abuse. The percentage of women with serious mental illness who have been subjected to abuse is truly astounding. In one recent study of 131 women in an outpatient clinic for people with chronic mental illness, 45 percent had been sexually abused, 51 percent had been physically abused, and 22 percent had experienced neglect during childhood. Two of 3 women reported abuse in some form.[123] Yet women who have experienced abuse report that clinicians either ignore their history of abuse or ascribe the woman's emotional problems to an entirely different problem.[124]

What effect have antidiscrimination laws had on these practices?

To date, very little. The nation's antidiscrimination laws have long prohibited discrimination on the basis of race and gender. They have been on the books for thirty years, yet they have rarely if ever been invoked to challenge discriminatory practices in the mental health or mental retardation systems. One can only speculate on the reasons for this: differential treatment is often difficult to detect; proving it in a court of law can be a daunting task, especially in view of the likely defense that the practitioner exercised appropriate clinical judgment in each individual case; and it is hard to figure out an appropriate remedy for the harm that has been inflicted. After all, the goal is to get the right diagnosis and treatment; once that is accomplished, people ask no more of the system.[125]

Nonetheless, there is precedent for challenging racially and ethnically disparate treatment in the mental disability service system. In one noteworthy and longstanding case, African American and Hispanic children successfully challenged their disproportionate placement in special schools for emotionally disturbed children.[126] Litigation and other forms of advocacy may bring similar results for other people with mental disabilities whose civil rights have been violated on the basis of race, ethnicity, or gender.

Notes

1. Perlin, *On Sanism*, 16 Southern Methodist University Law Review 373 (1992).

2. Fisher, *Disclosure, Discrimination, and the ADA*, unpublished paper, quotation reprinted in United States Congress Office of Technology Assessment, *Psychiatric Disabilities, Employment and the Americans with Disabilities Act*, OTA-BP-BBS-124 (1994) at 68.

3. 29 U.S.C. § 701 and following.

4. Pub. L. No. 100-430, 102 Stat. 1619 (1988), codified at 42 U.S.C. § 3601 and following.

5. 42 U.S.C. § 12101 and following.

6. 42 U.S.C. § 12101(b)(1).

7. S. Rep. No. 116, 101st Cong., 1st Sess. 20 (1989). The background and meaning of the integration mandate is discussed in Cook, *The Americans with Disabilities Act: The Move to Integration*, 64 Temple Law Review 393 (1991).

8. 42 U.S.C. § 12101(a)(2).

9. 56 Federal Register 35703 (July 26, 1991).

10. 42 U.S.C § 12102(2).

11. 42 U.S.C. § 12211(b). Congress also said, gratuitously, that homosexuality and bisexuality are not disabilities.

12. 42 U.S.C. § 12210(b).

13. 29 U.S.C. § 793 and 794.

14. For an overview of employment of people with psychiatric disabilities, see Office of Technology Assessment, *supra*.

15. Rutman, *How Psychiatric Disability Expresses Itself as a Barrier to Employment*,

Resource Paper presented at Consensus Validation Conference, "Strategies to Secure and Maintain Employment for People with Long-Term Mental Illness," National Institute on Disability and Rehabilitation Research (1992).

16. Mancuso, *Case Studies on Reasonable Accommodations For Workers with Psychiatric Disabilities* (California Department of Mental Health 1993).

17. Rutman, *supra.*

18. Blanck, *Empirical Study of the Employment Provisions of the Americans with Disabilities Act: Methods, Preliminary Findings and Implications,* 22 New Mexico Law Review 119, 186–89 (Tables 6 and 7) (1992).

19. Kirszner, Baron & Rutman, *Employer Participation in Supported and Transitional Employment for Persons with Long-Term Mental Illness,* Final Report to the National Institute of Rehabilitation and Disability Research, Matrix Research Institute (1992); Blanck, *Empirical Study of the Employment Provisions of the Americans with Disabilities Act, supra.*

20. School Board of Nassau County v. Arline, 480 U.S. 273, 287 (1986).

21. For a guide to employment discrimination provisions of the Americans with Disabilities Act, see Haggard, *Reasonable Accommodation of Individuals with Mental Disabilities and Psychoactive Substance Abuse Disorders under Title I of the Americans with Disabilities Act.* 43 Journal of Urban and Contemporary Law 343 (1993). Mental Health Law Project, *Mental Health Consumers in the Work Place: How the Americans with Disabilities Act Protects You Against Employment Discrimination* (1992); Mancuso, *Reasonable Accommodation for Workers with Psychiatric Disabilities,* 4 Psychosocial Rehabilitation Journal 3 (1990); Zuckerman, Debenham & Moore, *The ADA and People with Mental Illness, A Resource Manual for Employers,* American Bar Association and National Mental Health Association (1993).

22. Allen v. Heckler, 780 F.2d 64 (D.C. Cir. 1985).

23. 42 U.S.C. § 12111(8).

24. For discussions of reasonable accommodations for people with mental disabilities, see Harp, *A Crazy Folks' Guide to Reasonable Accommodation* (1992); Mancuso, *Case Studies on Reasonable Accommodations for Workers with Psychiatric Disabilities, supra.* Mancuso, *Reasonable Accommodation for Workers with Psychiatric Disabilities;* National Institute on Disability and Rehabilitation Research, *Consensus Validation Conference: Strategies to Secure and Maintain Employment for People with Long-Term Mental Illness* (1992); Zuckerman, Debenham & Moore, *supra. See also* Haggard, *Reasonable Accommodation of Individuals with Mental Disabilities and Psychoactive Substance Abuse Disorders under Title I of the Americans with Disabilities Act,* 43 Journal of Urban and Contemporary Law 343 (1993).

25. Equal Employment Opportunity Commission. *A Technical Assistance Manual on the Employment Provisions (Title I) of the Americans with Disabilities Act* (1992) at III-9.

26. For a discussion of the development of a reasonable accommodation for a salesperson with bipolar (manic depressive) disorder, see Blanck, Handley, Andersen, Wallach & Tenney, *Implementing Reasonable Accommodations under ADR under the ADA: The Case of a White-Collar Employee with Bipolar Mental Illness,* 18 Mental and Physical Disability Law Reporter 458 (1994).

27. 42 U.S.C. § 12112(c)(2).

28. 42 U.S.C. § 12112(c)(3). *See* Feldblum, *Medical Examinations and Inquiries under the Americans with Disabilities Act: A View from the Inside,* 64 Temple Law Review 521 (1991).

29. 42 U.S.C § 12112(b)(4).

30. Mancuso, *Case Studies on Reasonable Accommodations For Workers with Psychiatric Disabilities, supra*; Office of Technology Assessment, *supra*.

31. 42 U.S.C. § 12112(b)(6).

32. 42 U.S.C. § 12112(b)(7).

33. 42 U.S.C. § 12111, 12113(b).

34. 29 C.F.R. § 1630.2(r).

35. 42 U.S.C. § 12101(5).

36. 29 C.F.R. §§ 1630.2(r), 1630.15(b)(2).

37. Doe v. Colautti, 592 F.2d 704 (3d Cir. 1979); Doe v. Devine, 545 F. Supp. 576 (D.D.C. 1982), *aff'd on other grounds* 703 F.2d 1319 (D.C. Cir. 1983).

38. Equal Employment Opportunity Commission, Interim Enforcement Guidance, EEOC Notice N-915.002 (1993).

39. 42 U.S.C. § 12132.

40. 42 U.S.C. § 12131.

41. The list of forms of discrimination is taken from regulations issued by the United States Department of Justice, 38 C.F.R. § 35.130.

42. Letter from Louis W. Sullivan, Secretary of Health and Human Services, to Barbara Roberts, Governor of Oregon, August 3, 1992, with attached memorandum. Oregon revised the plan to eliminate reliance on quality of life and resubmitted it to HHS. It was then approved.

43. Concerned Citizens to Save Dreher Park Center v. City of West Palm Beach, 846 F. Supp. 986 (S.D. Fla. 1994).

44. *Id.* at 992.

45. Easley v. Snider, No. 93-0224 (E.D. Pa. 1993); *see also* Bosteder v. Soliz, No. 93201817A (Sup. Ct. of Thurston Co., Wash.). *But see* Marshall v. McMahon, 22 Cal. Reptr. 2d 220 (Cal Ct. App. 1993) (decided under § 504 of the Rehabilitation Act).

46. Easley v. Snider, 36 F.3d 297 (3d Cir. 1994).

47. Dees v. Austin Travis County Mental Health and Mental Retardation, No. A 93 CA 525 SS (W.D. Tex. 1994).

48. 28 C.F.R. § 35.130(d).

49. Helen L. v. Didario, 46 F.3d 325, 338 (3d Cir. 1995).

50. Traynor v. Turnage, 485 U.S. 535 (1985).

51. Jackson v. Fort Stanton Hosp. and Training School, 757 F. Supp. 1243 (D.N.M. 1990), reversed in part on other grounds, 964 F.2d 980 (10th Cir. 1992); Homeward Bound v. Hissom, No. 85-C-437-E (N.D. Okla. 1987).

52. 469 U.S. 297 (1985).

53. South Carolina Department of Disabilities and Special Needs, Department of Mental Health, Department of Social Services and Bazelon Center for Mental Health Law, *Implementing the ADA in South Carolina to Ensure Access for People with Mental Disabilities* (1994).

54. Clark v. Virginia Board of Bar Examiners, 880 F. Supp. 430 (E.D. Va. 1995); Ellen S. v. Florida Board of Bar Examiners, No. 94-0429-CIV-KING (S.D. Fla. 1994); Medical Society of New Jersey v. Jacobs, 93-3670 (WGB), (D.N.J. 1993); *In re* Underwood, Docket No. BAR-03-21 (Maine Supreme Judicial Court December 7, 1993); *In re* Petition of Frickey, (Sup. Ct. of Minnesota 1994).

55. *See generally* Piltch, Katz & Valles, *The Americans with Disabilities Act and Professional Licensing,* 17 Mental and Physical Disability Law Reporter 556 (1993).

56. Stanley v. Illinois, 405 U.S. 645 (1972).

57. Brakel et al., *supra,* at 509. They cite a Texas clerk who was asked about inquiries on these subjects. The clerk is reported to have replied, "Are you serious? How can I ask a person if he's crazy?" *Id.* citing Allen, Ferster & Weihofen, *Mental Impairment and Legal Incompetency 303 (1968).*

58. Hayman, *Perceptions of Justice: Law, Politics and the Mentally Retarded Parent,* 103 Harvard Law Review 1201 (1990); Note, *Retarded Parents in Neglect Proceedings: The Erroneous Assumption of Parental Inadequacy,* 31 Stanford Law Review 785 (1979).

59. *In re* Welfare of JJB, 390 N.W. 2d. 274 (Minn. 1986).

60. *See, e.g.,* Wright v. Alexandria Division of Social Services, 433 S.E. 2d 500 (Va. App. 1993) (allows evidence of mental retardation in the context of the effect of retardation on developing parenting skills; *In re* Lori D., 510 A.2d 421 (R.I. 1986)(allows denial of parental rights based on consideration of mental illness or mental retardation).

61. Hayman, *Perceptions of Justice, supra*; Stefan, *Whose Egg Is It Anyway?: Reproductive Rights of Incarcerated, Institutionalized and Incompetent Women,* 13 Nova Law Review 404 (1989). *See* Wisconsin *ex rel.* Torrance P. v. Raymond C., 522 N.W.2d 243 (Wisc. Ct. of App. 1994) (substituted judgment for incompetent woman authorizing abortion).

62. 42 U.S.C. § 12182(b)(1)(B).

63. A complete list of public accommodations is found at 42 U.S.C. § 2181(7).

64. The ADA makes an exception for places that have five or fewer rooms and are occupied by the owner. 42 U.S.C. § 12191(7)(A).

65. *See* 28 C.F.R. § 36.212.

66. *Id.*

67. University Interscholastic League v. Buchanan, 848 S.W. 2d 298 (Tex. Ct. of App. 1993). Two federal courts of appeals, however, ruled against a student in similar cases. Sandison v. Michigan High School Athletic Ass'n, 64 F.3d 1029 (6th Cir. 1995); Pottgen v. Missouri State High School Activities Ass'n, 40 F.3d 926 (8th Cir. 1994).

68. Park v. University of North Carolina at Wilmington, No. 93-750-5-D (E.D.N.C. 1993).

69. Southeastern Community College v. Davis, 442 U.S. 397 (1979).

70. City of Cleburne v. Cleburne Living Center, 473 U.S. 432 (1985).

71. Pub. L. No. 100-430, 102 Stat. 1619 (1988), codified at 42 U.S.C. §§ 3601–19, 3631, and 28 U.S.C. §§ 2341–42. Unlike the Rehabilitation Act, the Fair Housing Amendments Act is not limited to recipients of federal financial assistance.

72. For an analysis of the impact of the Fair Housing Amendments Act and its relationship to prior efforts to prohibit discrimination against people with mental disabilities, see Kanter, *A Home of One's Own: The Fair Housing Amendments Act of 1988 and Housing Discrimination Against People with Disabilities,* 43 American University Law Review 925 (1994); Simring, *The Impact of Federal Antidiscrimination Laws on Housing for People with Mental Disabilities,* 59 George Washington Law Review 413 (1991).

A booklet for laypeople describing the rights of people with disabilities under the Act is Bazelon Center for Mental Health Law, *What Does Fair Housing Mean to People with Disabilities* (1993).

73. The definition of disability in the Fair Housing Act is virtually identical to the

definition of disability in the ADA. It includes impairments, such as mental retardation and psychiatric conditions, that substantially limit one or more major life activities. It also includes people with a record of a disability or who are regarded by others as having a disability. The definition excludes people who are current unlawful users of controlled drugs; former or recovering drug abusers are covered, however. *See* United States v. Southern Management, 955 F.2d 914 (4th Cir. 1992).

74. United States v. Scott, 788 F. Supp. 1555 (D. Kansas 1992); People Helpers Foundation v. Richmond, 781 F. Supp. 1132 (E.D. Va. 1992).

75. There is an exception for housing specifically developed for a group of people with disabilities. In that case, the question would be asked to determine whether the applicant qualifies for the unit.

76. 24 C.F.R. § 100.202(c).

77. Cason v. Rochester Housing Authority, 748 F. Supp. 1002 (W.D.N.Y. 1990).

78. 42 U.S.C. § 3604(f)(9). However, if a reasonable accommodation would eliminate the threat to health or safety or to the physical structure, the landlord has an obligation to provide it.

79. 42 U.S.C. § 3604(f)(3)(A). The Fair Housing Act also contains accessibility requirements for all multifamily units for four or more families built for occupancy March, 1991 or later. 42 U.S.C. 3604(f)(3)(C). The Department of Housing and Urban Development has written guidelines for accessibility. Providers of assisted housing are required by Section 504 of the Rehabilitation Act to bear the costs necessary to make their housing programs structurally accessible.

80. 42 U.S.C. § 3604(f)(3)(C).

81. Majors v. Housing Authority of DeKalb County, 652 F.2d 454 (5th Cir. 1981); Whittier Terrace Associates v. Hampshire, 532 N.E. 2d 712 (Mass. Ct. App. 1989).

82. Citywide v. Penfield, 409 N.E.2d 140 (Mass. 1991). *See also* Roe v. Sugar River Mill Associates, 820 F. Supp. 636 (D.N.H. 1993)(person whose occupancy may pose a direct threat to others may not be excluded unless housing provider determines that it cannot make a reasonable accommodation that would alleviate the threat).

83. Horizon House Developmental Services v. Township of Upper South Hampton, 804 F. Supp. 683 (E.D. Pa. 1992), *aff'd* 995 F.2d 217 (3d Cir. 1993); United States v. Village of Marshall, 787 F. Supp. 1555 (D. Kansas 1992).

84. *See, e.g.,* Oxford House v. City of St. Louis, 843 F. Supp. 1556 (E.D. Mo. 1994); Oxford House v. Town of Babylon, 819 F. Supp. 1179 (E.D.N.Y. 1993); United States v. City of Plainfield, 769 F. Supp. 1329 (D.N.J. 1991); United States v. City of Taylor, 798 F. Supp. 442 (E.D. Mich. 1992). The Fair Housing Act contains an exemption allowing reasonable regulation of the maximum number of occupants allowed to occupy a dwelling. In City of Edmonds v. Oxford House, No. 94-23 (U.S. May 15, 1995), the Supreme Court held that this exemption does not apply to ordinances limiting the number of unrelated people in a dwelling.

85. Stewart B. McKinney Foundation, Inc. v. Town Plan and Zoning Commission of Fairfield, 790 F. Supp. 1197 (D. Conn. 1992); Oxford House v. City of Cherry Hill, 799 F. Supp. 450 (D.N.J. 1991); Easter Seals Society of New Jersey v. Township of North Bergen, 798 F. Supp. 228 (D.N.J. 1992).

86. Marbrunak v. City of Stow, 974 F.2d 43 (6th Cir. 1992); Potomac Group Home v. Montgomery County, 823 F. Supp. 1285 (D. Md. 1993). In United States v. City of

Philadelphia, 838 F. Supp. 223 (E.D. Pa. 1993), the court found that the duty of reasonable accommodation prevented enforcement of a rule requiring a back yard where a side yard existed. *See also* Bangerter v. Orem City Corp. 46 F.3d 1491 (10th Cir. 1995) (zoning rule requiring 24-hour supervision of residents unlawful unless city can show that it is necessary to avoid a direct threat).

87. *Potomac Group Home v. Montgomery County, supra.*

88. Federation v. Town of Oyster Bay, CV93-2070 (ADS) (E.D.N.Y. 1994).

89. Martin v. Constance, 843 F. Supp. 1321 (E.D. Mo. 1994).

90. Metalsky v. Mercy Haven, Inc. 156 Misc. 2d 558, 594 N.Y.S. 2d 24 (N.Y. Sup. Ct. 1993). *See also* Daniels v. Christofeletti, 542 N.Y.S. 2d 482 (1992); Carr v. Friends of the Homeless, No. 89-LE 3942-S (Hampden County, Mass. Housing Court 1990); Serrezze v. YWCA of Western Mass 30 Mass. App. 639, 572 N.E. 2d 581 (1991). *Compare* Helping Out People Everywhere v. Deitch, 589 N.Y.S. 2d 744 (1992) (shelter provider which "licensed" residents on a day-to-day basis did not create status of tenant or roomer, even though individual had remained fifteen months).

91. Housing and Community Development Act of 1992, Pub. L. No. 102-550, §§ 621 et seq.

92. See 24 C.F.R. pts. 880, 881, 883, 884, and 886, 59 Fed. Reg. 22916 (May 3, 1994) (assisted housing) and 24 C.F.R. pts. 945 and 960, 59 Fed. Reg. 17652 (April 13, 1994) (public housing).

93. For a summary of these provisions, see Mental Health Law Project, *Mental Health Developments*, 26 Clearinghouse Review 1079 (1993). For a broader description, see Milstein, *The New Segregation of Elderly and Mentally Ill Tenants in Publicly Supported Housing*, 2 Housing Center Bulletin No. 2 (August 1993).

94. The number for people with hearing impairments is 1-800-927-9275.

95. *In re* the Treatment and Care of Infant Doe, No. GU8204-004A (Ind. Cir. Ct., Apr. 12, 1982), *cert. denied sub nom.*, Infant Doe v. Bloomington Hosp., 464 U.S. 961 (1983).

96. Wisconsin v. Yoder, 406 U.S. 205, 233–34 (1972).

97. Bowen v. American Hospital Association, 476 U.S. 610 (1986).

98. *Id.* In a case brought by the American Hospital Association and others, the Court sidestepped the critical questions concerning the provider's obligations and instead focused on the fact that the record in the case showed no instances where the parents failed to consent to the withholding of treatment. Under these circumstances, it held, there was no justification for the rules under Section 504. Still, the Court acknowledged that discrimination could be involved if the hospital and its staff are implicated in the decision to terminate treatment solely because the infant has a disability. As a result, the decision left the important questions undecided.

99. 42 U.S.C. § 5101-5.

100. 42 U.S.C. § 5101.

101. 42 U.S.C. § 5102.

102. Annas, *The Rights of Patients, supra*, at 213.

103. *Id.* at 214.

104. Burt, *The Treatment of Handicapped Newborns: Is There a Role for Law?* 1 Issues in Law and Medicine 279, 289 (1986).

105. *Id.* at 290.

106. 50 Fed. Reg. 14,889 (1985) (codified at 45 C.F.R. app. to pt. 1340).

107. 42 U.S.C. § 1395dd.

108. Matter of Baby K., 16 F.3d 590 (4th Cir. 1994).

109. Snowden & Cheung, *Use of Inpatient Mental Health Services by Members of Ethnic Minority Groups,* 45 American Psychologist 347 (1990); Rosenthal & Carty, *Impediments to Services and Advocacy for Black and Hispanic People with Mental Illness* (Mental Health Law Project 1990); Lindsay & Paul, *Involuntary Commitments to Public Mental Institutions: Issues Involving the Overrepresentation of Blacks and Assessment of Relevant Function,* 106 Psychological Bulletin 171 (1989); Lindsey, Paul & Mariotto, *Urban Psychiatric Commitments: Disability and Dangerous Behavior of Black and White Recent Admissions,* 40 Hospital and Community Psychiatry 286 (1989); Ramm, *Over-Committed,* 17 Southern Exposure 14 (1989).
The Lindsay & Paul study looked at a sample of 45,000 patients and found that in fourteen of the sixteen jurisdictions studied, blacks were involuntarily committed more frequently than whites. Ramm found that in Florida, African Americans were involuntarily committed five times as frequently as whites.

110. Lawson, Hepler, Holladay & Cuffel, *Race as a Factor in Inpatient and Outpatient Admissions Diagnosis,* 45 Hospital and Community Psychiatry 72 (1994).

111. *See,* e.g., Jones & Gray, *Problems in Diagnosing Schizophrenia and Affective Disorders Among Blacks,* 37 Hospital and Community Psychiatry 61 (1986); Neighbors, Jackson, Campbell et al., *Problems in Diagnosing Schizophrenia and Affective Disorders: A Review and Suggestion for Research,* 25 Community Mental Health Journal 61 (1986); Bell & Mehta, *Misdiagnosis of Black Patients with Manic Depressive Illness,* 73 Journal of the National Medical Association 141 (1981) and 72 Journal of the National Medical Association 101 (1980); Thomas & Sillin, *Racism and Psychiatry* (1972).

112. Lawson, Hepler, Holladay & Cuffel, *supra.*

113. Bell & Mehta, *supra.*

114. Glazer, Morgenstern, & Doucette, *Race and Tardive Dyskinesia Among Outpatients at a CMHC,* 45 Hospital and Community Psychiatry 38 (1994). These researchers sought to determine whether covarying demographic factors like age and socioeconomic status could explain the correlation. The authors found three covariates but statistical analysis led them to conclude that "the other three covariates explained very little of the crude effect of race."

115. Glazer, Morgenstern & Doucette, *supra.*

116. Flaherty & Meagher, *Measuring Racial Bias in Inpatient Treatment,* 137 American Journal of Psychiatry 379 (1980).

117. Bond, DiCandia & MacKenzie, *Response to Violence in a Psychiatric Setting: the Role of the Patient's Race,* 14 Personality and Social Psychology Bulletin 448 (1988). Other studies, however, find less evidence of disproportionate use of seclusion and restraint against African Americans. Lawson, Yesavage & Werner, *Race, Violence and Psychopathology,* 45 Journal of Clinical Psychiatry 294 (1989).

118. Adebimpe, *Race, Racism and Epidemiological Surveys,* 45 Hospital and Community Psychiatry 27 (1994).

119. Rosenthal & Carty, *supra.*

120. Apfel & Handel, *Madness and Loss of Motherhood: Sexuality, Reproduction and Long-Term Mental Illness* (1993).

121. Nicholson, Geller, Fisher & Dion, *State Policies and Programs that Address the Needs of Mentally Ill Mothers in the Public Sector*, 44 Hospital and Community Psychiatry 484 (1993).

122. *Id.*

123. Muenzenmaier, Meyer, Struening & Ferber, *Childhood Abuse and Neglects Among Women Outpatients with Chronic Mental Illness*, 44 Hospital and Community Psychiatry 666 (1993).

124. Stefan, *The Protection Racket: Rape Trauma Syndrome, Psychiatric Labeling, and the Law*, 88 Northwestern University Law Review 1271, 1312–19 (1994).

125. *See* Wing, *Title VI and Health Facilities: Forms without Substance*, 30 Hastings Law Journal 137 (1978).

126. Lora v. Board of Education, 623 F.2d 248 (2d Cir. 1980).

VI

The Right to Treatment and Services

The existence and scope of a right to treatment have been among the most widely discussed issues in mental disability law for three decades. To many, the idea seems only just: if a person desires mental health care or habilitation,[1] society ought to provide it.

But the details are surprisingly complicated. Who has such a right? Who must provide it? Where? And at whose expense? What is the standard for measuring the adequacy of any treatment that is provided? Does the right to treatment include housing and supportive services in the community? What recourse does a person have to enforce a right to treatment if it has been violated? Who decides these questions?

The debate about these and related issues has been fierce. At its root the right to treatment is an assertion that the government has an obligation not just to protect institutionalized individuals or leave them alone, but to provide services that will improve their lives. There is no reference in the Constitution to a right to treatment for people with mental disabilities or anyone else. In a society where access to basic health care is not considered a legal right, the concept of a constitutional right to treatment for people with mental disabilities requires some special justification.

Paradoxically, the right to treatment is, in practice, among the most widely recognized *moral* rights. The idea that people confined in institutions have a right to treatment or habilitation is acknowledged in some form by the laws of virtually every state and, more importantly, in the minds of an increasing number of administrators of these facilities. And if there is a right to treatment in institutions, does it not follow that such a right should exist in the community as well? In chapter 5, we considered how antidiscrimination law could affect access to medical care for people with mental disabilities. This chapter will discuss other approaches to these questions, beginning with the constitutional right to treatment and then considering the laws that Congress and the states have enacted creating entitlements to services, income, housing, health care, and education.

THE ORIGINS AND SCOPE OF THE RIGHT TO TREATMENT

What are the origins of the right to treatment?

The first serious discussion of a right to treatment began in the 1960s largely in response to appalling conditions in state psychiatric hospitals and institutions for people with mental retardation. At the time, a great many of these facilities were overcrowded and understaffed, offering only custodial care in the most degrading, unsanitary, and stultifying conditions. Even in the best of these institutions, the most common sight was of people congregated for hours in day rooms in front of a television set no one watched—the dead end of life. At the time, many "experts" in the field thought that protective custodial confinement—asylum in its best sense—was the most one could expect for the majority of the inmates of these institutions, the "chronic" and "incurable" "cases" locked in the back wards of facilities for "imbeciles" and "idiots." By the 1950s and 1960s, new theories of care and treatment were emerging. For mental retardation, Wolf Wolfensberger and Gunnar Dybwad, among others, promoted the developmental model, arguing that people with mental retardation are able to learn or be "habilitated," acquiring skills useful for living in the world.[2] Depending on the individual, these can range from personal hygiene and self-care to cooking and cleaning to money management and working. They also preached the theory of "normalization," urging that the more people with mental retardation live like others in the community, the greater their capacity to adopt behaviors and acquire skills the community values.[3]

In psychiatry, too, the idea that mere custodial care was appropriate for people with serious mental disorders had lost its dominance, especially after the discovery of antipsychotic medication in the 1950s. Treatment, not mere confinement, was seen as not only possible but essential. Visionaries in community mental health demonstrated that, with proper treatment and supports, people with psychiatric disabilities could live in the community.

It was against this background of deplorable institutional conditions and profound change in the fields of mental health and mental retardation that the right to treatment was born. The fact that most individuals confined in institutions were there on the authority of the state lent even greater urgency to the perceived need for a legal basis to establish a right to treatment. Couldn't the state be required to do something to improve their lives in exchange? In 1960, Morton Birnbaum, a doctor and lawyer, published a paper in the American Bar Association's journal entitled "The Right to Treatment."[4] A great deal of scholarly interest ensued, followed by litigation to develop a constitutional right to treatment and apply it to the worst of these institutions.

What are some of the legal bases for the right to treatment?

The legal analysis begins with the Fourteenth Amendment to the Constitution, which guarantees that the government will not deprive a person of liberty without due process of law.[5] A state's act in civilly confining an individual with a mental disability in an institution constitutes a deprivation of liberty. Does the state have an obligation to provide something in return? Is that something treatment?

The right to treatment was first recognized by a court in 1966 in *Rouse v. Cameron*, a case involving a man who had been committed to a mental institution after having been found not guilty by reason of insanity. In his petition for release from the hospital, Rouse argued that if he was not released, he was entitled to receive more treatment than the facility had provided. Finding that "the purpose of involuntary confinement is treatment, not punishment,"[6] and that the law under which Rouse was committed guaranteed him treatment, the court held that the state must live up to that purpose and provide Rouse appropriate treatment. Writing for the court, Judge David Bazelon also suggested that the Constitution itself might provide a basis for a right to treatment.

A few years later, the United States Supreme Court held that the Constitution prohibits confining a man found incompetent to stand trial unless there is a likelihood that institutionalization will result in progress toward the restoration of competence. As the Court said, "At the least, due process requires that the nature and duration of commitment bear some reasonable relation to the purpose for which the individual is committed."[7]

The first decision to find a constitutional right to treatment was *Wyatt v. Stickney,* a 1971 case in which an Alabama federal court held that, in exchange for the massive deprivation of their liberty, people institutionalized for a mental illness "have a constitutional right to receive such individual treatment as will give each of them a reasonable opportunity to be cured or to improve his or her mental condition."[8] The court reasoned that where individuals have committed no crime and have been confined solely because of a mental disability, the purpose of confinement must be treatment, not punishment. Adopting what has come to be known as the quid pro quo theory (literally "something for something"), the court ruled that the state must provide such individuals with treatment in exchange for the loss of their liberty.

In a later order the court ruled that people with mental retardation have similar rights to "such individual habilitation as will give each of them a realistic opportunity to lead a more useful and meaningful life and to return to society."[9] *Wyatt* also held that treatment must comply with the principle of "the least restrictive alternative," that is, that form of involuntary care least restrictive of a person's liberty.[10] This principle is discussed more fully in chapter 2.

The term *treatment* covers a broad range of services that the state must provide to the individuals it confines to improve their physical or mental condition and to offer training in self-care and other skills. In order to satisfy the requirements of the right to treatment, the institution must have enough space, materials, and trained staff members to provide the necessary services. The court order in *Wyatt* addressed minimal staff-patient ratios, minimum hours of therapy, the use of restrictive procedures, food quality, and much more. Many of these standards are reproduced in appendix A.

Wyatt implemented treatment and habilitation rights through an individualized plan for each person that describes the kinds of services the individual needs, how they are to be provided and by whom, and how progress will be evaluated. The standard for mental health treatment plans, which was updated in 1992, provides for an individualized treatment plan developed with the active participation of the patient that is based on (1) a statement of the individual's specific problems and needs; (2) a statement of the individual's strengths; (3) a statement of the least restrictive treatment conditions necessary to achieve the purposes of commitment and the goals of the treatment plan; (4) a description of intermediate and long term treatment goals, with a timetable for achieving them; (5) a specification of staff responsibility and a description of proposed staff involvement; (6) specific and measurable criteria, written in understandable terms, for release to a less restrictive treatment condition and discharge; (7) a notation of therapeutic tasks and labor to be performed; (8) an assessment of restrictions on physical activity based on medical condition; and (9) an individualized discharge plan that identifies the residential, clinical, social, and vocational services the patient will require on discharge.[11] Progress must be recorded in the chart according to specified schedules, and the plan must be reviewed and updated as appropriate no less than every three months. A quality assurance procedure such as peer review must also be in place to assess, among other things, the need for continued hospitalization.

The requirements for habilitation plans for people with mental retardation are similar. The plans must be based on an individualized evaluation, the establishment of goals, the development of a program to meet those goals, and a process for assessing whether they have been achieved. The overarching objective is normalization through a habilitation program that maximizes the resident's abilities to cope with the environment and develops and realizes his or her fullest potential. *Wyatt's* approach to the habilitation of people with mental retardation, moreover, explicitly raised questions concerning the relationship between habilitation and institutionalization. For example, one standard provides that admission to the facility is inappropriate unless institutionalization is the least restrictive habilitation setting feasible and services and programs in the community cannot afford the individual adequate habilitation. Consistent with the principle of the least restrictive alternative, the *Wyatt* standards require the institution to attempt to move residents (1) from more to less structured living; (2) from larger to smaller facilities; (3) from larger to smaller living units; (4) from group to individual residence; (5) from segregated from the community to integrated into community living; and (6) from dependent to independent living.[12]

The quid pro quo approach was not the only theory of the right to treatment advanced during the 1970s. In another influential ruling involving the notorious Willowbrook State School, a facility that was the source of one of Geraldo Rivera's first television exposes, a federal court in New York found that institutionalized persons have a constitutional right to protection from harm.[13] This concept derived in part from the Eighth Amendment to the Constitution, which guarantees protection against cruel and unusual punishment.[14] The court reasoned that the state had an obligation to prevent people in its custody from suffering the barbaric conditions of Willowbrook and that residents could only be protected from harm if treatment or habilitation were made available to them.

The right to protection from harm raised the more profound question whether institutions could ever be run in such a way as to protect their residents from harm. From the start of right to treatment litigation, many advocates had urged that rights could be protected only if alternative sites as well as methods of treatment were developed. The Willowbrook litigation ultimately led to the closing of the facility and its replacement with small group residences and community-based programs. Many other cases followed, and—especially in the field of mental retardation—right to treatment litigation often explicitly sought to close large institutions and replace them with community-based programs.[15]

Other legal theories supporting alternatives to institutions as part of a right to treatment appeared. For example, the right to placement in the least restrictive placement, a product of the reformed civil commitment laws discussed in chapter 2, led to arguments to develop community-based alternatives to institutional care. One early case found that one of the newly enacted civil commitment laws imposed an obligation to develop a full array of community-based alternatives to psychiatric hospitalization to meet the needs of people who are either involuntarily committed or at risk of involuntary commitment.[16]

The Supreme Court never directly addressed these theories of a right to treatment. In 1975 it decided *O'Connor v. Donaldson*,[17] a case that both influenced the development of the right to treatment and established a constitutional standard for civil commitment, as discussed in chapter 2. Kenneth Donaldson had been involuntarily confined by the State of Florida for fifteen years and sued for money damages and for his release on the ground that he was not dangerous, could survive safely in the community with the help of family or friends, and was receiving no treatment at all. Although hailed by many at the time as a right to treatment case, *O'Connor* did not directly decide whether the Constitution recognizes a right to treatment. Instead, it held that Donaldson must be released because he was not dangerous and was receiving no treatment. The Court ruled that "without more"—the "more" interpreted to mean treatment—the state could not confine a person who was not dangerous and who was capable of surviving outside of the institution with the help of willing and responsible family members or friends.[18]

The decision raised as many questions as it answered. Is there a right to treatment and, if so, what is its scope? Because the Court addressed its concern about the right to treatment only negatively, requiring release in the absence of treatment, these questions were left undecided.[19] Nevertheless, lower courts continued to recognize a constitutional right to treatment and to require reform of institutional practices.

Seven years after it decided *O'Connor*, the Supreme Court returned to the question of a right to treatment. In *Youngberg v. Romeo*, the mother of a thirty-three-year-old man with profound mental retardation sued the staff of an institution, claiming that they had not provided the training and habilitation required to enable her son to avoid self-injury and assaults by others. As a result he suffered numerous injuries and spent a great deal of time in physical restraints. The Supreme Court took the opportunity presented by *Youngberg v. Romeo*[20] to outline the general scope of the constitutional right to treatment, a right that remains in place today.[21]

THE RIGHT TO TREATMENT IN INSTITUTIONS TODAY

The right to treatment in institutions occupies a paradoxical place in mental disability rights today. On the one hand, it has become well established, recognized not only under the Constitution but in statutes enacted by state legislatures throughout the country. On the other hand, the practice of long-term institutionalization that provided the initial catalyst for the development of a right to treatment is rarely defended on clinical or programmatic grounds except for people who are violent. The circumstances of long-term institutional confinement often defeat the goals of habilitation and treatment, and normalization in community living cannot occur. The traits that are rewarded in institutions, such as passivity, submissiveness, and dependence, are at odds with the characteristics needed for success in the community.

Nevertheless, many people with mental disabilities still remain in institutions. In 1992, after a generation of deinstitutionalization, about one-half of all people with mental retardation who did not live at home lived in facilities of sixteen or more beds.[22] The average daily census of state psychiatric hospitals still hovers around 100,000 people. The right to treatment affords these people the rights to services that may help improve their condition and that will, at the very least, maintain the skills they had when they entered the institution.

As explained in chapter 2, the numbers of people treated in acute care inpatient facilities has grown enormously in the past decades. Although not devised with these settings in mind, the right to treatment is relevant to them as well, ensuring appropriate treatment plans, controls on the use of medication, plans for discharge, and other treatment rights.

What rights do people in state facilities have to minimally adequate treatment under the Constitution?

In *Youngberg v. Romeo* the Supreme Court held that an involuntarily confined man with mental retardation who had suffered injuries "on at least 63 occasions"[23] while institutionalized, had a constitutional interest in safe conditions of confinement, freedom from undue restraint, and "minimally adequate" training necessary to achieve these ends.[24] Tying the right to treatment to the deprivation of liberty, the Court ruled that if treatment could minimize or avoid injuries and the use of restraint, the state has an obligation to provide it. For Nicholas Romeo, minimally adequate training consisted of "additional training programs, including self-care, [which] were needed to reduce his aggressive behavior."[25]

The right to minimally adequate treatment recognized in *Youngberg* is more extensive than might first appear, requiring treatment "which is reasonable in light of the identifiable liberty interests and the circumstances of the case."[26] It guarantees staff in sufficient numbers[27] and with appropriate knowledge and training[28] to provide needed interventions. The right can encompass many forms of treatment designed to enhance a person's ability to function with autonomy and without state interference. At a basic level it includes self-care skills, such as grooming, toileting, eating, and dressing;[29] training in the exercise of self-control;[30] training in walking or communication (e.g., speech therapy), since these skills will enable people to exercise their liberty interests;[31] and psychiatric therapies to avoid physical restraint or institutionalization. It can apply as well to the manner in which medications are prescribed and monitored, the mix of therapies appropriate to an individual's needs, and other interventions tied to a person's liberty interests.

The further a particular form of treatment is from a restraint of liberty, though, the less likely it is that the state will be constitutionally obligated to provide it. For example, there is some debate whether vocational training is required. The argument for its inclusion is that vocational training and community living skills bring greater independence—and hence greater individual liberty—and are thus a necessary element of minimally adequate habilitation.[32]

A second and equally important facet of the right to treatment is the prevention of deterioration. Deterioration can be a consequence of long-term institutionalization, often characterized by a lack of positive social interactions as well as a lack of reinforcement of existing skills. It may also include the emergence of inappropriate patterns of behavior that may be designed to get more attention, to protect oneself from harm, or simply to provide diversion from the tedium of institutional life. Deterioration can also appear as the loss of self-care and community-living skills, increased dependence, learned helplessness, or physicial decline. In his concurring opinion in *Youngberg*,[33] Justice Harry Blackmun wrote that the right to minimally adequate training should include whatever training is required to preserve the basic self-care skills that individuals had before they entered the institution.[34] Although Justice Blackmun's opinion is not binding, lower courts have uniformly agreed that the right to be protected from deterioration is a part of the right to minimally adequate treatment to protect against regression, loss of skills, and the development of "harmful or inappropriate habits (such as head-banging, feces eating, eye-gouging, and biting)."[35] This principle is also incorporated in the Medicaid regulations governing intermediate care facilities for people with mental retardation.[36] One court has taken this right a step further to require the state to assure that individuals are given sufficient training to match the skills they would have developed had they never been confined.[37]

How is minimally adequate treatment determined?

The standard the Supreme Court adopted in *Youngberg* for ascertaining when the right to minimally adequate treatment has been violated is quite different from the approach lower courts took in *Wyatt, Willowbrook*, and other prior cases. Unlike those decisions, the Court did not establish an objective standard to define the parameters of the right to treatment—for example six hours of daily programs and a ratio of one direct care staff person to every six residents.[38] Nor did it recognize a constitutional right to treatment in the least restrictive setting.[39]

Instead, the Court declared that a treatment decision is presumptively correct if it was made by a professional and does not substantially deviate from professional judgment, standards, or practices in the field. Departing from traditional practice in defining a constitutional right, the Court declined to decide what minimally adequate treatment is, ruling that such a determination should be left to the judgment of professionals. The term "professional" includes anyone whose education, training, or experience provide the knowledge necessary to make the decision in question, such as a doctor, nurse, psychologist, or physical therapist.[40]

At first glance, this deference to professionals may appear sensible, but in fact it undercuts the idea of a constitutional right, since the judge is required to defer to the very professionals whose practices are being challenged.[41] There is no violation if other experts or even most professionals agree that a certain different form of treatment would be best for the individual,[42] unless no standard in the profession would support the challenged professional's conduct.

An illustration of the consequences of the *Youngberg* approach and how it differs from past decisions is a case in which a hospital's patients proved that its treatment plans were generated by a computer, without any effort to tailor them to the particular needs of individuals. The plans lacked individualized objectives for each patient and particularized plans needed for therapy and were not updated appropriately. Following the *Youngberg* approach, the court held that the plans did not violate the constitutional right to minimally adequate treatment because they did not constitute a substantial departure from professional standards in the field. However, the court did agree that they violated the *Wyatt* standards, which by then had been enacted into state law.[43]

The Supreme Court did leave some room to challenge the care provided by a professional. Although the decision of a professional treating an individual is entitled to a presumption of validity,[44] the court can hear testimony from other professionals that the decision represents "such a substantial departure from accepted professional judgment, practice or standards as to demonstrate that the person responsible did not base the decision on such a judgment."[45] A substantial departure from professional judgment can be shown in any of three situations: first, where no judgment was made at all, e.g., something happened without anyone authorizing it; second, where the decision was not *in fact* made by a qualified professional, that is, by someone with the training, education, and experience in the relevant professional field to make these judgments;[46] or third, where the judgment, decision, or practice violates well-accepted standards in the field.[47]

The last category is the most important. A professional has been held to have violated the standard where the judgment, decision, or practice undertaken was made not for professional reasons, but because of bias, administrative, or bureaucratic convenience, expediency, financial exigency, or punishment. Significant departure from state regulations or recognized professional standards in the field can also amount to a violation of the right to minimally adequate treatment.

For example, courts have found a violation of professional judgment where professionals confined people with developmental disabilities but no diagnosis of mental disorder in state psychiatric hospitals, gave them excessive doses of inappropriate antipsychotic drugs designed to treat mental disorders, and failed to monitor the side effects of those drugs.[48] In addition, when an institution's own professionals recommend a course of treatment for an individual and those recommendations are not followed, the institution may be found to violate the professional judgment standard.

Except in these types of cases, the professional judgment standard provides significant insulation to operators and staff of state facilities from claims of violation of the right to treatment. On the other hand, the professional judgment standard can become a significant advocacy tool when the professionals in the institution become allies of institutionalized people in fighting bureaucratic and financial obstacles to professionally acceptable treatment.

Do people admitted voluntarily have a constitutional right to treatment?

People who enter a facility on their own rather than through state coercion can, in theory, leave as they please so are not deprived of their liberty by the state. Since the right to minimally adequate treatment is derived from individual liberty interests, a person whose liberty is not at stake has no such right.

As discussed in chapter 2, however, the theory does not hold up well in practice. The distinction between voluntary and involuntary status often exists more in a notation on a chart than in the life of the person whose chart it is. Many people do not understand what their inpatient status is. Others, while classified as voluntary, are subject to coercion in the decision to enter the facility or in the staff's response to a request to leave it. In fact, in many states, a person admitted voluntarily is not even permitted to leave without giving two or three days notice, during which time the facility can begin involuntary commitment proceedings. In still other cases, living in an institution is a result of the absence of alternatives; the "choice" to enter an institution occurs only when all other options have been exhausted. Finally, as the Supreme Court recognized in *Zimermon v. Burch*, discussed in chapter 2, some individuals classified as voluntary patients are not competent to consent to admission.

For these reasons, for many years courts made no distinction between the treatment rights of voluntary and involuntary residents.[49] A 1989 decision of the Supreme Court holding that people who are not in state custody have no constitutional rights to state-provided services[50] cast doubt on these decisions. Courts have now split on the question of whether the realities of life in institutions are to be put aside in favor of a formalistic approach that looks exclusively at whether the person is legally in the custody of the state.[51] The more thoughtful judges have refused to apply this wooden distinction, reasoning that a person is, for all practical purposes, in custody regardless of legal status if liberty is truly restrained.[52] Simply put, where voluntary status is a legal fiction, *Youngberg* should apply.

Do any other federal laws require that treatment be provided?

Yes. Three important federal laws require that certain institutionalized people receive appropriate habilitation or treatment. The federal Developmental Disabilities Act requires that each state that receives funds under the Act for serving people with developmental disabilities must have a habilitation plan for each person it serves with a developmental disability.[53] The plan by and large must follow *Wyatt*-type requirements: it must be in writing, be based on participation by the resident, contain long-term habilitation goals and intermediate habilitation objectives describe strategies for reaching the goals and objectives, and identify the people who will assist in implementing the strategies. The plan must then be implemented.[54]

Second, as explained in chapter 5, Section 504 of the Rehabilitation Act and the Americans with Disabilities Act preclude an institution from offering treatment and services to some residents, but not others, on the basis of the severity of their disability. This prohibition on discrimination is particularly important for people with multiple disabilities (e.g., deafness and mental illness or mental retardation) or especially severe disabilities, where the facility wants to save funds by offering only custodial care for these individuals. Such a policy clearly discriminates on the basis of disability and is unlawful.[55]

Third, people with developmental disabilities in facilities that receive some of the billions of Medicaid dollars to fund institutional care have very specific treatment and habilitation rights. The Medicaid program provides funding to support habilitation in a residential setting for people with mental retardation in facilities called intermediate care facilities for the mentally retarded (ICF/MRs). Three-fourths of the people in ICF/MRs reside in facilities larger than sixteen beds, although the number of small ICF/MRs is steadily increasing.

These facilities must comply with rules for "active treatment" established by the federal Medicaid agency, the Health Care Financing Administration. Compliance is monitored by both the Health Care Financing Administration and by agencies that operate the state Medicaid program. If the facilities do not comply, the Medicaid funds for the facility may be terminated.

These regulations provide that no one may be admitted to the facility who is not in need of the level of care and restrictiveness the facility offers. Each resident of an intermediate care facility for the mentally retarded is entitled to

a continuous active treatment program, which includes aggressive, consistent implementation of a program of specialized and generic training, treatment, health services and related services . . . directed toward—
(i) the acquisition of the behaviors necessary for the client to function with as much self-determination and independence as possible; and
(ii) the prevention or deceleration of regression or loss of current optimal functional status.[56]

The regulations stress that training must be individualized to meet each person's specific needs and must require a full range of services to meet them, including occupational and physical therapy, self-care and social skills training, medical care, and much more. The habilitation plan is the essential glue of the right to habilitation. The right to an individual program plan guarantees that an individual will be assessed within a short time of entering an institution, his or her needs will be identified, and programs will be developed to meet those needs.[57] Within thirty days, the interdisciplinary treatment team must identify presenting problems and their causes, the person's strengths, developmental, and behavioral management needs, and the need for services. These needs must be determined without regard to services actually available and must include physical, nutritional, sensory-motor affective, speech and language, cognitive and social development and adaptive behaviors, independent living skills, and vocational skills necessary to function in the community. The team, with participation by the individual for whom the plan is being developed (or the person's legal guardian), must then develop a plan stating specific objectives necessary to meet the person's needs and specifying methods to be used to achieve those objectives, the schedule for use of the method, and the person responsible for the program.

Each person has a right to receive the habilitation necessary to achieve the objectives identified in the program plan, and all staff members who work with the person must help to implement the program.[58] In addition, the facility must document the individual's progress at least annually and review the plan whenever the person achieves a goal or is obviously failing to progress.[59]

Do state laws guarantee people in psychiatric institutions and mental retardation facilities a right to treatment or habilitation?

States are free to provide their citizens with a right to treatment beyond the basic federal constitutional guarantees, and in fact many do. In states that have an enforceable statutory right to treatment, the debate about the scope and interpretation of the constitutional right is largely irrelevant.

For example, many states have adopted detailed requirements for treatment in psychiatric facilities. In other cases, even though state statutes are silent, departmental regulations guarantee treatment rights. These provisions vary from state to state but almost uniformly provide far more detail about the treatment that is required and the process that must guide treatment decisions than *Youngberg* would mandate. Some of these state codes or regulations are based explicitly on the standards developed in *Wyatt*.

In Montana, for example, the state code requires institutions to provide mental health care that is "suited to the needs of the person" and "skillfully and humanely administered with full respect for the person's dignity and personal integrity."[60] In New Hampshire, the state mental health code "create[s] a right for those patients involuntarily committed to a State hospital and concomitantly imposes a duty upon employees of the State hospital to provide adequate and humane treatment."[61] Connecticut law requires that "Each patient shall be treated in accordance with a specialized treatment plan suited to his disorder."[62]

Many states have similar mandates for the habilitation of institutionalized people with mental retardation. In general, these laws require interdisciplinary assessments of a person's needs and the development of a habilitation plan to meet those needs. That plan must be implemented and then updated periodically. The Illinois definition of habilitation is typical: "an effort directed toward alleviation of developmental disability or toward increasing a developmentally disabled person's level of physical, mental, social, or economic functioning." It may include evaluation, medical services, residential and day care, special living arrangements, training, education, sheltered employment, protective services, and counseling.[63] People in facilities for developmental disabilities are entitled to a habilitation plan within fourteen days that includes goals, a timetable for accomplishing the goals, necessary services, a description of the intended role of the family, and the name of the person responsible for supervising the individual's habilitation. The plan must be reviewed every thirty days.[64] Furthermore, each person shall receive an annual review of the need for continued residence,[65] and prior to discharge the facility director shall prepare a post-discharge plan that is consistent with the individual's habilitation goals.[66]

Other states have similar statements of the right to treatment or habilitation, often including detailed requirements for treatment or habilitation plans, interdisciplinary planning and a full range of therapies. Custodial treatment is thus not only professionally unacceptable; it is no longer legally permissible.

Moreover, unlike the *Youngberg* professional judgment standard, state standards generally require that care be more than "minimally adequate." Some courts have expressed the requirement as "meaningful treatment,"[67] interpreted by one court to require treatment "consistent with good medical practice." The court also said that "meaningful treatment thus requires not only basic custodial care but also an individualized effort to help each patient by formulating, administering and monitoring a 'specialized treatment plan' as expressly mandated by" the state's statute.[68] Thus, state standards are not as deferential to the judgments of professionals as the *Youngberg* standard and do not require proof that the practice or decision is a "substantial departure" from professional standards. The result is that substandard treatment practices may violate state law even when they do not violate constitutional requirements.

As a practical matter, then, what does the right to treatment or habilitation mean for someone who is in an institution?

Despite variations in state statutes, federal regulations, and other sources of law and accreditation,[69] the right to treatment or habilitation in an institutional setting can be boiled down to a few essential elements.

First, everyone is entitled to a fully developed, individualized, professionally acceptable treatment plan that is based on an appropriate diagnosis and provides for a full range of services relevant to the diagnosis and the person's needs. The plan must be implemented according to professional standards and reviewed at necessary intervals. The goal is a plan that is responsive to individual needs.

Second, in designing the plan, less restrictive rather than more restrictive interventions must be chosen.

Third, the person must have a full opportunity to participate in the development and revision of the plan. Participation is essential to respect the dignity of the individual and to enable those developing the plan to learn from the individual's own experience which interventions are helpful and which are not. The individual must receive enough information to make informed judgments and participate fully in the treatment planning process. The individual's right to participate should not be restricted by doubts about the person's competence, since even incompetent people can express preferences and desires.

Fourth, the interventions used cannot be restricted to those that are convenient or simple, such as medication. Rather, the person has a right to therapies that meet his or her individual needs.

Fifth, the facility must have sufficient numbers of trained staff to implement the plan properly.

Sixth, there must be adequate controls on the use of medication, including rules for noting medication information in the chart, periodic professional review of all medication administered, and monitoring for side effects. Medication may not be used for the convenience of staff, as punishment, or as a substitute for other appropriate treatment.

Seventh, the plan must be directed toward discharge. That is, it must be premised on the idea that the goal of habilitation or treatment is discharge to a noninstitutional setting. The treatment plan should address discharge explicitly and provide a timetable for accomplishing it.

Are all these rights enforceable?

Yes. Rights are meaningless without a means to enforce them. This section focuses on methods for vindicating treatment rights. Chapter 7 discusses the right of access to advocates and the means for enforcing other rights of people in institutions and communities.

First, through advocacy at the facility itself. The initial, and often most effective strategy to enforce treatment rights is through advocacy with staff at the facility itself. Insufficient or inadequate treatment or discharge plans, lack of habilitation programs or therapies, inappropriate use or monitoring of medication, and other violations can and should be addressed in the first instance to the professionals and administrators at the facility.

Because of its formal requirements for participation, the treatment or habilitation planning process can be an effective vehicle for voicing concerns about the type or quality of interventions offered.[70] It need not be the only vehicle, however. Discussions and formal complaints through quality assurance and other institution-based peer review committees can also be effective to insist on respect for treatment rights.

Second, through state or federal regulatory or oversight agencies responsible for monitoring quality of care. Institutions are subject to extensive state regulation. When they receive federal funds, as so many do, they must comply with standards regarding the use of those funds. The regulatory and oversight agencies conduct both regularly scheduled reviews and receive and investigate complaints alleging violations of standards.

For example, compliance with the ICF/MR regulations discussed in this chapter is monitored by both state Medicaid agencies and by the federal Health Care Financing Administration. Federal and state agencies perform reviews of compliance with standards periodically, the results of which are obtainable through state and federal freedom of information laws. If the agency finds that a facility has failed to comply with rules regarding treatment or habilitation, it can order a plan of correction for the facility or, in egregious cases, cut off federal funds. Other Medicaid and Medicare standards are applicable to hospitals, nursing homes, and other facilities and have similar oversight mechanisms.

These agencies also accept individual complaints of inappropriate treatment or habilitation. Anyone can file a complaint with the regional office of the Health Care Financing Administration, which is part of the Department of Health and Human Services, concerning services funded by Medicaid or Medicare. In the case of Medicaid, complaints may also be filed with the state Medicaid agency, whose offices are usually listed in the telephone directory. If the agency fails to respond, a member of Congress may be able to offer assistance.

Other state or local agencies may also regulate the facility. It is important to understand the state regulatory mechanisms and the complaint procedures they use. As discussed in chapter 7, a protection and advocacy agency or other advocacy group can also assist individuals or families seeking to enforce treatment or habilitation rights.

Third, through private accreditation agencies, such as the Joint Commission on Accreditation of Healthcare Organizations (JCAHO). The joint commission is the private organization that establishes standards for the accreditation of private and publicly operated psychiatric hospitals and other health care facilities serving people with mental illness.[71] Many of these standards are contained in manuals covering particular kinds of facilities, such as the Accreditation Manual for Mental Health, Chemical Dependency and Mental Retardation/Developmental Disabilities Services. JCAHO also publishes scoring guidelines by which it measures compliance with its standards.

Many facilities consider accreditation to be advantageous as a means of recruiting staff and patients, obtaining third party reimbursement for care, satisfying state legislators, or increasing their prestige in the community. Serious violations of standards can jeopardize that accreditation. Thus, it is useful to become familiar with these standards and if a facility is accredited, to write directly to JCAHO and other accredited agencies if treatment or habilitation standards are not being met.

Fourth, through independent oversight agencies operated by the state. Some states have oversight bodies, such as the Mental Disabilities Board of Visitors in Montana and the New York State Commission on Quality of Care for the Mentally Disabled, that have no enforcement authority but can identify violations of standards for treatment or habilitation and pressure facility administrators to comply with their obligations.

Fifth, through federal administrative enforcement of federal rights. As discussed in chapter 4, the Department of Justice has authority to enforce Titles II and III of the Americans with Disabilities Act. The Justice Department may also bring lawsuits against states if the institutions they operate show a pattern or practice of egregious or flagrant violations of the rights of their residents.[72] The address of the Justice Department is contained in appendix B. Finally, the Office for Civil Rights of the

Department of Health and Human Services may receive complaints for violations Section 504 of the Rehabilitation Act by any facilities that receive federal funds.

Sixth, through the courts. A court may enforce constitutional or statutory rights at the behest of a person whose rights have been violated. These may be individual cases or class action cases brought on behalf of a group (or all) of the individuals in a facility who have been deprived of their treatment rights. Dozens of class actions have resulted in orders for appropriate treatment in psychiatric institutions or mental retardation facilities. In one relatively recent case, the court found that treatment was not adequate because the facility failed to implement adequate behavior management programs that resulted in otherwise unnecessary chemical and physical restraints; training programs were not individualized to meet the residents' individual specific needs; the facility did not adequately teach functional skills; there was not enough physical space available for training activities; and the materials used were not appropriate for the age of the people living in the institution.[73] Additional information about bringing lawsuits and gaining access to advocates to represent institutionalized people is contained in chapter 7.

Seventh, through organizing and protest. The most effective of all strategies is often through the time-tested means of political action. Public exposure through the media, letter-writing campaigns to public officials, well-attended meetings with responsible decision makers, and myriad other forms of protest not only can bring more attention to the deficiencies than formal enforcement methods but can often exert greater pressure to correct them.

THE RIGHT TO TREATMENT IN NURSING HOMES, JAILS, AND PRISONS

Do people in a nursing home who have mental disabilities have rights to appropriate treatment and services?

Yes, as long as the nursing home receives Medicare or Medicaid funds.[74] Residents of nursing homes have the right to:

- *A resident assessment.* Within fourteen days of the person's arrival and at least annually thereafter (and also after a significant change in the person's condition), the nursing home must perform an assessment by an interdisciplinary team, coordinated by a registered nurse. The assessment must include an evaluation of skills and needs in the areas of daily routines, cognition (thinking), communication, health, and mental health.

• *A care plan.* The assessment must lead to an individualized plan of care that explains how the nursing home will meet the person's medical, nursing, mental health, and other needs.

• *Services.* The nursing home must provide specialized rehabilitative services to attain or maintain the highest practicable physical, mental, and psychological well-being of each resident. These include medical, dental, rehabilitation (e.g., physical therapy, speech therapy), medication, mental health, and social services that are responsive to the person's needs as identified in the assessment and reflected in the plan of care.[75]

A nursing home resident has the right to participate in the development of a plan of care, including the right to review and copy records relating to it and to be informed of proposed courses of treatment, as well as the right to refuse a particular course of treatment.

What mental health services must a nursing home provide? Who must provide them?

The nursing home must provide counseling, group therapy and other services. In addition, the state—not the nursing home—has the obligation to provide "specialized services." For people with mental retardation, these include habilitation designed to improve the person's level of functioning. Specialized services for people with psychiatric disabilities are more limited, amounting to hospitalization when the resident is experiencing an acute episode.

How may treatment rights in nursing homes be enforced?

Every state has a nursing home ombudsman to investigate and resolve problems concerning violations of rights and quality of care in nursing homes. The nursing home must post the phone number and address of the ombudsman office. It is also available through the Eldercare Locator, 1-800-677-1116.

Do incarcerated people have a right to mental health treatment?

Yes, although prison and jail administrators have great leeway in deciding what treatment to provide. The number of incarcerated people with psychiatric disabilities or mental retardation has soared. According to a survey conducted by the National Alliance for the Mentally Ill (NAMI) and Public Citizen's Health Research Group, on any given day, more than 30,000 people, or 7.2 percent of jail inmates, have a serious mental illness such as schizophrenia, manic depression, or major depression.[76] A General Accounting Office survey concluded that between 6 and 14 percent of prison inmates have major psychiatric disorders.[77] Estimates of the number of prison inmates with mental retardation range from 10 to 30 percent.[78]

The NAMI/Public Citizen investigation also reported that in one way or another, 17 states explicitly authorize the use of jails to hold people for civil commitment hearings and that 43 percent of jails surveyed reported holding a person with a serious psychiatric disability in the absence of criminal charges. Although one court has upheld the constitutionality of the use of jails to confine people awaiting civil commitment proceedings, as long as they have separate units for this purpose and meet certain other conditions,[79] we disagree. The justification for involuntary civil commitment includes the premise that its purpose is treatment. Even if the jail offers medication, it is hardly an appropriate setting for treatment.

The fate of people with mental disabilities in correctional facilities is frightening: they are vulnerable to abuse, exploitation and attack, worsening of psychiatric symptoms, loss of contact with support systems, and even death through assault or suicide. But the legal standard for treatment is very low. The only requirement of prison administrators is that they may not be "deliberately indifferent" to inmates' health care needs,[80] including needs for mental health treatment and habilitation. The deliberate indifference standard is even weaker than the professional judgment standard of *Youngberg*, but it nevertheless has some teeth. Jails and prisons must make mental health treatment, including medication, available to inmates, take precautions against suicides, and offer some minimal habilitation program.[81] They have no obligation, however, to do what may be best for the person's mental health.

THE RIGHT TO SERVICES IN THE COMMUNITY

For the past three decades federal, state, and local governments have failed to finance or develop a full range of community-based services needed by people with mental disabilities, including social skills training, therapy, housing, outreach, advocacy, crisis intervention, case management, peer counseling, substance abuse treatment, and support.[82] From a moral, social policy, and clinical viewpoint, long-term institutional care is rapidly becoming an expensive anachronism, yet it is kept alive by traditional funding streams, the inability to finance alternatives, and by the fact that many of the people who remain institutionalized have been there for so long that their lives have been written off by society.[83]

Confronted by the persistence of institutionalization of people with mental disabilities, and faced as well by such manifestations of shortages of community-based services as homelessness and the phenomenon of adults with mental disabilities living with aging parents, people with mental disabilities and their advocates have sought to establish a right to services in the community. Why, they argue, must an individual be confined in an institution—the most restrictive and expensive setting for treatment—in order to gain an entitlement to services? Wouldn't the establishment of a right to treatment in the community provide essential services in a humane and cost-effective way, without waiting for a crisis that results in institutionalization? Why should people with mental disabilities who have not been institutionalized as children lose the right to services once they have completed school?

Part of the problem stems from a Supreme Court ruling that held that government has no constitutional duty to provide services to individuals who are not in its custody.[84] People confined in institutions are; those voluntarily receiving outpatient services are not. As a result, the development of a right to services in the community turns largely on the creation and enforcement of statutory entitlements. Although an all-encompassing statutory right to services has yet to be passed, Congress and numerous state legislatures have enacted programs that entitle people with mental disabilities to receive substantial benefits and services. This section examines some of these entitlements.

The Right to Mental Health and Mental Retardation Services

Under federal law, is there a right to treatment in the community for people who are currently institutionalized?

The answer is a highly qualified yes. As discussed above, the articulation of a right to treatment inevitably brought with it claims for treatment and habilitation outside institutions. The very first cases exposing the horrors of the nation's most infamous institutions in the 1970s, such as Willowbrook in New York and Pennhurst in Pennsylvania, sought and often achieved closure or massive downsizing and an entitlement to community-based services. A critical component of the court orders in these cases was continued judicial supervision over the state's compliance efforts to ensure that former residents received appropriate and high-quality community services. In some of these early cases, courts are still struggling to bring about the substitution of community services for institutional ones. In states that lacked court orders or strong leadership to prod them into compliance, community services have typically lagged.[85] Meanwhile, literally dozens of other courts have issued orders requiring the development of community services for people once housed in institutions.

These early cases were all based on an interpretation of the right to treatment. One of the *Wyatt* mental health standards, for example, provides for a right to transitional care after discharge, including psychiatric day programs, out-patient treatment, treatment at home, and care in a psychiatric ward at a general hospital.[86] Another calls for discharge planning. Other courts have relied on constitutional or statutory requirements for placement in the least restrictive setting as a basis for ordering a full range of community-based services including housing, vocational, and support programs; health and psychiatric care, and others.[87]

In recent years, reinterpretations of the law by a more conservative judiciary have slowed this movement. The courts have generally held that there is no broad right under the Constitution[88] or federal antidiscrimination laws[89] to the creation of less restrictive services in the community, such as housing, transitional services, rehabilitation, vocational services, health care, and other essential components of a community-based system of mental health or mental retardation services. Indeed, it is commonplace in the field of mental disability law to hear that no such right exists. Despite the jurisprudential setbacks on which these statements are based, persistent advocates and judges who are willing to confront massive systemic failure have crafted orders mandating a range of services in the community for people formerly institutionalized. In the past half-dozen years, cases in North Carolina,[90] Oklahoma,[91] New Mexico,[92] Montana,[93] and elsewhere have, on a wide variety of legal grounds, resulted in orders to provide community-based services as an alternative to institutionalization to large classes of people with mental disabilities. Elsewhere, states have entered into sweeping agreements to plan individualized community-based services for thousands of people who are now institutionalized.[94]

In recent years, two legal arguments have proven most successful in forcing states to develop alternatives to institutional confinement for people with mental disabilities. First, judges have relied on the professional judgment standard articulated in the *Youngberg* case. They reason that where a qualified professional within a government-operated institution determines that the only professionally acceptable form of treatment for an institutionalized person is a set of community-based services, but none are available, the government has a constitutional obligation to develop alternative services in the community.[95]

This conclusion follows from the logic of the professional judgment rule itself, where the professional's opinion is the means for gauging compliance with constitutional requirements. As one court put it: "An individual confined to an institution against his best interests is unduly restrained to the same extent that an individual shackled to his wheelchair is unduly restrained. If professional judgment dictates that community placement is necessary in the best interest of the individual, then the individual has a constitutional right to such placement and continued confinement in the institution constitutes undue restraint."[96] The place of financial considerations in determining the deference due professional judgment in decisions concerning the appropriateness of community services remains unsettled. One trial court denied they had any place at all: "The residents are entitled to treatment recommended by a qualified professional whose judgment is unsullied by consideration of the fact that the state does not provide funding for appropriate services in the community."[97] The court of appeals, however, rejected so sweeping a decision, observing that "A professional determination that excludes all considerations of costs and available resources could easily become impossible for the state to implement within justifiable budgetary limitations."[98] On the other hand, it warned that the state may not impose "overly extensive cost restrictions in individual cases."[99] The resolution of the cost dilemma, the court suggested, was to thrust the decision back to the state to devise alternative means of providing minimally adequate treatment in accordance with the judgments of professionals in a way the state could manage. In short, while the state need not proceed as though cost is irrelevant, it may not avoid constitutional obligations by citing expense.

This is consistent with the approach taken in cases involving court-approved agreements to expand community-based mental health and retardation services, where courts have required the executive branch of the state to make good faith efforts to secure adequate funding from the legislature before making cuts in services.[100]

A second set of arguments for access to community-based services for institutionalized people derives from Section 504 of the Rehabilitation Act[101] and the Americans with Disabilities Act.[102] Although these laws require only reasonable changes in programs to ensure meaningful access to people otherwise qualified for the programs and not the creation of new programs for those not previously served,[103] they are nevertheless germane to the question of a right to community-based services.

As described in chapter 4, antidiscrimination laws may be used to challenge the denial of services to a particular group of individuals based on discriminatory criteria. All too often, for financial or programmatic reasons, planners "skim" institutions, developing community-based alternatives for the residents with the least severe disabilities, while multiply disabled or more severely disabled residents remain institutionalized. Both Section 504 and the ADA prohibit the denial of meaningful access to community-based programs to institutionalized persons, based on the nature or severity of their disability.[104] In one case, the court concluded: "The severity of Plaintiffs' handicaps is itself a handicap which, under Section 504, cannot be the sole reason for denying plaintiffs access to community programs. . . . Defendants' failure to accommodate the severely handicapped in existing community programs while serving less severely handicapped peers is unreasonable and discriminatory."[105]

In addition, a public entity's duty to make reasonable modification of its rules and practices, as discussed in chapter 5, requires the state to provide services and supports that will enable persons with more severe disabilities to benefit from community programs already offered to people with less severe disabilities. The fact that the state or local government may have to spend money to remedy this discrimination is no excuse for failing to do so.[106]

The second antidiscrimination argument goes to the heart of the purpose of the ADA. As described in chapter 5, the main purpose of the Act is to integrate people with disabilities into all facets of community life by enabling them to gain access to social services, benefits, and other social programs. The regulations issued by the Justice Department under the ADA further this purpose by requiring a public entity to provide programs and activities "in the most integrated setting appropriate to the needs of qualified individuals with disabilities."[107]

The concept of integration can be interpreted to require the state to take affirmative steps to enable people with disabilities to live appropriately in the community rather than be confined in institutions. Taking the argument a step further requires an end to long-term institutional confinement altogether,[108] since segregation itself can be a form of prohibited invidious discrimination.[109] Shortly after the ADA became effective, the state of Pennsylvania asked a court to relieve it of the obligation the court had previously imposed to develop community-based services for people with mental retardation who were formerly housed in the Pennhurst State School, a large institution that was now closed. It argued that neither the Constitution nor any other law imposed a legal obligation to provide these services. The court rejected the state's motion, and in the process commented: "Further, the Commonwealth neglects to point out that in enacting the Americans with Disabilities Act of 1990, Congress affirmed that 504 [of the Rehabilitation Act of 1973] prohibits unnecessary segregation and requires reasonable accommodations to provide opportunities to include all state and local programs, regardless of the receipt of federal financial assistance."[110]

One court, though, expressed skepticism that the ADA requires government to meet the integration mandate by closing institutions and designing appropriate community-based services for people with mental disabilities. In that case, former residents of inpatient psychiatric hospitals in Massachusetts claimed that the ADA's integration requirement prohibited the Department from placing them in housing exclusively for people with psychiatric disabilities and refusing to provide services to individuals with dual diagnoses of mental illness and substance abuse. The court held that "nothing in the ADA requires that a specific proportion of housing placements provided by a mental health agency be in 'integrated' housing." It also rejected the claim that agencies could not exclude services with a particular disability, here a dual diagnosis. "An agency does not obligate itself to make services available to persons with different or complicating disabilities by treating individuals with a single disability."[111]

The meaning of the ADA's integration mandate is one of the most intriguing questions in mental disability rights today. The idea, if taken seriously, has the potential to break through the separation, in thought and in fact, of people with mental disabilities from society. Or it could prove yet another empty promise to people who have been stigmatized and excluded for so long.

Do people with mental disabilities who do not live in an institution have a constitutional right to community-based services and housing?

Generally not. All the attention the law devotes to the question of whether institutionalized people have a right to obtain community-based services does not affect the huge number of people with mental disabilities living outside state institutions (or on the verge of discharge from them) without adequate or any access to services. As discussed above, people not in the custody of the state have no rights to services under the Constitution[112] and no constitutional protection against cuts state and local governments make in budgets for existing community-based services.[113] Some advocates have successfully contended that the state owes former residents of facilities a duty of continuing care to the extent the state's role in their lives remains active, such as through staff planning and monitoring of daily activities in community-based facilities.[114] The court found, however, that generalized state budget cuts, if rationally planned, do not violate this obligation.

Do people with mental disabilities have rights to community-based services under any other laws?

Indeed they do. Just as we saw in the discussion of rights in institutions, rights have many sources, including those conferred by state and federal laws. The continuing deprivations of housing and basic services for people with mental disabilities—whether they are living in family situations difficult for everyone in the household, in filthy board and care homes, in shelters, or on the street—has led to a continuing search for a non-Constitutional legal basis to assert rights to community housing and services.

Just as state laws often prescribe the rights of people in institutions, many states describe in great detail the kinds of services that must be made available to people with mental disabilities in the community.[115] To take but two examples, in Georgia, the statute governing mental retardation services establishes in its declaration of purpose that the state "recognizes the capacity of all of its citizens, including those who are mentally retarded, to be both personally and socially productive; and it further recognizes its obligation to provide aid in the form of a coordinated system of community facilities, programs, and services to mentally retarded citizens so that they may achieve a greater measure of independence and fulfillment and more fully enjoy their rights of citizenship."[116] The state, taking the county plans into account, must publish state disability services plans including outpatient services, day and other partial hospitalization programs, day training and work activity centers, residential services, emergency, consultation, education, and training services.[117]

In Illinois, the Department of Mental Health and Developmental Disabilities must create a service system that will

strengthen the disabled individual's independence, self-esteem and ability to participate in and contribute to community life; to insure continuity of care for clients; to enable disabled persons to access needed services, commensurate with their individual wishes and needs . . . , to prevent unnecessary institutionalization and the dislocation of individuals from their home communities; to provide a range of services so that persons can receive these services in settings which do not unnecessarily restrict their liberty; and to encourage clients to move among settings as their needs change.[118]

The language and legally binding effects of these state-imposed requirements vary considerably.[119] In some cases, even a specific statement of services to be provided has been held not to create any enforceable rights.[120] Other courts, however, have viewed statutes worded very generally as mandating a comprehensive array of services in large metropolitan areas like Phoenix and Denver.[121] In the Denver case, a court interpreted a Colorado statute providing for care and treatment "to secure for each person who may be mentally ill such care and treatment as will be suited to the needs of the person" to mean that any person receiving evaluation or treatment under the statute is entitled to adequate care and treatment in the community.[122] In Phoenix, the court found that the mental health system was fragmented and disjointed, a product of violations of duties assigned to state agencies, the county, and the state hospital. The state failed to assure coordinated services, the state hospital discharged patients without medication, medical records, or notification to any other agency; and the county was not providing adequate community mental health services. It ordered a plan to overhaul the system to remedy the violations.[123]

Other judges have interpreted state laws requiring discharge plans to require states to fulfill the housing and service proposals in the plan.[124] For example, in one recent case, a court interpreted a common statutory requirement that people discharged from a psychiatric hospital have a service plan to obligate the government to make sure that they have adequate housing available to them; the order did not appear to require the development of housing when none is available.[125] And still others have enforced the obligation to fund services required by state law.[126] In general, the more clearly the obligation is set forth in the state's statute—such as a requirement of an adequate discharge plan—the more likely a court will find enforceable rights to adequate services for individuals or for entire classes of people with mental disabilities. It is imperative to read the state law concerning mental health and mental retardation services very closely, paying particular attention to the degree of discretion to provide needed services the state legislature has left to its officials.

Do children with mental disabilities have rights to services in the community?

Yes, and far more than adults do. In the first place, children with disabilities are entitled to a free, appropriate public education, a right discussed later in this chapter. School districts are required to provide children with both an educational program designed to meet their individual needs and related services to help them learn.

About 40 percent or more of children who are removed from their families and placed in foster care have serious emotional and behavioral problems[127] Many of these children virtually lose their childhood as they bounce from placement to placement. In many states, troubled child welfare systems have come under attack for unnecessarily removing children from their families and for failing to meet federal statutory requirements to use reasonable efforts to keep families together. One case in particular focused on the needs of children with emotional and behavioral disorders and brought about a landmark settlement.

The case, *R.C. v. Hornsby*, was brought on behalf of a class of children with emotional and behavioral disorders in Alabama. The case challenged the state's failure to provide the in-home and community-based support and treatment services that would enable these children to remain with their families and out of foster care. The children alleged that their constitutional rights to family integrity and minimally adequate mental health care had been violated and also that their specific rights under the federal Adoption Assistance and Child Welfare Act had not been complied with.[128] That law requires child welfare agencies to make reasonable efforts to keep families together and to place children in state custody in the least restrictive, familylike setting available.

The case never came to trial. Instead, the state agreed to a settlement requiring a wide range of in-home and community-based services to the children to avoid their being taken into state custody.[129] The decree begins with a statement of principles embracing family support, empowerment, and choice and proceeds to a specific set of requirements designed to meet the needs of emotionally disturbed children. The settlement, for example, requires the state to assure that families be full participants in the planning and delivery of services and to make all relevant services available to them. As a result, the number of children in the Alabama child welfare system has steadily declined.

R.C. may well become the same kind of model for services for children with emotional and behavioral problems who commonly are either institutionalized or removed from families as *Wyatt, Willowbrook, Pennhurst,* and *Brewster* were for adults with psychiatric disabilities and mental retardation in the 1970s and 1980s. *R.C.* dovetails as well with efforts to redirect mental health services for seriously emotionally disturbed children from institutions to homes and communities. In 1992 Congress enacted a new program to enable selected states and local governments to create a full range of home- and community-based mental health services for children, including diagnosis and assessment, outpatient care, day treatment, intensive in-home support services, respite care for families, and other services.[130] The program remains very small in scope but may become a model for the future.

The Right to Income

The complexities of the right to treatment discussed in the preceding section are a product of the limitations inherent in a system of rights that seeks only to protect people from government. American society remains a long way from recognizing rights under the Constitution to be provided with life's basic needs, including food, clothing, and shelter.

Yet people with mental disabilities do have rights to income support provided through Social Security Act programs established by Congress. Indeed, they have two kinds of rights: the right to receive benefits according to eligibility criteria established by Congress and the Social Security Administration; and the right to be protected from arbitrary, discriminatory, or irrational decisions by the Social Security Administration.

The rules governing these programs are too long, cumbersome, and complicated to discuss in detail here. The Social Security Administration publishes descriptions of its programs, and many reference manuals and guidebooks are available to help guide people through the process.[131] An advocate to help on a Social Security or SSI claim can be located through a local legal services organization, protective and advocacy agency, or through the National Organization of Social Security Claimants' Representatives. The last consists primarily of lawyers and advocates in private practice who represent claimants in Social Security cases. It can be reached at 1-800-431-2804.

What income-support programs exist under the Social Security Act for people with mental disabilities?

Congress has created two income-support programs for people who, on account of disability, are not able to work. One is *Social Security Disability Insurance (SSDI)*,[132] which pays Social Security benefits to people with disabilities who have paid enough taxes through the Federal Insurance Contributions Act (FICA) to be eligible for benefits. Generally, an adult whose disability began in childhood and whose parent is retired or deceased can also receive Social Security based on the contributions of the parent to the Social Security program.

The monthly SSDI benefit depends on how large the person's contributions have been. Like Social Security retirement and survivor's benefits, the size of the monthly check does not depend on the amount of the recipient's income, assets, or other indicator of financial need; rich and poor alike are entitled to benefits that vary only with the amount of contributions into the system. The maximum monthly benefit is more than $1,000 per month. Because this program was established under Title II of the Social Security Act, these benefits are often referred to as Title II benefits.

The second program is *Supplemental Security Income (SSI)*,[133] also known as Title XVI benefits after the title of the Social Security Act where the program is established. SSI benefits are available to adults and children with disabilities. The childhood rules evaluate whether the child has a disability severe enough to qualify for benefits.

Although SSI and SSDI have identical rules for deciding whether someone is sufficiently disabled to receive benefits, the financial rules and the benefits paid are very different. SSI is an income support program for the poor, people too poor in fact to have contributed any (or very many) FICA taxes. In 1996 the maximum federal benefit under SSI was $470 a month. This payment does not bring a person even to the poverty level, so some states supplement this federal payment.

Because SSI is a program for the poor, it is operated like welfare programs. It restricts the amount of income a person can earn and the value of assets a person can have and still remain eligible for benefits. Further, Social Security reduces the amount of the monthly benefit check if the recipient does have other income. The rules for counting income and reducing benefits are very complex, and after reviewing the brief discussion below we recommend consulting one of the resources listed in the notes or contacting the Social Security Administration for information about financial eligibility.[134]

In many cases, a person has paid Social Security taxes in an amount that only yields a very small monthly benefit check. If the person's income and assets are low enough, the person can receive SSI as well as SSDI.

What kind of disability must an adult have to be eligible for benefits?

Despite the complexity of these programs, the basic rule for both SSDI and SSI is easily stated: an adult is eligible if, because of a mental or physical condition that is expected to last at least one year or result in death, he or she cannot engage in substantial gainful activity. In general, substantial gainful activity means competitive work. Put most simply, a person who is unable to work on account of a mental condition is eligible for benefits.

Most of the application process for SSDI and SSI is devoted to figuring out if the applicant can work. Social Security asks for information about the applicant's medical condition, recent experience in the work place, and names of doctors to contact, then turns the information over to a special state agency called a disability determination service (DDS) to determine whether the applicant meets the rules for SSDI or SSI. To begin, the Social Security Administration assumes that a person who earns even as little as $500 a month from employment (sheltered or supported employment income is viewed differently) is not disabled.

If the applicant earns less than $500 a month, a disability examiner at the DDS reviews all the medical and functional evidence and compares it with a list of symptoms and skills relating to work (for example, the ability to follow and carry out instructions and the ability to concentrate) for each major medical condition. Mental conditions for which there is a "listing" include organic mental disorders, psychotic disorders, depression, mental retardation, anxiety disorders, personality disorders, and somata-form (psychosomatic) problems.[135]

Except for an applicant with an IQ of less than 70, in which case the applicant is automatically found disabled,[136] the disability examiner then decides whether the evidence shows that the applicant has limitations in functioning stemming from the condition that render the person unable to work.[137] In general, in assessing the ability to work, SSA looks at criteria such as the ability to concentrate, to complete tasks, to maintain social relationships, and to live independently.

Determinations of disability are based not on face-to-face contact with Social Security or DDS personnel but on reviews of paper records. The state DDS often requires applicants to be examined by a physician on contract to the agency, but even then receives only written reports. The agency's evidence collection practices leave a lot to be desired, so it is worthwhile to submit all the evidence about the applicant's condition, especially about the characteristics that make it impossible to work. Social Security is required to consider nonmedical as well as medical evidence, so that social workers, counselors, family, friends, and others may contribute to the record that Social Security and the disability examiner assemble.

What kind of disability must a child have to be eligible for SSI?

As this book goes to press, Congress is considering major changes in the SSI program for children. We recommend contacting the Social Security Administration for details about current eligibility rules, which may differ from those discussed in this section.

The SSI program pays cash benefits to children on the basis of a disability. In addition, children with disabilities are eligible for Social Security benefits in the same manner as other survivors of a deceased wage-earner or as a dependent of a wage-earner with a disability.

SSI can be a very important source of additional cash benefits for low-income families and, in most states, guarantees the child's eligibility for Medicaid. SSI's family income rules permit many working families, as well as very poor ones, to receive benefits.

Children are disabled by the standards of the SSI program if they have an impairment and accompanying restrictions in age-appropriate behaviors and abilities contained in a list of disabilities prepared by the Social Security Administration. Each disability on the list is referred to as a "listing." These listings include conditions such as mental retardation, autism, attention deficit hyperactivity disorder, mood disorders, and a host of psychiatric conditions. If a child has a condition included in the listings and the child is financially eligible, benefits are granted.

Two enormous changes have taken place in the SSI program for children with disabilities in recent years, resulting in an increase in the number of children receiving benefits from fewer than 300,000 children in 1989 to almost 900,000 five years later. First, in the case of *Sullivan v. Zebley*[138] the Supreme Court ruled that the Social Security Administration's method of determining childhood disability violated the Social Security Act. Under the old scheme, if a child's condition was not a listed impairment, the child was not eligible for benefits. The Supreme Court said this procedure was unlawful because it denied each child an individual assessment of the effect of the disability on the child's development and functioning. As of this writing, however, Congress is considering legislation that would eliminate the requirement of an individual functional assessment.

Second, in the same year *Zebley* was decided, the Social Security Administration revised the rules for children with mental impairments,[139] more than half the children receiving SSI benefits. The new rules were designed to realistically assess disability due to a mental impairment in a child, based on information gathered from modern developmental pediatrics and child psychiatry. The rules are tailored both to the child's age and to particular conditions such as anxiety, autism, attention deficit hyperactivity disorder, mental retardation, and others. The new rules contain special guidelines for infants and toddlers that assess cognitive/communicative functions, motor development, social interaction, and responsiveness to stimuli.[140] Taken together, the rule changes have altered the SSI program from one that was so limited and frustrating to parents seeking benefits that few families could take advantage of it to one that is accessible to all low-income children with severe disabilities.

What are the financial requirements for SSDI and SSI?

Social Security Disability Insurance. As mentioned above, to receive Social Security benefits, a person must have contributed to the Social

Security system through payroll taxes for the required number of quarters to achieve what Social Security calls "insured status." The Social Security Administration can help determine who has contributed to the system sufficiently to qualify for SSDI benefits. Other income and financial resources do not figure at all in eligibility for Social Security benefits.

Alternatively, a person can become eligible for Social Security benefits if the applicant has a disability that manifested itself before the age of twenty-two, is over eighteen and has a parent receiving Social Security benefits or a parent who was fully insured at the time of death. Many people with mental retardation qualify for this benefit, which is sometimes referred to as the "adult disabled child" benefit.

Supplemental Security Income. As indicated above, Supplemental Security Income is a means-tested program, and there are strict rules regarding income and resources. These limits affect not only basic eligibility for benefits but the size of the check the beneficiary receives. The greater the applicant's income, the smaller the check.

To receive SSI, an adult may not have more than $446 in monthly *countable* earned income. We stress the word *countable* because the Social Security Administration has complex rules for figuring out what income counts for SSI purposes. For example, the first $20 in unearned income (for example, interest paid by a bank) does not count. Similarly, SSA does not count the first $65 in earned income plus an additional $20 if that amount has not been deducted from unearned income. After that, it counts only half of earned income. In addition, Social Security takes into consideration certain work expenses and does not count money set aside under an approved "plan for achieving self-support." Finally, a set of complicated rules is used to determine how to count various kinds of in-kind assistance, such as the value of housing provided by another, and other items of income.[141]

SSI's resource rules are also strict and complicated. A person seeking SSI benefits cannot own more than $2,000 in property such as bank accounts, real estate, stock, and other property. Here, too, there are many exceptions, including the value of a home, household goods, equipment required because of medical conditions, a car if necessary for medical reasons, and certain insurance policies.[142]

The SSI financial rules for children are somewhat different. Financial eligibility decisions for children are based on the income and assets of the child's parent or parents and the number of children in the household who have no disability (if more than one child has a disability, the income limits increase). As in the adult program, certain income is not counted. The parents and child combined can have up to $5,000 in resources after excluding the value of the house, the car needed to obtain medical care, and certain other assets.

Can a recipient of SSDI or SSI continue to receive benefits while trying to work?

Disability benefits should not, by design or effect, lead to lifelong dependence. Instead, they should be structured to provide support for the time when the recipient cannot work while containing financial incentives for a return to work and avoiding punishment of those who try to work and fail. Both the SSDI and SSI programs have incentives to return to work, but they are unfortunately inadequate to accomplish their purpose.

People receiving Social Security benefits are permitted what is called a "trial work period." Here is how it works. For a total of nine months in any five-year period, a recipient who earns more than $200 is entitled to continue to receive Social Security benefits. After nine months of this trial work, Social Security benefits end, though Medicare benefits continue an additional thirty-six months. The obvious problem here is that the nine months do not have to be consecutive. If, for example, a person works for two months in year one and cannot continue, he or she has only seven months of trial work left for the next four years.

SSI offers more attractive incentives for going back to work. Instead of paying full benefits in the beginning and then totally cutting them off, SSI allows a recipient to keep a certain amount of SSI benefits until a designated limit (just under $1,000 in 1994) is reached, regardless of how long the person has worked. The SSI work incentive program also allows a person to maintain eligibility for Medicaid indefinitely, even after earning too much to receive cash benefits, as long as income remains below a certain amount.[143]

SSI also has a program that encourages people to set aside money for education, training, and other supports necessary to go to work called a plan for achieving self-support (PASS). The PASS program is effective in allowing people not only to invest in their future without losing benefits but to use income and resources that might otherwise make them ineligible for SSI at all to gain self-sufficiency. In return, SSI benefits will be paid. Unfortunately, people often do not know about and thus do not take advantage of this simple program.

What appeal rights exist if Social Security denies benefits?

All too often, Social Security unjustifiably denies an application for Social Security or SSI disability benefits. The Social Security Act permits applicants to appeal the denial of benefits all the way to the federal courts. The appeal process contains a number of sequential steps, none of which can be skipped. Unless there is a very good excuse, each step must be taken within a strictly specified time period, usually sixty days from the date of the last decision.

The first essential step of the appeal is called "reconsideration." This step involves Social Security or the DDS staff taking a second look at the application. New evidence can be submitted at this stage but success is fairly rare. If the claim is denied on reconsideration, the applicant can file an appeal within sixty days of receiving notice of denial for a hearing before an administrative law judge.

This step holds more promise, since it is the first time the applicant gets to appear in person before the decision maker. The administrative law judge, moreover, is a person who is far more independent (though not completely so) of Social Security than the examiners who make the prior decisions. Most important of all, the applicant is permitted to present evidence and have a lawyer or other representative at a real hearing. It is a good idea to have such a representative.

If the applicant loses before the administrative law judge, the next appeal—again, it must be filed within sixty days of receiving notice of the administrative law judge's decision—is to a body called the Social Security Appeals Council, whose job is to review the decisions made by administrative law judges. After that, appeal may be made to the United States District Court.

What rights do recipients have if Social Security seeks to terminate disability benefits?

Recipients have the right to a hearing. Social Security may seek to terminate benefits for a variety of reasons, such as its belief that the recipient is no longer disabled. The appeal and hearing procedures are the same as those for denials of benefits. During the course of an appeal of a proposed termination of SSI, benefits continue, although Social Security can seek to recover them if it prevails in the appeal. Social Security benefits, however, will be discontinued while the appeal goes forward. If the appeal is successful, back benefits will be awarded from the time of termination.

What other income supports exist for people with disabilities?

Some states have general assistance or disability benefit programs, but they rarely pay as much as SSI or SSDI. Veterans may be eligible for benefits available through the Veteran's Administration.[144]

Can Social Security deprive a person of the right to control benefits?

Yes. It can appoint what is called a representative payee to receive the check and administer the benefits if it believes that the recipient's mental or physical condition prevents the person from properly managing the benefits. For children, custodial parents or guardians are the first choice in representative payee, followed by a list of preferences in the event the custodial parent or guardian cannot or will not perform this role. In addition, disability beneficiaries who receive payments because of alcohol or drug addiction must have a representative payee.

The representative payee is supposed to spend the check on the beneficiary, buying food, clothing, shelter, and items for personal comfort. Beyond these general obligations, the representative payee has a great deal of leeway in the use of the funds. Unfortunately, the representative payee program has operated poorly, with many reports of payees stealing or misusing benefit checks and of Social Security refusing to issue checks where no representative payee can be found.[145]

Further, no due process accompanies appointment of a representative payee. Social Security can appoint the representative payee without seeking a guardian or conservator through a court. It is then up to the person for whom a representative payee has been appointed to appeal the decision through the usual appeal procedure.

Still, there are some safeguards against improper appointment of a representative payee and against the payee's misuse of disability checks.[146] For example, the payee must account to SSA annually as to how the money has been spent.

The Right to Housing

We know from the experiences of people with mental disabilities—no different, in fact, from the experience of everyone else in society—as well as from social science research that stable housing is the single most important element to a settled and satisfying life in the community. The lack of housing in the community for people with mental disabilities remains a serious barrier to their integration into society. The residential circumstances of persons with psychiatric disabilities in terms of affordability, crowding, physical conditions of the housing, and quality of the neighborhood are worse than the population at large, even when corrected for income.[147]

Indeed, after a decade's debate on the relationship between housing, deinstitutionalization, and homelessness among people with psychiatric disabilities, a national Task Force on Homelessness and Severe Mental Illness assembled under the auspices of the federal Interagency Council on the Homeless found that lack of affordable housing, particularly the dwindling supply of single room occupancy and other inexpensive units, contributed extensively to homelessness among people with mental illness.[148] The single room occupancy losses alone amounted to a million units.[149] At the same time, the value of the monthly Supplemental Security Income check that so many people with mental disabilities depend on for housing has diminished so considerably that it is insufficient to rent an efficiency or one-bedroom apartment under HUD's affordability guidelines in *any* of the nation's more than 2,500 counties.[150]

For people with mental retardation, despite a policy favoring community-based housing as an alternative to institutions, billions of dollars of federal Medicaid funds continue to pour into institutions housing people with mental retardation. Complex and restrictive have rules limited the effectiveness of provisions for redirecting some of these funds for community-based alternatives.

Finally, as discussed in chapter 5, openly expressed discrimination against people with mental disabilities makes it difficult to gain access to available housing.

Is there any hope in this dismal picture? The most promising development is the movement toward normalized housing, such as apartments and single room occupancy units, and away from congregate living. New concepts, such as "normalized housing" and "housing with supports," emphasize enhancing the autonomy and dignity of people with mental disabilities by supporting them in their own homes or apartments rather than in a program facility. This approach can open up the nation's supply of housing to people with mental disabilities, making the tiny inventory of "specialized" units no longer the only housing available to them.

Is there a right to housing for people with mental disabilities?

If by this question we mean, "does the government have an obligation to assure that each person with a mental disability is adequately housed?" the answer is no. There exists no constitutional or statutory right to housing in the United States that can be enforced through a court. Despite the absence of such a categorical right to housing and despite the limited funds available under the programs described, the need for housing is so compelling—especially in light of homelessness—that people with mental disabilities have not given it up. If a general right to housing does not exist, innovative arguments can be put forth identifying specific circumstances where a right can be said to exist. We discuss them not because they are well established rights but because somewhere, at sometime, a court has agreed that such a right exists.

The right to a discharge plan that includes housing. As discussed above, many states require that a psychiatric patient discharged from a hospital be given a discharge plan that describes the person's needs and how those needs will be met upon discharge. If that plan is to be more than a meaningless piece of paper or the infamous "Greyhound therapy"—giving the discharged patient a bus ticket—the discharge plan must describe real housing and real services. That means that the state must assure that each person discharged is provided housing.

The highest court in New York State recognized that the city of New York is required to "prescribe and assist in locating adequate and appropriate housing for about-to-be-discharged mentally ill patients" and to follow appropriate discharge plans in the process.[151] The court qualified this statement, though, by saying that the obligation did not require the local government to develop new housing for people who are to be discharged in order to meet their needs.

The right to be placed in a less restrictive setting than a hospital when professional judgment so demands. As explained earlier in the chapter, the professional judgment standard the Supreme Court used in the *Youngberg* case has been employed not only defensively, to insulate practices within an institution from outside scrutiny, but affirmatively to provide community-based services to individuals professionals believe are needlessly confined in state facilities. This argument has not translated into a specific right to housing, but providing housing has always been included as among the services the state is obligated to provide.

Rights under an order to develop community-based services. Lawsuits have been brought in major cities such as Phoenix, Washington, D.C., and Denver attacking the failure of the responsible governments to develop a system of community-based services for people with mental illness. The judges in these cases, recognizing that housing is an essential component of any such system, have ordered that housing be provided to persons with mental illness who are homeless or otherwise without housing.[152]

While not qualifying as rights—because a person has no entitlement to them—a number of programs have been enacted by Congress specifically to increase the supply of housing for people with mental disabilities. Funding levels for these programs are determined annually by Congress. They include Section 8, Section 811 Housing for People with Disabilities, and Shelter Plus Care, among others. Each has different features and different eligibility requirements.[153] Many states have housing programs for people with mental disabilities as well.

The Right to Medical Assistance: Medicaid and Medicare

Medicaid

As this book goes to press, Congress is considering major changes in the Medicaid program. Proposals under consideration include placing limits on its status as an entitlement and replacing it with a block grant. If any of these proposals are enacted, Medicaid will differ substantially from the program that existed in the recent past.

Medicaid has represented the sorry alternative to a right to health care in the United States for certain low-income people. Financed by state and federal funds and administered by the states under rules the federal government establishes, Medicaid provides health benefits for certain low-income children and adults. It also pays for nursing homes for elderly or disabled persons who are indigent and for intermediate care facilities for people with mental retardation.

Medicaid is notorious for its inadequate coverage of people living below the poverty level. In 1990 fewer than half of all Americans living below the poverty level received Medicaid benefits at any time during the year.[154] Medicaid is also well known for Byzantine bureaucratic requirements, inadequate reimbursement rates that discourage health providers from participating in the program, and restrictions in covered services. Nevertheless, it remains a source of billions of dollars of health benefits for people with mental disabilities.

Moreover, reforms in Medicaid enacted during the past decade made it important to people with mental disabilities. The early and periodic screening, diagnosis, and treatment (EPSDT) component of Medicaid enabled many mental health services to be made available to children that would otherwise be unavailable under the state's Medicaid program. The future of EPSDT, however, is uncertain. Some "waiver" programs— waiving the requirements that would otherwise be applied—enabled funds otherwise spent in institutions to finance community-based programs for people with mental illness and mental retardation. Other waiver programs, giving states great flexibility in shaping Medicaid programs, may reduce access to mental health services. Chapter 5 contains a discussion of the impact of the Americans with Disabilities Act on Medicaid.

What exactly is Medicaid?

Medicaid is a system of financing health services for eligible low-income people. One of the reasons it is so complicated is that Medicaid is a federal program administered by state agencies. Some of the services are required under federal law, such as medically necessary services for children. Others may be provided at the option of the state, according to a plan it adopts and files with the federal government. In very poor states, the federal government contributes about 80 percent of the money for Medicaid; in the wealthiest states, it splits the costs equally. People eligible for Medicaid never see or gain access to Medicaid funds. The money is paid directly to health care providers. The Medicaid recipient has only a card showing eligibility.

Who is eligible for Medicaid?

In all but twelve states, anyone who receives SSI is eligible for Medicaid.[155] Children who receive Aid to Families with Dependent Children (AFDC) are automatically eligible. So are pregnant women and children through age five with income up to 133 percent of the federal poverty level, children born after September 30, 1983, whose family income is below 100 percent of the poverty level; children in foster care and special needs adoptions; and certain other children.

After these mandated groups, as of early 1996, states may choose to cover certain people if they wish, including:

• Pregnant women and infants up to age one with incomes up to 185 percent of the federal poverty level

• People living in institutions who have income and resources below certain thresholds

• Children with serious disabilities who require the level of care provided by a nursing home or hospital that could be given outside such a facility[156]

• People with disabilities whose incomes are above the SSI threshold but below the federal poverty level[157]

• "Medically needy" people—those people who meet program requirements for SSI (age or disability) or AFDC, have more resources or income than the programs allow, but who have high medical costs[158]

Are homeless people eligible for Medicaid?

Yes. A state may not deny a person a Medicaid card based solely on the lack of a permanent address.[159] Indeed, it must take affirmative steps to make Medicaid cards available to people who are homeless or do not have a permanent home or mailing address.[160]

What medical services are paid by Medicaid?

Medicaid mandates that every state offer certain health services and states to offer additional health services. Among the mandatory services are inpatient and outpatient hospital services, laboratory and x-ray services, physician services, nurse midwife services, rural health clinic services, family planning services, and—a service whose future is in doubt—early and periodic screening, diagnosis, and treatment services (EPSDT) for children.[161]

If it chooses, a state can also offer important other services. Some of these are traditional medical services, such as dental and vision care, physical and occupational therapy, prescription drugs, eyeglasses, prosthetic devices, and speech, hearing, and language disorder services.[162] Other innovative services a state can offer are especially important to people with mental disabilities. These include case management services, rehabilitation, home- and community-based care for functionally disabled individuals, and community-supported living arrangement services. Advocates for people with mental disabilities should press the state to assure that its Medicaid Plan includes these services, especially in new managed care programs.

For both optional and mandatory services except EPSDT, states can limit the amount, duration, and scope of the services it provides. This means, for example, that a state can limit the number of visits to a certain type of health professional and the number of days of hospital coverage it will reimburse.[163]

We noted above that Medicaid pays a huge amount of money for institutional care. Typical of Medicaid, though, it does this in inconsistent ways. It pays the costs of institutionalizing people with mental retardation through ICF/MRs as long as the person is approved for this level of care. But Medicaid in the past did not reimburse care at a psychiatric hospital for people between the ages of twenty-one and sixty-five (it paid for care in a psychiatric hospital for children and elderly people). This exclusion for "institutions for mental diseases," was designed to prevent states from shifting most of the costs of running their state psychiatric hospitals to Medicaid, but it also applied to private psychiatric hospitals and to nursing homes that house a majority of people with a diagnosis of mental illness. Psychiatric wards in general hospitals, however, were not excluded from reimbursement under this provision. The exclusion is being reconsidered by Congress.

Can Medicaid deny coverage for psychiatric drugs?

No. In the late 1980s, when the antipsychotic medication Clozaril became available in the United States, many states refused to cover it under Medicaid because it was very expensive. Courts held this refusal to cover unlawfully discriminated against people who sought the medication based on their condition.[164]

What is EPSDT and why is it so important?

As indicated above, one of Medicaid's mandatory services is early and periodic screening, diagnosis, and treatment for Medicaid-eligible children under age twenty-one, known as EPSDT. Despite its bureaucratic terminology, EPSDT is important because it essentially eliminates optional Medicaid service categories for children, instead requiring that *any medical service indicated by a physical or mental examination of a child (known as a "screen") must be made available to the child.*[165]

Children may receive mental health services even if those services are not otherwise covered under the state's Medicaid Plan. Many states do limit mental health services for children, so EPSDT is a key to gaining for children what they need.

Congress is now considering changes in Medicaid that would eliminate the requirement that states offer EPSDT to all eligible children. If this happens, states can still maintain the program if they wish. There is good reason for them to keep EPDST, especially as states move to managed care arrangements for Medicaid recipients. Screening and early treatment are a means of prevention of serious health conditions and thus can lead to both improved health and lower costs.

How can Medicaid help adults with mental retardation seeking community-based services?

For many years, Medicaid has been the single largest funder of residential facilities for people with mental retardation, pouring billions of dollars into them. These ICR/MRs were once virtually all large institutions. In 1977, 99 percent of all federal Medicaid funds dedicated to intermediate care facilities for people with mental retardation were spent on state institutions or privately operated facilities with sixteen or more beds. As the movement toward community-based services developed, the Medicaid program began to support smaller facilities, so that by 1992, the percentage of Medicaid funds spent on these large facilities declined to 74 percent.[166]

In addition, in 1981 Congress enacted a law that enables states to spend Medicaid funds to provide services in the community for people with mental retardation (and certain others) who would otherwise be institutionalized.[167] This "home and community-based waiver" makes non-institutional services available to people with mental retardation in states that take advantage of it. It enables people to select from a menu of services corresponding to their individual needs rather than requiring the individual to adapt to the services offered by a particular agency or facility. The menu includes case management, homemakers, home health aides, personal care, residential habilitation, day habilitation, respite care, supported employment, transportation, adaptive equipment and home modification, as well as occupational, speech, physical, and behavioral therapists. By 1992 the program served more than 60,000 people at a cost approaching a billion dollars.[168]

What are Medicaid managed care plans?

The rapidly increasing cost of the Medicaid program has led many states to require Medicaid recipients to enroll in a managed care plan. Although these plans have many variations, in mental health they usually involve an arrangement in which the state pays a fixed sum of money to an organization that agrees to provide mental health services for a defined population (e.g., low-income people with serious mental illness) in a particular geographic area. This contrasts with past practice, where a provider of services simply billed the Medicaid agency for each service provided to an eligible recipient. Under the new system, the managed care entity must approve all services to be made available to each recipient.

If designed with significant consumer and family input and implemented with adequate resources (including other state mental health funds), managed care in public mental health programs can offer a number of benefits. It can bring about greater flexibility in the use of resources, including a shift from institutions to less expensive community-based services, focus on the services people want, rather than on those providers decide to offer, and force greater attention on outcomes. But managed care in the public sector also raises a host of potential problems. Managed care companies lack experience with children with serious emotional disturbance, homeless people, and people who need long-term rehabilitation and support. Managed care entities often have financial incentives to deny services. Managed care may also lead to increased use of involuntary treatment.[169] It is therefore critical for anyone concerned with the quality of mental health services to seek to participate in decisions concerning the development and implementation of managed care systems.

What rights need to be protected in managed care systems?

As in other settings, participants in managed care plans should have the right to be free from discrimination, the right to participate in treatment decisions, the right to refuse services, the right to confidentiality, and other rights discussed elsewhere. But managed care raises special rights issues because of the nature of the organization of services.

One of the principal concerns is "disenrollment," or exclusion from the plan. Managed care plans must be prohibited from disenrolling a participant for refusing a treatment or from seeking one form of treatment rather than another. Disenrollment should also be prohibited where the participant misses appointments or exhibits difficult behavior if that behavior is related to the person's disability.[170]

In addition, it is critical for managed care plans to have effective grievance procedures that enable people to challenge service denials and other concerns quickly and effectively. These grievance procedures should include both appeals within the managed care entity and the opportunity to appeal to an outside decision maker. Participants should have access to outside advocates to assist in this process.[171]

How does a person apply for Medicaid benefits?

Medicaid is administered by a state health or social services agency. In thirty-one states and the District of Columbia, an application for Supplemental Security Income is automatically considered an application for Medicaid, and eligibility for Medicaid will follow if the SSI applicant is granted. In seven other states, although an SSI recipient is automatically eligible for Medicaid, a separate application must be filled out. In the remaining states and in cases where a person is not eligible for SSI, the person must apply directly for Medicaid benefits. If the application is denied, the applicant has the right to appeal and appear at a hearing before an Administrative Law Judge. Further appeal is available before a Medicaid board of review and to a court in the state in which the application was filed.

Medicare

Medicare is the familiar, huge program that pays many health care costs for people over the age of sixty-five. It is not limited to older Americans; a person who has received Social Security Disability Insurance benefits for two years is also eligible. Thus it can be an important source of payment for medical care for people with mental disabilities who receive SSDI. With minor exceptions, children are not eligible for Medicare.

Is Medicare like Medicaid?

Medicare is nothing like Medicaid. In the first place, like Social Security, it is available to all people who fit into its eligibility category, regardless of income. Second, it is exclusively a federal program, so it escapes the complexities that are a product of Medicaid's state administrative and program variations, especially its optional services. Third, it is far more generous than Medicaid in its payment schedule. Fourth, Medicare beneficiaries must contribute to the costs of medical care through premiums, copayments, and deductibles, just like ordinary insurance. Finally, it has a more strictly medical orientation than Medicaid, consisting of hospital insurance (Part A) and supplementary medical insurance (Part B). It does not reimburse needed community support services like case management and psychiatric rehabilitation and pays for skilled nursing home care only for a brief period of recovery after hospitalization.

What benefits does Medicare have for mental health care?

Medicare pays for mental health treatment in a general hospital on the same basis as for other medical conditions, usually up to ninety days in each benefit period. It limits payments to psychiatric hospitals, however, to 190 days in a lifetime, less if the person first becomes eligible for Medicare while in a psychiatric hospital. The outpatient benefit in Part B pays 80 percent of the costs of physician services for evaluations and for brief visits to manage medication. Psychotherapy with a psychiatrist, social worker, and psychologist and "partial hospitalization"[172] are covered but require a 50 percent copayment.

Can a person be eligible for Medicare and Medicaid?

Yes. In fact about 25 to 30 percent of all people with disabilities who receive Medicare are covered by Medicaid as well because they meet Medicaid's financial eligibility rules. Medicaid will also pay Medicare premiums, deductibles, and copayments for people whose income is below the poverty level.

The Right to Education

As this book goes to press, Congress is considering changes in the Individuals with Disabilities Education Act. Proposals under consideration include stream-lining the due process requirements and giving schools greater leeway in discipline cases. If these changes are enacted, a child's rights under IDEA may differ in certain respects from the description contained in this section.

It has only been within the last generation that society recognized that all children, not just those who fit into some preconceived norm, are entitled to education. In the not so distant past, many children with mental retardation were routinely excluded from the public schools altogether and children with emotional disorders were suspended from school or sent out of state. Quality education was well beyond their reach. As the movement to establish and protect the rights of people with mental disabilities took hold, challenges to exclusion from the schools was high on the agenda. Two seminal cases brought in the early 1970s gained recognition of important rights. *Pennsylvania Association for Retarded Citizens v. Pennsylvania*[173] held that before children with mental retardation are denied admission to or excluded from school, they have a right to notice and an opportunity to be heard. *Mills v. Board of Education*[174] established that the Constitution's equal protection and due process clauses forbid a school district from excluding children with disabilities from participating in public education. Federal legislation implementing these rights soon followed.

The enactment of Section 504 of the Rehabilitation Act in 1973[175] and, even more critically, the Education for All Handicapped Children Act (now called the Individuals with Disabilities Education Act or IDEA)[176] in 1975 opened the nation's public schools to children with disabilities. In 1990 the Americans with Disabilities Act expanded the equal access mandate still further by establishing the right of people with disabilities to be free from discrimination in settings ranging from preschools to higher education.[177]

These rights and the educational opportunities they have brought have enabled millions of children to prepare for productive and fulfilling lives as educated adults. Paradoxically, though, the rapid and enormous growth of school districts' special education programs spawned by these laws has brought with them large school bureaucracies sometimes more attuned to their own procedures than to the needs of the child. Perseverance and advocacy are therefore essential to enable these educational rights to be fulfilled.

Do children with disabilities have a right to education in the public schools?

Yes. Section 504 and IDEA mandate that every child with a disability receive a free and appropriate public education. Although the requirements of Section 504 and IDEA overlap significantly, there are also important differences relating to children with substance abuse problems and emotional disturbances. For clarity and simplicity, the discussion of elementary and secondary education focuses principally on IDEA and considers issues arising under Section 504 as they relate specifically to children with mental disabilities.[178]

The child's educational program may consist of specialized instruction together with related aids and services provided by the school. Related services consist of transportation to and from school in vehicles that are physically accessible and other nonmedical[179] "developmental, corrective and other supportive services . . . as may be required to assist a child with disabilities to benefit from special education."[180] The child with a disability must receive an education in accordance with an individualized educational program (IEP) designed especially to meet his or her educational needs.

What children have rights to special education and related services?

All children and young adults with disabilities[181] between the ages of three and twenty-one who need special education in order to benefit from their schooling are covered by IDEA.[182] In addition, in 1986 Congress enacted another provision of IDEA, called Part H, that encouraged states to provide comprehensive health and developmental services and family support to infants and toddlers experiencing developmental delays. Although states are not required to participate, once a state enters its fifth year of federally funded Part H planning, infants and toddlers have an entitlement to screening, evaluation, and early intervention services provided through an individualized family service plan.[183] All the states have chosen to establish the entitlement, but implementation has been erratic and virtually no state has yet developed the capacity to reach all eligible children.

Section 504 has even broader coverage than IDEA. For example, the U.S. Department of Education has taken the position that chemical dependence is not a health impairment rendering a child eligible for special education and related services under IDEA.[184] But Section 504 includes people who are addicted to drugs or alcohol as persons with disabilities unless they are current users of illegal drugs.[185] They are therefore entitled to an evaluation, determination of educational needs, and a program of special education and related services.

What is an individualized education plan, and how is it developed?

The individualized education plan, or IEP, is the key to the law. The plan is developed following a multidisciplinary evaluation of the child's strengths and needs—a process that must be repeated at least every three years or more often if the child's needs require.[186] For example, major developmental or behavioral changes may trigger a new evaluation. The evaluation must assess the child in all areas of suspected disability, including health, vision, hearing, social and emotional status, general intelligence, academic performance, communication skills, and where appropriate, drug and alcohol abuse. A school system cannot use a single test or evaluation tool and must follow required procedures for children suspected of having learning disabilities. Tests and evaluations must be nondiscriminatory and provided in the child's native or dominant language.[187]

Upon completion of the evaluation and at least annually thereafter, the school system must design an individualized program of education that meets the child's individual needs. The IEP does this by stating the child's current level of performance, specifying the child's annual educational goals with short-term measurable objectives and, most important, describing the particular special education and related services necessary to enable the child to meet those goals.

The plan must be detailed enough to say when the special programs will begin, the duration of the service, and the extent to which the education will take place in a setting integrated with nondisabled children.[188] It must also explain how and when the child's progress will be measured. For children age sixteen and older, the IEP must also specify the "transition services" to be provided the child. These are defined as activities that promote movement to situations such as post-secondary education, vocational training, employment, and adult services.[189]

The Supreme Court has recognized the importance of the IEP and established minimal standards by which to measure its adequacy. It must meet two fundamental criteria: first, that it is developed to assure full evaluation, planning, and parental participation; and second, that it is "reasonably calculated to enable the child to receive educational benefits."[190] Under IDEA, a school system is not obligated to develop a plan designed to maximize the child's potential, although some states impose this standard. In all cases, the school system must develop an IEP that enables the child to make reasonable educational progress.

What are the related mental health services a child is entitled to receive in the public schools?

For children with mental or developmental disabilities, related services can include psychotherapy, counseling with the child and family, parent training and counseling on matters relating to the child's development, rehabilitation counseling, occupational therapy, therapeutic recreational programs, and many others.[191] Psychotherapy is not specifically mentioned in the statute or regulations, but courts have generally recognized it as a related service in appropriate cases.[192] Under IDEA, substance abuse counseling can also be a related service but only if the child is eligible for special education and related services because of a disability other than substance abuse and the problem interferes with the child's ability to receive benefits from those services. Like other related services, only substance abuse services that are considered nonmedical are covered. Under Section 504, school districts have an obligation to provide counseling for eligible children with disabilities.

Related services for emotionally disturbed children are premised on the belief that their education must include services that extend far beyond traditional notions of education. They must help the child function independently, both at school and in the home and community, often through teaching general behaviors useful well beyond the classroom.[193] Thus, emotionally disturbed children should have a right to related services such as behavior therapy and parent training at home as well as in school, since the behaviors in and out of school are so closely linked.

Unfortunately, while these rights are beginning to be recognized by the courts, most school districts are far from meeting the educational and emotional needs of children with serious mental health problems.[194] They often prefer to send a child out of the public school altogether—often to a residential program far from home—rather than meeting the child's real needs through counseling, family services, and behavioral management.

Does the child with a mental disability have a right to be educated in a regular classroom?

Yes, with limited exceptions. This is one of the most important, but controversial aspects of IDEA. IDEA's vision is that children with disabilities will receive an appropriate education, participate fully in academic and extracurricular activities, and be integrated into the mainstream of school life to the maximum extent appropriate to the child's needs. As the Supreme Court put it, this means education of children with disabilities with nondisabled children whenever possible.[195]

IDEA provides a clear statutory right of children with disabilities to be educated with their nondisabled peers and creates a presumption that they will be educated in the regular classroom.

To the maximum extent appropriate, children with disabilities, including children in public or private institutions or other care facilities, are educated with children who are not disabled and that special classes, separate schooling, or other removal of children with disabilities from the regular education environment occurs *only when the nature or severity of the disability is such that education in regular classes with the use of supplementary aids and services cannot be achieved satisfactorily.*[196]

It is no excuse to deny inclusion based on the school system's educational theories or philosophy.[197] As one court said, "all children with disabilities need access to integrated experiences where they learn to function effectively." Integrated education increases "the opportunities for individuals to become fully-functioning, co-equal members of society."[198]

Thus, under IDEA, integrated, inclusive education is supposed to be the norm except when it is not possible. Unfortunately, this vision of IDEA is far from being fulfilled, despite the fact that legally the burden is on the school district if it believes that supports are not available to permit the child to participate in regular classes. Segregation of children with disabilities remains commonplace. A 1992 report to Congress from the Department of Education found that nearly two-thirds of the state plans submitted to the department were not in compliance with the mainstreaming requirements of IDEA. It reported that only 26 percent of school age children with mental retardation nationwide were placed in regular classrooms for at least 40 percent of the school day. In the most segregated state, New Jersey, only 2.35 percent of children with mental retardation were in these classes.[199]

There is growing legal support for strict interpretation of the right of a child with a disability to be educated in the regular classroom, accompanied by appropriate supports and services.[200] The courts have emphasized that before segregating children with disabilities, schools must determine whether education in the regular classroom can be achieved satisfactorily if accompanied by supplementary aids and services such as resource rooms, behavior modification programs, speech and language therapy, or itinerant teachers.[201] As one court wrote, "placement in other than a regular class is a fall-back choice made only *after* it is determined that placement in regular classes will be unsuccessful."[202] In making that decision, schools must consider a number of factors, including the entire range of supplemental aids and services available, the educational benefits available to the child in the regular classroom compared with those in a separate class, and the possible disruption of the regular class if the child with a disability is placed in it.

In one case, a school district declined to allow an eight-year-old child with Down's syndrome and severe cognitive and communicative disabilities to be placed in a regular class, saying that his low level of intellectual functioning and disruptive behavior precluded him from participating. It proposed sending him to a special class for multiply disabled children in another school district. Instead of accepting the school district's claims, the court looked at what it had actually done—and not done—for the child. The school had not developed a curriculum plan or a behavior management program and had not provided adequate special education support to the teacher, deficiencies that may have exacerbated the child's behavior problems. The school also had not taken advantage of what the court described as "professionally recognized methods and techniques by which educational experiences in regular classrooms can be modified so students . . . can benefit from participating in them, without interfering with the education of nondisabled students."[203] Further, the court found that the child's disruptive behaviors could not be used as an excuse to exclude him where the school had made no serious effort to devise means to ameliorate them.[204]

Decisions like these, especially combined with the mandate of the Americans with Disabilities Act to provide services "in the most integrated setting appropriate to the needs of the individual,"[205] begin to fulfill the right to an integrated education.

Can a child with special education needs be placed in another school or location where the school she would otherwise attend is unable to provide her an appropriate education?

Yes. This is the flip side of the integration mandate and reflects a tension in IDEA between inclusion and programs individually designed to meet a child's needs. As Professor Martha Minow has written, this tension reflects a choice "between specialized services and some degree of separate treatment on the one side and minimized labeling and minimized segregation on the other."[206] As illustrated above, IDEA resolves this tension by choosing inclusion whenever possible. But if is not possible through supplementary aids and services, the school district is obligated to find an appropriate program. If the placement is a residential program, the school district must pay not only the costs of the educational program but room and board as well. Indeed, a great deal of the litigation growing out of IDEA has concerned disputes about whether the child will be placed in such a program after parents, having witnessed the inadequacies of the programs offered their child by the school district, seek a special placement, for example, in a school for children with learning disabilities.

For children with severe mental health problems, disputes often arise concerning reimbursement for placement of children in mental health facilities such as psychiatric hospitals or residential treatment centers. When a child is placed in a private residential facility necessary for the child to receive an appropriate education, IDEA regulations provide that school districts must pay only for nonmedical services, as well as room and board.[207] On the other hand, if the placement is for primarily "medical" reasons, then schools are only obligated to pay the costs of special education and related services. Whether a placement is for medical or educational reasons is not always easy to determine, particularly when the child is placed in a mental health facility.

Some courts have denied reimbursement altogether for placements in mental health facilities,[208] others have said all the care was covered,[209] but the majority have sought to distinguish between the medical (not covered by IDEA) and nonmedical services (covered by IDEA) in the facility.[210] The Center for Law and Education has identified a number of factors courts appear to consider in determining whether reimbursement through IDEA is available, including whether the initial reason for the placement was an acute psychiatric episode or a situation where the child was medically stable, whether the residential facility is certified as a special education facility, whether the therapies are designed toward improving adjustment and performance in school, whether the services are the product of an IEP process, and whether the focus of the placement is for treatment of the psychiatric condition or for special education in a therapeutic setting.[211]

These disputes, however, mask the real issue, which is that education and related services for children with mental health problems should be dealt with, if at all possible, in the home, the local school, and the community. The conflicts about reimbursement for residential psychiatric placement are in many cases a product of the failure to design appropriate educational programs for children with serious emotional problems in a local school. As Theresa Glennon has argued, rather than debating whether these children are "bad" or are seriously ill and in need of treatment, schools need to address the children's problems as learners, and design programs that will enable them to obtain the emotional and social skills that are essential to their ability to grow into productive adults.[212]

Can parents be reimbursed for the costs of placing the child in a private school that meets the child's needs?

Yes, if the placement is provided for by the child's IEP. IDEA's mandate of free appropriate public education for children with disabilities means that if a school district itself cannot provide the appropriate program, it must pay the costs of a program provided by a capable public or private school. Many parents, frustrated by a school's inability or unwillingness to provide an appropriate educational program for their child, and not wanting to wait for completing the appeal process under

IDEA while the child's life goes by, enroll the child in a private program. They then seek reimbursement for the costs. Do they have a right to be reimbursed?

The answer is a qualified yes. They may be reimbursed if a hearing officer or court later decides that the school district's plan did not provide an appropriate education for the child and that the child's private placement is appropriate.[213] Reimbursement may be paid even if the private placement, though appropriate, does not meet all of IDEA's requirements.[214] Parents, though, act at their own risk. They will be reimbursed for their unilateral decision only if the hearing officer or court later determines that the program the school offered the child did not meet the child's needs and that the private placement does.

In making the decision about appropriateness, courts will take into account the student's right to be integrated into a regular school, which can conflict with parents' desire for a specialized private educational placement. For example, one court refused reimbursement for parents' placement of an emotionally disturbed child in a psychiatric institution. Aside from assessing the public school's program for the child, which included one-on-one instruction and interaction with nondisabled peers that led to educational and behavioral progress, the court noted that the institutional placement amounted to a far greater restriction of the child's liberty. It therefore denied reimbursement.[215]

What rights do children with mental disabilities have in school discipline proceedings?

Children with emotional or behavioral problems are suspended or otherwise excluded from school at alarming rates. School administrators have the authority to impose discipline,[216] but discipline may not be used to undermine the right of a child with a disability to a free, appropriate public education. School authorities must deal with the behavior of a child with a disability by seeking to ameliorate the behavior, not by expelling the student.[217] Further, schools may not discipline a child whose behavior can be traced to the failure of the school district itself to provide for the special needs of the child, whether the child has been previously identified as a child with a disability or not.

IDEA places both procedural and substantive limitations on the school's ability to exclude a child with a disability from its programs. Under IDEA a change in a child's placement can be made only through specific procedures, including notice to the parents and an opportunity to contest it.[218] In the case of *Honig v. Doe*,[219] the Supreme Court decided that a school's effort to suspend or exclude a student with a disability for more than ten days amounts to a change in educational placement. To make this change, the school district must convene the child's IEP team and follow IDEA's rules and procedural safeguards regarding a change in placement. These include notice of the proposed change, including a statement in understandable language of the reasons for the proposed change in placement, and an opportunity to be heard. All the details of the procedures must be explained to the parents. If they complain, the child has a right to remain in the current placement until the administrative appeal procedures and review by a court are completed.[220] The Court said that the "stay-put" rule prevents a school from unilaterally excluding children with disabilities from school for more than ten days for disciplinary reasons, even if they are considered dangerous and disruptive; instead, the school must keep the child in the current placement, and hence in school, until the reevaluation and IEP process has been completed. As Justice Brennan wrote, "Congress very much meant to strip schools of the unilateral authority they had traditionally employed to exclude disabled students, particularly emotionally disturbed students, from school."[221]

The right to education in the least restrictive environment is also implicated in school discipline. Long-term suspension or exclusion, including home teaching or residential placement, can impede the child's social development and isolate him or her from school peers. This does not mean that the severely disruptive child can never be excluded from the local school, but only where the child's behavior is so impaired that the needs of the child cannot be met and the education of other students is significantly compromised.[222]

Finally, the right to be protected against discrimination under Section 504 is implicated in school discipline cases, since students may not be punished on the basis of their status. Even if a student with a disability is not eligible for services under IDEA, Section 504 requires that the student be reevaluated before any significant change in placement and be given an opportunity before a hearing. Section 504 also prohibits suspension of ten days or more when the behavior of the student is an element of or related to the student's disabling condition or the result of an inappropriate educational program.[223]

Section 504 also has important implications for students who have never been referred for evaluation for special education or have no need for special education but who are considered behavior problems to the school. Disciplining students labeled a behavior problem or sending them to a special school or program may deny them the right to an evaluation and special education services if they in fact have a disability.

The school is not powerless to deal with imminent dangerous behavior by a student. In emergencies, schools can use such procedures as detention and timeout, and in extreme cases, where the student poses an immediate threat of injury to self or others, the school can suspend a student for up to ten days.[224] The school can reconvene the child's IEP team, which may review the child's IEP, propose revisions (e.g., alternative behavioral strategies), or may seek parental consent to a temporary alternative placement. If the parent disagrees with the proposal to remove him from the current educational placement, the school district can apply to a court for permission to prevent a dangerous child from attending school. It may not, however, seek to circumvent IDEA by referring the student to a juvenile or family court.

In addition, a 1990 amendment to Section 504 allows school districts to take disciplinary action against a student with a disability who currently is engaging in the illegal use of drugs and alcohol to the same extent as it would take against nondisabled students. In such cases, the due process procedures provided under Section 504, i.e., reevaluation before change in placement and due process review, do not apply.[225] If the student is eligible for services under IDEA, though, all IDEA's protections remain in place.

What rights do parents and children have in the process of devising an educational program for a child?

IDEA was designed to give parents a vital, participatory role in designing the educational program for their child. Sometimes, however, IDEA's complex and elaborate procedures are used by schools to disempower parents rather than to include them, as when interdisciplinary team members, who far outnumber parents, browbeat or intimidate parents into accepting the school's recommendations. Parent training in special education is a critical component of success in the special education process.

If a parent is not available to participate in the process, another adult, a "surrogate parent," is supposed to be appointed to fulfill the parental role under IDEA. The surrogate parent is supposed to look out for the best interests of the child and have the knowledge and skills to make sure that those interests are protected.[226]

Evaluation. Parental involvement in the development of a child's program begins with the evaluation of the child. Parents must be given notice of the proposal to evaluate a child and asked to consent to the first evaluation for special education.[227] If the parent refuses to consent, and the school district wants to proceed anyway, it must either follow state law requirements (e.g., obtain a court order) if the state law addresses the issue or use the due process hearing procedure under IDEA.

A parent who disagrees with the school district's evaluation, or who simply wants another, independent assessment, has the right to obtain one. Unless an independent evaluation is required by state law, the evaluation may be paid for by the parents, but under certain circumstances the school district must pay for it.[228] In addition, if a parent disagrees with the school's evaluation of the child, the parent has a right to another evaluation at public expense unless the school contests the need for such an evaluation at a hearing. Sometimes, however, states impose requirements on independent evaluations (e.g., who may conduct them, how much they cost) as conditions before reimbursing their costs. Once an additional evaluation is conducted, it must be considered by the school district.

Development of IEP. It is fundamental to IDEA that parents participate and collaborate in the development of the IEP. The initial IEP is supposed to be developed at a meeting involving the child's teacher, evaluator, or person knowledgeable about the child's evaluation and results; an administrator, and a parent—and the child when appropriate. The school district has the responsibility for setting up the meeting, arranging a mutually convenient time, and providing proper notice to parents concerning the purpose of the meeting and a list of people who will attend. Sometimes, parents are presented with a completed IEP at the meeting. *IDEA prohibits this practice.*[229]

At the meeting, the child's evaluation, educational progress, and other matters are reviewed and form the basis for determining the kind of programming and services that will be provided the child. The IEP is developed and a placement recommended. The IEP is supposed to determine the child's placement, not the other way around, and a school district violates IDEA if it develops an IEP around a placement it has already decided upon.

Revisions to IEP. During the course of a school year, the IEP may need to be revised. The school must include the parent in any revisions as fully as in the development of the initial IEP. Parents also have a right to seek a change in the IEP or placement at any time if they believe it is not meeting the child's needs. If the school district refuses to make either the specific changes the parent seeks or to revise the IEP generally, or if the parent objects to the school's proposed changes, the parent may complain and have a due process hearing.

Annual and periodic review of IEP. The school district must initiate a meeting with parents and other relevant people to review the child's IEP as often as necessary and at least once a year. Here, too, the school must include the parents as full partners, providing them with appropriate notice and an opportunity to participate, just as in the development of the initial IEP.

Access to records. Parents have the right to see and make copies of all educational records concerning their child. School systems must honor requests to see records promptly.[230]

What rights do parents and children have if they disagree with the school's proposed program or placement?

One of IDEA's central features is its effort to assure that parents not only participate in the process of their child's IEP but have an opportunity to challenge school district decisions before an impartial hearing officer. IDEA confers extensive due process rights on parents regarding decisions about evaluations, programs, and placements. Though often cumbersome and time-consuming, these procedures are designed to assure that every parent gets an opportunity to contest decisions before a decision maker who is not a school system representative seeking to save money, exclude difficult children, or fit a child into its existing programs.

Notice of hearing rights. Whenever a school proposes or refuses to identify, evaluate, or change the educational placement of the child or provide appropriate education to her, the school district must give notice to parents. Besides all the other requirements for the notice, it must describe how the parent may challenge the decision and how much time the parent has to do so.

Hearings. A hearing may be conducted by a hearing examiner for the local school district or the state education agency as the state determines. The parents' rights before and during the hearing include all of the following:

• The right to be informed of the availability of free or low-cost legal assistance

• The right to an impartial hearing officer, who may not be an employee of the school district, the state education agency, or other agency involved in the child's care

• The right to be represented by a lawyer and to receive other assistance at the hearing from experts in special education

• The right to subpoena witnesses, present evidence and cross examine witnesses

• The right to notice of evidence to be submitted to the hearing five days in advance (a reciprocal obligation)

• The right to a proceeding open to the public if the parent so chooses

• The right to a transcript or recording of the hearing

• The right to a decision in writing explaining the reasons for the decision and the facts on which it was based within forty-five days of the date the hearing is requested (this deadline may be extended by hearing officers and often is)

If the hearing has been conducted at the school district level, parents have a right to appeal to the state education agency, which reviews the record of the hearing and renders an independent decision in the case within thirty days of the time it is received.

Judicial review. A parent who is not satisfied with the decision of the state education agency may obtain further review of the decision in federal court. The time for filing the civil action in federal court is determined by state law.

Courts do not start from scratch. Under most circumstances, the judge considers only the evidence developed in the due process hearing, although IDEA does permit additional evidence to be introduced in the federal court proceeding. The court also must give "due weight" to the results of the administrative decision.[231] Nevertheless, the courts have a great deal of authority to protect a child's rights under IDEA. They can order a change in a child's placement, order a particular program or related service, require reimbursement of parents for unilateral placement actions they take and can even require "compensatory education," additional educational services to make up for deficiencies in past programs for a child. These services may include special education programs after a child reaches the age of twenty-one.[232]

Attorneys fees. Attorneys fees may be reimbursed to parents who prevail either in due process hearings, in court, or in the process of settling disputes before a due process hearing.[233] However, if a school district makes a written settlement offer more than ten days before a due process hearing and the parents refuse it, the hearing officer may deny attorneys' fees if the officer finds that the relief the parents obtained in the hearing is not more favorable than the settlement offer, unless the parents were substantially justified in refusing it. A similar rule applies to cases that reach court.

In addition to these rights, any person who believes the school district has discriminated against a child on the basis of disability may file a complaint within 180 days with the Office of Civil Rights of the Department of Education. The agency is supposed to investigate the complaint and seek an informal resolution. If it cannot, it can take legal action.

The Right to Vocational Rehabilitation Services

Congress is considering changes in the federally established and state-administered vocational rehabilitation program described here. Some proposals under consideration would eliminate all federal requirements.

People with disabilities, even severe disabilities, are often able to work, but in order to obtain the vocational skills necessary to get a job, they often need training and rehabilitation. It was for that purpose that Congress enacted the Rehabilitation Act[234] and annually provides funds to state rehabilitation agencies to provide these services.

A variety of approaches to vocational rehabilitation for people with mental disabilities exist, including employment skills training, supported employment, transitional employment, and others, but because of funding limitations they reach only a small fraction of the people with mental disabilities who need access to these services. Moreover, vocational rehabilitation programs have a long and sorry history of either excluding people with serious mental disabilities from their programs entirely by labeling them "unemployable" or else offering them so few programs and resources as to render them worthless to recipients. People with more severe or multiple disabilities often are rejected out of hand.

When they are accepted, vocational rehabilitation programs often demean people with mental disabilities, offer them training only for menial jobs, and give them virtually no opportunity to control their own destiny.

Their goals and aspirations are often ignored in favor of some notion of "appropriateness." One man writes of his experience: "I applied for services from DVR about a year after I left the hospital and was accepted as a client. I wanted to get a high school diploma, go to college, then law school. I very much wanted to advocate for the rights of people in psychiatric institutions. I was told that DVR would pay for me to go to a high school equivalency course, but they felt that a trade school was more appropriate for me than college or law school. My own choice was not respected."[235]

What approach does the Rehabilitation Act now take for people with mental disabilities, including severe mental disabilities?

Although funding remains a major obstacle to the availability of these services, Congress has recently taken steps to remedy discrimination, steering, devaluation, and exclusion from vocational rehabilitation programs. It did this not only by expanding eligibility for services but by setting forth detailed principles, standards, and rules designed to enable people to gain independence and to enable their values and preferences to drive the service system. In 1992 amendments to the Rehabilitation Act designed to harmonize the Act with the ADA, Congress articulated the purpose of the law "to empower individuals with disabilities to maximize employment, economic self-sufficiency, independence, and inclusion and integration into society" through "state-of-the art programs of vocational rehabilitation" that "respect individual dignity," and promote "personal responsibilities, self-determination and pursuit of meaningful careers, based on informed choice."[236]

Congress backed these values with new principles and requirements to respect individual choices, encourage individual growth, and develop individual skills.

The principles are as follows:

• Individuals with disabilities, including individuals with the most severe disabilities, are generally presumed to be capable of engaging in gainful employment, and the provisions of individualized vocational rehabilitation services can improve their ability to become gainfully employed.

• Individuals with disabilities must be provided the opportunities to obtain gainful employment in integrated settings.

• Individuals with disabilities must be active participants in their own rehabilitation programs, including making meaningful and informed choices about the selection of their vocational goals and objectives and the vocational rehabilitation services they receive.

• Families and natural supports can play an important role in the success of a vocational rehabilitation program but only if the individual with a disability requests, desires, or needs such supports.

• Qualified vocational rehabilitation counselors, other qualified rehabilitation personnel, and other qualified personnel facilitate the accomplishment of the employment goals and objectives of an individual.

• Individuals with disabilities and their advocates are full partners in the vocational rehabilitation program and must be involved on a regular basis and in a meaningful manner with respect to policy development and implementation.

• Accountability measures must facilitate and not impede the accomplishments of the goals and objectives of the program, including providing vocational rehabilitation services to, among others, individuals with the most severe disabilities.[237]

These principles are supposed to be put into place in every state vocational rehabilitation program. Instead of allowing the agency to deny services by labeling a person unemployable, the agency is obligated to assume that, with appropriate services and supports, individuals with disabilities can be trained for employment. Indeed, the rehabilitation agency is now under a heavy burden to justify denial of services by showing by "clear and convincing evidence" that a person is incapable of benefiting from vocational rehabilitation services.[238]

People with mental disabilities[239] are eligible for services. So are the people with severe disabilities, defined as someone "who has a severe physical or mental impairment which seriously limits one or more functional capacities (such as mobility, communication, self-care, self-direction, interpersonal skills, work tolerance, or work skills) in terms of employment outcome," whose rehabilitation can be expected to take an extended period of time, and who has one or more of certain listed disabilities, including mental illness and mental retardation.[240] Thus people with the type or severity of mental disability that led to their exclusion in the past are now eligible for vocational rehabilitation services.

The inclusion of people with severe disabilities, whose vocational outcome is uncertain, changes the entire focus of vocational rehabilitation from a program that "creams" the most easily rehabilitated to one that presumes that all people with disabilities can be trained for work. Whether this effort to transform vocational rehabilitation programs will succeed remains to be seen. Vocational rehabilitation agencies have proven extraordinarily resistant to change, but the tools for change have now been put in place.

What services do vocational rehabilitation agencies offer?

The state vocational rehabilitation agency is obligated to offer vocational and support services considered necessary to enable people with disabilities to work. The services must be tailored to meet individual needs in a manner consistent with the principles of self-determination and normalization. The wide array of services they must offer includes evaluations, guidance, physical and mental restoration services—including diagnosis and treatment for mental and emotional disorders—counseling, referrals, transportation for rehabilitation, personal assistance, supported employment, and other services. Tuition and books are also covered if these cannot be obtained from other sources.

The personal assistance and supported employment services reflect the broad scope of vocational rehabilitation in this new era. Supported employment, for example, takes place in integrated settings and can include, among other services, on-site intensive job skills training and social skills training.[241] They go far to transcend the traditional approach of offering services only to those who can step into a competitive position with no assistance or support at all.

How are the services determined and planned?

Vocational rehabilitation services are supposed to be consumer driven in every sense. The vocational rehabilitation agency must base its services on a plan developed for each person, called an individualized written rehabilitation program (IWRP). The program is developed jointly by the rehabilitation counselor and the person seeking services. Among many other requirements, the program must state the person's rehabilitation goals, the immediate rehabilitation objectives, an assessment of the expected need for post-employment services, the specific vocational services to be provided, the on-the-job and related personal assistance services to be provided, the time frame for providing the services, and the evaluation procedures and schedule for determining whether goals and objectives have been met.

To make sure the individual seeking rehabilitation determines the services offered, the IWRP must include a statement in the person's own words (or in the words of the person's parent, guardian, advocate, or other representative, if appropriate) describing how the person was informed about, and participated in choosing among, rehabilitation service alternatives and how he or she participated in determining goals and objectives for rehabilitation.[242]

The IWRP must meet a number of other requirements as well. For example, it must include information about other related services and benefits that may be available through other federal, state, and local programs that will help the person meet vocational rehabilitation goals. And it must explain the availability of advocates to assist in the process through the client assistance program (CAP). Finally, the IWRP must be reviewed and updated annually.

What if a person is found ineligible for services or is dissatisfied with the vocational rehabilitation services offered?

A person who is denied services or does not receive services responsive to his or her needs may appeal to an impartial hearing officer under procedures each state establishes. New evidence may be presented at this hearing concerning eligibility for services and the scope of appropriate services. At the hearing, the person is entitled to be represented by counsel, to present witnesses, and to cross examine witnesses.

Are advocates available to help people through the vocational rehabilitation process?

Yes. People who apply for vocational rehabilitation services may take advantage of client assistance programs (CAPs) charged with representing people in vocational rehabilitation proceedings. The addresses and phone numbers of these agencies are listed under Protection and Advocacy programs in appendix B.

CAPs are in the business of informing and advising clients of their rights to vocational rehabilitation services and assisting them both legally and practically. The scope of assistance includes determining eligibility for services, working out the individualized written rehabilitation plan, determining what services will be available, negotiating disagreements with rehabilitation counselors, and, of utmost importance, providing legal representation in rehabilitation and work-related disputes through the appeal process and in other matters.

Consistent with the purpose of the Rehabilitation Act, CAPs have responsibilities beyond helping people work out problems with the rehabilitation agency. They must inform individuals with disabilities of their rights under Title I (nondiscrimination in employment) of the Americans with Disabilities Act, "especially with regard to individuals with disabilities who have traditionally been unserved or underserved by vocational rehabilitation programs,"[243] including racial and ethnic minorities. The CAPs are also authorized to provide assistance and advocacy with respect to claims of discrimination based on disability in the private sector. This includes filing lawsuits against employers who discriminate. They can also assist with other benefit and service programs that concern rehabilitation and work. CAPs can be of enormous help to people applying for vocational rehabilitation services because they provide a source of advice and help independent of the vocational rehabilitation agency itself.

NOTES

1. In this chapter, we use the word *treatment* to include habilitation.

2. *See* Ass'n for Retarded Citizens of North Dakota v. Olsen 561 F. Supp. 473, 488 n. 20 (D.N.D. 1982), *aff'd on other grounds,* 713 F.2d 1384 (8th Cir. 1983) (citing Accreditation Council for Services for Mentally Retarded and Other Developmentally Disabled Persons, *Standards for Services for Developmentally Disabled Persons* (1981)).

3. Wolfensberger, *Normalization* (1972).

4. Birnbaum, *The Right to Treatment,* 46 American Bar Association Journal 499 (1960).

5. The Fourteenth Amendment to the United States Constitution, states in section one that "No state shall . . . deprive any person of life, liberty, or property without due process of law."

6. Rouse v. Cameron, 373 F.2d 451, 452 (D.C. Cir. 1966).

7. Jackson v. Indiana, 406 U.S. 715, 738 (1972).

8. Wyatt v. Stickney, 325 F. Supp. 781, 784 (M.D. Ala. 1971), *aff'd sub nom* Wyatt v. Aderholt, 503 F.2d 1305 (5th Cir. 1974).

9. Wyatt v. Stickney, 344 F. Supp 387, 390 (M.D. Ala. 1972).

10. For a general discussion of the least restrictive alternative principle, see Herr, Arons & Wallace, *Legal Rights and Mental Health Care* (1983), ch. 6.

11. The treatment plan requirement is outlined under mental health standards in appendix A.

12. Wyatt mental retardation standards are also contained in appendix A.

13. New York State Association for Retarded Children v. Carey, 393 F. Supp. 715 (E.D.N.Y. 1975) (consent decree).

14. The Supreme Court has in recent years held that the Eighth Amendment does not apply to these institutions, but only to people who are sentenced for criminal offenses.

15. Ferleger, *Anti-Institutionalization and the Supreme Court,* 14 Rutgers Law Journal 595 (1983).

16. Dixon v. Weinberger, 405 F. Supp. 974 (D.D.C. 1975). *See also* Brewster v. Dukakis, No. 76-4423-F (D. Mass. 1978) (consent decree).

17. 422 U.S. 563 (1975).

18. 422 U.S. at 576.

19. The Court said that there was no "reason now to decide whether mentally ill persons dangerous to themselves or to others have a right to treatment upon compulsory confinement by the state, or whether the state may compulsorily confine a non-dangerous mentally ill individual for the purposes of treatment."

20. 457 U.S. 307 (1982).

21. The Supreme Court also recognized a constitutional right to adequate food, shelter, clothing, and medical care. These are discussed in chapter 7.

22. Braddock et al., *The State of the States in Developmental Disabilities,* Institute on Disability and Human Development, University of Illinois at Chicago (1994) Table 2. To put these figures in perspective, however, just fifteen years earlier, in 1977, 86 percent of people with mental retardation in out-of-home placements lived in facilities of 16 or more beds, and only 7 percent lived in settings of 6 or fewer persons.

23. Youngberg v. Romeo, supra, 457 U.S. at 310 (1982).

24. 457 U.S. at 318.

25. 457 U.S. at 319.

26. 457 U.S. at 319 n. 25.

27. Jackson v. Fort Stanton Hosp. and Training School, 757 F. Supp. 1243, 1307 (D.N.M. 1990), rev'd in part 964 F.2d 980 (10th Circ. 1992). *Wyatt* and other early cases established minimum staff rations but cases decided under the *Youngberg* standard have shied away from them.

28. Thomas S. v. Flaherty, 699 F. Supp. 1178, 1192–93 (W.D.N.C. 1988), *aff'd* Thomas S. by Brooks v. Flaherty, 902 F.2d 250 (4th Cir. 1990), *cert. den.* 111 S. Ct. 373 (1990). The obligation extends to assuring that all direct care staff are sufficiently trained to meet the needs of the people in the facility and to avoid exposing them to risk of harm. *Jackson v. Fort Stanton, supra,* at 1308.

29. Hooker, *Non-Deterioration of Self-Care Skills in Institutionalized Mentally Retarded Persons: Youngberg and Its Progeny,* 14 Law and Psychology Review 239 (1990).

30. Ass'n for Retarded Citizens of North Dakota v. Olsen, *supra,* 561 F. Supp. at 484.

31. *Id.*

32. *Thomas S. v. Flaherty, supra,* at 1193–94.

33. A concurring opinion is one written by a member of the court who agrees with the result of the case but has separate or additional reasons for reaching that result.

34. *Youngberg v. Romeo, supra,* at 327 (Blackmun, J., concurring).

35. Society for Goodwill to Retarded Children v. Cuomo, 737 F.2d 1239, 1251 (2d Cir. 1984). *See also* Griffith by Griffith v. Ledbetter, 711 F. Supp. 1108, 1111–12 (N.D. Ga. 1989); Alessi v. Commonwealth of Pennsylvania, Department of Public Welfare, 710 F. Supp. 127, 135 (E.D. Pa. 1989), *rev'd on other grounds,* 893 F.2d 1444 (3d Cir. 1990).

36. 42 C.F.R. § 483.440(a)(1).

37. Clark v. Cohen, 794 F.2d 79, 96 (3d Cir. 1986) (Becker, J., concurring), cert. denied 479 U.S. 962 (1986).

38. Willowbrook Consent Judgment, *New York State Association for Retarded Children v. Carey, supra.*

39. *See* Lelsz v. Kavanaugh, 807 F.2d 1243 (5th Cir. 1987); *Society for Goodwill to Retarded Children v. Cuomo, supra;* Phillips v. Thompson, 715 F.2d 365 (7th Cir. 1983).

40. *Youngberg v. Romeo, supra,* at 322 n. 30. It would not, however, include an untrained mental health aide or custodial employee such as a janitor. Shaw by Strain v. Strackhouse 920 F.2d 1135, 1146–47 (3d Cir. 1990).

41. *See* Stefan, *Leaving Civil Rights to the 'Experts': From Deference to Abdication Under the Professional Judgment Standard,* 102 Yale Law Journal 639 (1992).

42. Society for Goodwill to Retarded Children v. Cuomo, Griffith by Griffith v. Ledbetter, 711 F. Supp. 1108, 1110 (N.D. Ga. 1989).

43. Ihler v. Chisholm, No. ADV-88-383 (Montana First Judicial District 1991).

44. *Id.* at 322. *See also* Washington v. Harper, 110 S. Ct. 1028 (1990) (state psychiatrists are appropriate decision makers to determine when government's interest in forcibly medicating prisoners outweighs prisoners' liberty interests).

45. 457 U.S. at 323 (footnote omitted).

46. *Jackson v. Fort Stanton Hosp. and Training School, supra,* at 1309 (professional psychology staff inadequately supervised and trained when there was no chief psychologist to supervise the psychology staff, who were not competent in many areas of psychology).

47. Youngberg v. Romeo, 457 U.S. at 323.

48. Thomas S. by Brooks v. Flaherty, 902 F.2d 250, 252 (4th Cir. 1990) (quoting *Thomas S. v. Flaherty, supra*).

49. *Ass'n for Retarded Citizens of North Dakota v. Olsen, supra,* at 484. *See also* N.Y. State Ass'n for Retarded Children, Inc. v. Rockefeller, 357 F. Supp. 752, 762 (E.D.N.Y. 1973) ("voluntary" admission of minor child on petition of parents may be treated as involuntary absent evidence that child's interests have been fully considered); *Thomas S. v. Flaherty, supra,* at 1191.

50. DeShaney v. Winnebago County Department of Social Services, 489 U.S. 189 (1989).

51. Doe v. Public Health Trust of Dade County, 696 F.2d 901 (11th Cir. 1983); *see also* Hanson v. Clarke County, 867 F.2d 1115, 1120 (8th Cir. 1989); (*Youngberg* holding does not apply with equal weight to those who have been voluntarily institutionalized); *but see* Goebel v. Colorado Department of Institutions, 764 P.2d 785, 797 (Colo. 1988); *Society for Goodwill to Retarded Children v. Cuomo, supra,* at 1250 (residents entitled to minimally adequate training whether voluntary or involuntary).

52. Halderman v. Pennhurst State School and Hospital, 784 F. Supp. 215 (E.D. Pa.), *aff'd* 977 F.2d 568 (3d Cir. 1972); United States v. Pennsylvania, 832 F. Supp. 122

(E.D. Pa. 1993); cases following *DeShaney* holding that, in some circumstances, voluntary patients may have no or fewer rights under *Youngberg* include Dorothy J. v. Little Rock School District, 7 F.3d 729 (8th Cir. 1993); Fialkowski v. Greenwich Home for Children, 921 F.2d 459 (3d Cir. 1990); Doe v. Public Health Trust of Dade County, 696 F.2d 901 (11th Cir. 1983); also Hanson v. Clarke County, 867 F.2d 1115, 1120 (8th Cir. 1989); Martin v. Voinovich, 840 F. Supp. 1175 (S.D. Ohio 1993).

53. 42 U.S.C. § 6023. See Garrity v. Gallen, 522 F. Supp. 171 (D.N.H. 1981).

54. These requirements may be enforced by courts. Martin v. Voinovich, 840 F. Supp. 1175 (S.D. Ohio 1993); Mihalcik v. Lensink, 732 F. Supp. 299 (D. Conn. 1990); Nicoletti v. Brown, 740 F. Supp. 1268 (N.D. Ohio 1987); Gieseking v. Schafer, 672 F. Supp. 1249 (W.D. Mo. 1987). Other provisions of the Developmental Disabilities Act, including its "Bill of Rights," create no enforceable rights, however. Pennhurst State School and Hospital v. Halderman, 451 U.S. 1 (1981).

55. *Jackson v. Fort Stanton Hosp. and Training School, supra.*

56. 42 C.F.R. § 483.440(a)(1).

57. *Id.* § 483.440(c)

58. *Id.* § 483.440(d).

59. Id. § 483.440(e),(f)(i),(ii).

60. Montana Code, § 53-21-101(1).

61. Chasse v. Banas, 399 A.2d 608, 610 (N.H. 1979).

62. Gen. Stats., § 17-206c.

63. Ill. Ann. Stat. 91✢ § 1-111.

64. *Id.* § 4-309.

65. *Id.* § 4-310.

66. *Id.* § 4-703(a).

67. *Mahoney v. Lensink,* 569 A. 2d 518, 527 (Conn. 1990); Ihler v. Chisholm, No. ADV-88-383 (Mont. Dist. Ct. 1991).

68. *Mahoney v. Lensink, supra.*

69. The Joint Commission on the Accreditation of Healthcare Organizations, a private body, accredits many inpatient facilities. To obtain accreditation, the facility must comply with standards for treatment and many other conditions of life in the facility.

70. *See* Schwartz et al., *Protecting the Rights and Enhancing the Dignity of People with Mental Disabilities: Standards for Effective Legal Advocacy,* 14 Rutgers Law Journal 541, 576 (1983).

71. The address of the Joint Commission on the Accreditation of Healthcare Organizations is One Renaissance Boulevard, Oakbrook Terrace, IL 60181.

72. Civil Rights of Institutionalized Persons Act, 42 U.S.C. § 1997.

73. *Jackson v. Fort Stanton Hosp. and Training School, supra.*

74. These rights are a product of the Omnibus Budget Reconciliation Act of 1987, 42 U.S.C. § 1395i-3(a)–(h)(Medicare) and 42 U.S.C. § 1396r(a)–(h)(Medicaid). For a discussion of whether the person with a mental disability should be in a nursing home at all, see ch. 2.

For a booklet describing the rights of people with mental disabilities in nursing homes, see *Elders Assert Their Rights* (Bazelon Center for Mental Health Law 1993). For a more comprehensive manual, see Mental Health Law Project and Legal Counsel for the Elderly, *Enforcing the Rights of Older People with Mental Disabilities, Volume I: Representing Nursing Home Residents* (1992).

75. 42 U.S.C. § 1395i-3(b)(4)(A)(i)(Medicare); 42 U.S.C. § 1396r(b)(4)(A)(i) (Medcaid). *See* Rubenstein, Rovner & Pepper, *What Federal Law Requires for Nursing Home Residents' Psychological Well-Being* (Bazelon Center for Mental Health Law 1992).

76. Torrey et al., *Criminalizing the Seriously Mentally Ill: The Abuse of Jails as Mental Hospitals.* A joint report of the National Alliance for the Mentally Ill and Public Citizen's Health Research Group (1992).

77. United States General Accounting Office, *Mentally Ill Inmates: Better Data Would Help Determine Protection and Advocacy Needs* Pub No. GAO/GGD-91-35 (1991).

78. Brackel, Parry & Weiner, *The Mentally Disabled and the Law* (3d ed. 1985) at 737.

79. Boston v. Lafayette County, 743 F. Supp. 462 (N.D. Miss. 1990).

80. Estelle v. Gamble, 429 U.S. 97 (1976).

81. The leading case, concerning the entire Texas prison system, is Ruiz v. Estelle, 503 F. Supp. 1265, 1345, (S.D. Tex. 1980), *affirmed in part and reversed in part* 679 F.2d 1115 (5th Cir. 1982), *cert. denied* 460 U.S. 1042 (1983). More recent cases include Smith v. Jenkins, 919 F.2d 80 (9th Cir. 1991); White v. Napoleon, 897 F.2d 103 (3d Cir. 1990); Eng v. Smith, 849 F.2d 80 (2d Cir. 1988); Langley v. Coughlin, 715 F. Supp. 522 (S.D.N.Y. 1989).

There is a great deal of writing about treatment rights of prisoners with psychiatric disabilities and mental retardation. The following represents a small sample. See Cohen & Dvoskin, *Inmates with Mental Disorders: A Guide to Law and Practice,* 16 Mental and Physical Disability Law Reporter 339 (1992) and 16 Mental and Physical Disability Law Reporter 462 (1992); Reed, *Legal Rights of Mentally Retarded Offenders: Hospice and Habilitation,* 25 Criminal Law Bulletin 411 (1989); Brenner & Galanti, *Prisoners' Rights to Psychiatric Care,* 21 Idaho Law Review 1 (1985); Note, *"And Some Grow Mad, and All Grow Bad:" Prisoners' Constitutional Right to Receive Psychiatric Treatment,* 11 New England Journal of Criminal and Civil Confinement 160 (1985); Rotman, *Do Criminal Offenders Have a Constitutional Right to Rehabilitation?,* 77 Journal of Criminal Law and Criminology 1023 (1986).

82. For a discussion of deinstitutionalization see chapter 2.

83. Elderly people represent 23 percent of the population of state psychiatric hospitals. *See* Jones & Kanter, *Advocating for Freedom: The Community Placement of Elders from State Psychiatric Hospitals,* 23 Clearinghouse Review 444 (1989). *See also* Streicher v. Prescott, 663 F. Supp. 335 (D.D.C. 1987).

84. *DeShaney v. Winnebago County Department of Social Services, supra.*

85. New York provides a striking example of the contrast between systems that were subject to court orders and those that were not. As a result of nineteen years of court supervision of the Willowbrook Consent Judgment, *New York State Association for Retarded Children v. Cuomo, supra,* which required the closing of the Willowbrook State School and the creation of a network of community services, the state's system of caring for people with mental retardation has shifted from one that relied almost exclusively on institutions to a largely community-based service system. Although there are still waiting lists for services, the network of existing community residences and support services for

people with mental retardation is many years ahead of the community service system for people with psychiatric disorders.

86. Wyatt mental health standards. *See* appendix A.

87. *Dixon v. Weinberger, supra; Brewster v. Dukakis, supra.*

88. P.C. v. McLaughlin, 913 F.2d 1033 (2d. Cir. 1990); S.H. v. Edwards, 860 F.2d 1045 (11th Cir. 1988), *modified* 886 F.2d 292 (11th Cir. 1989); Lelsz v. Kavanaugh, *supra* 815 F.2d 1034 (5th Cir.) *cert. denied* 108 S. Ct. 44 (1987); Society for Goodwill for Retarded Children, *supra;* Woe v. Cuomo, 729 F.2d 96 (2d Cir. 1984), *cert. denied* 469 U.S. 936 (1985); Phillips v. Thompson, 715 F.2d 364 (7th Cir. 1983).

89. *Phillips v. Thompson, supra;* Kentucky Association for Retarded Citizens v. Conn., 674 F.2d 582 (6th Cir. 1982); Williams v. Secretary of Executive Office, 609 N.E. 2d 447 (Mass. 1993) ("deinstitutionalization with subsequent services may be highly desirable for individuals in plaintiffs' position, such services are not required as a matter of law by the ADA").

90. *Thomas S. v. Flaherty, supra.*

91. Homeward Bound v. Hissom, No. 85-C-437-E (N.D. Okla. 1987).

92. *Jackson v. Fort Stanton Hosp. and Training School, supra.*

93. *Ihler v. Chisholm, supra.*

94. *See, e.g.,* Coffelt v. Department of Developmental Services, No. 916401 (Cal. Sup. Ct. 1994); Joan S. v. Gudeman, No. 91-C-727 (E.D. Wisc. 1994); Parrant v. Stewart, No. 89087653CV (Utah Dist. Ct. 1993).

95. *Clark v. Cohen, supra; Thomas S. v. Flaherty, supra;* Not all courts, however, have agreed with this approach. *See, e.g., S.H. v. Edwards, supra.*

The *Youngberg* standard also protects people against discharges not made with professional judgments. For example, where a person was transferred from a state hospital to a night care unit at a detoxification center, and no professional felt that this placement was consistent with his treatment plan, a court found that he did not receive minimally adequate treatment. Thomas S. v. Morrow, *supra,* 781 F.2d at 375.

96. Lelsz v. Kavanaugh, 629 F. Supp. 1487, 1494–95 (N.D. Tex. 1986).

97. *Jackson v. Fort Stanton Hosp. and Training School, supra.*

98. Jackson v. Fort Stanton Hosp. and Training School, 964 F.2d 980, 992 (10th Cir. 1992).

99. *Id.*

100. Brewster v. Dukakis, 675 F.2d 1, 4 (1st Cir. 1982). *See also, Goebel v. Colorado Department of Institutions, supra* (Court could direct implementation of plan until funds ran out; defendants would then have obligation to bring inadequacy of funding to legislature's attention); Arnold v. Department of Health Services, 160 Ariz. 593, 775 P.2d 521 (1989). (lack of funds inadequate reason when defendants never established impossibility of providing statutorily required services).

101. 29 U.S.C. § 794. The Rehabilitation Act prohibits discrimination on the basis of disability to recipients of federal financial assistance. It is discussed in chapter 4.

102. 42 U.S.C. § 12101 and following. *See* chapter 4.

103. Kentucky Ass'n for Retarded Citizens v. Conn., 674 F. 2d 582 (6th Cir. 1982), *cert denied* 459 U.S. 1041 (1982); Sabo v. O'Bannon, 586 F. Supp. 1132 (E.D. 1984); Goebel, 764 P.2d at 805. *See also* Garrity v. Gallen, 522 F. Supp. at 209.

104. Jackson v. Fort Stanton Hosp. and Training School, *supra,* 757 F. Supp. at

1298. *See also* Martin v. Voinovich, 840 F. Supp. 1175 (S.D. Ohio 1993); Conner v. Branstad, 839 F. Supp. 1346 (S.D. Iowa 1993); Halderman v. Pennhurst State School and Hospital, 784 F. Supp. 215 (E.D. Pa. 1992).

105. Jackson v. Fort Stanton Hosp. and Training School, *supra,* 757 F. Supp. at 1299.

106. *Id. See also Martin v. Voinovich, supra.*

107. 28 C.F.R. § 35.130(d).

108. *See* Cook, *The Americans with Disabilities Act: The Move to Integration,* 64 Temple Law Review 393, 399–403 (1991).

109. Homeward Bound v. Hissom, No. 85-C-437-E (N.D. Okla. 1987).

110. Halderman v. Pennhurst State School and Hospital, 784 F. Supp. 215 (E.D. Pa. 1992).

111. Williams v. Secretary of Executive Office, 609 N.E. 2d 447 (Mass. 1993). *See also* Conner v. Branstead, 839 F. Supp. 1346, 1357 (S.D. Iowa 1993).

112. *DeShaney v. Winnebago County Department of Social Services, supra.*

113. Philadelphia Police and Fire Association v. City of Philadelphia, 874 F.2d 156 (3d Cir. 1989); McNamara v. Dukakis, 762 F. Supp. 959 (D. Mass. 1990).

114. *McNamara v. Dukakis, supra.*

115. *See* Perlin, *State Constitutions and Statutes as Sources of Rights for the Mentally Disabled: The Last Frontier?,* 20 Loyola of Los Angeles Law Review 1249 (1987); Costello & Preis, *Beyond Least Restrictive Alternative: A Constitutional Right to Treatment for Mentally Disabled Persons in the Community,* 20 Loyola of Los Angeles Law Review 1527 (1987).

116. Ga. Code Ann. § 88-502.388-601(a).

117. *Id.* § 88-606.

118. Ill. Ann. Stat. 91½ § 2-102(a).

119. The variation in state laws mandating community-based services is discussed in Brackel, Parry & Weiner, *Mental Disability and the Law* (3d ed. 1985) at 626–27.

120. Matter of W.N., 828 P.2d 378 (Mont. 1992); Mental Health Association in California v. Deukmejian, No. B014479 (Ct. App. 1986).

121. Arnold v. Department of Health Services, 160 Ariz. 593, 775 P.2d 521 (1989); Goebel v. Colorado Department of Institutions, 764 P.2d 785 (1988).

122. Goebel v. Colorado Department of Institutions, *supra,* 764 P.2d at 796.

123. *Arnold v. Department of Health Services, supra.*

124. The ICF/MR regulations also provide that the facility must "provide a post-discharge plan of care that will assist the client to adjust to the new living environment." 42 C.F.R. § 483.440(b)(5)(ii).

125. Heard v. Cuomo, 80 N.Y. 2d 684, 594 N.Y.S. 2d 675, 610 N.E. 2d 348 (1993).

126. Ohio *ex rel.* Cottrill v. Meigs County Board of MR and DD, 621 N.E.2d 728 (Ohio Ct. App. 1993).

127. House Select Committee on Children, Youth, and Families, *No Place to Call Home: Discarded Children in America,* H.R. Rep. No. 101-395, 101st Cong., 2d Sess. 1990.

128. The Adoption Assistance and Child Welfare Act requires states to use reasonable efforts to prevent out-of-home placement of children and reunify children with families once separation has occurred. 42 U.S.C. §§ 620–28, 670–79a. As this book went to press, however, Congress was considering major revisions to this law, including replacing its detailed rules with a block grant to the states without a family preservation mandate.

129. R.C. v. Hornsby, No. 88-H-1170-N (M.D. Ala. June 5, 1991) (consent decree).

The case is described in greater detail in Burnim, Jackson, Milstein & Pepper, *Developments in Mental Disability Law in 1991*, 25 Clearinghouse Review 1218, 1229–31 (1992).

130. Comprehensive Community Mental Health Services for Children with Serious Emotional Disorders, 42 U.S.C. § 290.

131. These include Bloch, *Federal Disability Law and Practice* (1994); Bush, *Social Security Disability Practice* (1994); Hall, *Social Security Disability Practice*; Legal Counsel for the Elderly, *Disability Practice Manual for Social Security and SSI Programs*; Lybarger & Onerheim, *An Advocate's Guide to Surviving the SSI System* (1985); National Organization of Social Security Claimants' Representatives, *Social Security Practice Guide* (1993).

For information about children's SSI benefits, see Bazelon Center for Mental Health Law, *The Advocate's Guide to SSI for Children* (2d ed. 1995).

132. 42 U.S.C. § 401 and following.

133. 42 U.S.C. § 1381 and following.

134. The regulations governing the two program set out eligibility and other requirements in detail. Social Security Disability Insurance regulations are found in volume 20 of the Code of Federal Regulations Part 404 and SSI regulations are in the same volume, part 416.

135. For an overview of the rules, see Rubenstein, *SSA Issues New Listings Governing Mental Impairments*, 19 Clearinghouse Review 715 (1985). In the past benefits were available for a disability as a result of drug or alcohol addiction, but Congress is considering legislation that would eliminate eligibility on account of addiction.

136. 20 C.F.R. § 404.1520a.

137. The process by which a state disability determination agency does this is somewhat complex. It first tries a short-cut, looking at whether the person has the serious limitations in the ability to work that are contained in the listing itself. If not, the agency goes on to see whether the person's ability to work is severely restricted by any work-related limitations in the ability to function. This latter step is called the determination of "residual functional capacity."

138. 110 S. Ct. 885 (1990).

139. 55 Fed. Reg. 51208 (Dec. 12, 1990).

140. For a discussion of the new mental impairment rules and the impact of Zebley, see Bazelon Center for Mental Health Law, *supra.*

141. For a description of the income rules for adults, see National Senior Citizens Law Center, *Representing Older Persons* (1990) Lybarger & Onerheim, *An Advocate's Guide to Surviving the SSI System, supra.*

142. *Id.*

143. A description of this program can be obtained from the Social Security Administration entitled *Red Book on Work Incentives—A Summary Guide to Social Security Work Incentives for People with Disabilities*, SSA Pub. No. 64-030 (1991). *See also* Shelton, *Work Incentives for Persons with Disabilities under the Social Security and SSI Programs*, 28 Clearinghouse Review 236 (1994).

144. *See* Wildhaber, Abrams, Stichman & Addlestone, *Veterans Benefit Manual: An Advocates Guide to Representing Veterans and the Their Dependents*, (National Veterans Legal Services Project 1991).

145. *See* Briggs v. Sullivan, 886 F. 2d 1132 (9th Cir. 1991).

146. 20 C.F.R. § 416.601–.665.

147. Newman, *The Housing and Neighborhood Conditions of Persons with Severe Mental Illness,* 45 Hospital and Community Psychiatry 338 (1994).

148. Federal Task Force on Homelessness and Mental Illness, *Outcasts on Main Street* (1992). For a thorough review on the relationship between mental illness, discrimination, and housing, see Perlin, *Competency, Deinstitutionalization and Homelessness: A Story of Marginalization.* 28 Houston Law Review 64 (1991).

149. United States Department of Health and Human Services, *The Homeless: Background, Analysis and Options.* Briefing Paper prepared by the HHS Working Group on the Homeless and submitted to the U.S. House of Representatives Subcommittee on Intergovernmental Relations and Human Resources, 1984.

150. McCabe et al., *A National Study of Housing Affordability for Recipients of Supplemental Security Income,* 44 Hospital and Community Psychiatry 494 (1993).

151. *Heard v. Cuomo, supra.*

152. *Arnold v. Department of Health Services, supra, Goebel v. Colorado Department of Institutions, supra,* Dixon v. Kelly, No. 74-285 (D.D.C. January 27, 1992) (consent order).

153. For up to date information about these programs, contact a local public housing authority, mental health or mental retardation agency, or community development corporation. State mental health and mental retardation agencies, as well as the Department of Housing and Urban Development, are also a source of information.

154. House Subcommittee on Health and the Environment of the Committee on Energy and Commerce, *Medicaid Source Book: Background Data and Analysis (A 1993 Update),* prepared by the Congressional Research Service, Committee Print 103-A, 103d Cong., 1st Sess. 1993 at 3.

155. The twelve states, known as 209(b) states after the section of the Medicaid law permitting the exclusion, are Connecticut, Hawaii, Illinois, Indiana, Minnesota, Missouri, New Hampshire, North Carolina, North Dakota, Ohio, Oklahoma, and Virginia.

156. Twenty states have exercised this option.

157. Six states and the District of Columbia have exercised this important option. They are Florida, Hawaii, Massachusetts, Nebraska, New Jersey, and Pennsylvania.

158. Thirty-six states exercise this option, but each state can establish its financial criteria for eligibility as long as the income limit is below 133 1/3 percent of the state's maximum AFDC payment.

159. 42 U.S.C. § 1396a(b)(2).

160. 42 U.S.C. § 1396a(a)(48).

161. This is not a complete list of mandatory services.

162. This list of optional services is also incomplete.

163. *See* Alexander v. Choate, 469 U.S. 297 (1985).

164. Visser v. Taylor, 756 F. Supp. 501 (D. Kan. 1990); Alexander L. v. Cuomo, 588 N.Y.S.2d 85 (N.Y. Sup. Ct. 1991); Doe v. Palmer, No. C90-4101 (N.D. Iowa 1991).

165. This feature of EPSDT was created by Congress in 1989 in § 6403 of the Omnibus Budget Reconciliation Act of 1989, Pub. L. No. 101-239.

166. Braddock et al., *supra.*

167. 42 U.S.C. § 1396n(c).

168. Braddock et al., *supra.*

169. Bazelon Center for Mental Health Law, *Managing Managed Care for Publicly Financed Mental Health Services* (1995).

170. *Id.*

171. *Id.*

172. Partial hospitalization refers to a program where an individual spends part of a day in an intensive program in a hospital or community mental health center.

173. 344 F. Supp. 1257 (E.D. Pa. 1971), *modified* 343 F. Supp. 279 (E.D. Pa. 1972).

174. 348 F. Supp. 886 (D.D.C. 1972).

175. 29 U.S.C. § 794. The Department of Education has issued detailed regulations to implement Section 504's general nondiscrimination requirement in the context of public education.

176. This law is commonly known as Public Law 94-142 and is codified at 20 U.S.C. § 1400 and following. The federal regulations under IDEA flesh out the requirements of the law. They are contained in 34 C.F.R. pt. 300.

177. Nondiscrimination in higher education is discussed in the chapter on discrimination.

178. There are many guidebooks that can provide additional detail about the rights of children with disabilities in the public schools. For an introduction to the law, we recommend Ordover & Boundy, *Education Rights of Children with Disabilities, A Primer for Advocates* (Center on Law and Education, 955 Massachusetts Ave., Cambridge, MA 02139, 1991). A longer analysis is Turnball, *Free Appropriate Public Education: The Law and Children with Disabilities* (1986). A guide written specifically for parents and teachers is Anderson, Chitwood & Hayden, *Negotiating the Special Education Maze, A Guide for Parents and Teachers* (2d ed. 1990).

179. Medical services are excluded as a related service unless they are diagnostic or for evaluation. 20 U.S.C. § 1401(a)(7). Health-related supportive services, even if apparently medical in nature, that are provided by a nurse or other nonphysician are not excluded under this exception. In Irving Independent School District v. Tatro, 468 U.S. 883 (1984), for example, the Supreme Court held that a school district must provide clean intermittent catheterization every three to four hours to a child who needs it.

180. 20 U.S.C. § 1401(a)(17).

181. IDEA lists covered disabilities, including mental retardation, learning disability, serious emotional disturbance, autism, and traumatic brain injury. In addition, other health impairments that lead to the need for special education or related services are covered. 20 U.S.C. § 1401(a)(1).

182. If serving young adults ages eighteen to twenty-one is inconsistent with state law or practice or under a court order, however, the local school district is not required to. 20 U.S.C. § 1412(2)(C).

183. The definition of child with a disability is broader under Part H than under the rest of IDEA. Children who have received early intervention services under Part H may continue to receive special education services between ages three and five even if they do not meet IDEA's narrower definition of eligibility.

184. However, if the child has another condition that renders her eligible for services under IDEA and has a substance abuse problem that interferes with the ability to benefit from special education, related services must address the substance abuse problem.

185. The ADA amended Section 504 to exclude a person who is currently engaging in the illegal use of drugs. However, the exclusion does not apply to individuals who have successfully completed a supervised drug rehabilitation program or who otherwise have ceased engaging in illegal drug use. People currently participating in a supervised drug rehabilitation program are also covered by 504. 29 U.S.C. § 706(8)(C)(ii).

186. 20 U.S.C. §§ 1412(2)(c) and 1414(a)(1)(A).

187. 34 C.F.R. §§ 300.532(a), (b); 300.533(a)(1).

188. 20 U.S.C. § 1401(a)(20).

189. 20 U.S.C. § 1401(a)(19).

190. Board of Education v. Rowley, 458 U.S. 176, 206–7 (1982).

191. 20 U.S.C. § 1401(a)(17).

192. Clovis Unified School District v. California Office of Administrative Hearings, 903 F.2d 635 (9th Cir. 1990); Max M. v. Illinois State Board of Education, 629 F. Supp. 1504 (S.D.N.Y. 1984); T.G. v. Board of Education of Piscataway, 576 F. Supp. 420 (D.N.J. 1983), *aff'd* 738 F.2d 420 (3d Cir.), *cert. denied* 469 U.S. 1086 (1984); Papagoda v. State of Connecticut, 528 F. Supp. 68 (D. Ct. 1981); Doe v. Anrig, 651 F. Supp. 424 (D. Mass. 1987).

There has been some disagreement among the courts, however, whether psychotherapy provided by a psychiatrist is a related service covered by IDEA or a "medical" service not covered by IDEA. Darlene L. v. Illinois State Board of Education, 568 F. Supp. 1340 (N.D. Ill. 1983); McKenzie v. Jefferson, 566 F. Supp. 404 (D.D.C. 1983) (psychiatrist's services not covered); Tice v. Botentour County School Board, 908 F.2d 1200 (4th Cir. 1990) (psychiatrist's services covered).

193. David D. v. Dartmouth School Committee, 775 F.2d 411 (1st Cir. 1985).

194. *See* Koyanagi & Gaines, *All Systems Failure: An Examination of the Needs of Children with Serious Emotional Disturbance* (National Mental Health Association and Federation of Families for Children's Mental Health, 1993); Glennon, *Disabling Ambiguities: Confronting Barriers to the Education of Students with Emotional Disabilities,* 60 Tennessee Law Review 295 (1994).

195. Board of Education v. Rowley, 458 U.S. 176, 202 (1982).

196. 20 U.S.C. § 1412(5)(B)(emphasis added).

197. Roncker v. Walter, 700 F.2d 1058 (6th Cir. 1983).

198. Oberti v. Board of Education of the Clementon School District, 801 F. Supp. 1392 (D.N.J. 1992), *affirmed* 995 F.2d 1204 (3d Cir 1993).

199. *Fourteenth Annual Report to Congress on the Implementation of the Individuals with Disabilities Education Act,* cited in Oberti v. Board of Education, 995 F.2d 1204, 1214 (3d Cir. 1993).

200. *E.g.,* Greer v. Rome City School District, 950 F.2d 688 (11th Cir. 1991), *opinion withdrawn and remanded on other grounds,* 956 F.2d 1025 (11th Cir. 1992), *reinstated* 974 F.2d 173 (11th Cir. 1992); *Oberti v. Board of Education, supra,* at 1204; Daniel R.R. v. State Board of Education, 874 F.2d 1036 (5th Cir. 1989).

201. *Oberti v. Board of Education, supra; Daniel R.R. v. State Board of Education, supra.* Moreover, even if this goal cannot be achieved and education outside a regular classroom is necessary, school districts still have an obligation to mainstream the child to the maximum extent possible.

202. Holland v. Board of Education, 786 F. Supp. 874, 882 n. 9. (E.D. Cal. 1992), *aff'd sub nom.* Sacramento City Unified School District v. Rachel H., 14 F.3d 1398 (9th Cir.), *cert. denied* 114 S. Ct. 2679 (1994).

203. *Oberti v. Board of Education of the Clementon School District, supra,* at 1404.

204. *See also* Chris D. v. Montgomery School District, 735 F. Supp. 922, 743 F. Supp. 1524 (M.D. Ala. 1990).

205. 42 U.S.C. § 12182(b)(1)(B).

206. Minow, *Learning to Live with the Dilemma of Difference: Bilingual and Special Education,* 48 Law and Contemporary Problems 157, 181 (1985).

207. 34 C.F.R. § 300.302.

208. *E.g.,* Clovis Unified School District v. California Office of Administrative Hearings, 903 F.2d 635 (9th Cir. 1990).

209. *E.g., Papagoda v. State of Connecticut, supra.*

210. Babb v. Knox County School System, 705 F.2d 800 (6th Cir. 1992). The school district claimed the expenses for three hours of classes and intensive mental health services were medical not educational services and thus not within IDEA's purview. The court said the school district was wrong and that special education services include instruction provided in a hospital and the related psychological and counseling services it provided. *See also Tice v. Botentour County School Board, supra;* Taylor v. Honig, 910 F.2d 627 (9th Cir. 1990).

211. Ordover & Boundy, *supra,* at 25.

212. Glennon, *supra.*

213. School Committee of Burlington v. Department of Education of Massachusetts, 471 U.S. 359 (1985).

214. Florence County School District Number Four v. Cater, 114 S. Ct. (1993).

215. Teague Independent School District v. Todd L., 999 F.2d 127 (5th Cir. 1993).

216. All school discipline in the public schools must comport with students' rights to due process of law. Goss v. Lopez, 419 U.S. 565 (1975).

217. *Chris D. v. Montgomery School District, supra.*

218. Section 504, moreover, requires reevaluation prior to any proposed change in educational placement.

219. 108 S. Ct. 592 (1988).

220. 20 U.S.C. § 1415((e)(3).

221. 108 S. Ct. at 604.

222. 34 C.F.R. § 300.552.

223. *See* discussion of applicability of Section 504 in Ordover & Boundy, *supra.*

224. 108 S. Ct. at 605.

225. 29 U.S.C. § 706(8)(C)(iv).

226. 20 U.S.C. § 1415(b)(1)(B).

227. IDEA has very specific requirements for the content of all notices sent to parents. Where applicable, the notice must contain a description of the proposed action, the reasons why the action is proposed, the alternatives considered and rejected, a description of the evaluation procedures and a full explanation of the procedural safeguards available to the parent. The notice must be written in clear and understandable language and, where applicable, in a language other than English.

228. The rules governing when the school district must pay for the evaluation are contained in 34 C.F.R. § 300.503.

229. 20 U.S.C. § 1401(a)(20).

230. 28 C.F.R. § 300.562. *See also* Family Educational Rights and Privacy Act, 20 U.S.C. § 1232(g), which gives families the right to challenge and amend incorrect records.

231. *Board of Education v. Rowley, supra,* at 206.

232. Pihl v. Massachusetts Department of Education, 9 F.3d 184 (1st Cir. 1993).

233. 20 U.S.C. § 1415(e)(4),

234. 29 U.S.C. § 701 and following.

235. Harp, *Empowerment of Mental Health Consumers in Vocational Rehabilitation,* in *Strategies to Secure and Maintain Employment for People with Long-Term Mental Illness,* Consensus Validation Conference of the National Institute of Disability and Rehabilitation Research, Resources Papers (1992).

236. 29 U.S.C. § 701, as added by Pub. L. No. 102-569 § 101.

237. 29 U.S.C. § 720(a), added by Pub. L. No. 102-569 121(a)(2).

238. 29 U.S.C. § 722(a)(4)(A).

239. People who are currently engaged in the unlawful use of drugs are not considered people with disabilities for the purposes of eligibility for vocational rehabilitation services. 29 U.S.C. § 706(8)(C)(i).

240. 29 U.S.C. § 706(15)(A).

241. 29 U.S.C. § 706(33) and (34).

242. 29 U.S.C. § 722(b)(1)(B)(x).

243. 29 U.S.C. § 732(a).

VII

Rights in Everyday Life in Institutions and the Community

Not long ago, when television cameras first found their way into state institutions for people with developmental disabilities, they revealed images as stark and memorable as those of concentration camps: filthy, naked, sometimes malnourished patients tied to beds, feces smeared on walls, routinized staff beatings of residents. In the 1970s those images, the inevitable scandals that accompanied them, and the portrayal of institutions in novels and films such as *One Flew Over the Cuckoo's Nest* led to litigation and reform and to demands for the protection of the rights of people kept inside the walls of institutions.

Most of the snake pits are gone, and the place of long-term institutions in the lives of people with mental disabilities has diminished. Fewer than half the number of people with mental disabilities live most of their lives in state institutions as when the last edition of this book was published. In part, this is a product of the changes in values, clinical practice, and knowledge that include designing ways of avoiding hospitalization, even for people in crisis, through the use of mobile outreach teams, crisis houses with peer support, intensive case management, and other strategies. Indeed, the avoidance of hospitalization is typically used as a measure of success in the assessment of community-based mental health programs. Similarly, many community-based mental retardation programs seek to address problem behaviors in the settings in which they occur rather than, as in the past, sending people to "behavior units" inside an institution.

These developments do not tell the entire story. Many of the people who remain in institutions have been there for two or three decades, sometimes longer. Moreover, while their average daily census has declined, each year state hospitals admit hundreds of thousands of people who remain for weeks, months, and sometimes years. And these figures represent but a small segment of the acute care admissions to all inpatient facilities for psychiatric treatment, now more than two million people annually.[1] So in this age of deinstitutionalization, a great many people still find themselves institutionalized.

It is still possible to find barbarities in institutional practice. Violence, abuse, and injuries are still far more common than is reasonably acceptable. Investigation and oversight agencies issue numbing reports of abuses. One recent case revealed the practice of keeping civil patients in prison cells for twenty-three hours a day or keeping patients in seclusion so others can go to lunch.[2] In another, people in a psychiatric emergency room were forced to sleep on plastic chairs, radiators, and even on waiting room floors for days until an inpatient bed became available.[3] The more dominant feature of these facilities, though, is that life remains controlled, restrictive, and often excruciatingly boring. For any institution is, by definition, a bureaucracy, inevitably structured in large part around its own needs rather than those of its patients.[4]

Anyone who has been hospitalized for a physical illness has an inkling of the problem. Hospitalization for physical illness, though, provides but a glimpse of life in a facility for people with mental disabilities. Even when hospitalization is clinically defensible, state psychiatric hospitals, large intermediate care facilities for people with mental retardation, nursing homes, psychiatric wards in general hospitals, and even the most posh private psychiatric hospitals are highly regimented environments. Rules govern when to eat and when to go outside, when to go to bed and what possessions are allowed. Writing a letter, engaging in sexual activity, even voting, become difficult and sometimes impossible. Sanctions for noncompliance with rules can be severe, including restraints on whatever personal liberty remains, like the right to leave the ward.

These restrictions are often defended on clinical grounds, for example, to "reduce stimulation" or "to encourage socialization skills." The true basis for the rule may be more complex, involving staffing patterns and shift requirements, safety, and administrative needs. These may be legitimate concerns, but it often becomes impossible to sort out when a restriction is therapeutic and when it is merely a rationalization for controlling large numbers of people living together in a closed environment or serving the convenience of the staff.

Administrators are often loathe to acknowledge that factors other than clinical need come into play in their decisions. So sometimes the world of the institution takes on an Orwellian quality, where every restriction, every punishment, every intervention is labeled therapeutic and hence is immune to challenge. It is this pervasive invocation of therapeutic justifications for stultifying institutional practices, rather than deliberate abuse, that is so characteristic of daily life in institutions today and makes the demand for definition and protection of rights as important as ever. At the same time, these facts raise the question of whether any large institution can be run well enough to protect people's rights.

The story has yet another chapter. Even people who are not confined in institutions do not escape violations of rights by the operators of programs in which they participate. Expectations that susceptibility to harm, neglect, or abuse would end once a person resides in the community have been dashed by board and care homes that are run as restrictively as any institution and by programs that fail to protect their participants from harm. So many of the rights once considered relevant only to institutional life are necessary in the community as well. In addition, some rights, like the right to vote and the right to confidentiality of and access to records, are as central for people living in communities as they are to people living in institutions.

This chapter discusses rights in the context of daily life in institutions and community programs. Some of these rights have been discussed in earlier chapters, including the rights to treatment and services, to informed consent, to refuse treatment, and to be free of discrimination. The remaining issues, including conditions of daily existence, protection from harm and abuse, civil rights, the use of restrictive procedures, access to advocates, and rights to records, are discussed here.

THE ORIGINS AND SCOPE OF RIGHTS OF INSTITUTIONALIZED PEOPLE

Do institutionalized people have rights? Where do they come from?

People institutionalized by the state have rights that derive from the Constitution. Obtaining judicial recognition of these rights, though, took great courage and struggle. As David and Sheila Rothman observed in *The Willowbrook Wars,* a story of one the first cases seeking to establish these rights, Orrin Judd, the federal judge who first heard the case, found it easier to issue an injunction against the American bombing of Cambodia than to find in the Constitution rights that could be a basis to curb abuse of people locked in the Willowbrook State School.[5]

The same case that brought about a right to treatment, *Wyatt v. Stickney*,[6] also recognized rights in state-operated facilities and remains the fount of much of our thinking about them even today. *Wyatt* recognized rights to have decent food in a humane living environment, to protection from harm, to communicate and maintain relationships with people in the world outside, to be free of experimental treatment in the absence of adequate consent, to religious practice, to be served by qualified and trained personnel, to be free of restrictive interventions, and to be prepared for discharge.

Despite resistance, backlash, second thoughts, reinterpretation of constitutional requirements, and a more conservative judiciary, the *Wyatt* standards have endured as the quintessential statement of rights for people with mental disabilities in state institutions. Many of the standards have been adopted as state law by legislatures or through regulations issued by state mental health or mental retardation agencies.[7] They influenced nonbinding model bills of rights enacted by Congress for people in developmental disability[8] and psychiatric institutions.[9] They also provided the conceptual framework for the bill of rights Congress established for residents of nursing homes funded by Medicaid and Medicare.[10] *Wyatt* also influenced standards for the protection of rights in residences funded by Medicaid called intermediate care facilities for people with mental retardation, (ICF/MRs), described in chapter 6.[11] These facilities may be large or small, institutions or homes, publicly or privately run. Because of their continuing importance, the rights recognized in *Wyatt* are reproduced in appendix A.

By the time the Supreme Court first considered the rights of institutionalized people with mental disabilities in the *Youngberg*[12] case in 1982, their importance was already well established. Aside from recognizing a right to minimally adequate treatment, the Supreme Court held in *Youngberg* that institutionalized persons confined in state facilities have rights to food, clothing, shelter, safety, protection from harm, and freedom from undue restraints. *Youngberg*, however, took the same approach to these rights as it did to minimally adequate treatment, as described in chapter 6: as long as the relevant decision has been made on an individual basis by a responsible and qualified professional in accordance with professional

standards rather than for reasons of punishment or administrative convenience, the action taken does not violate anyone's constitutional rights.[13]
Under the professional judgment standard, the very professionals whose
conduct is at issue and who may indeed be the source of the claimed
violation of rights are insulated from independent judicial decisions.[14]

Following *Youngberg*, courts have deferred to the judgments of professionals in matters relating not only to treatment and ward management
but to core aspects of liberty such as protection against unwarranted
seclusion and restraint and searches and seizures.[15] But *Youngberg* cannot
apply equally to all rights. Although, as we discuss below, *Youngberg*
has some application to free speech questions in institutions, the First
Amendment's guarantee of freedom of speech cannot be completely subject
to professional control. The right to vote is completely outside the realm
of the professional judgment standard. Professional or ward staff have no
discretion to take this right away for disciplinary reasons, because they
believe the individual is not "ready" or able to exercise the right, or because
the treating physician thinks it is contraindicated.

Rights recognized by state law generally are not subject to the professional judgment standard at all. These statutes and regulations can always
be changed, but while they are on the books, they often provide greater
protection of basic freedoms to confined individuals than rights deriving
from the Constitution. It is not uncommon now for a court to decide
that a facility has violated rights or standards recognized under state law
but not federal constitutional rights.

As a result of all these developments, it is no longer sufficient to speak
in general terms about the rights of institutionalized people with mental
disabilities. The critical question is whether and how these rights truly
constrain the staff of institutions. Do they really protect people from
arbitrary or unwanted exercise of authority by staff? Or are they just a
comforting veneer that can be shattered in an instant at the whim of
institutional personnel? Each right must be analyzed separately, with an
examination of the source of the right and the degree to which the
professional judgment standard is applicable.

Two further points deserve emphasis. First, the rights one has may
depend on whether the facility is public or private. People have constitutional rights only against government action. Occasionally, private facilities
undertake government functions, such as holding people involuntarily
committed by courts, and a strong case can be made that constitutional

rights should apply in those facilities as well.[16] Even where the constitution does not apply, however, state and federal law protecting people in institutions, such as the Medicaid ICF/MR regulations, often apply to both public and private facilities.

Second, health care providers have legal obligations to the people they care for beyond the protection of constitutional and statutory rights. They have the same legal duty under the common law as any other provider of medical or habilitation services to act reasonably toward the people under their control and to refrain from intentionally harming them. If a provider does not exercise due care, it may be held liable for malpractice and be required to compensate the individual who has suffered harm from the provider's negligence. Indeed, the legal standard for showing negligence is generally lower than for showing a violation of constitutional rights. In a negligence case, it is usually no defense for an institutional staff member to show that he or she acted in a "professional" manner. Rather, the provider must establish reasonable conduct in accord with an objective standard of care.[17]

THE RIGHT TO SAFETY AND PROTECTION FROM HARM

Do people in public institutions have a right to safe conditions?

Yes.[18] This seems self-evident; the fact that it must be articulated shows the frequency of harms to residents of institutions. The right encompasses a safe physical structure, adequate protection from fire, a clean and sanitary environment that is adequately ventilated and kept at temperatures necessary for health, food that is disease free, sufficient supervision to prevent injuries, and safe feeding practices for residents with severe physical disabilities (e.g., residents cannot be fed while they are lying down because of the risk of choking). In one case, the staff argued that even worse injuries would occur if these residents were to live at home, but the court disagreed. "The question is not what setting would be most unsafe, but whether the state must bear responsibility for unsafe conditions in its schools. We hold that it must."[19]

Residents also have a right to protection from physical and mental abuse by staff or other residents, as well as from self-injury and self-abuse.[20] Violations include corporal punishment, staff abuse, wounds inflicted on patients, and failure to terminate staff members who engage in assault.[21]

People in institutions also have a right to protection from suicide.[22] The right to protection from harm also mandates the use of adaptive equipment to prevent the physical deterioration of nonambulatory individuals (such as exercise equipment that will help people who can't walk or exercise themselves to retain their muscle strength). Finally, it includes freedom from inappropriate drugs or drugs given in excessive doses or inadequately monitored for adverse effects.[23]

Do institutionalized people have a right to protection from unwanted sexual activity?

Yes. The right to protection from harm includes the right to protection from sexual assault or abuse by other patients or residents as well as from staff. Protection against sexual exploitation and assault remains inadequate. Evidence suggests that rapes of patients have been common[24] but severely underreported.[25] And when sexual abuse is reported, it is often either not investigated or is mishandled because of the failure of staff members to differentiate between consensual sexual activity and abuse.[26] A great deal more needs to be done to protect institutionalized people from sexual abuse than merely stating they have rights.

What steps must a facility take when safety is jeopardized?

A facility has an obligation to investigate incidents that jeopardize safety and to take steps to prevent their recurrence. The Medicaid regulations, for example, require facilities to report and investigate allegations of mistreatment and to ensure that further abuse does not take place while an investigation is in progress.[27]

THE RIGHT TO NECESSITIES: FOOD, CLOTHING, SHELTER, AND MEDICAL CARE

Is there a right to adequate food, shelter, clothing, and medical care?

Yes.[28] The evidence in the original *Wyatt* litigation showed that the state of Alabama spent less than fifty cents per person on food each day, that it allowed food to be prepared in unsanitary conditions, and that in one facility it permitted the staff to feed fifty-four boys from one bowl and nine plates. Extensive regulation and oversight have been put in place to ensure that institutions provide the necessities of life to the people who live in them. They must serve an adequate amount of food that is safe and of decent quality. They must adhere to special dietary needs of residents. For example, the Medicaid regulations[29] require that each person in an ICF/MR receive a balanced and varied diet in appropriate quantities under the supervision of a dietician. The facility must serve people in dining areas in upright positions to prevent them from choking on their food.[30]

The right to shelter requires the facility to provide clean space that is adequately heated, ventilated, and lit and that remains free of asbestos and pests. Staff must monitor hot water and fire safety systems and maintain sanitation.[31] Rooms should be of adequate size, occupancy should not exceed licensed capacity, and enough space and equipment must be available for appropriate services.[32] No court has gone so far as to suggest that each person must have a private room. The Medicaid regulations require, however, that there be no more than four people to a room.[33]

Clothing must be appropriately individualized and clean and must fit the person who wears it.[34] In the not very distant past, patients were required to wear ill-fitting jumpsuits, prison or military clothing, or even pajamas, a reinforcement of the degradation associated with institutionalization. They now have a right to adequate clothing of their choice[35] along with a place to store it.[36]

An institution must ensure that the services of a physician are available at all times, on site or by contract.[37] A facility must have a sufficient number of physicians and nurses, provide dental care, maintain infectious diseases and mortality rates within a normal range, and monitor medications and their side effects. It must maintain charts in accord with medical standards,[38] administer drugs by qualified personnel, and otherwise keep drugs locked under proper conditions at all times.[39] It must protect people against communicable diseases and offer appropriate care to individuals who have these diseases, including AIDS.

The rights to adequate food, clothing, and shelter extend beyond meeting people's physical needs. These rights are also subject to the principle of normalization. Thus, institutionalized people have a right to make some personal decisions concerning what they will eat[40] as a means of exercising some modicum of control over their daily lives. They have the right to personalize their areas[41] and the right to reasonable access to private space.[42] Pictures and posters on the walls, furniture that varies from room to room, and various other individualized touches that make the institution look more like a home than a prison may seem too trivial to qualify as rights, but in fact deeply affect a person's experience. Similarly, the institution must provide " 'adaptive' clothing, or clothing modified to suit a person's physique or to help her learn how to dress herself properly."[43] This is important because "the failure to provide adaptive clothing may deny . . . residents an opportunity to retain basic self-care skills such as dressing and toileting themselves."[44]

Life in an institution, however, renders true normalization impossible and hence limits the rights to food, clothing, and shelter in important ways. In one case, for example, a court held that no violation of the right to adequate food occurs where more aggressive residents grab food from other residents, as long as it is not a common occurrence.[45] Another illustration is a facility's ability to regulate clothing or jewelry it deems unsafe. These may include not only sharp jewelry but watches, belts, and other items of clothing.

THE RIGHTS OF CITIZENSHIP AND CIVIC LIFE

One of the pervasive myths about people with mental disabilities is that they are too crazy or impaired to participate in the life of their nation or community, to be paid for working, or to engage in the normal activities of life. Social science research as well as common observation challenges the stereotype. One study, for example, showed that the majority of patients confined in a state psychiatric hospital, almost all of whom had diagnoses of psychotic or major affective disorders, had opinions about operations of the 1991 Gulf War similar to those of the American public.[46]

Nevertheless, the simplest activities of life that enable a person to participate in civic life, including making a phone call, sending and receiving mail, reading books, seeing visitors, going outside, getting exercise, and smoking can either disappear or be recharacterized as a "privilege" to be earned once a person is confined in an institution. Hence courts, legislatures, and administrative agencies have had to articulate the rights to fresh air and exercise, to make telephone calls, receive visitors, and send and receive mail.[47] The scope of the right to maintain contact with the outside world, though, is subject to interpretation both by administrators and courts. One appellate court overturned a trial court's ruling that people confined in an institution had a right to go shopping, to go to restaurants, and to visit recreational facilities in the outside community. Instead of recognizing how important these activities are to provide a modicum of normal life to institutionalized people, the court instead mocked them. "We cannot say that the state deprives an individual of a liberty interest when it fails to provide enough field trips."[48]

Other civil rights are more fully recognized and protected under state law, particularly those less intimately connected to everyday life in the facility. These include the right to enter into contracts, to manage one's financial affairs, to associate with others, to marry, and to divorce. The one right that remains sacrosanct is access to a lawyer or advocate.

Do people confined in institutions have the right to vote?

Yes. Since voting is a fundamental right of citizenship,[49] the right to vote cannot be denied on account of hospitalization or institutionalization,[50] although as a practical matter exercising that right can be difficult because the right to register and vote is often ignored by hospital administrators.[51] In 1993, Congress enacted legislation to make voter registration easier (the "Motor Voter" law, so named because it provided for voter registration in connection with the acquisition or renewal of a driver's license). The law requires states to permit registration by mail[52] and requires public and private agencies to register voters if they provide state-funded programs primarily for persons with disabilities.[53] The latter could well include state psychiatric and mental retardation institutions.

Is there a right to religious freedom in an institution?

One of the most basic of constitutional rights is the First Amendment guarantee of the free exercise of religion. At a minimum, people confined in public institutions are entitled to practice their religion or abstain from religious worship if they so choose. Approximately two-thirds of the states also have enacted statutes or regulations that extend protections of religious freedom to private facilities as well. The scope varies from broad guarantees of the right to worship, to the right to reasonable accommodations for transportation to nearby religious services. A number of states expressly authorize a right to visit with members of the clergy at all times, while several specifically allow institutionalized people access to sacred texts. Consistent with these principles, facilities should grant access to religious publications and materials, make reasonable accommodation of dietary requirements, and allow reasonable attendance at religious services and visits by members of the clergy. Facilities should also scrupulously protect those who choose not to practice a religion.

Perhaps because the right to religious freedom is so widely recognized, there has been little litigation in this area.[54] In one case, an involuntarily committed Christian Scientist successfully sued to prevent a municipal hospital from forcing her to take psychotropic medication in violation of her religious beliefs. Affirming the principle that a competent person's freedom of worship may be restricted only where there is a "grave and immediate danger to interests which the state may lawfully protect," a federal appeals court upheld the woman's right to refuse treatment as long as she was not dangerous to herself or others.[55] This principle applies equally to the refusal of other forms of medical treatment, such as blood tests and transfusions.

Do involuntary residents have a right to freedom of expression and association?

Yes. All residents, whether voluntarily or involuntarily admitted, have the right to communicate and associate freely with others for social, personal, political, or religious reasons. These rights are protected by the First Amendment to the Constitution, as well as by the constitutions and statutes of most states.[56]

For many years, institutions severely limited the communication rights of residents. In some cases, mail, telephone, and visitation rights were withdrawn at the time of commitment, and inmates were required to earn them back as part of a privilege system of discipline rather than as part of a treatment plan. In other instances, officials arbitrarily curtailed these rights on the grounds that communication with other inmates or the outside world would be "antitherapeutic." Although many treatment professionals sincerely believed that the exercise of First Amendment rights interfered with residents' treatment, others imposed such restrictions as a means of control, to eliminate dissent, or for their own convenience.

The first institutional conditions cases, such as *Willowbrook*[57] and *Wyatt*,[58] established the principle that institutionalized people with mental disabilities have the general right to communicate with others inside and outside the institution. Subsequently, courts have reaffirmed and elaborated on these rights, including the right to reasonable visitation, the use of telephones, uncensored incoming and outgoing mail, and access to advocates, counsel, and the legal system.[59] They have emphasized, for example, that arbitrary restrictions on visitation, such as allocation of visiting hours to particular persons[60] or severe limits on visiting hours,[61] are not tolerated. Although the Supreme Court has yet to decide a case directly raising these issues, it has enunciated the basic principles underlying these rights. In *Youngberg*, the Court ruled that certain basic constitutional rights survive confinement, "even for penal purposes." People who are involuntarily committed "may not be punished at all" and therefore, one may reasonably infer, are entitled to at least the same rights as convicted prisoners.[62] Adopting this reasoning, some courts have applied rights developed in prison cases to restrictions in the field of civil commitment.[63] Under this analysis, a restriction on an inmate's constitutional rights must be related to a substantial and legitimate institutional purpose and should be no greater than is necessary to achieve that purpose.[64] For example, a hospital may not eliminate or reduce an individual's visiting rights because of insufficient staffing, as punishment for misbehavior, or for the staff's convenience. Nor can the restriction sweep too broadly. Typically, the institution must have substantial security or treatment concerns that can only be addressed by narrowly limiting a particular right.

As a general rule, involuntarily committed people have a right to frequent visits by people of their own choosing, (including lawyers and advocates), reasonable access to a telephone, and to make and distribute materials such as newsletters within the institution. They may also send and receive sealed mail; contact lawyers, advocates, judges, or governmental agencies; and invite people from outside the institution to speak to them about their rights as confined persons.

The most common justification for limiting visitors, monitoring mail, or curbing telephone privileges is the assertion that these measures are a necessary part of the individual's treatment plan.[65] Although courts are reluctant to permit restrictions on free speech and association, they occasionally permit limited infringements in the relatively rare circumstances where a hospital can show that a particular restriction furthers a substantial governmental interest, is a legitimate and essential part of an individual's treatment, and no other, less restrictive means are appropriate. Thus, despite the general rule that involuntarily committed people have a right to send and receive mail freely, a federal court in Oregon upheld a hospital's right to censor certain outgoing mail of an involuntarily committed forensic psychiatric patient who had been sending "mass mailings" containing "outrageous accusations and lurid language relating to his treatment." The hospital had begun censoring all of the inmate's mail as part of a treatment plan designed to teach him to ventilate his anger at confinement through other means. The court, however, ruled that these restrictions were overly broad and violated his First Amendment right to send uncensored mail to public officials, government agencies, advocacy groups, and attorneys. It also ordered the hospital to send the individual copies of each notice of censorship and the justification for each piece of mail it censored.[66]

One of the more creative uses of the First Amendment took place in New York in 1987. A homeless woman who lived on the sidewalk on New York's fashionable Upper East Side was among the first people committed as part of a highly publicized program to confine homeless street people with mental disorders under a controversial commitment standard promulgated by the city's mayor. No sooner was she picked up than New York City issued a press release describing her condition in unflattering terms, albeit under a pseudonym. The woman, who called herself Billie Boggs, was incensed and tried to contact several television and newspaper reporters to present her side of the story. The hospital refused to allow her access to the media, professing concern for the woman's privacy rights and barring the reporters she had called from visiting her. The following day she complained to the judge presiding at her commitment hearing that her First Amendment rights had been being violated. The hospital then reversed its position and made space available for her to hold press conferences as needed.[67] Through frequent contacts with the media, Ms. Boggs was able to break the city's monopoly on information about her case and influence the public's perception of homeless people with mental disorders.

Do people in institutions have the right to sexual expression and reproductive choice?

Put this way, the question seems bizarre. Doesn't everyone have a fundamental right to sexual expression, at least as long as it does not violate laws against rape, incest, and other unlawful sexual practices? The Supreme Court has said time and again that the right to reproductive choice is fundamental. But stereotypes about people with mental disabilities have rendered restrictions of sexual expression one of the hallmarks of life for people with mental disabilities who are institutionalized. One of the *Wyatt* standards provides for the opportunity for suitable interaction with members of the opposite sex, but only a handful of states adopted it, and some that did ultimately repealed it.[68]

Sex takes place in institutions, as it does everywhere else, but the subject is hardly discussed.[69] When it is discussed at all, sexual activity often masquerades as a treatment issue, to be allowed or forbidden as the professional staff sees fit. Professionals sometimes assume the authority to decide whether sex in general or in a particular instance is "good" for the individual and some have developed criteria for making the decision.[70] These theories may be right or wrong, but the decision to interfere with consensual sexual relationships remains a violation of a fundamental right. Courts, fearful of entering the arena, are deferential to these judgments, even to the point of allowing staff to decide whether sexually explicit reading material should be allowed.[71]

On the other hand, questions about regulation of sexual expression are often complicated by the duty of institutional personnel to protect residents from harm and from sexual exploitation, especially those whose competence to make decisions related to sexual activity is uncertain. Although administrators and clinicians should not prohibit sexual activity on "therapeutic" grounds, they have an obligation to protect residents. Sometimes these judgments are difficult ones, but it is unfortunately true that many institutionalized people are deprived of both sets of rights.

Sexual and reproductive rights within institutions are finally gaining some attention. Competent women in institutions have the same right to access to contraception, to carry a pregnancy to term,[72] and to obtain an abortion under *Roe v. Wade* as noninstitutionalized women do, although the procedures for implementing these rights are often vague or ad hoc.[73]

Do residents have a right to be paid for their labor?

Yes. Work, it is said, is a key to personal dignity, and people with mental disabilities now have the civil right to equal opportunity in employment. But work that is forced or unpaid is dehumanizing,[74] degrading, humiliating, and exploitive. As late as the early 1970s, a survey revealed that 32,000 of the 150,000 people in facilities for mentally retarded people worked, but only 20 percent received more than $10 per week, and 30 percent received no pay at all.[75] The unpaid or marginally paid patient labor that was once the hallmark of institutional life is now gone, a product of the simple principle that one must be paid for one's work.

Thirty years ago, courts determined that compulsory, uncompensated work by a person with a mental disability confined to an institution is involuntary servitude and violates the Thirteenth Amendment to the

Constitution.[76] Despite a later interpretation of the Thirteenth Amendment that narrowed its scope to encompass only physical or legal coercion,[77] we can safely say that forcing people to work without pay remains a violation of the Constitution. Following *Wyatt's* prohibition of uncompensated work that benefits the institution,[78] most state laws and regulations and federal ICF/MR regulations prohibit uncompensated work that amounts to more than routine personal housekeeping.[79]

Are institutionalized people entitled to the minimum wage?

Yes, as long as the person is performing work at a competitive level. The nation's minimum wage law, the Fair Labor Standards Act, applies to people confined in institutions as long as the institution derives a benefit from the labor and the person does productive work.[80] The fact that the work may have therapeutic value may not be taken into account in determining wages. The only exceptions are for personal housekeeping and for crafts kept by the individual.

Regulations issued by the Department of Labor[81] recognize that not all labor performed by persons living in institutions is performed according to competitive standards. So they allow pay at subminimum wage levels (but not less than 50 percent of minimum wage) for individuals whose productive capacity is impaired to the extent that they cannot earn minimum wages. No minimum rate is applicable, however, for up to a year for participants in evaluation or training programs for individuals whose productive capacity is inconsequential.

In order to pay less than minimum wage, the facility must obtain a certificate from the Department of Labor allowing it to do so. There are a number of categories in which a certificate may be offered, including evaluation and training, individual exceptions, work activities center, and group minimum wage. The first three require wages commensurate with productivity; group minimum wage must pay at least 50 percent of the minimum wage.

The Medicaid regulations governing ICF/MRs also require that people who work be "compensated for their efforts at prevailing wages and commensurate with their abilities."[82]

Must former patients working at facilities be granted the benefits other workers have?

Yes. A number of states operate programs to employ former patients in the facility where they once lived. These programs may suspend the usual civil service requirements in hiring and give special preferences to these individuals. Once hired, though, they may not be placed in a special class of employee that denies them benefits other civil service workers enjoy.[83] This rule amounts to nothing more than the application of the principle of nondiscrimination to employees hired through an affirmative action program.

Must involuntarily confined people pay the costs of their confinement?

Almost all states have statutes that require individuals, their families, and their estates to pay the costs of both voluntary and involuntary institutionalization. This practice is often justified under the legal fiction that even people admitted involuntarily enter into an implied contract with the institution to provide for their care and treatment. Otherwise, it is asserted, they would be unjustly enriched by having received services for which they did not pay. Yet many people who have been involuntarily confined object to paying for what they consider to be the equivalent of a prison. In their view, the deprivation of liberty can be a singularly unenriching experience, particularly when confined in state institutions that are overcrowded and understaffed and offer meager and frequently inadequate treatment. Ironically, prisoners generally do not have to pay for their criminal confinement.

By and large, these statutes have withstood constitutional challenge. Some courts, however, have required institutions to demonstrate that the services they provided were minimally adequate. For example, a New York court refused to allow the state to collect payment from a father who entrusted his profoundly retarded, multiply handicapped daughter to the care of the Willowbrook State School, where she received "little or no care and grossly inadequate maintenance."[84] In addition, there is generally no obligation to pay for involuntary confinement that was subsequently found by a court to be unwarranted.[85]

Finally, a state may not bill individuals in a discriminatory or retaliatory manner. One court ruled that New York State could not bill individuals who sued the state mental health agency for the full cost of institutionalization where it usually assessed charges only to the extent it believed that patients had the ability to pay.[86] Fearing that they could be liable for the entire amount of the bills if they continued the litigation, the plaintiffs considered withdrawing their lawsuits. The court struck down the rule on the ground that New York's practice had a chilling effect on the plaintiffs' rights of free speech and access to the courts.

Are families liable for the cost of their relatives' care?

Yes. All but three states have statutes that hold family members liable for the cost of institutionalization of their relative with a mental disability if the relative is unable to pay.[87] Generally, this obligation covers parents, spouses, and adult children, although in some cases parental liability ends when an individual reaches the age of majority.[88] In addition, some courts have held that third party relatives are liable only if they have received express notice of their financial responsibility.[89]

SECLUSION AND RESTRAINT

Our images of the snake pits of the past often include a patient wearing a straightjacket, locked in a tiny room, or tied spread-eagle to a bed. To the general public, that image is no more contemporary than the shootout at the OK Corral. Unfortunately, the public is wrong. Seclusion and physical restraint remain the wild west of institutional psychiatry. They are neither long gone nor adequately controlled. They are used in state psychiatric hospitals, private facilities, and psychiatric wards of general hospitals. And they are dangerous. A review of New York State institutions revealed that there were 111 reported deaths associated with seclusion or restraint between 1984 and 1993.[90] A survey of 1,000 patients conducted in connection with that review revealed that, of the 54 percent of respondents who were secluded or restrained, 62 percent reported unnecessary force, psychological abuse, ridicule, or threats by staff.[91] Recent litigation against psychiatric institutions has brought to light instances where individuals have been kept tied to a bed for days at a time and in seclusion rooms for months on end, where seclusion or restraint is used as a form of staff retaliation, and where people were locked in seclusion to allow others to go to a party.[92]

Even strong adherents of the use of seclusion and restraint as psychiatric procedures recognize how problematic they are, both in terms of physiological dangers and psychological impact. One of its strongest defenders, Thomas Gutheil, concedes that in some settings "seclusion may represent a serious treatment failure and defeat; an ambivalently held, conflicted procedure of dubious civil-rights validity; or a clumsily performed, unpracticed brawl, leaving a host of injuries and grudges in its wake."[93]

Proponents of seclusion and restraint argue that they are last ditch efforts to avoid imminent harm, invoked only when there is literally no other option. The data suggest otherwise, that facilities that choose to forgo seclusion and restraint, or invoke it only sparingly, can do so without untoward consequences. Studies indicate that the frequency and duration of these procedures vary enormously from one institution to another. In the New York study, 16 percent of the facilities surveyed did not use seclusion or restraint at all in the month studied, while 39 percent used seclusion and restraint 40 or more times.[94] Other studies also show similarly significant variations in use. Efforts to account for these wide variations suggest that the frequency of seclusion and restraint appears to have far more to do with the attitudes and philosophies of institutional staff and the adequacy of staff training than with patient demographics or behavior.[95] Some defenders of seclusion and restraint have suggested that low use of seclusion or restraint may be compensated for by increased unscheduled use of antipsychotic medication,[96] but the evidence suggests that this is not so. Rather, the same facilities that use seclusion and restraint only sparingly, if at all, generally respect individual rights and avoid "as needed" medication.[97]

These data confirm what many professionals and facilities have demonstrated, that seclusion and restraint can be avoided. For example, as a result of abuses uncovered in the *Willowbrook* case, New York State banned the use of seclusion in mental retardation facilities in 1975.[98] Nearly twenty years later, the state Office of Mental Retardation and Developmental Disabilities reports that its institutions and community facilities have been able to address even the most difficult behavioral challenges with individualized treatment plans and without the need for seclusion.[99]

Greater respect for individual rights and interventions like simple positive reinforcement and encouragement, staff-patient interaction, even going for a walk off the unit, can be effective in reducing or eliminating the use of (or claimed need for) seclusion or restraint. Leadership and firm policy can also reduce its frequency. After the deaths in New York led to an effort to reduce the use of seclusion and restraint, one of the hospitals turned to methods of dealing with problem behaviors like rewards for good behavior and, as one administrator put it, "more individual attention."[100]

In facilities for persons with mental retardation, institutional reform litigation has been more successful in curbing the inappropriate use of seclusion and restraint. Seclusion is rare and the physical restraints used typically allow a person some mobility. Restraints tend to be used as a means to protect others from aggressive behavior (e.g., hitting, scratching, kicking) or to prevent self-abuse (e.g., head-banging, rocking). Still, controversy surrounds their use not only because of the restrictions they impose but because they may be improperly used as a substitute for training to eliminate the unwanted behavior.

What is seclusion? What is restraint? What are chemical restraints?

Seclusion generally means involuntary placement in a locked room, generally one designated for that purpose. Seclusion rooms are typically very small and contain no furniture (except possibly a bed) or other objects. The barrenness is said to protect against suicide attempts. Seclusion room doors often have windows through which staff can observe the individual placed in the room.

Seclusion is usually distinguished from timeout, which involves placement in an unlocked room to decrease stimulation. In facilities for persons with developmental disabilities, however, the phrase *timeout* includes placing a person in a room from which he cannot leave. In those circumstances, though, the rules require a staff member to be present or, if the door is closed, a locking mechanism that requires constant physical pressure to engage.[101]

Physical restraint is the tying or strapping of a person to an object to prevent bodily movement. Common methods include four point restraints, in which a person is strapped to a bed or chair by arms and legs; five point restraints, which add a strap to the waist; cuffs or straps on the hands that permit the person to walk but prevent the use of arms; and the posey vest or straightjacket, which locks arms and hands inside the vest. Other facilities use chair restraints and other unorthodox methods and devices. A few facilities use handcuffs, which are not a clinically appropriate means of restraint and should only be used where an individual is under arrest.[102]

The term *chemical restraints* refers to the administration of strong antipsychotic medications as a way of controlling behavior. Chemical restraints are generally unlawful. Restrictions on the use of chemical restraints are difficult to enforce because so many people are given antipsychotic medication for the purpose of improving behavior. The difference between appropriate medication and chemical restraint is often as much a metaphysical as a legal or medical question. So while many laws and regulations still forbid the use of chemical restraints,[103] they are of almost no practical value in protecting anyone's rights.[104]

It is perhaps for that reason that current ICF/MR regulations refrain from any consideration of chemical restraints and instead try to identify the specific harms the use of antipsychotic medications may bring to an individual. They state that medications used for behavior control must not be given in doses that interfere with a person's daily activities, must be integrated into the person's individual program plan, and may not be used until "it can be justified that the harmful effects of the behavior clearly outweigh the potentially harmful effects of the drugs."[105]

The situation is different in nursing homes, where antipsychotic drugs have long been used as a way of controlling unwelcome behaviors like making noise, wandering, or mild aggressiveness toward other residents, even when the individual being medicated lacks any psychiatric diagnosis. Nursing homes that receive Medicaid or Medicare funds are now forbidden from using drugs for behavior control and from using a psychotropic drug in a dose larger than necessary to achieve the purposes for which it is indicated.[106] Indeed, the concern about the misuse of these drugs is so great that nursing homes receiving Medicaid or Medicare funds must have an outside expert review their drug regimens at least annually.

What is the most common justification for the use of seclusion and restraint?

As a short-term, emergency measure to protect the patient or others from the risk of imminent physical harm, usually when the individual is violent. This use of seclusion and restraint is justified solely to protect people against injury and does not purport to have a therapeutic purpose. The United Nations Principles for the Protection of Persons with Mental Illness and for the Improvement of Mental Health Care,[107] adopted in late 1991, adhere to the view that seclusion or restraint can be used only "when it is the only means available to prevent immediate or imminent harm to the patient or others."[108] About a dozen states also have laws restricting the use of seclusion or restraint to circumstances where violence is imminent; a revised *Wyatt* standard, adopted in 1992, agrees.[109] Many advocates have urged that this be the only ground for the use of physical restraints.[110]

In mental retardation facilities governed by Medicaid rules, restraints may be used on an emergency basis—that is, when "absolutely necessary to protect the client or others from injury." The emergency use of timeout is forbidden.[111]

What other justifications for the use of seclusion and restraint do professionals assert?

Mental health professionals have been imaginative in justifying the use of seclusion and restraint even where there is no serious risk of harm to the patient or others. The principal reasons given for the use of seclusion and restraint include:

To prevent serious disruption of the treatment program or significant damage to the physical environment. The use of seclusion and restraint for this purpose has been endorsed by the American Psychiatric Association.[112] Sometimes this rationale is described through the euphemism that dominates the field, to protect "disruption of the therapeutic milieu." The obvious problem here is that this justification places no identifiable limits on the use of seclusion or restraint. It has been applied to people who simply refuse to participate in ward activities (part of the "treatment program"). Further, it is difficult at best to distinguish this supposedly clinically appropriate use of seclusion or restraint from impermissible grounds such as staff convenience or punishment of the patient. The result of such fluid professional standards is the absence of any constraint on individual staff behavior and potential abuse of patients.

For this reason, the use of seclusion for disruption of the treatment environment must be viewed with careful scrutiny. A mere notation in the chart that the patient is secluded to preserve the therapeutic milieu should never justify so drastic a deprivation of liberty and should be contested immediately.

As a means of behavioral therapy, as a part of a planned, usually written system of rewards and punishments (e.g., contingent restraint) to eliminate destructive, violent or self-abusive behavior. The use of physical restraints for behavioral purposes has been advocated for psychiatric patients to change destructive or violent patterns of behavior,[113] but its use is particularly prominent as a means of behavior training in mental retardation. The use of timeout rooms and physical restraints like gloves, helmets, and other devices that prevent self-abuse or hitting others remain far from uncommon.

The rules governing Medicaid-funded facilities for people with mental retardation permit the use of timeout and physical restraints for behavioral training purposes but with elaborate safeguards. In the first place, the facility must have a set of written policies and procedures concerning behavior management, listing authorized behavioral interventions for inappropriate behavior in a hierarchy of most positive to most restrictive and requiring that the least intrusive means be employed first. The policy must also set criteria for the use of timeout rooms and physical restraints, list the staff members authorized to use them, and provide a mechanism for monitoring them. Next, the restraint may not be employed on an ad hoc basis, but only if an "integral part of the individual program plan that is intended to lead to less restrictive means of managing and eliminating the behavior for which the restraint is applied."[114] This means that the proposed use of the procedures will be reviewed in advance by the interdisciplinary staffing team and later by outsiders such as human rights committees, family members, and accreditation and monitoring bodies.

There is a great deal of controversy about the use of restraints as a technique for behavior modification, stirring impassioned debates in professional journals. Restraints can interfere with training in appropriate behavior, are uncomfortable at best and quite painful at worst, and, once authorized, not easily controlled. One practical—and human rights—issue should not be forgotten: the safeguards available in academic research settings are rarely present in the typical institution. The use of restraints as a behavioral technique thus inevitably raise human rights issues and are prohibited in some states and heavily regulated in others.

To decrease "stimulation" or to provide "structure" to a person's life. According to the American Psychiatric Association, seclusion (but not restraints) may be used to decrease stimulation or gain relief from sensory overload.[115] This standard is also too vague to be fully understandable.

What constitutional and other legal limitations exist on the use of seclusion and restraint?

The Constitution guarantees that individuals in state custody will not be subject to unreasonable restrictions on their bodily movements. As the Supreme Court put it in the context of placing prisoners in isolation rooms, "Liberty from bodily restraint always has been recognized as the core of the liberty protected by the Due Process Clause."[116] In *Youngberg*, the Supreme Court for the first time addressed the use of restraints in a state facility for people with mental disabilities. It held that the Constitution guarantees residents "freedom from undue restraint." This means that the state may not restrain people except to the extent professional judgment deems necessary to ensure the person's safety or to provide training.[117] As in other applications of the professional judgment standard, the judgment of the professional is presumptively valid.

It is also clear when no professional judgment justifies the use of seclusion and restraint: for punishment, for the convenience of the staff,[118] as a substitute for lack of sufficient staff,[119] to ward off potential violence where there is no basis for believing the particular restrained individual will be violent,[120] and in ways that interfere with a treatment program.[121] It may not be ordered in the chart PRN ("as needed").[122]

Seclusion and restraint may not be used in place of a treatment program. As one court put it, "it is a substantial departure from professional standards to rely routinely on seclusion and restraint rather than systematic behavior techniques such as social reinforcement to control aggressive behavior."[123] Further, the fact that a facility labels seclusion and restraint as "treatment" rather than as punishment cannot justify them. Nor may restrictive procedures be used because professionals have failed to employ appropriate techniques to control disturbed people.

In *Milonas v. Williams,*[124] for example, the court held that seclusion practices at a school for disturbed boys were unconstitutional because the permissible reasons for the procedure were not within accepted professional standards. "The use of the term out of control as a justification for the basically uncontrolled discretion in subjecting juveniles to the P-Room [seclusion] . . . permitted unreasonably harsh school responses to the conduct of disturbed boys."

The application of *Youngberg* casts serious doubt on the constitutionality of some common uses of seclusion and restraint. Even under that deferential standard, the legal basis for using seclusion or restraint to regulate the therapeutic environment or to decrease stimulation is questionable, since the professional standards are so vague as to be virtually incapable of application.

Do limitations exist on the manner in which seclusion and restraint are implemented?

Yes. If the grounds for the use of restraints and seclusion remain broad, strict safeguards for their use exist. The main safeguards required by the Constitution and state laws include the following:

1. *Seclusion or restraint may be employed only if less restrictive interventions have been attempted.*

The Constitution requires a facility to use less restrictive methods of intervention before resorting to seclusion or restraint.[125] As we have already seen, the requirement that less intrusive means of behavioral control be attempted before restraints are employed is built into the regulations governing facilities for persons with mental retardation funded by Medicaid.[126] These means are as diverse as the individuals for whom the restrictive technique is considered.

2. *Seclusion and restraint may be authorized on a psychiatric unit only by a physician and in mental retardation facilities only by appropriately qualified professionals.*

The potential for medical complications from the use of seclusion or restraint has resulted in the requirement that these interventions be authorized only by a qualified professional,[127] and in mental health facilities, only by a psychiatrist after examination of the patient.[128] While courts have held that emergency seclusion or restraint will inevitably be initiated by nurses or other qualified professionals on the scene, these staff members must immediately notify a psychiatrist who must examine the patient and review the decision.[129] Telephone consultation is insufficient.[130]

One court explained the reason for the requirement of immediate examination:

The evidence established that the first three hours of seclusion/restraint is a crucial period for physician examination because violent episodes may be the result of inappropriate medications, which could be corrected immediately, thus relieving the patient's violent or aggressive behavior. This is particularly true when the patient is new to the Hospital or the unit and is not well known by staff, or does not have a prior history of requiring seclusion/restraint, or has recently had a change in medication. It is in circumstances such as these that the professional judgment of a psychiatrist is necessary to evaluate the situation and determine if other interventions may be effective. Such examination also serves as a further check on the patient's actual need for such restrictive intervention.[131]

3. *An order for seclusion or restraint must be time-limited.*

Because of the restrictiveness of seclusion and restraint, minimal professional standards permit an order to be valid for no more than twelve hours.[132] In addition, the individual must be released when the conditions that led to the episode have subsided. As the United Nations Principles for the Protection of Persons with Mental Illness and for the Improvement of Mental Health Care state, "seclusion or restraint shall not be prolonged beyond the period which is strictly necessary."[133]

In mental retardation facilities funded by Medicaid, a resident may not be placed in a timeout room for more than one hour, and an order for restraints imposed as an emergency measure is valid for no longer than twelve hours.[134]

4. *While in seclusion or restraints, the individual's condition must be monitored and recorded in the chart.*

As explained earlier, these are potentially dangerous procedures, and patients must be monitored by nursing staff carefully, usually at no less than fifteen-minute intervals.[135]

5. *An outside representative should be told of the incident.*

Although not yet recognized under American law or practice, the United Nations Principles hold that a personal representative must be given notice of the physical restraint or seclusion of a patient. This safeguard is in an entirely different category from the others, since it brings an outsider into the picture who can witness what the staff is doing as well as observe the individual's behavior.

6. *The facility must have in place review procedures to assure that seclusion and restraint are used properly.*

In addition to the individual safeguards, the facility must have review procedures designed to assure that seclusion and restraint are not used either for improper reasons or without complying with mandated procedures.[136] These reviews should include a random investigation of individual patient charts as well as special methods for keeping track of all incidents of seclusion or restraint, such as monitoring of alternative interventions tried, length of time in seclusion or restraint, and appropriate watch over the patient's condition.

CONFIDENTIALITY OF AND ACCESS TO RECORDS[137]

Medicine has long recognized the privacy of the physician-patient relationship. One's health is an intimate matter and should be no one else's business. The stigma associated with mental health treatment or with residential placement for mental retardation is unfortunately so great that another person's mere knowledge of the fact of treatment, institutionalization, or hospitalization can result in ostracism, discrimination, or worse.

So it is essential to have the right not only to keep the records of mental health treatment private but also to prevent the unwanted disclosure of the fact of having been treated.

As the world becomes more technologically sophisticated, these rights are especially important, though increasingly difficult to assure. Insurance companies, for example, collect vast amounts of information about medical history. Medical information services learn—and share with others—the ways that people are treated and what conditions they have.

Are communications between patients and clinicians confidential?

Yes. The general rule is that treatment records, including statements made to a doctor or therapist, are confidential. Although there is not as yet a constitutional right to confidentiality, virtually every state has enacted laws limiting the disclosure of private communications between doctors, therapists, and other clinicians and their patients, unless the patients expressly authorize their release.[138] Some states also have statutes that forbid the release of records or information concerning inpatient treatment of people with mental disabilities without their consent. In addition, statutory privileges[139] exempt confidential communications between doctors or other clinicians and their patients from disclosure in court. Similarly, Medicaid regulations governing ICF/MRs prohibit the disclosure of any information about a resident without the consent of the resident or the resident's authorized agent.

Codes of ethics of professionals such as psychiatrists and psychologists require that patient records be kept secret. The general ethical rule of these professions is that written or verbal information conveyed by the client to the professional in the course of a professional relationship must be kept confidential. The rule of confidentiality is based both on the need for trust that must develop between patients and therapists and the recognition of privacy as an end in itself. These codes of professional conduct do not generally have the force of law, but rather represent professional standards of conduct, sometimes embedded in professional licensing laws.[140]

There are, however, exceptions to the rule of confidentiality, where, for example, the costs of care are paid by Medicaid, Medicare, or another government program; the information is needed for commitment proceedings; the patient has expressly waived confidentiality or has done so implicitly in a court proceeding by raising a claim or defense in which the patient's mental state is at issue; or the clinician is under a legal duty to make disclosure, such as in situations involving child abuse or neglect or a duty to warn another person or other government authorities of potential harm from the patient.

The last exception has been greatly debated in recent years. The right to confidentiality may cease to exist where a therapist believes a patient is likely to commit a violent act against another person. In many states the therapist has what has been called a "duty to warn" either the intended victim or the police. This duty stems from the California Supreme Court's decision in the famous case of *Tarasoff v. Regents of the University of California*.[141] *Tarasoff* held that where a therapist engaged in outpatient treatment of an individual (and thus without a custodial relationship to the patient) learns that the patient intends to inflict harm on a third party, the therapist has a duty to warn a third party or take other steps to protect the possible victim.

The Court articulated the duty in this way.

When a therapist determines, or pursuant to the standards of his profession should determine, that his patient presents a serious danger of violence to another, he incurs an obligation to use reasonable care to protect the intended victim against such danger. The discharge of this duty may require the therapist to take one or more of various steps, depending upon the nature of the case. Thus, it may call for him to warn the intended victim or others likely to apprise the victim of the danger, to notify the police, or to take whatever steps are reasonably necessary under the circumstances.[142]

One difficulty with discharging this duty is ascertaining when a person is likely to commit violence against another person, e.g., when the duty is triggered. But the California Supreme Court gave short shrift to this problem, stating that "the professional inaccuracy in predicting violence cannot negate the therapist's duty to protect the threatened victim."[143] The therapist must exercise that "reasonable degree of skill, knowledge, and care" exercised by other therapists in like circumstances.[144] *Tarasoff* has spawned dozens of cases throughout the country, with many variations on when confidentiality may or must be breached, what alternatives the therapist may select in lieu of notifying the purported victim (e.g., initiating civil commitment proceedings), and what behavior may trigger the duty to warn. About a dozen states have enacted special statutes to answer these questions.

Another proposed exception to the rule of confidentiality has garnered interest in recent years. That proposal would permit agencies that provide mental health services to an individual to share those records with other mental health agencies without obtaining permission from the individual. For example, a community mental health center serving a person may seek to obtain records of the person's hospitalization without having to obtain the person's consent because obtaining that consent is administratively difficult, too time-consuming, or impossible because the person refuses. This desire to share information between agencies is understandable and often has the laudable goal of providing good treatment. That desire, though, provides insufficient reason to abandon the principle of confidentiality that has been a hallmark of modern medical ethics and practice and is central to the protection of individual privacy. Most states still prohibit disclosures between agencies without the individual's consent, but there is increasing pressure to change their laws.

What are the remedies for violation of the duty of confidentiality?

There are several remedies for violations of confidentiality. Individuals can file a complaint with the state licensing body as well as with the clinician's professional association. They can also sue for damages for breach of an implied contract or violation of the common-law duty of confidentiality and trust.[145]

Can a person be required to give up the right to the confidentiality of information about hospitalization or medical treatment?

Sometimes a person must waive the right to confidentiality and allow someone else to see treatment records. Health insurance companies, for example, routinely ask individuals to waive the right to confidentiality so that they can consider reimbursement for services rendered by a medical provider. Life insurance companies usually demand access to all medical records before they will offer a policy. In addition, waiver of the right to confidentiality is often a condition of receiving public benefits that are offered only to people with a disability. For example, the Social Security Administration requires a person applying for Social Security Disability Insurance to release her medical records.

Similarly, filing a lawsuit claiming either that problems in a person's current mental condition are the responsibility of another (e.g., obstetrician's negligence caused mental retardation) or that an individual's mental condition was caused by someone else's negligence (placement in physical restraints led to recurring nightmares) requires waiver of the right to confidentiality.

Are there limits to the extent patients can be required to waive confidentiality of records in return for another benefit?

Yes, if the waiver discriminates on the basis of disability. As discussed in chapter 5, the Fair Housing Act prohibits a landlord from asking a person to provide medical records in order to obtain an apartment or other housing. Similarly, a neighborhood association cannot demand records of residents of a group home as a condition of zoning approval for the residence. The ADA protects applicants for employment from coercive demands to waive the right to confidentiality. An employer cannot ask a prospective employee whether he or she has a disability, or the nature or extent of the disability, or for access to medical records until after a preliminary offer of employment is made, and then this inquiry and access is subject to restrictions as discussed in chapter 5. Finally, applicants for licenses should be protected from routine demands for their medical records.

Do individuals have a right of access to their records?

Although almost every state grants patients access to their medical records, a number of states make exceptions for psychiatric records. The most typical justification is that disclosure would be "countertherapeutic" because it could harm the patient and discourage relatives and others from coming forward with information that is essential to the individual's treatment. However, in states where access is liberally granted, there is little evidence that this has been the case. More often, the withholding of medical records serves no purpose other than to shield the patient from negative staff comments contained in the chart. In recent years this paternalistic double standard has slowly given way to a stronger recognition of patients' rights.

Yet, even in jurisdictions that recognize a legal right of access to mental health records, that right is often qualified. For example, the District of Columbia has a law governing mental health records that permits a provider to deny access where a clinician reasonably believes that nondisclosure is necessary to protect the patient from a substantial risk of imminent psychological impairment or to protect a patient or another individual from a substantial risk of imminent and serious physical injury.[146] Although the patient is required to receive notice of this decision and may appeal, the very concept is so vague as to be silly. The physician is given virtually unbridled authority to define "psychological impairment" and to make a decision that the person is likely to suffer harm simply by seeing the record.

Often the only way to gain access to records is to seek them through an advocate, attorney, or another doctor. A facility is usually required to release records to a physician or lawyer even when it will not provide them to the person whose life they describe.

Courts have been reluctant to declare a broad constitutional right of access to psychiatric records. Unless one can show a compelling need for the records, such as use at a criminal competency hearing[147] or in a proceeding to obtain government benefits,[148] courts generally will not require disclosure.[149] Nor, as described in chapter 2, is there an established right of access to one's treatment records for use at a commitment hearing.[150] Rather, granting access to the individual's attorney has been deemed to satisfy the requirements of due process.

RIGHTS IN COMMUNITY PROGRAMS

Many community programs for people with mental disabilities offer high-quality services and are respectful of individual rights. Nevertheless, the idea of the "community" as invariably a safe and nurturing place for people with mental disabilities has lost much of its romance. The abuse and neglect characteristic of life in institutions has migrated to some programs in the community, particularly in board and care homes that are as institution-like and remote from oversight as rural state hospitals once were. As Ann Braden Johnson has shown, state deinstitutionalization policies were often accompanied by a bargain with the devil: loosening regulation of board and care or adult homes, allowing unscrupulous operators to maximize their profits by exploiting and neglecting their residents in return for taking discharged patients in the first place.[151]

Even community-based programs that started with noble goals can deteriorate into organizations that abuse the rights of participants through control and regimentation as thorough as is found in institutions. People are told where they can live, which visitors can be brought into their homes, when and what they can eat, what programs they participate in, and when they must leave.

Do people with mental disabilities in the community have the rights to safety and protection from harm?

Yes. Individuals in community-based programs are generally not in state custody, so they have no constitutional rights. During the past two decades, though, state and local governments have enacted laws protecting the rights of people in community-based programs. Many of these protections derive from the lengthy, complex set of community standards in the case of *Wuori v. Zitnay*,[152] governing the deinstitutionalization of developmentally disabled people in Maine. The standards represent an adaptation of the *Wyatt* standards for community-based programs, covering not only treatment and programming but civil rights, protection from harm, adequacy of living conditions, privacy, nutrition, and other aspects of life in the community.

Today, the level of protection of people with mental disabilities living in the community in general depends on their living circumstances and the level of resident functioning. Supervised congregate residences like board and care or adult homes are licensed and highly regulated by state or municipal governments.[153] These rules tend to fall into three categories: (1) administrative matters like educational or training qualifications for staff; medical coverage for residents; minimum staffing ratios; admission, transfer, and discharge rules; the safeguarding of resident property and record-keeping; (2) rules governing residents' everyday lives, from the use of physical restraint and behavioral modification to diets, amenities in residents' rooms, and the availability of rehabilitation programs and social services; and (3) safety issues, such as fire safety rules, medication storage, stability of physical structure, lighting, heat, ventilation, insulation, water supply, fire safety, and bathing and toilet facilities. Typically, civil and criminal penalties may be imposed for violations and, in extreme cases, withdrawal of the license to operate. Unfortunately, licensing agencies are notorious for their lackadaisical enforcement.

People living in semi-independent settings like apartments without on-site supervision leased by a mental health or mental retardation agency are usually not protected by the kind of specialized health and safety regulations applied to adult homes. Nevertheless, the agency responsible for the program may have a duty under the state laws or regulations or the common law to protect the people in the programs it runs. And individuals living completely independently have a right not to be subjected to sexual advances by a therapist.

Finally, many states have rules governing community mental retardation programs—including nonresidential programs—that are similar to those now common in institutions. The District of Columbia, for example, regulates the use of restrictive interventions like behavior modification programs involving the use of aversive stimuli and seclusion in a locked room. Medication is also strictly regulated, with rules specifying who may administer medication and subjecting a person's medication regimen to regular review and mandating a termination date for any prescription of psychotropic medication, not to exceed thirty days.[154]

What rights to personal autonomy does a person with a mental disability have in community-based programs?

The same as other members of society. The civil rights of people in institutions have migrated to community-based programs. State and local laws and regulations often include bills of rights for people with mental disabilities in community programs that require participation in developing a treatment or habilitation program, guarantee the freedom to associate with friends of one's choice, privacy, communication, access to advocates, and other rights relating to personal autonomy in everyday life.

Still, community-based programs are often highly structured and statements of rights are usually designed not to interfere with that structure. Further, just as institutions are run to meet their own needs and constraints, so are community programs. Thus, for example, it is not uncommon for people to be locked out of their homes during the day as a means of saving staffing costs in a supervised residence. This practice destroys the basic right to choose when to stay at home and when to leave. Similarly, "house rules," such as locking the front door at a certain time, may render it impossible to take advantage of social opportunities in the evening.

The rights to autonomy and independence, moreover, must be harmonized with the duty to protect vulnerable persons. Respect for the civil rights of vulnerable persons should not be used as an excuse to neglect them. A state investigative agency found, for example, that a supportive apartment program serving seventy-two people with developmental disabilities summarily discharged people from the program, failed to assure adequate medical and mental health services, failed to report and investigate serious incidents, and did not appropriately supervise residents or intervene when their behavior was abusive or dangerous. The provider defended itself partly on the ground that it was encouraging choice and empowerment. The investigating agency commented in response, "Serving these individuals well requires an ability to formulate and implement creative solutions to problems—an ability which rests on a clear understanding in any particular cases when the line between empowerment and neglect has been crossed."[155]

ACCESS TO ADVOCATES AND REDRESS FOR VIOLATIONS OF RIGHTS

Rights are meaningless unless they are respected and, if violated, capable of being enforced. We know from difficult and lengthy experience that rights are only as strong as the ability to insist on adherence to them and on the strength of advocacy for their protection. That is why rights and advocacy go hand in hand.

What mechanisms and resources exist to protect the rights of people with mental disabilities in institutions and the community?

Protection of rights begins—but does not end—with the individual whose rights are at stake. Advocacy for one's own rights is essential. That advocacy means questioning those in authority and insisting on respect for the rights typically listed on the walls of institutions, but often ignored. Self-advocacy is also a part of the process of gaining self-respect and independence. It is empowering in the best sense, enabling people to gain control over their fate. Organizations like People First, for people with developmental disabilities, and self-help organizations of people with psychiatric disabilities prove the power of self-advocacy. Families and friends can play an important supportive and, at times, proactive role in advocacy for people with mental disabilities.

Virtually every facility and program serving people with mental disabilities has a grievance procedure. These procedures vary greatly, but usually have in common a complaint form that is directed at someone in authority at the facility or program. Some institutions designate particular employees to assist individuals in filing or resolving grievances; others have formally established "internal" advocates, a term used to distinguish them from the "external" advocates who are not employees of the facility and who act with considerably more independence than the internal advocates.

Generally speaking, grievance procedures are best for handling day-to-day issues like the need for information about medication from the physician, difficulties with daily routines, access to ground privileges, schedules, and other similar matters. More serious problems like abuse and discrimination are not likely to be resolved through grievance procedures.

Often, the limitations of internal grievance procedures have much to do with the very situations of people with mental disorders confined in institutions, and sometimes in communities as well. One court described this situation well. Speaking of people confined in psychiatric facilities, it first noted characteristics that often make it difficult for them to exercise their rights:

The mentally ill are vulnerable to abuse and neglect because many mentally ill individuals have difficulty recognizing that they have rights and will not necessarily identify even the most egregious abuse as a violation of their rights. Even if cognizant of their rights, many of these individuals have difficulty assessing whether their rights have been violated and may have difficulty identifying P & A[156] as a resource to remedy rights violations. In addition, both the effects of medications and of mental illness may cause confusion and problems with memory, making it difficult to remember and explain possible rights violations after the lapse of several days. . . .

Some patients, by virtue of their illness and because of personal characteristics unrelated to mental illness, may not be willing to ask questions about their rights publicly or until they have had an opportunity to develop a degree of trust towards the advocate.[157]

In addition, the court recognized that the characteristics of the facility and its leadership can also make protection of rights difficult. It noted that residents "are apt to be deterred if facilities for making a private call are not available or if the nature of the call must be revealed to the institution's staff in order to gain access to a private phone. Many institutionalized residents are reluctant or afraid to take actions that might incur the displeasure of staff who control nearly every aspect of their daily life."[158]

For these reasons, every state has external advocates whose job it is to investigate rights violations on behalf of people with mental disabilities who live in institutions and in the community, to investigate violations of their rights, and to help them find a means for redress. These external advocates work for independent agencies that do not report to the director of the facility. They are known as "protection and advocacy" agencies, or "P&As," after the laws Congress enacted to create them, and now exist in every state, territory, and the District of Columbia. The name, address, and phone numbers of the P&A in each state is listed in appendix B.

The P&As were established in the mid-1970s and originally were charged with representing people with developmental disabilities in institutions and communities. Under that mandate, they challenged conditions in institutions, helped children with developmental disabilities obtain access to education, and engaged in other activities to assist people with mental retardation and other developmental disabilities to protect their rights. In the years since, Congress has expanded their mandate. They now have the obligation to provide assistance to individuals in the vocational rehabilitation process, as discussed in chapter 6, to represent people with psychiatric disabilities confined or recently released from psychiatric hospitals, and to provide assistance to people with disabilities, including mental disabilities, in the community. So whether the problem involves seclusion in a psychiatric hospital, the denial of Social Security benefits, or exclusion from a community-based program, the P&As have the authority to help, limited only by the budgets and priorities set by the individual P&As.

Other resources may be available as well. Legal services organizations often represent people with mental disabilities in matters relating to Social Security and SSI benefits, housing, and other aspects of life in the community or institutions. As discussed in chapter 6, nursing home residents may contact the Office of the Long-Term Care Ombudsman to investigate and resolve problems concerning violations of rights and quality of care in nursing homes. Some states have specially designated agencies, such as the New York State Commission on the Quality of Care for the Mentally Disabled and the Montana Board of Visitors, who have the responsibility to periodically investigate conditions in institutions and community-based programs. This obligation may include visits by experts to facilities and discussions with the people confined as well as assistance in the resolution of individual complaints.

Advocacy, family, and consumer organizations can often provide assistance as well. Chapters of the Arc, formerly the Association for Retarded Citizens, Mental Health Associations, the Alliance for the Mentally Ill, and other organizations of families and advocates exist in virtually every state as do organizations of consumers of services.

Finally, the Civil Rights Division of the Department of Justice is charged by Congress with investigating and remedying "egregious" violations of rights of institutionalized people.[159] The Justice Department can be alerted to violations by a letter addressed to the Special Litigation Section in the Civil Rights Division of the Department of Justice.

May those in charge of an institution restrict the access of external advocates to the facility?

Absolutely not. Institutional staff may not deny confined individuals the right of access to assistance with advocacy and with the right to consult with a lawyer. In order to make the right of access effective, external advocates must be able to get into the facility. Accordingly, the facility must allow them in, whether the staff likes it or not. Lawyers, too, are generally not subject to limitations on visiting hours as long as they come at a reasonable hour.

This means that an institution may not monitor correspondence, telephone calls, meetings, or other communications between attorneys and their clients and must provide an area where they can carry on private discussions outside the presence of hospital staff members. An institution may not restrict attorney-client communications for "therapeutic" reasons.

The right to communicate with counsel is part of a broader right to "meaningful access to the courts,"[160] guaranteed by the First Amendment right to petition the government for the redress of grievances.[161] Although the right to counsel is constitutionally required only at commitment hearings,[162] people subject to commitment have a right of access to resources that will enable them to bring writs of *habeas corpus*, civil rights complaints, and other claims related to their confinement to the attention of a court. One federal court of appeals ruled that this can be achieved through either the availability of counsel to assist in completing the legal papers or access to a law library. After finding that a Colorado hospital had chosen not to make available any law library materials, the court ordered the state to ensure the availability of a lawyer through the completion of a federal *habeas corpus* petition or civil rights complaint, "including necessary research and consideration of the facts and the law."[163]

Institutionalized people nevertheless often experience much difficulty gaining access to external advocates. This difficulty is a product of the isolation of institutions, limited access to phones and other means of communication, and, for more impaired residents, lack of ability to make the initial advocacy contact. Sometimes staff actively discourage residents from contacting external advocates. As a result, external advocates must have access to the facilities even in the absence of a request for help from a particular, identifiable client.

Many states and facilities have fought against permitting access by advocates without an individual request. After the protection and advocacy agency issued a damning report about conditions in a facility, the state of Mississippi sought to impose the following restrictions on the protection and advocacy agency: the P&A could not interview a resident on the same visit as initial record review; it had to give twenty-four-hour notice to the institution whenever it sought to interview a new client and provide the legal office with "probable cause" that violations of rights had occurred; the facility reserved the right to ask the client whether a staff member could be present at the interview; and after the interview, the client was "debriefed" in an effort to find out what had transpired between the advocate and the client. The P&A successfully challenged these onerous restrictions as a violation of the statute establishing the protection and advocacy program. In overturning the state's rules, the court of appeals noted that they had a "chilling effect of gigantic proportions" on the ability to protect and enforce residents' rights and represented an effort to render protection of rights "comatose if not moribund."[164]

Likewise, in New Mexico, after the P&A issued a highly critical report about conditions in a state psychiatric facility, the state prohibited it from interviewing a potential client until the client signed a request form asking to see a P&A advocate or the P&A provided written evidence of a complaint or claim. The facility also obstructed access to records and imposed a slew of bureaucratic obstacles before a visit could be scheduled. The court decided not only that the statute establishing the advocacy program guarantees access, but that this access is essential to protect a constitutional right—the right of meaningful access to the courts.[165] The ruling is important because it not only recognizes the constitutional dimensions of the right of access but applies to advocates besides protection and advocacy agencies.

What are the remedies for violations of rights?

If a rights violation cannot be resolved through a facility's internal grievance system, state or federal regulatory oversight, the intervention of a civil rights agency, or another less formal avenue, a lawyer can file a legal claim on behalf of the aggrieved individual in court. If the violation is proven, the court can issue an injunction, or order, requiring the facility to cease or cure it. An injunction can be as broad as necessary to remedy the harm and to assure that the violation is not repeated in the future. To guarantee compliance, courts often retain a supervisory role over their injunctive orders for many years. A violation of an injunction is punishable by contempt, which can result in further orders of the court, fines, and the appointment of special masters to oversee compliance.

An injunction can address the violations themselves as well as the conditions that brought them about. It can require such corrections as the hiring of more staff, improvement in quality assurance, medication reviews, and restrictions on the use of seclusion and restraint. The power to issue an injunction has also been the source of the courts' authority to require that individuals be discharged and provided for in the community when that is the only effective remedy for the violation of rights.

It is unfortunately quite rare for people who have suffered physical injury or other harms on account of violations of their rights to receive money damages. The availability of damages is a complex subject, depending on such factors as whether the facility is public or private, who committed the harm, what legal immunities from the payment of damages the guilty actors have, whether budgetary constraints led to the violation,[166] the degree to which state law permits compensation by government, and many other factors.[167] Despite these obstacles, individuals have obtained damages for abuse, for violations of the right to be free of inappropriate seclusion or restraint, and for other violations that cause harm to the individual. Damages have also been awarded when an institutions's negligence results in serious harm or death to a resident. In one case, a man with mental retardation was awarded $600,000 to compensate him for beatings by staff that led to permanent injuries;[168] in another, a court awarded $50,000 for pain and suffering to a person whose attempted suicide resulted in permanent spinal injuries;[169] and in another, a jury awarded $250,000 to a woman with severe mental retardation and a long history of serious behavior problems who was improperly restrained for years in a psychiatric facility.[170] In one notable case, the pervasive violation of the rights of all individuals confined in a forensic unit led to a settlement awarding damages for everyone subjected to the conditions.[171]

Notes

1. National Institute of Mental Health, *Mental Health United States 1992.*
2. Ihler v. Chisholm, No. ADV-88-383 (Montana First Judicial District 1991).
3. *See* Lizotte v. New York City Health Hospitals Corporation, No. 85 Civ. 7548 (S.D.N.Y. 1992).
4. *See* Goffman's classic study of institutions, *Asylums* (1961).
5. Rothman, *The Willowbrook Wars* 69–71 (1984).
6. 344 F. Supp. 373 (M.D. Ala. 1972).
7. State laws on the rights of institutionalized people with mental disabilities are surveyed in Brown & Smith, *Mental Patients' Rights: An Empirical Study of Variation Across the United States,* 11 International Journal of Law and Psychiatry 157 (1988) and in Lyon, Levine & Zusman, *Patients' Bills of Rights: A Survey of State Statutes,* 6 Mental Disability Law Reporter 178 (1982). An up-to-date list is also found in Perlin 2 *Mental Disability Law: Civil and Criminal* 954–55 (1989).
8. Developmentally Disabled Assistance and Bill of Rights Act, 42 U.S.C. § 6010.
9. The Bill of Rights for Mental Patients. 42 U.S.C. 9501, 10841.
10. The rights of people in nursing homes are contained in the Omnibus Reconciliation Act of 1987, 42 U.S.C. § 1395i-3(a)–(h) for Medicare and 42 U.S.C. § 1396r(a)–(h) for Medicaid. The regulations issued by the Health Care Financing Administration of the Department of Health and Human Services are contained in 42 C.F.R. pts. 442 and 483.

For a booklet explaining the rights of people with mental disabilities in nursing homes, see Bazelon Center for Mental Health Law, *Elders Assert Their Rights* (1993). A more comprehensive multivolume manual on the subject is Bazelon Center for Mental Health Law and Legal Counsel for the Elderly, *Enforcing the Rights of Older Persons with Mental Disabilities* (1993).

11. These are found at 42 C.F.R. § 483.420(a).
12. 457 U.S. 307 (1982).
13. Stefan, *What Constitutes Departure from Professional Judgment?*, 17 Mental and Physical Disability Law Reporter 207 (1993).
14. *See* Stefan, *Leaving Civil Rights to the 'Experts': From Deference to Abdication Under the Professional Judgment Standard,* 102 Yale Law Journal 639 (1992).
15. Cameron v. Tomes, 783 F. Supp. 1511 (D. Mass. 1992) (strip and oral cavity search not justified by professional judgment); *Ihler v. Chisholm, supra* (room searches professional justifiable).
16. Despite the logic of this argument, the courts still disagree about this proposition. *Compare* Harvey v. Harvey, 949 F.2d 1127 (11th Cir. 1992); Spencer v. Lee, 864 F.2d 1376 (7th Cir. 1989), *with* Rubenstein v. Benedictine Hospital, 790 F. Supp. 390 (N.D.N.Y. 1992).
17. Shaw by Strain v. Stackhouse, 920 F.2d 1135, 1140 (3d Cir. 1990).
18. Youngberg v. Romeo, 457 U.S. at 315. State law and federal regulations also typically recognize the right to safe conditions.
19. Society for Goodwill to Retarded Children v. Cuomo, 737 F.2d 1239, 1246–47 (2d Cir. 1984).

20. Valentine v. Strange, 597 F. Supp. 1316 (E.D. Va. 1984); Ass'n for Retarded Citizens of North Dakota v. Olsen, 561 F. Supp 470, 472 (D.N.D. 1982). 42 C.F.R. § 483.420(d)(1).

21. Jackson v. Fort Stanton Hosp. and Training School, 757 F. Supp. 1243, 1307 (D.N.M. 1990) rev'd in part on other grounds 964 F2d 980 (10th Cir. 1992). *See* 42 C.F.R. § 483.420(d)(1).

22. Harper v. Cserr, 544 F.2d 1121 (1st Cir. 1976); Gann v. Schramm, 606 F. Supp. 1442 (D. Del. 1985).

23. Thomas S. v. Flaherty, 699 F. Supp. 1178, 1200 (W.D.N.C. 1988), aff'd Thomas S. by Brooks v. Flaherty, 902 F.2d 250 (4th Cir. 1990), cert. den. 111 S. Ct. 373 (1990). For Medicaid-funded mental retardation facilities, see 42 C.F.R. § 483.420(a)(5) and (6).

24. Jennings, Jennings, Somer & Burstein, *A Parent's Survey of Problems Faced by Mentally Ill Daughters*, 38 Hospital and Community Psychiatry 668 (1987). Chamberlain, *Issues in Fertility Control for Mentally Retarded Female Adolescents: Sexual Activity, Sexual Abuse, and Contraception*, 73 Pediatrics 445 (1984).

25. Stefan, *Whose Egg Is It Anyway? Reproductive Rights of Incarcerated, Institutionalized and Incompetent Women*, 13 Nova Law Review 405 (1989).

26. Sundram & Stavis, *Sexual Behavior and Mental Retardation*, 17 Mental and Physical Disability Law Reporter 448 (1993).

27. 42 C.F.R. § 483.420(d)(2),(3), (4).

28. *Youngberg v. Romeo, supra. See* 42 C.F.R. §§483.460, 483.480.

29. 42 C.F.R. § 483.410 *et seq.*

30. 42 C.F.R. § 483.480.

31. Jackson v. Fort Stanton Hosp. and Training School, *supra*, 757 F. Supp at, 1260–61. *See also* 42 C.F.R. § 483.470 for conditions of participation: physical environment requirements for ICF/MRs. *See also* Society for Goodwill to Retarded Children v. Cuomo, 737 F.2d 1239, 1244 (2d Cir. 1984). *See also* Scott v. Plante, 691 F.2d 634, 637 (3d. Cir. 1982)(claim of subhuman conditions submitted to jury when there was evidence that person was confined in such conditions for twenty-four years because of defendants' inattention to their normal professional responsibilities).

32. 42 C.F.R. § 483.470(g)(1).

33. 42 C.F.R. § 2483.470(b)(1)(iii).

34. *Society for Goodwill to Retarded Children v. Cuomo, supra*, at 1245; *Jackson v. Fort Stanton Hosp. and Training School, supra*, at 1259.

35. Ass'n for Retarded Citizens of North Dakota v. Olsen, *supra*, 561 F. Supp. at 486, 491.

36. *Ass'n for Retarded Citizens of North Dakota v. Olsen, supra*, at 491–92. *See also* 42 C.F.R. § 483.470(c)(2) (requiring storage space for client's personal belongings in ICF/MR bedrooms).

37. Society for Goodwill to Retarded Children v. Cuomo, *supra*; 42 C.F.R. § 483.460(a)(1).

38. *Jackson v. Fort Stanton Hosp. and Training School, supra*, at 1264. *See also* 42 C.F.R. § 483.460. *See* Annas, *The Rights of Patients*, ch. 10.

39. 42 C.F.R. § 483.460(k),(l).

40. *Ass'n for Retarded Citizens of North Dakota v. Olsen, supra*, at 486.

41. *Jackson v. Fort Stanton Hosp. and Training School, supra,* at 1260–61.

42. *Id.*

43. *Society for Goodwill to Retarded Children v. Cuomo, supra.*

44. *Id.*

45. *Id.* at 1244.

46. Geller et al., *State Hospital Patients' Views about Operation Desert Storm,* 43 Hospital and Community Psychiatry 833 (1992).

47. *See, e.g., Thomas S. v. Flaherty, supra. See* 42 C.F.R. § 483.420 concerning the rights of people in intermediate care facilities for people with mental retardation. As to right to have an opportunity to exercise and have outdoor recreation, see N.Y. State Ass'n for Retarded Children, Inc. v. Rockefeller, 357 F. Supp. 752, 765 (E.D.N.Y. 1973). According to one court, "this right obligates the state to provide capable retarded residents with reasonable opportunities to make trips into the outside communities." *Ass'n for Retarded Citizens of North Dakota v. Olsen, supra,* at 486.

48. *Society for Goodwill to Retarded Children v. Cuomo,* at 1247.

49. Bullock v. Carter, 405 U.S. 134 (1972).

50. A few states have laws on the books that do not permit institutionalized persons to vote, but these are likely unconstitutional. In Manhattan Citizens Group v. Bass, 524 F. Supp. 1270 (S.D.N.Y. 1981), the court held that a New York law that disqualified people with mental disabilities from voting in the absence of an adjudication of incompetence was unconstitutional. *See also* 42 C.F.R. § 483.420(a)(3) (right of people in Medicaid-funded mental retardation facilities to exercise rights as citizens of the United States).

51. *See* Note, *Mental Disability and the Right to Vote,* 88 Yale Law Journal 1644 (1979). Many states place restrictions on the right to vote, including denial of the franchise to people adjudicated incompetent. While it has been suggested that this restriction, too, may be unconstitutional, Brakel, Parry & Weiner, *The Mentally Disabled and the Law* 446 (3d ed. 1985), Congress appeared to reinforce this restriction in the Motor Voter legislation, since it permits states to remove voters names from registration lists on the ground of mental incapacity under state law. 42 U.S.C. § 1973gg-4(a)(3)(B).

52. 42 U.S.C. § 1973gg-6.

53. 42 U.S.C. § 1973gg-5(a)(2)(B).

54. There has, however, been litigation involving the free exercise rights of prisoners. People with mental disabilities confined in institutions have no lesser right than convicted prisoners and therefore should enjoy at least the same rights. *See Youngberg v. Romeo, supra,* at 324.

55. Winters v. Miller, 446 F.2d 65, 69–70 (2d Cir. 1971), *cert. denied,* 404 U.S. 985 (1971) citing, West Virginia v. Barnette, 319 U.S. 624, 639 (1943).

56. *See, e.g.,* Thomas S. by Brooks v. Flaherty, *supra,* 699 F. Supp. at 1203–4; *Ass'n for Retarded Citizens of North Dakota v. Olsen, supra,* at 492 (1982).

57. New York State Association for Retarded Children v. Carey, 393 F. Supp. 715 (E.D.N.Y. 1975). Section A of the Steps, Standards, and Procedures of the Willowbrook Consent Judgment states, *inter alia:*

"Residents shall be provided with the least restrictive and most normal living conditions possible. This standard shall apply to . . . movement, use of free time and contact and communication with the outside community." The judgment also required the posting of a document listing the "legal and civil rights of residents."

58. 344 F. Supp. at 379 (involuntarily confined persons have "an unrestricted right to send sealed mail" and to receive sealed mail from their attorneys, private physicians and other mental health professionals, from courts, and government officials and have "the right to receive sealed mail from others" and "the same rights to visitation and telephone communications as patients at other public hospitals," except "to the extent that . . . the Qualified Mental Health Professional responsible for . . . a particular patient's treatment plan" writes an order imposing special restrictions).

59. *See, e.g., Ass'n for Retarded Citizens of North Dakota v. Olsen, supra,* at 492 ("mentally retarded residents possess a right to free association . . . requir[ing] . . . state to provide residents who are capable of communicating, reasonable opportunities to communicate with others both inside and outside the institution where they reside"); *Ward v. Kort,* 762 F.2d 856, 860 (10th Cir. 1985) (involuntarily committed psychiatric patients have right to availability of either law library facilities or counsel "on a reasonable basis."); *Society for Goodwill to Retarded Children v. Cuomo, supra,* at 1300 (institution for people with mental retardation must provide improved "family visitation areas"), vac. in light of Pennhurst State School v. Halderman, 465 U.S. 89 (1984), *Society for Goodwill to Retarded Children v. Cuomo, supra,* dism. as moot because defendants will voluntarily implement court order, 103 F.R.D. 168, 169 (E.D.N.Y. 1984).

A discussion of the right of access to the courts and counsel can be found later in this chapter.

60. *Society for Goodwill to Retarded Children v. Cuomo, supra; Cameron v. Tomes, supra,* at 1511, 1523 (no professional judgment in prohibiting grandchildren's visits).

61. *Ihler v. Chisholm, supra.*

62. 475 U.S. at 315–16. Because of the great deference accorded First Amendment rights, infringements of speech and associational interests are subjected to more exacting scrutiny than the Court afforded to the rights considered in *Youngberg.*

63. *See, e.g., Ward v. Kort, supra* (involuntary psychiatric patients have same right as prisoners to "meaningful access to the courts").

64. *Martyr v. Bachik,* 770 F. Supp. 1406 (D. Or. 1991) (insanity acquitee) (preliminary injunction), *Martyr v. Mazur-Hart,* 789 F. Supp. 1081 (D. Or. 1992) (permanent injunction). *See also* Procunier v. Martinez, 416 U.S. 396, 413–14 (1974), *rev'd in part,* Thornburgh v. Abbott, 490 U.S. 401 (1989) (establishing standard for censorship of prisoner mail; *Thornburgh* modified the standard for incoming mail for reasons of security).

65. For example, the Medicaid regulations state that the facility must ensure that "clients have access to telephones with privacy for incoming and outgoing local and long distance calls except as contraindicated by factors identified within their individual program plans. 42 C.F.R. § 483.420(a)(10).

66. *Martyr v. Bachik, supra.* Subsequently, an Oregon appeals court held that, regardless of the treatment rationales offered by the facility staff, state law prohibited them from opening and censoring Mr. Martyr's outgoing mail. Martyr v. Oregon, 883 P.2d 237 (Or. Ct. App. 1994).

67. Because the hospital ultimately recognized Ms. Boggs's right to communicate and associate with members of the media, there was no litigation on this issue. For general information concerning the case of Billie Boggs, whose real name was Joyce Brown, see chapter 2.

68. Perlin, 2 *Mental Disability Law: Civil and Criminal* Supp. 207 n. 266.3 (1993);

Lyon, Levine & Zussman, *Patient's Bills of Rights: A Survey of State Statutes,* 6 Mental Disability Law Reporter 178 (1982).

69. For a discussion of the right to sexual expression, see Perlin, *Hospitalized Patients and the Right to Sexual Interaction: Beyond the Las Frontier?* 20 New York University Review of Law and Social Change 517 (1993–94); and Stefan, *Dancing in the Sky Without a Parachute: Sex and Love in Institutional Settings* in *Choice and Responsibility* (C. Sundram, ed. 1994).

In most instances, the subject is not even brought up. Medicaid's regulations governing people in intermediate care facilities for people with mental retardation, for example, require that the facility allow clients to "associate and meet privately with individuals of their choice," 42 C.F.R. § 483.420(a)(7), but make no specific reference to sexual activity. The regulations do provide, however, that a married couple living in ICF/MR have the right to share a room. 42 C.F.R. § 483.420(a)(13).

70. *See,* for example, Binder, *Sex Between Psychiatric Inpatients,* 57 Psychiatric Quarterly 121 (1985); Keitner & Grof, *Sexual and Emotional Intimacy Between Psychiatric Inpatients: Formulating a Policy,* 32 Hospital and Community Psychiatry 188 (1981); Saunders, *The Mental Health Professional, the Mentally Retarded and Sex,* 32 Hospital and Community Psychiatry 717 (1981). Some clinicians are beginning to recognize both the fundamental nature of the right and even claim therapeutic value for it. Welch, *Sexual Behavior of Hospitalized Chronic Psychiatric Patients,* 42 Hospital and Community Psychiatry 855 (1991).

71. *Ihler v. Chisholm, supra.*

72. Foy v. Greenblott, 141 Cal. App. 3d 1, 190 Cal. Rptr. 84 (1983).

73. Stefan, *Whose Egg Is It Anyway? supra,* at 436–37. *See also* In re Jane A., 629 N.E.2d 1337 (Mass. App. 1994) (incompetent woman).

74. This was the description by the court in Wyatt v. Stickney, 344 F. Supp. at 375.

75. Friedman, *The Mentally Handicapped Citizen and Institutional Labor,* 87 Harvard Law Review 567 (1974), citing Richardson, *A Survey of the Present Status of Vocational Training in State Supported Institutions for the Mentally Retarded* 4, 11–12 (July 1972).

76. Johnson v. Henne, 355 F.2d 129 (2d Cir. 1966); Johnston v. Ciccone, 260 F. Supp. 553 (W.D. Mo. 1966).

77. United States v. Kozminski, 487 U.S. 931 (1988).

78. *See* appendix A.

79. *See* 42 C.F.R. § 483.420(a)(8).

80. Souder v. Brennan, 367 F. Supp. 808 (D.D.C. 1973). A Supreme Court decision in 1976 held that the Commerce Clause of the Constitution precluded application of the Fair Labor Standards Act to state facilities. National League of Cities v. Usery, 426 U.S. 528 (1976). As a result, the minimum wage law was no longer applied to patient labor at state-owned institutions. National League of Cities v. Usery was overruled a decade later in Garcia v. San Antonio Metropolitan Transit Authority, 469 U.S. 528 (1985), and it is now clear that the Fair Labor Standards Act applies.

81. The regulations applicable to patient labor appear at 29 C.F.R. § 529 and following.

82. 42 C.F.R. § 483.420(a)(8).

83. Allen v. Heckler, 780 F.2d 64 (D.C. Cir. 1985).

84. State Dept. of Mental Hygiene v. Schneps, 408 N.Y.S.2d 980 (App. Term 1st Dep't. 1978). *See also* State v. Stavola, 523 N.Y.S.2d 189 (3d Dep't. 1987).

85. *See, e.g.,* State *ex rel.* Memmel v. Mundy 75 Wis. 2d 276, 249 N.W. 2d 573 (1977) (because there was no valid commitment order, plaintiffs could not be considered committed for any purpose and thus were not liable for cost of their care).

86. Acevedo v. Surles, 778 F. Supp. 179 (S.D.N.Y. 1991).

87. Brakel, Parry & Weiner, *supra,* at 74, Tables 2.17 and 2.18.

88. *Id.*

89. *Id.,* citing Estate of Hinds v. State, 394 N.E.2d 943 (Ind. Ct. App. 1979); *reh'g denied and remanded,* 390 N.E.2d 172 (Ind. Ct. App. 1979); South Carolina Dep't of Mental Health v. Turbeville, 257 S.E.2d 493 (S.C. 1979).

90. New York State Commission on Quality of Care for the Mentally Disabled, *Restraint and Seclusion Practices in New York State Psychiatric Facilities* (1994).

91. New York State Commission on Quality of Care for the Mentally Disabled, *Voices from the Front Line: Patients' Perspectives and Restraint and Seclusion Use* (1994). The survey was not randomized but based on a mail survey. Slightly more than one-third of the surveys were returned.

The survey also found that 78 percent of respondents reported no examination by a physician; lack of periodic bathroom, exercise, meal, and water breaks; no monitoring by staff; excessive time in restraint or seclusion; and poor regulation of seclusion room temperature.

92. *Ihler v. Chisholm, supra.*

93. Gutheil, *Review of Individual Quantitative Studies* in *The Psychiatric Uses of Seclusion and Restraint* (K. Tardiff ed. 1984) at 129.

94. New York State Commission on the Quality of Care, *Restraint and Seclusion Practices, supra.*

95. New York State Commission on Quality of Care, *supra;* Betemps, Somoza & Buncher, *Hospital Characteristics, Diagnoses, and Staff Reasons Association with Use of Seclusion and Restraint,* 44 Hospital and Community Psychiatry 367 (1993); Betemps, Buncher & Oden, *Length of Times Spent in Seclusion and Restraint by Patients at 82 VA Medical Centers,* 43 Hospital and Community Psychiatry 912 (1992); Way & Banks, *Use of Seclusion and Restraint in Public Psychiatric Hospitals: Patient Characteristics and Facility Effects,* 41 Hospital and Community Psychiatry 75 (1990); Carpenter, Hannon, McLeary & Wanderling, *Variations in Seclusion and Restraint Practices by Hospital Location,* 39 Hospital and Community Psychiatry 418 (1988); Okin, *Variation among State Hospitals in the Use of Seclusion and Restraint,* 36 Hospital and Community Psychiatry 648 (1985).

96. Gutheil & Tardiff, *Indications and Contraindications for Seclusion and Restraint* in *The Psychiatric Uses of Seclusion and Restraint* (K. Tardiff ed. 1984).

97. New York State Commission on the Quality of Care, *Restraint and Seclusion Practices, supra.*

98. 14 NYCRR 27.7(b).

99. Interview with Thomas Maul, Commissioner of the New York State Office of Mental Retardation and Developmental Disabilities, Sept. 22, 1994.

100. N.Y. Times, Aug. 1, 1994 at B2.

101. 42 C.F.R. § 483.450(c)(1)(iii).

102. *See Lizotte v. New York City Health and Hospitals Corporation, supra.*

103. For example, the congressional findings in the Developmental Disabilities Act still prohibits "excessive use of chemical restraints" as well as the use of "such restraints as punishment, or as a substitute for a habilitation program or in quantities that interfere with services, treatment, or habilitation." 42 U.S.C. § 6009(3)(B)(iv).

104. *See e.g., Jackson v. Fort Stanton Hosp. and Training School, supra,* at 1307.

105. 42 C.F.R. § 483.450(e)(3).

106. 42 U.S.C. § 1395i-3(c)(1)(A)(ii)(Medicare); 42 U.S.C. 1396r(c)(1)(A)(v) (II) (Medicaid). *See generally* Burger, *An Ombudsman's Guide to Effective Advocacy Regarding the Inappropriate use of Chemical and Physical Restraints* (National Citizens Coalition for Nursing Home Reform 1990).

107. Principles for the Protection of Persons with Mental Illness and for the Improvement of Mental Health Care, General Assembly 119, 46th Sess., December 17, 1991.

108. *Id.* Principle 11.

109. Wyatt by and through Rawlins v. King, 793 F. Supp. 1058, 1077–79 (M.D. Ala. 1992).

110. *See, e.g.,* Saks, *The Use of Mechanical Restraints in Psychiatric Hospitals,* 95 Yale Law Journal 1836 (1986).

111. 42 C.F.R. § 483.450(c)(l)(i).

112. American Psychiatric Association, Task Force Report 22, *Seclusion and Restraint* (1985).

113. *See, e.g.,* Liberman & Wong, *Behavior Analysis and Therapy Procedures Related to Seclusion and Restraint,* in *The Psychiatric Uses of Seclusion and Restraint* (Kenneth Tardiff ed. 1984).

114. 42 C.F.R. § 483.450(d).

115. American Psychiatric Association Task Force Report 22, *supra.*

116. Greenholtz v. Nebraska Penal Inmates, 442 U.S. 1, 18 (1979) (Powell, J., concurring); *see also Youngberg v. Romeo, supra,* at 316.

117. *Youngberg v. Romeo, supra.*

118. Restraining individuals for staff convenience does not necessarily involve bad faith. It may be a consequence of the organization of the facility. But it is still prohibited if the only justification is staff convenience. In one recent case, the municipal operator of a psychiatric emergency room agreed to end the practice of using handcuffs routinely on patients waiting (often for days) for evaluation and admission, limiting the use of these restraints unless the patient is under arrest or will cause immediate serious harm to himself or others. *Lizotte v. New York City Health and Hospitals Corporation, supra.*

Another court found that "excess locking of doors, locking of otherwise ambulatory persons into wheelchairs and failing to put on leg braces for individuals who can walk with their assistance violates . . . residents' freedom from undue restraint." *Society for Goodwill to Retarded Children v. Cuomo, supra,* at 1247.

Not all courts, however, have been rigorous in enforcing the restriction on use of restraints for staff convenience. One court upheld the locking of clients in their rooms while staff ate so as to preserve order at staff meal times was found not to violate these rights. Johnson by Johnson v. Brelje, 701 F.2d 1201, 1209–10 (7th Cir. 1983).

119. *Jackson v. Fort Stanton Hosp. and Training School, supra*, at 1307 (residents restrained to toilets because insufficient staff available).

120. *Cameron v. Tomes, supra.*

121. *See, e.g*, 42 C.F.R. § 483.450(b)(3).

122. Wyatt by and through *Rawlins v. King, supra*; *Ihler v. Chisholm, supra*, slip op. at 31. *See also* 42 C.F.R. § 483.450((d)(3) (regulations governing Medicaid-funded mental retardation facilities).

123. Thomas S. v. Flaherty, *supra*, 669 F. Supp. at 1189; *See also* Santana v. Collazo II, 793 F.2d 41, 45 (1st Cir. 1986); Ihler v. Chisholm, *supra.*

124. 691 F.2d 931, 942 (10th Cir. 1982).

125. *Thomas S. v. Flaherty, supra*, at 1189; *See also Santana v. Collazo II, supra*; *Ihler v. Chisholm, supra*; *Wyatt by and through Rawlins v. King, supra.*

126. 42 C.F.R. § 483.450(b)(iii).

127. *Youngberg v. Romeo, supra*; Ferola v. Moran, 622 F. Supp. 814 (D.R.I. 1985).

128. *Wyatt by and through Rawlins v. King, supra* (other physicians only permitted to authorize seclusion and restraint if they receive significant training in psychiatry); Ihler v. Chisholm, *supra.*

129. *Wyatt by and through Rawlins v. King, supra*; Wells v. Franzen, 777 F.2d 1258, 1261–62 (7th Cir. 1985). The American Psychiatric Association standard requires the psychiatrist to see the patient usually within one hour and never in more than three. The APA makes an exception, however, for individuals who have a long history of episodic violence and experience in seclusion and restraint. They must nevertheless be examined by a physician as soon as possible.

130. *Ihler v. Chisholm, supra.*

131. *Id.*

132. American Psychiatric Association Task Force Report 22, *supra. But see Wyatt by and through Rawlins v. King, supra* (Wyatt permits eight hours as the maximum length of such an order).

133. *Wyatt by and through Rawlins v. King, supra*; Principles for the Protection of Persons with Mental Illness, *supra*, § 11(11).

134. 42 C.F.R. § 483.450(c)(2).

135. *See* American Psychiatry Association Task Force Report 22, *supra*; 42 C.F.R. § 483.450(d)(4); *Wyatt by and through Rawlins v. King, supra.*

136. *Ihler v. Chisholm, supra.*

137. This is a relatively abbreviated consideration of this subject. For a more extensive discussion of the right to confidentiality, see Annas, *The Rights of Patients* (1989).

138. Brakel, Parry & Weiner, *The Mentally Disabled and the Law, supra*, at 462.

139. A privilege is a legal term for the right to withhold information from compelled disclosure by a court order.

140. For example, in the District of Columbia, willful violation of the duty of confidentiality renders the person subject to sanctions under the licensing law. D.C. Code 2-3305.14(16).

141. There were two decisions in *Tarasoff*, the first at 529 P.2d 553, 118 Cal. Rptr. 129 (1974) and the second at 551 P.2d 334, 131 Cal. Rptr. 12 (1976).

142. 551 P.2d at 352–53, 131 Cal. Rptr. 32–33.

143. 551 P.2d at 346, 131 Cal. Rptr. at 26.

144. 51 P.2d at 340, 131 Cal. Rptr. at 32.

145. *See, e.g.*, McDonald v. Clinger, 446 N.Y.S.2d 801 (4th Dept. 1982); Doe v. Roe, 400 N.Y.S.2d 668 (Sup. Ct. N.Y. Co. 1977).

146. D.C. Code §§ 6-2016(a)(1), 2042.

147. *See* U.S. v. Dannon, 481 F. Supp. 152 (W.D. Okla. 1979).

148. *See, e.g.*, Thorton v. Schweiker, 663 F.2d 1312 (5th Cir. 1981).

149. *See* Gotkin v. Miller, 514 F.2d 124 (2d Cir. 1975).

150. *See, e.g.*, Project Release v. Prevost, 766 f.2d 960 (2d Cir. 1982).

151. Johnson, *Out of Bedlam, the Truth about Deinstitutionalization* 120–23 (1990).

152. No 78-80-SD (D. Maine July 14, 1978). The complete set of Wuori standards is found in Perlin, 2 *Mental Disability Law: Civil and Criminal* § 7.28 at 696.

153. Indeed, federal law requires that states establish and enforce standards for board and care homes, foster homes, or other group living arrangements in which a significant number of recipients of Supplemental Security Income live. These standards must address admissions policies, safety, sanitation, and protection of civil rights. 42 U.S.C. § 1382e(e)(1). Regulations promulgated by the Department of Health and Human Services require that the state provide an authority to establish, maintain, and enforce the standards. Enforcement must include periodic inspections and complaint investigations. 45 C.F.R. § 1397.10 and 20. *See* Wolford by Mackey v. Lewis, 860 F. Supp. 1123 (S.D.W.Va. 1994).

154. D.C. Code §§ 6-1965, 1966, 1968, 1970(d).

155. New York State Commission on Quality of Care for the Mentally Disabled, *Crossing the Line from Empowerment to Neglect: The Case of Project L.I.F.E.* (1994).

156. The abbreviation stands for "Protection and Advocacy," independent agencies discussed in the following pages.

157. Robbins v. Butke, 739 F. Supp. 1479, 1486 (D.N.M. 1991).

158. *Id.*

159. Civil Rights of Institutionalized Persons Act, 42 U.S.C. § 1997.

160. *Ward v. Kort, supra.*

161. Bill Johnson's Restaurants, Inc. v. NLRB, 461 U.S. 731, 741 (1983); Acevedo v. Surles, 778 F. Supp. 179 (S.D.N.Y. 1991).

162. *See* chapter 3. Some state constitutions require assignment of counsel in other proceedings, such as involuntary medication hearings. *See, e.g.*, Rivers v. Katz, 67 N.Y. 2d 485 (1986).

163. *Ward v. Kort, supra*, at 860–61.

164. Mississippi Protection and Advocacy v. Cotten, 929 F. 2d 1054, 1058–59 (5th Cir. 1991).

165. *Robbins v. Butke, supra.*

166. Youngberg v. Romeo, *supra*, 457 U.S. at 323. Moreover, even if there is evidence that budgetary constraints existed, a jury should be allowed to decide whether these constraints actually caused the violation of the person's rights. Scott v. Plante, 691 F.2d 634, 637 (3d Cir. 1982). If the violation was not a result of the budgetary constraints, the professional may be found liable under the professional judgment standard.

167. For a discussion of suits for damages, see Schwartz, *Damage Actions as a Strategy*

for Enhancing the Quality of Care of Persons With Mental Disabilities, 17 New York University Review of Law and Social Change 651 (1989–90). Schwartz has also prepared an annotated list of cases in which damages have been sought for people with mental disabilities, available from the Center for Public Representation, Northampton, MA (revised May, 1994).

168. Savidge v. Fincannon, 836 F.2d 898 (5th Cir. 1987).

169. Heck v. Commonwealth, 387 Mass. 336, 491 N.E. 2d 613 (1986).

170. McCartney v. Barg, Civil Action No. C83-26 (N.D. Ohio 1988).

171. *Ihler v. Chisholm, supra.*

VIII

The Legal System

For many persons, law appears to be magic—an obscure domain that can be fathomed only by the professionals initiated into its mysteries. People who might be able to use the law to their advantage sometimes avoid the effort out of awe for its intricacies. But the main lines of the legal system, and of the law in a particular area, can be explained in terms clear to the layperson.

What does a lawyer mean by saying that a person has a legal right?

Having a right means that society has given a person permission—through the legal system—to secure some action or to act in some way that she or he desires. For example, a woman might have a right to an abortion, a job applicant the right to employment free from discrimination, or a person accused of a crime the right to an attorney.

How does one enforce a legal right?

The concept of enforcing a right gives meaning to the concept of the right itself. While the abstract right may be significant because it carries some connotation of morality and justice, enforcing the right yields something concrete—the abortion, the job, the attorney.

A person enforces a right by going to some appropriate authority—often, a judge—who has the power to take certain action. The judge can order the people who are refusing to grant the right to start doing so, on pain of a fine or jail if they disobey.

The problem with the enforcement process is that it will often be lengthy, time-consuming, expensive, frustrating, and may arouse hostility in others—in short, it may not be worth the effort. On the other hand, in some cases it is not necessary to go to an enforcement authority in order to implement a right. The officials may not realize that a right exists and may voluntarily change their actions once the situation is explained to them. Further, the officials may not want to go through the legal process either—it may be expensive and frustrating for them also.

Where are legal rights defined?

There are several sources. The prime sources are the constitutions of the federal and state governments. Rights are further defined in the statutes or laws passed by the United States Congress and by state and city legislatures. They are also set forth in the written decisions of federal and state judges. Congress and state and local legislatures have also created institutions called administrative agencies to enforce certain laws, and these agencies interpret the laws in decisions and rules that further define people's rights.

Are rights always clearly defined and evenly applied to all people?

Not at all. Because so many different sources define people's rights and because persons of diverse backgrounds and beliefs implement and enforce the law, there is virtually no way to enforce uniformity. Nor do statutes that set forth rights always do so with clarity or specificity. It remains for courts or administrative agencies to interpret and to flesh out the details. In the process of doing so, many of the interpreters differ. Sometimes, two courts will give different answers to the same question. Whether or not a person has a particular right may depend on which state or city he or she lives in.

The more times a particular issue is decided, the more guidance there is in predicting what other judges or administrative personnel will decide. Similarly, the importance of the court or agency that decides a case and the persuasiveness of its reasoning will help determine the impact of the decision. A judge who states thoughtful reasons will have more influence than one who offers poor reasons.

In sum, law is not a preordained set of doctrines, applied rigidly and unswervingly in every situation. Rather, law is molded from the arguments and decisions of thousands of persons. It is very much a human process, of trying to convince others—a judge, a jury, an administrator, the lawyer for the other side—that one view of what the law requires is correct.

What is a case or decision?

Lawyers often use these words interchangeably, although technically they do not mean the same thing. A *case* means the lawsuit started by one person against another, and it can refer to that lawsuit at any time from the moment it is begun until the final result. A *decision* means the written opinion in which the judge declares who wins the lawsuit and why.

What is meant by precedent?

Precedent means past decisions. Lawyers use precedent to influence new decisions. If the facts involved in a prior decision are close to the facts in a new case, a judge will be strongly tempted to follow the former decision. She is not, however, bound to do so and, if persuasive reasons are presented to show that the prior decision was wrong or ill-suited to changed conditions in society, the judge may not follow precedent.

What is the relationship between decisions and statutes?

In our legal system, most legal concepts originally were defined in the decisions of judges. In deciding what legal doctrine to apply to a case, each judge kept building on what other judges had done. The body of legal doctrines created in this way is called the *common law.*

The common law still applies in many situations, but increasingly state legislatures and the Congress pass laws "statutes" to define the legal concepts that judges or agencies should use in deciding cases. The written decisions of individual judges are still important even where there is a statute because statutes are generally not specific enough to cover every set of facts. Judges have to interpret their meaning, apply them to the facts at hand, and write a decision; that decision will then be considered by other judges when they deal with these statutes in other cases. Thus it is generally not enough to know what a relevant statute defines as illegal; you also have to know how judges have interpreted the statute in specific situations.

What different kinds of courts are there?

The United States is unique for its variety of courts. Broadly speaking, there are two distinct court systems: federal and state. Both are located throughout the country; each is limited to certain kinds of cases, with substantial areas of overlap. Most crimes are prosecuted in state courts, for instance, although a number of federal crimes are prosecuted in federal courts. People generally use state courts to get a divorce, but they must sue in federal court to establish rights under certain federal laws.

In both federal and state court systems one starts at the *trial* or *lower* court level, where the facts are "tried." This means that a judge or jury listens and watches as the lawyers present evidence of the facts that each side seeks to prove. Evidence can take many forms: written documents, the testimony of a witness on the stand, photographs, charts. Once a judge or jury has listened to or observed all the evidence presented by each side, it will choose the version of the facts it believes, apply the applicable legal doctrine to these facts, and decide which side has won. If either side is unhappy with the result, it may be able to take the case to the next, higher-level court and argue that the judge or the jury applied the wrong legal concept to the facts or that no reasonable jury or judge could have found the facts as they were found in the trial court and that the result was therefore wrong.

What are plaintiffs and defendants?

The *plaintiff* is the person who sues—that is, who complains that someone has wronged him or her and asks the court to remedy this situation. The *defendant* is the person sued—the one who defends against the charges of the plaintiff. The legal writing in which the plaintiff articulates her or his basic grievance is the *complaint,* and a lawsuit is generally commenced by filing this document with a clerk at a courthouse. The defendant then responds to these charges in a document appropriately named an *answer.*

One refers to a particular lawsuit by giving the names of the plaintiff and defendant. If Mary Jones sues Smith Corporation for refusing to hire her because she is a woman, her case will be called *Jones v. Smith Corporation* (*v.* stands for versus, or against).

What is an administrative agency?

Agencies are institutions established by either state or federal legislatures to administer or enforce a particular law or series of laws and are distinct from both courts and legislature. They often regulate a particular industry. For example, the Federal Communications Commission regulates the broadcasting industry (radio and television stations and networks) and the telephone and telegraph industry, in accordance with the legal standards set forth in the Federal Communications Act.

Agencies establish legal principles, embodied in rules, regulations, or guidelines. *Rules* are interpretations of a statute and are designed to function in the same way as a statute—to define people's rights and obligations in a general way but in a more detailed fashion than the statute itself. Agencies also issue specific decisions in cases, like a judge, that apply a broad law or rule to a factual dispute between particular parties.

How does one find court decisions, statutes, and agency rules and decisions?

All these materials are published and can be found in law libraries. In order to find a desired item, one should understand the system lawyers use for referring to, or citing, these materials. For example, a case might be cited as *Watson v. Limbach Company,* 333 F. Supp. 754 (S.D. Ohio 1971); a statute, as 42 U.S.C. § 1983; a regulation, as 29 C.F.R. § 1604.10(b). The unifying factor in all three citations is that the first number denotes the particular volume in a series of books with the same title; the words or the letters that follow represent the name of the book; and the second number represents either the page or the section in the identified volume. In the examples above, the *Watson* case is found in the 333d volume of the series of books called *Federal Supplement* at page 754; the statute is found in volume 42 of the series called the *United States Code* at section 1983; the regulation is in volume 29 of the *Code of Federal Regulations* at section 1604.10(b).

There are similar systems for state court decision. Once the system is understood, a librarian can point out where a particular series of books is kept so that the proper volume and page or section can be looked up. It is also important to check the same page or section in material sometimes inserted at the back of a book, since many legal materials are periodically updated with "pocket parts." A librarian will explain what any abbreviations stand for that are unclear.

Given this basic information, anyone can locate and read important cases, statutes, and regulations. Throughout this book, such materials have been cited when deemed important. Although lawyers often use technical language, the references cited usually can be comprehended without serious difficulty, and reading the original legal materials gives people self-confidence and a deeper understanding of their rights.

What is the role of the lawyer in the legal system?

A lawyer understands the intricacies and technicalities of the legal system and can maneuver within it. Thus lawyers know where to find out about the leading legal doctrines in a given area and often how to predict the outcome of a case based on a knowledge of those doctrines. A lawyer can advise a client what to do: forget about the case, take it to an administrative agency, sue in court, make a will, and so on. A lawyer also helps take the legal actions that the client wants.

How are legal costs determined and how do they affect people's rights?

The cost of using the legal system is predominantly the cost of paying the lawyer for his or her time. Since the cost has become prohibitive even for middle-class individuals, many people are not able to assert their rights, even though they might ultimately win if they had the money to pay a lawyer for doing the job.

Is legal action the only way to win one's legal rights?

By no means. Negotiation, education, consciousness raising, publicity, demonstrations, organization, and lobbying are all ways to achieve rights, often more effectively than through the standard but costly and time-consuming resort to the courts. In all these areas, it helps to have secure knowledge of the legal underpinnings of your rights. One has a great deal more authority if one is protesting illegal action. The refrain "That's illegal" may move some people in and of itself; or it may convince those with whom you are dealing that you are serious enough to do something about the situation—by starting a lawsuit, for instance.

APPENDIX A
Rights of Institutionalized People under Wyatt v. Stickney

APPENDIX B
Resources

Appendix A

Rights of Institutionalized People under Wyatt v. Stickney

This appendix contains excerpts of the standards recognized in *Wyatt v. Stickney* for people confined in institutions for people with mental disabilities. The standards were originally established in 1972 and are reported at 344 F. Supp. 373, 379 (M.D. Ala. 1972) (people with mental illness) and 344 F. Supp. 387, 395 (M.D. Ala. 1972) (people with mental retardation). Both sets of standards were amended in 1980, and the mental health standards were amended again in 1992. The latter are published in Wyatt by and through Rawlins v. King, 793 F. Supp. 1058, 1071 (M.D. Ala. 1992).

For convenience and clarity, the standards are listed in alphabetical order by subject, not in the order they appear in the court orders. These excerpts omit some definitions and details. Condensed portions are indicated by a summary in brackets.

Standards Governing Care and Treatment in Psychiatric Facilities

Definitions

A *qualified mental health professional* (1992) [includes a psychiatrist; a doctoral level clinical psychologist; a master's level clinical psychologist with specialized training in abnormal behavior, two years experience under the supervision of a doctoral level clinical psychologist; a master's level social worker with two years of experience under the supervision of a QMHP; and a registered nurse with training and two years of experience in psychiatric nursing.]

The *Extraordinary Treatment Committee* (1992) [consists of individuals appointed by the court, including consumers and/or expatients, to deal with the medical, psychological, psychiatric, legal, social and ethical issues involved in hazardous or extraordinary treatments.]

Standards

Access to and Confidentiality of Records (1992)
Confidentiality of the patient record shall be protected. . . . The following
shall have access to a patient's record: (a) the patient; (b) the patient's guardian;
(c) individuals properly authorized in writing by the patient or the patient's
guardian; (d) attorneys for the plaintiff class and their designated agents; (e) the
[protection and advocacy agency]; and (f) properly authorized employees of the
Department of Mental Health.

Access to Counsel and Health Professionals
Patients shall have an unrestricted right to visitation with attorneys and with
. . . health professionals.

Aversive Procedures (1980)
No patient shall be subjected to any aversive conditioning or other systematic
attempt to alter his behavior by means of painful or noxious stimuli, except
under the following conditions:
A. A program of aversive conditioning has been recommended by a Qualified
Mental Health Professional ("QMHP") trained and experienced in the use of
aversive conditioning. This recommendation shall be made in writing with detailed clinical justification and an explanation of which alternative treatments
were considered and why they were rejected. The recommendation must be
concurred in by another Qualified Mental Health Professional trained and experienced in the use of aversive conditioning and approved by the superintendent
or medical director of the facility.
B. The patient has given his express and informed consent in writing to the
administration of aversive conditioning. It shall be the responsibility of the
treating psychiatrist to provide the patient with complete and accurate information
concerning the nature and effects of aversive therapy, to assist the patient in
comprehending the significance of such information, and to identify any barriers
to such comprehension. The written consent signed by the patient shall include
a statement of the nature of the treatment consented to; a description of its
purpose, risks, and possible side effects; and a notice to the patient that he has
the right to terminate his consent at any time and for any reason.
C. No aversive conditioning shall be imposed on any patient without the
prior approval of the Extraordinary Treatment Committee, . . . whose primary
responsibility it is to determine, after appropriate inquiry and interview with the
patient, whether the patient's consent to such therapy is, in fact, knowing,
intelligent, and voluntary and whether the proposed treatment is in the best
interest of the patient. . . .

D. The patient shall be represented throughout all proceedings including the signing of his consent and the deliberations of the Extraordinary Treatment Committee, by legal counsel appointed by the Extraordinary Treatment Committee. Counsel shall assure, among other things, that all considerations militating against the use of aversive conditioning have been adequately explored and resolved and that the patient is competent to consent to such treatment. . . .

E. [Written records of consent and approval must be kept.]

F. Aversive conditioning shall be administered only under the direct supervision of and in the physical presence of a Qualified Mental Health Professional trained and experienced in the use of aversive conditioning.

G. No patient shall be subjected to an aversive conditioning program which attempts to extinguish or alter socially appropriate behavior or to develop new behavior patterns for the sole or primary purpose of institutional convenience.

H. A patient may withdraw his consent or aversive conditioning at any time and for any reason. Such withdrawal of consent may be either oral or written and is to be given effect immediately.

Clothing

Patients have a right to wear their own clothes and to keep and use their own personal possessions except insofar as such clothes or personal possessions may be determined by a Qualified Mental Health Professional to be dangerous or otherwise inappropriate to the treatment regimen. The facility has an obligation to supply an adequate allowance of clothing to any patients who do not have suitable clothing of their own. Patients shall have the opportunity to select from various types of neat, clean, and seasonable clothing. Such clothing shall be considered the patient's throughout his stay in the facility. The facility shall make provision for the laundering of patient clothing.

Electroconvulsive Therapy (1992)

Patients may be administered electro-convulsive treatment (ECT) provided the following conditions are met prior to implementing each course of treatment:

The patient is 19 years of age or older; the treatment is prescribed by a licensed psychiatrist who has training regarding the appropriate use of ECT, has conducted a thorough mental and physical examination of the patient, and has reviewed the medical records available; [an] Extraordinary Treatment Committee concurs in the recommendation of treatment; . . . the clinical director of the facility has approved the decision to treat with ECT; the treatment is administered by a psychiatrist who is specially trained in the use of ECT. . . . regressive or depatterning electro-convulsive techniques are not utilized; complete, accurate, and contemporaneous records are maintained with respect to each administration of ECT; and consent has been obtained [as described below] . . . or the emergency administration of ECT is permitted. . . .

Consent to ECT. For a *competent* patient (i.e., a patient who is capable of giving informed consent to ECT):[1]

A. The patient has been fully informed by the treating psychiatrist (in language and in a manner appropriate to the patient's condition and capacity to understand) of the nature, risks and consequences of ECT, including the possibility of memory loss; of the patient's right to revoke his consent at any time, including during the course of the treatment; and of specific means by which the patient may revoke his consent (e.g., by orally informing the treating psychiatrist or other staff, by calling a specific telephone number, by returning a preprinted form, etc.); and

B. The patient has consented in writing to the treatment.

If the patient has been *judicially determined to be incompetent* to consent to treatment (e.g., a court has appointed for the patient a general guardian or a limited guardian with power to consent to treatment), and the patient has not regained competency before or during the proposed course of ECT treatment:

A. The patient has been informed of the nature of the treatment in language and in a manner appropriate to the patient's condition and capacity to understand; and

B. Consent has been obtained in writing from the patient's guardian[2] after the guardian [has been given the same information as the competent patient].

If the patient has been *judicially determined to be incompetent to consent to treatment . . . but the patient has regained competency before or during the proposed course of ECT treatment* (regardless of whether the patient's guardian has consented to the treatment), [the same procedures should be followed as for competent patients].

If a patient *has not been judicially determined to be incompetent to consent to treatment, but the treating psychiatrist believes the patient may not be competent to consent:*

A. The treating psychiatrist has caused a formal request (e.g., petition, motion, etc.) to be filed in a court of competent jurisdiction for adjudication of the patient's competence to consent to treatment;[3] and

B. Either (i) the court has appointed a guardian [and the procedures for incompetent patients are followed] or (ii) the court itself has authorized the treatment.

Emergency administration. Patients may be administered ECT in an emergency if

A. The treating psychiatrist has documented, and the Extraordinary Treatment Committee has found, that: (i) the patient is not competent to consent to treatment and is without a guardian; (ii) the patient's condition has deteriorated, (iii) the patient has failed to respond to alternative forms of treatment; (iv) a delay in treatment could reasonably be expected to jeopardize the life of the patient or to result in serious physical harm to the patient; and

B. The treating psychiatrist has (i) notified the Department's Internal Rights Advocacy and Protection Program of his or her decision; and (ii) been unable to secure a decision on the appointment of a guardian or a judicial authorization from a state court to administer ECT on an emergency basis, despite diligent efforts on his part and the part of legal counsel for the Department.[4]

If the treating psychiatrist believes that the patient may require additional ECT treatment in the future, the Department must make diligent efforts following the emergency treatment to obtain a judicial determination of whether the patient is competent to consent and, if it is determined that the patient is not competent, to obtain the appointment of a guardian to consent to treatment or a judicial authorization for future ECT treatments.

Review. The Department's Internal Rights Advocacy and Protection Program shall annually review all administrations of ECT (i.e., emergency administrations, administrations to consenting competent patients, and administrations to incompetent patients when a guardian or court has given consent).

Exercise and the Outdoors

Patients have a right to regular physical exercise several times a week [and to be furnished] facilities and equipment for such exercise. Patients have a right to be outdoors at regular and frequent intervals, in the absence of medical considerations.

Experimental Research

Patients shall have a right not to be subjected to experimental research without the express and informed consent of the patient, if the patient is able to give such consent, and of his guardian or next of kin, after opportunities for consultation with independent specialists and with legal counsel. Such proposed research shall first have been reviewed and approved by the institution's Human Rights Committee before such consent shall be sought. Prior to such approval the Committee shall determine that such research complies with the principles for research involving human subjects published by the American Psychiatric and Psychological Associations and with those required by the United States Department of Health and Human Services for projects supported by that agency.

Hazardous Procedures and Psychosurgery (1980)

No lobotomy, psychosurgery or other unusual, hazardous or intrusive surgical procedure designed to alter or affect a patient's mental condition shall be performed on any patient. . . . No patient . . . shall be subjected to any other extraordinary or hazardous technique or procedure not specifically mentioned herein unless the treating psychiatrist or the medical director of the facility has first obtained the written approval of the Extraordinary Treatment Committee to the utilization of such technique or procedure and the express and informed consent of the patient in writing to the administration of such treatment.

There shall be no coercion in any form with regard to the treatment of any patient by means of . . . extraordinary techniques. . . . Consent to any such form of treatment shall not be made a condition for receiving any type of public assistance, nor may it be a prerequisite to any health or social service or for admission or release.

Humane Environment

A patient has a right to a humane psychological and physical environment. . . . [F]acilities shall be designed to afford patients with comfort and safety, promote dignity, and ensure privacy. The facilities shall be designed to make a positive contribution to the efficient attainment of the treatment goals of the facility. . . . [The standards describe minimal requirements for resident units, toilets and lavatories, showers, day rooms, dining rooms, linen service, housekeeping, heat, fire and safety, water temperature, and refuse management.]

There must be special facilities for geriatric and other nonambulatory patients to assure their safety and comfort, including special fittings on toilets and wheelchairs. Appropriate provision shall be made to permit nonambulatory patients to communicate their needs to staff.

Labor

No patient shall be required to perform labor which involves the operation and maintenance of the facility or for which the facility is under contract with an outside organization. Privileges or release from the facility shall not be conditioned upon the performance of labor covered by this provision. Patients may voluntarily engage in such labor if the labor is compensated in accordance with the minimum wage laws of the Fair Labor Standards Act. . . .

Patients may be required to perform therapeutic tasks which do not involve the operation and maintenance of the facility, provided the specific task or any change in assignment is an integrated part of the patient's treatment plan and approved as a therapeutic activity by a Qualified Mental Health Professional responsible for supervising the patient's treatment; and supervised by a staff member to oversee the therapeutic aspects of the activity.

Patients may voluntarily engage in therapeutic labor for which the facility would otherwise have to pay an employee, provided the specific labor or any change in labor assignment is an integrated part of the patient's treatment plan and approved as a therapeutic activity by a Qualified Mental Health Professional responsible for supervising the patient's treatment; supervised by a staff member to oversee the therapeutic aspects of the activity; and compensated in accordance with the minimum wage laws of the Fair Labor Standards Act. . . .

Patients may be required to perform tasks of a personal housekeeping nature such as the making of one's own bed.

Payment to patients pursuant to these paragraphs shall not be applied to the costs of hospitalization.

Least Restrictive Conditions

Patients have a right to the least restrictive conditions necessary to achieve the purposes of commitment.

Mail

Patients shall have an unrestricted right to send sealed mail. Patients shall have an unrestricted right to receive sealed mail from their attorneys, private physicians, and other mental health professionals, from courts, and government officials. Patients shall have a right to receive sealed mail from others, except to the extent that the Qualified Mental Health Professional responsible for formulation of a particular patient's treatment plan writes an order imposing special restrictions on receipt of sealed mail. The written order must be renewed after each periodic review of the treatment plan if any restrictions are to be continued.

Managing One's Affairs

No person shall be deemed incompetent to manage his affairs, to contract, to hold professional or occupational or vehicle operator's licenses, to marry and obtain a divorce, to register and vote, or to make a will solely by reason of his admission or commitment to the facility.

Medical Care

Patients have a right to receive prompt and adequate medical treatment for any physical ailments.

Medication

Patients have a right to be free from unnecessary or excessive medication. No medication shall be administered unless at the written order of a physician. . . . The use of medication shall not exceed standards of use that are advocated by the United States Food and Drug Administration. Notation of each individual's medication shall be kept in his medical records. At least weekly the attending physician shall review the drug regimen of each patient under his care. All prescriptions shall be written with a termination date, which shall not exceed 30 days. Medication shall not be used as punishment, for the convenience of staff, as a substitute for program, or in quantities that interfere with the patient's treatment program.

Notices

Each patient and his family, guardian, or next friend shall promptly upon the patient's admission receive written notice, in language he understands, of all the above standards for adequate treatment. In addition a copy of all the above standards shall be posted in each ward.

Nutrition

Patients, except for the non-mobile, shall eat or be fed in dining rooms. The diet for patients will provide at a minimum the Recommended Daily Dietary Allowances as developed by the National Academy of Sciences. Menus shall be satisfying and nutritionally adequate. . . . Provisions shall be made for special therapeutic diets and for substitutes at the request of the patient, or his guardian or next of kin, in accordance with the religious requirements of any patient's faith. Denial of a nutritionally adequate diet shall not be used as punishment.

Privacy and Dignity

Patients have a right to privacy and dignity.

Quality Assurance/Release (1992)

Each facility shall have a Quality Assurance Program that provides for all treatment plans to be reviewed in accordance with JCAHO standards and a Utilization Review Program that requires that all patients be screened for appropriateness of admission to the facility [and continued hospitalization] according to specific criteria, including whether the patient meets the standards for commitment. . . . [In these determinations] the facility shall document the specific basis for a determination that a patient needs to be admitted or continues to need institutional care. [Whenever a patient is found not to require hospitalization any longer], the patient must be discharged immediately unless he or she agrees to continue treatment on a voluntary basis. Upon discharge, the patient will be linked to an appropriate community mental health center and given access to case management services unless not clinically indicated.[5]

Records

The record shall include at a minimum: [all information and progress reports required to be in the treatment plan], as well as
[Identification and legal status];
[History];

The chief complaints of the patient and the chief complaints of others regarding the patient. The chief complaints of others shall be discussed with the patient, and the patient's response shall be documented along with the complaints;

An evaluation that notes the onset of illness, the circumstances leading to admission, attitudes, behavior, estimate of intellectual function, memory function, orientation, and an inventory of the patient's assets in descriptive, not interpretative, fashion;

A summary of each physical examination that describes the results of the examination;

A detailed summary of each significant contact by a Qualified Mental Health Professional with the patient;

A signed order . . . for any restrictions on visitation and communication;

A signed order by a qualified physician for any physical restraints or seclusion . . . ;

A detailed summary of any extraordinary incident in the facility involving the patient to be entered by a staff member noting that he has personal knowledge of the incident or specifying his other source of information, and initialed within 24 hours by a QMHP;

A summary of the findings of the screen of appropriateness of admission and of the continued stay reviews . . . and a summary of any finding by the director or his or her appointed agent that the patient does not require inpatient treatment in accordance with the standards for commitment.

Religious Practice

The right to religious worship shall be accorded to each patient who desires such opportunities. Provisions for such worship shall be made available to all patients on a nondiscriminatory basis. No individual shall be coerced into engaging in any religious activities.

Seclusion and Restraint (1992)

Patients have a right to be free from seclusion and physical restraint. Patients may be placed in seclusion or physically restrained only (a) to prevent a patient from physically injuring himself/herself or others, (b) after alternative treatment interventions have been unsuccessful or after determining that alternative treatment interventions would not be practicable, and (c) when authorized by a written order of a qualified physician[6] who is physically present and has examined the patient. No order for seclusion or restraint may exceed eight hours.

[Exceptions to these rules] may be made in emergency situations when no qualified physician is available. In such situations, the use of restraint or seclusion may be implemented for up to one hour by a trained, clinically privileged, qualified registered nurse to prevent a patient from physically injuring himself/herself or others, after determining that alternative treatment interventions have been unsuccessful or would not be practicable. The nurse must be physically present and evaluate the patient's physical condition to the extent that it is feasible and document the evaluation in the clinical record. A qualified physician should be notified as soon as possible after the emergency episode of seclusion or restraint. A qualified physician should see the patient within four hours of the initiation of seclusion or restraint and preferably within one hour. The emergency episode of seclusion or restraint may be extended up to four hours (i.e., three hours beyond the initial one hour authorized by the qualified registered nurse) upon verbal order of a qualified physician if necessary to prevent a patient from physically injuring himself/herself or others and if, in the opinion of the qualified physician, alternative treatment interventions would be unsuccessful in preventing injury. After the emergency episode has extended for four hours, the patient must be released unless a qualified physician writes a new order for seclusion or restraint that meets the criteria [for seclusion or restraint]. All emergency seclusion or restraint orders (including any related documentation) must be reviewed and signed by a qualified physician within twelve hours of the initial use of seclusion or restraint.

All written orders for seclusion and restraint (including in emergency situations) shall include a clinical assessment of the patient, the alternative treatment interventions attempted, and criteria for the release of the patient which shall relate to the standard for seclusion or restraint . . . above. When the criteria for release have been met or at the end of the period set out in the order (whichever occurs first), the patient must be released unless the patient is then examined by a qualified physician who writes a new order for seclusion or restraint.

A documented observation shall be made of a patient in restraint or seclusion at least every fifteen minutes. The person making the observation shall be made aware of and shall take account of any special medical concerns regarding the patient. The patient must be given bathroom privileges at least every hour, must be bathed at least every twenty-four hours or more frequently if necessary, and must be provided meals and fluids on a regular basis. Vital signs shall be taken as clinically indicated. Patients in restraint shall be released for range of motion exercises as clinically indicated.

Seclusion and restraint shall not be used as punishment or for the convenience of staff or in a manner that causes undue physical discomfort, harm, or pain to the patient. [As needed] orders for seclusion and restraint are prohibited.

Socializing with the Opposite Sex

The institution shall provide, with adequate supervision, suitable opportunities for the patient's interaction with members of the opposite sex.

Staff (1992)

[QMHP] staff shall meet all licensing and certification requirements . . . for individuals in private practice. . . . [Other] staff shall meet licensing and certification standards for individuals in private practice. . . . [Non QMHP staff shall be under the supervision of a QMHP in the same discipline.] Staff members on all levels shall have regularly scheduled in-service training.

Telephone and Visitation

Patients shall have the same rights to visitation and telephone communications as patients at other public hospitals, except to the extent that the Qualified Mental Health Professional responsible for formulation of a particular patient's treatment plan writes an order imposing special restrictions. The written order must be renewed after each periodic review of the treatment plan if any restrictions are to be continued.

Transitional Care

. . . [Each involuntary patient released is entitled to] adequate transitional treatment and care. Transitional care and treatment possibilities include, but are not limited to, psychiatric day care, treatment in the home by a visiting therapist, nursing home or extended care, out-patient treatment, and treatment in the psychiatric ward of a general hospital.

Treatment Plans (1992)

Each patient shall have an individualized treatment plan developed by an assigned Treatment Team. The team shall actively involve the patient, and with the patient's permission, the patient's family, in developing the plan. [The plan must contain:]

(1) A statement of the nature of the specific problems and specific needs of the patient;

(2) A statement of the patient's strengths including skills and interests;

(3) A statement of the least restrictive treatment conditions necessary to achieve the purposes of commitment and the goals of the treatment plan;

(4) A description of intermediate and long term treatment goals which relate to involuntary commitment criteria, with a projected timetable for their attainment;

(5) A specification of staff responsibility and a description of proposed staff involvement with the patient in order to attain these treatment goals;

(6) Specific and measurable criteria for release to less restrictive treatment conditions, and specific and measurable criteria for discharge which relate to involuntary commitment standards. These criteria shall be written in nontechnical language and shall be explained to the patient in a manner appropriate to the patient's capacity to understand.

(7) A notation of any therapeutic tasks and labor. . . .

(8) An assessment by medical staff of any restrictions or limitations on physical activity;

(9) An individualized discharge plan developed concurrently with the individualized treatment plan that identifies the residential, clinical, social and vocational services the patient will require upon discharge.

A Qualified Mental Health Professional and a psychiatrist shall be responsible for supervising the implementation of the treatment plan, integrating the various components of the treatment program, reviewing the treatment plan on a regular and periodic basis, and recording the patient's progress. The QMHP shall be responsible for ensuring that the patient is released, where appropriate, into a less restrictive form of treatment. The QMHP shall ensure that, upon discharge, the patient is linked to an appropriate community mental health center and is given access to case management services.

Summaries of the patient's progress shall be recorded on a regular and periodic basis by a QMHP, [and shall include] a medication review . . . that specifically addresses, among other things, the extent to which the prescribed medication is achieving its intended purposes and the presence of unintended side effects. A summary of the extent and nature of the patient's work activity shall also be included, if applicable. The frequency and regularity with which the patient's progress is noted should be dictated by good clinical judgment. Factors affecting the exercise of such judgment should include changes in the patient's condition and/or the need to document observations that affect treatment planning. At a minimum, progress summaries shall be recorded as follows:

(1) Weekly summaries for patients in short-term treatment programs (programs of up to 180 days) and in adolescent treatment programs;

(2) Monthly summaries for patients in long-term treatment programs (programs of more than 180 days);

(3) Monthly summaries for geriatric patients.

Modifications in the individualized treatment plan shall be made by the Treatment Team as the need becomes evident through regular and periodic reviews. At a minimum, the treatment plan shall be reviewed at major key decision points in the patient's treatment, including: at the time of admission, transfer, and discharge; when there is a major change in the patient's condition; at the point of estimated length of treatment and thereafter based on that estimated length of treatment; and at least every three months.

Treatment Standards (1980)

All treatments . . . administered to patients . . . shall accord with the standards of quality and care reasonably expected by and of the medical and psychiatric professions.

STANDARDS GOVERNING CARE AND TREATMENT IN MENTAL RETARDATION FACILITIES

[The standards governing clothing, confidentiality, exercise and access to the outdoors, environment, experimental and hazardous treatment, labor, mail, managing one's affairs, medical care, nutrition, privacy, records, religion, socialization with the opposite sex, and staff are generally the same as the standards for psychiatric institutions listed above, with minor adjustments to take into account the specific needs of people with mental retardation. The following sections apply uniquely to people with mental retardation.]

Admission

No person shall be admitted to the institution unless a prior determination shall have been made that residence in the institution is the least restrictive habilitation setting feasible for that person. No mentally retarded person shall be admitted to the institution if services and programs in the community can afford adequate habilitation to such person. . . . Borderline or mildly mentally retarded persons shall not be residents of the institution. . . . Prior to his admission to the institution, each resident shall have a comprehensive social, psychological, educational, and medical diagnosis and evaluation by appropriate specialists to determine if admission is appropriate.

No person shall be admitted to any publicly supported residential institution caring for mentally retarded persons unless such institutions meets [these standards] or unless the chief administrator of such institution determines that the person, if allowed to remain in the community, is likely to cause serious injury to himself or others, or that the only alternative for providing adequate shelter, food and clothing for such person is jail.

Behavior Modification

No resident shall be subjected to a behavior modification program designed to eliminate a particular pattern of behavior without prior certification by a physician that he has examined the resident in regard to behavior to be extinguished and finds that such behavior is not caused by a physical condition which could be corrected by appropriate medical procedures. No resident shall be subjected to a behavior modification program which attempts to extinguish socially appropriate behavior or to develop new behavior patterns when such behavior modifications serve only institutional convenience.

Behavior modification programs involving the use of noxious or aversive stimuli shall be reviewed and approved by the institution's Human Rights Committee and shall be conducted only with the express and informed consent of the affected resident, if the resident is able to give such consent, and of his guardian or next of kin, after opportunities for consultation with independent specialists and with legal counsel. Such behavior modification programs shall be conducted only under the supervision of and in the presence of a Qualified Mental Retardation Professional who has had proper training in such techniques.

Electric shock devices shall be considered a research technique for the purpose of these standards. Such devices shall only be used in extraordinary circumstances to prevent self-mutilation leading to repeated and possibly permanent physical damage to the resident and only after alternative techniques have failed. The use of such devices shall be subject to the conditions [prescribed above and in accordance with standards on experimentation] and shall be used only under the direct and specific order of the superintendent.

Education

Residents shall have a right to receive suitable educational services regardless of chronological age, degree of retardation or accompanying disabilities or handicaps.

Habilitation and the Normalization Principle

Residents shall have a right to habilitation, including medical treatment, education and care, suited to their needs, regardless of age, degree of retardation or handicapping condition. Each resident has a right to a habilitation program which will maximize his human abilities and enhance his ability to cope with his environment. The institution shall recognize that each resident, regardless of ability or status, is entitled to develop and realize his fullest potential. The institution shall implement the principle of normalization so that each resident may live as normally as possible.

Habilitation Plans

Each resident shall have an individualized habilitation plan formulated by the institution. This plan shall be developed by appropriate Qualified Mental Retardation Professionals and implemented as soon as possible but no later than 14 days after the resident's admission to the institution. . . . Each individualized habilitation plan shall contain:

(1) A statement of the nature of the specific limitations and specific needs of the resident;

(2) A description of intermediate and long-range habilitation goals with a projected timetable for their attainment;

(3) A statement of, and an explanation for, the plan of habilitation for achieving these intermediate and long-range goals;

(4) A statement of the least restrictive setting for habilitation necessary to achieve the habilitation goals of the resident;

(5) A specification of the professionals and other staff members who are responsible for the particular resident's attaining these habilitation goals;

(6) [C]riteria for release to less restrictive settings for habilitation within the institution and, in appropriate cases, movement to less restrictive settings outside the institution, including criteria for discharge and a projected date for discharge.

In the interests of continuity of care, one Qualified Mental Retardation Professional shall be responsible for supervising the implementation of the habilitation plan, integrating the various aspects of the habilitation program, and recording the resident's progress as measured by objective indicators. This Qualified Mental Retardation Professional shall also be responsible for ensuring that the resident is released when appropriate to a less restrictive habilitation setting.

The habilitation plan shall be continuously reviewed by the Qualified Mental Retardation Professional responsible for supervising the implementation of the plan and shall be modified if necessary. In addition, six months after admission and at least annually thereafter, each resident shall receive a comprehensive psychological, social, educational and medical diagnosis and evaluation, and his habilitation plan shall be reviewed by an interdisciplinary team of no less than two Qualified Mental Retardation Professionals and such resident care workers as are directly involved in his habilitation and care.

Least Restrictive Setting

Residents shall have a right to the least restrictive conditions necessary to achieve the purposes of habilitation. To this end, the institution shall make every attempt to move residents from (1) more to less structured living; (2) larger to smaller facilities; (3) larger to smaller living units; (4) group to individual residence; (5) segregated from the community to integrated into the community living; (6) dependent to independent living.

Notices

The guardian or next of kin of each resident shall promptly, upon resident's admission, receive a written copy of all the above standards for adequate habilitation. Each resident, if the resident is able to comprehend, shall promptly upon his admission be orally informed in clear language of the above standards and, where appropriate, be provided with a written copy. The superintendent shall report in writing to the next of kin or guardian of the resident at least every six months on the resident's educational, vocational and living skills progress and medical condition. Such report shall also state any appropriate habilitation program which has not been afforded to the resident because of inadequate habilitation resources.

Personal Hygiene

Each resident shall be assisted in learning normal grooming practices with individual toilet articles, including soap and toothpaste, that are available to each resident; [personal hygiene is to be assured].

Physical Restraint

Physical restraint shall be employed only when absolutely necessary to protect the resident from injury to himself or to prevent injury to others. Restraint shall not be employed as punishment, for the convenience of staff, or as a substitute for a habilitation program. Restraint shall be applied only if alternative techniques have failed and only if such restraint imposes the least possible restriction consistent with its purpose. Only Qualified Mental Retardation Professionals may authorize the use of restraints.

Orders for restraints by the Qualified Mental Retardation Professionals shall be in writing and shall not be in force for longer than 12 hours. A resident placed in restraint shall be checked at least every 30 minutes by staff trained in the use of restraints, and a record of such checks shall be kept. Mechanical restraints shall be designed and used so as not to cause physical injury to the resident and so as to cause the least possible discomfort. Opportunity for motion and exercise shall be provided for a period of not less than ten minutes during each two hours in which restraint is employed. Daily reports shall be made to the superintendent by those Qualified Mental Retardation Professionals ordering the use of restraints summarizing all such uses of restraint, the types used, the duration, and the reasons therefore.

Protection from Harm

The institution shall prohibit mistreatment, neglect or abuse in any form of any resident. Alleged violations shall be reported immediately to the superintendent and there shall be a written record that: (1) Each alleged violation has been thoroughly investigated and findings stated; (2) the results of such investigation are reported to the superintendent and to the commissioner within 24 hours of the report of the incident. Such reports shall also be made to the institution's Human Rights Committee monthly and to the Alabama Board of Mental Health at its next scheduled public meeting.

Seclusion

Seclusion, defined as the placement of a resident alone in a locked room, shall not be employed. Legitimate "time out" procedures may be utilized under close and direct professional supervision as a technique in behavior-shaping programs.

Transition

Each resident discharged to the community shall have a program of transitional habilitation assistance.

NOTES

1. A psychiatrist may consider a patient to be "competent" when the psychiatrist reasonably believes the patient to be capable of giving informed consent to ECT.

2. As used in this standard, a "guardian" includes any person authorized by a court of competent jurisdiction to consent on behalf of the patient to the administration of ECT.

3. Each such formal request filed in court must ask the court to appoint counsel for the patient whose competence is at issue.

4. Requests filed with the court for the appointment of a guardian or judicial authorization to administer ECT must ask the court to appoint counsel for the patient whose competence is at issue.

5. In some of these cases, the person may not be mentally ill or may not require community mental health or case management services upon discharge.

6. [A psychiatrist or a licensed physician with specialized training in psychiatry.]

Appendix B

Resources

Books and Journals

Two comprehensive legal treatises concern the rights of people with mental disabilities. They are Samuel Jan Brackel, John Parry, and Barbara Weiner, *The Mentally Disabled and the Law*, published by the American Bar Foundation (1986); and Michael Perlin, *Mental Disability Law: Civil and Criminal* (3 vol. 1989), published by the Michie Company. The latter is updated with a supplement annually. In addition, Perlin has a condensed, one-volume version of his treatise issued by the same publisher. Michael Perlin, *Law and Mental Disability* (1994).

As is evident by its frequent citation here, another volume in this ACLU series, George Annas's *The Rights of Patients* (1989) is very helpful on issues that are only touched on here, including confidentiality, right to access to records, malpractice, human experimentation, and research.

The American Bar Association Commission on Mental and Physical Disability Law publishes a legal semimonthly journal, the *Mental and Physical Disability Law Reporter*, that contains reports on recent cases in the field. It also publishes *Mental Disability Law, a Primer* (5th ed. 1995). Other journals focusing on mental disability law include the *Bulletin of the American Academy of Psychiatry and Law* and the *International Journal of Law and Psychiatry*. The law governing the entitlements discussed in chapter 5 can be followed in *Clearinghouse Review*. Two useful medical-legal journals are *Law, Medicine and Health Care* and *Law and Human Behavior*. In addition, professional journals frequently contain articles on legal subjects.

Three reference books are useful. The American Association on Mental Retardation's *Mental Retardation: Definition, Classification, and Systems Support* (9th ed. 1992) by Ruth Luckasson et al. describes the current classification system used for people with mental retardation. The American Psychiatric Association's *Diagnostic and Statistical Manual of Mental Disorders* (4th ed. 1994) lists the criteria psychiatrists (and many other mental health professionals) use for diagnosing mental disorders. Finally, the *Physician's Desk Reference*, published annually by Medical Economic Data Production Company, Five Paragon Drive, Montvale, NJ 07645, lists the indications for, side effects of, and warnings about all prescription drugs approved by the Food and Drug Administration. It is available as well on CD-ROM.

FEDERAL AGENCIES

Department of Education
Office of Civil Rights
Washington, DC 20202
1-800-421-3481

Takes complaints about violations of rights of students under Section 504 of the Rehabilitation Act and Title II of the ADA.

Department of Housing and Urban Development
Office of Fair Housing and Equal Opportunity
Washington, DC 20410
1-800-669-9777 or 1-800-927-9275 TDD

Takes complaints of housing discrimination.

Department of Justice
Civil Rights Division
P.O. 66738
Washington, DC 20035-9998
ADA Information line 1-800-514-0301 or 1-800-514-0383 (TDD)

Receives and investigates complaints under Titles II and III of the Americans with Disabilities Act and the Civil Rights of Institutionalized Persons Act. Publishes handbooks on the ADA.

Equal Employment Opportunity Commission
1801 L Street, N.W.
Washington, DC 20507
For ordering documents:
1-800-669-3362
1-800-800-3302 TDD
For questions:
1-800-669-4000 (voice)
TDD: use relay service

Investigates complaints under Title I (private employment) of the ADA.

National Council on Disability
800 Independence Ave. S.W.
Washington, DC 20591
1-800-875-7814
(301) 577-7814 TDD

Provides analysis and advice to Congress and the President on disability-related issues and also issues reports on the ADA and other issues of concern to people with disabilities.

National Institute on Disbability and Rehabilitation Research (NIDRR)
NIDRR is part of the U.S. Department of Education and provides funds for ten ADA technical assistance centers.
ADA technical assistance nationwide
1-800-949-4232 (voice and TDD)

President's Committee on Employment of People with Disabilities
1331 F Street, N.W.
Washington, DC 20004
1-800-232-9675
Job Accommodation Network 1-800-526-7234

Provides national leadership on increasing employment opportunities for people with disabilities.

Social Security Administration
See phone book for local office.
1-800-772-1213
1-800-325-0778 TDD

NATIONAL ORGANIZATIONS

Alzheimer's Disease and Related Disorders Ass'n, Inc.
919 North Michigan Ave. Suite 1000
Chicago, IL 60611
(312) 335-8700
(312) 335-8882
1-800-272-3900

American Association on Mental Retardation
1719 Kalorama Road N.W.
Washington, DC 20009
(202) 387-1968

National association of professionals in the field of mental retardation. AAMR publishes books and articles on the definition and interpretation of mental retardation, among many other publications.

American Bar Association
Commission on Mental and Physical Disability Law
740 15th St., N.W.
Washington, DC 20005
(202) 662-1570

In addition to the *Mental and Physical Disability Law Reporter*, publishes manuals and guidebooks on involuntary civil commitment, the Americans with Disabilities Act and other subjects. The ABA also has a legal research service.

American Civil Liberties Union
132 West 43 Street
New York, NY 10036
(212) 944-9800

Organization concerned with protecting individual rights through the Bill of Rights and laws promoting equal rights and equal justice. Has affiliates in most states.

Autism Society of America
8601 Georgia Ave. Suite 503
Silver Spring, MD 20910
(301) 565-0433

Anxiety Disorders Association of America
6000 Executive Blvd. Suite 200
Rockville, MD 20852
(301) 231-8368

Bazelon Center for Mental Health Law (formerly Mental Health Law Project)
1101 15th Street, N.W.
Washington, DC 20005
(202) 467-5730
(202) 467-4232 TDD

National advocacy organization on behalf of people with mental disabilities. Publishes manuals, handbooks, and reports on rights of people with mental disabilities with respect to employment, housing, nursing homes, public benefits, Medicaid, and other subjects.

Disability Rights Education and Defense Fund
2212 6th Street
Berkeley, CA 94712
(510) 644-2555
ADA information 1-800-466-4243

National advocacy organization concerned with rights of people with disabilities. Operates ADA information line.

Federation of Families for Children's Mental Health
1021 Prince Street
Alexandria, VA 22314
(703) 684-7710

National Alliance for the Mentally Ill
200 N. Glebe Road
Arlington, VA 22203-3754
(703) 524-7600
1-800-950-6264

Organization composed principally of families of people with serious psychiatric disabilities, particularly schizophrenia and manic depression. Also has a consumer caucus.

National Association of Protection and Advocacy Systems
900 2nd Street N.E. Suite 211
Washington, DC 20002
(202) 408-9514
(202) 408-9521 (TDD)

National Depressive and Manic Depressive Association
730 North Franklin, Suite 510
Chicago, IL 60610
(312) 64200049
1-800-82-NMDA

National Down Syndrome Congress
1605 Chantilly Drive, Suite 250
Atlanta, GA 30324
(404) 633-1555

National Empowerment Center
130 Parker Street, Suite 20
Boston, MA 01843
1-800-POWER-2-U

Clearinghouse and technical assistance center for consumer organizations for people with psychiatric disabilities.

National Mental Health Association
1021 Prince Street
Alexandria, VA 22314
(703) 684-7722

National organization with state and local affiliates concerned with mental health services.

National Mental Health Consumers' Clearinghouse
311 S. Juniper St.
Philadelphia, PA 19107
(215) 735-6082
1-800-553-4539

Provides technical assistance to people with psychiatric disabilities on the ADA and other issues, training and referrals to local consumer groups.

The Arc
500 East Border Street
Arlington, TX 76010
(817) 261-6003
(817) 277-0553 TDD

National association, with many state and local chapters, composed primarily of families of people with mental retardation. The Arc nationally and locally publishes information about and advocates on behalf of people with mental retardation. Some local affiliates also run programs and housing for people with mental retardation.

United Cerebral Palsy Associations, Inc.
1660 L St. N.W.
Washington, DC 20036
(202) 776-0406 (voice/TDD)
1-800-872-5827

STATE-BASED ORGANIZATIONS

For each state, five organizations are listed: The Arc Chapter; the Protection and Advocacy agency; Mental Health Consumer Groups, the Alliance for the Mentally

Ill Chapter; the Mental Health Association affiliate and the Federation of Families for Children's Mental Health affiliate.

Where the Protection and Advocacy program has a separate Client Assistance Program under the Rehabilitation Act, it is designated as "CAP," and where it has separate programs for people with mental illiness and developmental disabilities, they are designated "MI" and "DD" respectively.

	The Arc	P & A	MH Assoc	Consumer Groups	Alliance for MI	Fed. of Fam.
ALABAMA	025/262-7688	205/348-4928 800/826-1675 CAP 205/281-8780	205/752-2689 800/264-6422	MHC of AL 800/264-6422	205/833-8336	205/664-1590
ALASKA	907/277-6677	907/344-1002 801/478-1234 CAP 907/333-2211	907/563-0880	MHC of AK 907/277-3817	907/277-1300	907/561-3127
ARIZONA	602/243-1787	602/274-6287	602/381-1591		602/244-8166	602/867-0310
ARKANSAS	501/375-7770	501/324-9215 800/482-1174	501/686-9000	P.E.O.P.L. 501/686-9273	501/661-1548	501/663-0886
CALIFORNIA	916/522-6619	916/322-5066 800/776-5746	916/557-1167	CA Netwk. of MH Clients 916/443-3232	916/567-0163	Fam. Network 415/564-0722 Matrix 415/499-3877 TASK 714/533-8275 United Adv. 415/752-4978
COLORADO	303/756-7234	303/722-0300	303/744-6718	SCCORE 303/762-4339	303/321-3104	No. CO FFCMH 303/223-3036 Kids MH Coal. 303/296-2400
CONNECTICUT	203/953-8335	203/297-4300 800/842-7303	800/842-1501	CT Dept. of MH 203/566-5837 800/842-1501	203/586-2319	203/529-6552

DELAWARE	302/996-9400	302/856-0038 CAP 302/698-9336 800/640-9336	302/656-8308	MH in DE 302/656-8308	302/427-0787	302/656-8308
DIS. OF COL.	202/636-2950	202/408-9514 [for referral]	202/265-6363	MH Consumers' League 3169 Mt. Pleasant St., NW Washington, DC 20010	202/546-0646	202/708-0239
FLORIDA	904/921-0460	904/488-9071 800/342-0823	305/379-2673	FL MH 904/455-2479 Consumer Council 305/663-8821 FL Cares 904/254-8821	904/222-3400	904/487-2460
GEORGIA	404/761-3150	404/885-1234 800/282-4538 CAP 404/657-3012	404/875-7081	800/297-6146	404/894-8860	404/756-0197
HAWAII	808/737-7995	808/949-2922	808/521-1846	Self-Help 808/926-0466	808/737-2778	808/553-5600
IDAHO	208/336-5353		208/334-0800	LAMP 208/334-0856	208/376-4304	208/683-2143
ILLINOIS	708/206-1930	312/341-0022 CAP 217/782-5374	312/368-9070	Recovery, Inc. 802 N. Dearborn Chicago, IL 60610	217/522-1403	708/354-1977

continued on next page

	The Arc	P & A	MH Assoc	Consumer Groups	Alliance for MI	Fed. of Fam.
INDIANA	371/632-4387	317/232-1150 800/622-4845	317/638-3501	KEY Org. 317/630-4210	317/236-0056	317/685-1276
IOWA	515/283-2358	515/278-2502 CAP 515/281-3957	319/557-8331		515/254-0417	515/576-1877
KANSAS	913/271-8783	913/776-1541 800/432-8276	816/822-7100	KS Mental Ill. Awareness Council 913/334-3491	913/233-0755	913/233-8732
KENTUCKY	502/875-5225	502/564-2967 800/372-2988 CAP 502/564-8035 CAP 800/633-6283	502/893-0460	Advocates Taking Action 502/245-5281	502/245-5284	502/868-0458
LOUISIANA	504/927-0764	504/522-2337 800/662-7705	504/343-1921		504/343-6928	504/893-4010
MAINE	207/872-6484	207/626-2774 CAP 207/622-7055	207/287-7200 207/777-2208	Portland Coalition 207/777-2208	207/622-5767	207/369-0542
MARYLAND	410/379-0400	410/235-4700 CAP 410/554-3221	410/235-1178	On Our Own 410/488-4480	410/467-7100 800/467-0075	Montgomery 301/317-1289 PSP 301/424-0656
MASSACHUSETTS	617/891-6270	MI 413/584-1644 CAP 617/727-7440 DD 617/723-8455	617/742-7452	Nat'l Empow 800/ POWER-2-U	617/426-2299	617/482-2915
MICHIGAN	517/487-5426	517/487-1755 CAP 517/373-8193	313/557-6777		313/355-0010	616/343-5896

367

MINNESOTA	612/827-5641	612/332-1441	612/331-6840	612/298-5351 612/222-2741	612/645-2948	612/827-3065
MISSISSIPPI	601/362-4830	601/981-8207 CAP 601/982-7051	601/992-1227			601/981-1618
MISSOURI	417/864-7887	314/991-1190	314/773-1399	MO AMI 314/993-6937	314/634-7727	314/388-3180
MONTANA	406/755-6588	406/444-3889 800/245-4743	406/442-4276		406/443-7871	406/657-2055
NEBRASKA	402/475-4407	402/474-3183 CAP 402/471-3656	402/423-6990	402/489-6239	402/477-2992	
NEVADA	702/423-4760	702/383-8150 800/992-5715 CAP 702/688-1440 CAP 800/633-9879	702/687-5943		702/254-2666	
NEW HAMP.	603/228-9092	CAP 603/228-0432	603/271-5000		603/225-5359	603/225-5359
NEW JERSEY	908/246-2525	609/292-1750 CAP 609/292-9742 800/792-8600	201/744-2500	C.S.P. NJ 201/780-1175	609/695-4554	210/677-3259
NEW MEXICO	505/883-4630	CAP 505/256-3100 CAP 800/432-4682	505/841-8978		505/254-0643	
NEW YORK	518/439-8311	518/473-7378 800/432-4682 518/473-4057	518/462-5439	MH Adv. Assoc. 800/293-3797 Project Release 212/679-0100	518/462-2000 800/950-3228	315/443-4323

continued on next page

	The Arc	P & A	MH Assoc	Consumer Groups	Alliance for MI	Fed. of Fam.
N. CAROLINA	919/782-4632	919/733-9250 800/821-6922 CAP 919/733-3364	919/981-0740	NC MH Consumers' 919/834-2285 800/326-3842	919/851-0063	919/851-0063
N. DAKOTA	701/223-5349	701/224-2972 800/472-2670 CAP 701/224-4625	701/255-3692		701/852-5324	
OHIO	614/487-4720	614/466-7264 800/282-9181 CAP 614/466-9956	614/239-6304	OH Adv. for MH 800/589-2603	800/686-2646	216/726-9570
OKLAHOMA	918/582-8272	918/664-5883 CAP 405/521-3756	918/585-1213	800/583-1264	405/330-0000 405/848-4330	
OREGON	503/581-2726	503/243-2081 CAP 503/378-3142	503/945-2800		503/370-7774	503/581-2047
PENNSYLVANIA	717/234-2521	717/236-8110 800/692-7443 CAP 215/557-7112	215/735-2465	PA MH Cons. Assoc. 717/291-9482	717/238-1514	215/735-2465
RHODE ISLAND	401/463-9191	401/831-3150	401/253-1945	401/861-9326	401/464-3060	401/736-8844
S. CAROLINA	803/489-7043	803/782-0639 800/922-5225 CAP 803/734-0457	803/799-0017	SC SHARE 803/252-7076	803/779-7849	803/852-4125
S. DAKOTA	605/224-8211	CAP 605/224-8294 800/658-4782	605/773-5991		605/697-7210 800/551-2531	
TENNESSEE	615/327-0294	615/298-1080	615/269-5355		615/531-8264	615/794-0467

TEXAS	512/454-6694	CAP 512/454-4816 800/252-9108	512/454-3706	Neches Crossing 512/459-7681	512/474-2225
UTAH	801/364-5060	801/363-1347 800/662-9080	801/531-8996	Utah AMI 801/584-2023	801/584-2023	801/272-1068
VERMONT	802/65-4014	802/863-2881 800/622-4555	802/734-7766	Vt. Psy. Survivors 800/564-2106	802/257-5546 800/639-6480	802/223-4917
VIRGINIA	804/649-8481	804/225-2042 800/552-3962	804/782-2225	Va. MH Consumers Assoc. 804/288-7326	804/225-8264	804/225-0002
WASHINGTON	206/357-5596	206/721-4049	206/783-9264		206/438-0211	206/697-3922
WEST VIRGINIA	304/422-3151	304/346-0847 800/950-5250	304/340-3512	WV MH Consumers Assoc. 304/529-2600	304/342-0497	304/233-5399
WISCONSIN	608/251-9272	608/267-0214 CAP 608/267-7422 CAP 800/362-1290	414/276-3122	Wisc. Net. of MH Consumers Route 3, Box 404 Ashland, WI 54806	608/257-5888	608/267-6888
WYOMING	307/237-9110	307/638-7668 800/821-3091	307/634-9653	Wyom. Coalition for Consumer Self-Advocacy 307/234-0440	307/234-0440	Uplift 307/778-8686